LANDOWNERSHIP
IN NEPAL

THIS VOLUME IS SPONSORED BY
THE CENTER FOR SOUTH AND SOUTHEAST ASIA STUDIES
UNIVERSITY OF CALIFORNIA, BERKELEY

MAHESH C. REGMI

LANDOWNERSHIP IN NEPAL

UNIVERSITY OF CALIFORNIA PRESS
Berkeley · Los Angeles · London

UNIVERSITY OF CALIFORNIA PRESS
Berkeley and Los Angeles, California

University of California Press, Ltd.
London, England

Copyright © 1976, by
The Regents of the University of California

ISBN 0-520-02750-7
Library of Congress Catalog Card Number: 74-77734

Old laws and rights, inherited,
From age to age, drag on and on
Like some hereditary disease
Steadily widening, growing worse.
Wisdom turns nonsense, good deeds prove a curse,
Your ancestors your doom!
The native right that's born with us,
For that, alas, no man makes room.

JOHANN WOLFGANG VON GOETHE
(1749–1832)

CONTENTS

	Foreword	xiii
	Preface	xv
Chapter 1.	The Kingdom of Nepal	1
	Size and Location	1
	Geographic Divisions	2
	Importance of Agriculture	4
	The Social Milieu	6
	The Historical Background	8
	The Panchayat System	9
	Recent Social and Economic Developments	10
	Slow Economic Growth	11
	Land and Economic Development	14
Chapter 2.	The State and the Land	15
	The *Raikar* System	16
	Birta	16
	Guthi	17
	Jagir	17
	Rakam	18
	The *Kipat* System	19
	Interrelationship of Different Forms of Land Tenure	20
Chapter 3.	Privileged Landownership: *Birta* Tenure	22
	Origin and Evolution of the *Birta* System	23
	Birta Grants during the Rana Period	26
	The Nature of the *Birta*-owning Class	26
	Vicissitudes of *Birta* Landownership	28
	Privileges and Obligations of *Birta* Landowners	33
	Birta and *Raikar*	37
	Privileged Landownership	38
Chapter 4.	Institutional Landownership: *Guthi* Tenure	46
	Form and Nature of *Guthi* Endowments	48
	Objectives of *Guthi* Land Endowments	50
	Area and Location of *Guthi* Land Endowments	56

CONTENTS

	Efforts toward Simplicity and Uniformity	135
	Collections in Cash	137
	Conversion Rates	138
	The *Bijan* System	139
	Land-Tax Assessments in the Tarai	142
	Land-Tax Rates in 1951	147
	Standardization of Grading Formulas	148
	Reorganization of the Land-Tax Assessment System	150
	Panchayat-Development Taxation	152
	Tax on Agricultural Income	153
Chapter 9.	Labor Services and Landownership	156
	Origin of the *Rakam* System	156
	Developments during the Rana Period	158
	Rakam and *Chuni* Peasants	160
	Rakam Obligations	161
	Land Redistribution and Allotment	162
	Tenurial Characteristics	164
	Critique of the *Rakam* System	166
	Recent Developments	168
	Abolition of the *Rakam* System	169
Chapter 10.	Property Rights in Land	170
	Traditional Nature of *Raikar* Landholding Rights	171
	Records of Rights	174
	Limitations on Property Rights in Land	177
	Developments after 1951	179
	Decline in Real Value of the Land Tax	180
	Property Rights in *Birta* Land	182
	Economic Differentiation	185
	Incidence of Tenancy	191
	Landlord-Tenant Relations	194
Chapter 11.	The Impact of Land Reform	197
	Objectives of Land-Reform Policy	197
	The 1964 Land-Reform Program	200
	Impact of the Land-Reform Program	207
	Land Reform and Class Coordination	213
	Forest-Land Policy	215
	Purchase of Landownership Rights	216
	A Compromise Formula	217
	The Objective of Land Reform	221

Chapter 12.	The Future Pattern of Landownership	224
	The Traditional Landed Elite	224
	The Role of Nonascriptive Landownership	225
	Land Reforms under the Panchayat System	227
	A Scheme for Panchayat Landownership	229
	Glossary	233
	Bibliography and Source Materials	237
	Index	249

TABLES

Table 1.	Area under Various Forms of Land Tenure, 1952	20
Table 2.	Tax-Assessment Rates on Newly Reclaimed Lands, 1934	136
Table 3.	Land-Tax Rates in the Tarai and Inner Tarai Districts	148
Table 4.	Current Rates of Land Taxation in Different Regions	151
Table 5.	Total Agricultural Holdings in Nepal and Share Thereof Cultivated by Tenants, 1961	193
Table 6.	Ceilings on Landholding in Different Regions	201
Table 7.	Agricultural Rents in Kathmandu Valley	205
Table 8.	Agricultural Rents in Some Tarai and Inner Tarai Districts	206
Table 9.	Rates of Compulsory Savings in Different Regions	206
Table 10.	Average Yields of Principal Crops in Kathmandu Valley, by Tenure Status	221

CHARTS

Chart 1.	Land Tenure	21
Chart 2.	Forms of Tax Assessment on *Khet* Lands in the Midland Region	134

FOREWORD

It would be appropriate to commence with a word of tribute to the author of this volume, Shri Mahesh C. Regmi, for he is truly a unique phenomenon in the intellectual and scholarly community in Nepal and one deserving of emulation. In the late 1950s, Shri Regmi made a decision that was almost inconceivable in Nepal at that time—to establish a *private* research and translation program without any assured sources of financial support from either the government of Nepal, a Nepali educational institution, or a foreign foundation. This was indicative not only of a proclivity for entrepreneurship rare in Nepal but also of an independence of mind and a dedication to scholarship.

It was my good fortune to fall into the hands of Shri Regmi during my first field trip to Nepal as a graduate student in 1957. Indeed, much of my initial socialization into that very alien but warm and hospitable society was a consequence of the close working relationship that developed between the two of us. Not that we agreed on everything—or even on most things. But the combination in Shri Regmi of an inherent skepticism, intellectual honesty, and a tolerant (if occasionally bemused) attitude toward a struggling foreigner trying desperately to comprehend the intricacies and subtleties of the Nepali political culture was just what was required.

This study of the land-tenure system in Nepal in a historical context is an excellent example of the author's dedication to scholarship in the true meaning of the term as well as of the persistence and thoroughness with which he approaches difficult research projects. It is the product of a decade or more of work in the copious but chaotic record resources on the subject matter in several government offices in Nepal. (One important by-product of his study was the substantial improvement in the organization, and hence the accessibility, of these records.)

Shri Regmi has used this mass of documentation from many different sources to derive general conclusions and to present a coherent history of the evolution of land-tenure policies, in realistic rather than formalistic terms. He then offers conjectures about the best strategies for development in the crucial agrarian system in contemporary Nepal. By doing so, he provides a model for similar studies not only in Nepal but also in other Third World countries in which the need to comprehend existing institutional structures before attempting to reform or abolish them is recognized increasingly, and in which the assumption that an institution is incidental to current development-needs if it is "traditional" is no longer accepted dogma. Discovering the past may be an academic enterprise; but using the past for innovational purposes is the most relevant scholarship. The latter is what Shri Regmi has accomplished in this definitive study which is, in my view, the most important volume yet published on Nepal.

LEO E. ROSE

PREFACE

This book has been written in the belief that "if the men of the future are ever to break the chains of the present, they will have to understand the forces that forged them."[1] Economic-development policies can be formulated and implemented effectively only if there is an adequate understanding of existing institutions, particularly agrarian institutions in countries such as Nepal. These policies often run counter to the interests of privileged groups in the society, and so what is advocated as reform is nothing else than old wine in new bottles. A study of landownership systems in Nepal is thus of more than academic interest.

The study represents an attempt to outline the institutional framework within which an important aspect of Nepal's economic life has functioned. Such an attempt needs no apology, for relations of production, particularly in the agrarian field, are a crucial factor determining the pace and level of economic development. Problems of agrarian relations and agricultural development, however, do not relate simply to the mechanics of economic growth. These problems have an equal impact on the social, political, and cultural life of the nation. Reforms in these fields, therefore, basically affect the social, political, and cultural attitudes of the people. For this reason, agrarian institutions are a field of study of equal interest to economists, sociologists, anthropologists, historians, and political scientists. The study seeks to present the basic outline of Nepal's agrarian system, which may facilitate research in these other fields as well.

The book begins with a short chapter on the geographical, historical, social, and economic background to the land problem of Nepal. The next chapter describes the traditional theory of *Raikar* land tenure, or state ownership of the land, and the various forms of land tenure that emerged in Nepal as a result of land grants and assignments or the state's recognition of the customary rights of certain ethnic commu-

[1]Barrington Moore, Jr., *Social Origins of Dictatorship and Democracy* (Penguin Books, 1967), p. 308.

nities. Chapters 3–5 are devoted to a historical analysis of *Birta* tenure (originating from land grants to individuals), *Guthi* tenure (growing out of land endowments to religious and philanthropic institutions), and *Jagir* tenure (stemming from assignments of lands to government employees and functionaries in lieu of emoluments). Communal landownership, which was confined to certain communities of Mongoloid origin in the hill region, is taken up in chapter 6. Chapter 7 explores the way in which the authority granted to village-level functionaries for land-tax collection and general land administration in the Tarai districts during the 1860s gradually developed as a form of landownership. The next two chapters deal with *Raikar* land taxation (chap. 8) and labor obligations traditionally attached to *Raikar* landownership (chap. 9). Chapter 10 is concerned with the evolution of the traditional concept of state ownership of *Raikar* land, which gradually gave way to a system of private ownership that gave rise to the development of a landlord-tenant nexus on lands of this tenure category. Against this background, chapter 11 examines the land-reform measures introduced since the overthrow of the Rana government in 1951, particularly since the introduction of the Panchayat system in 1961. The concluding chapter attempts to delineate basic trends in the evolution of Napal's land system in recent centuries and also presents the conceptual framework for remodeling the land system in keeping with the goals of the Panchayat system.

As the contents show, the basic data used in this book are partly the same as those used in the author's four-volume study, *Land Tenure and Taxation in Nepal* (published by the University of California Press in 1963–68). That study was the result of a piecemeal exploration of Nepal's land system over a period of eight years, which has helped the author to acquire a deeper understanding of the land system of Nepal in total perspective. It is, of course, for scholars to judge to what extent that understanding has contributed to the value of this study. The author would also like to stress the fact that the subjective element inevitably emerges in a work like this, so that other students may arrive at basically different findings and conclusions on the same data-base. No one would feel more delighted than the author if his work inspires the study and application necessary to reach such conclusions.

A formal expression of thanks to Dr. Leo E. Rose could scarcely be a fitting return for his support and encouragement in the preparation of this book. Thanks are due also to Dr. Ludwig F. Stiller, who, as a true friend and scholar, offered many helpful comments and stimulating criticisms. Professor Ernest Gellner, with his steady encouragement and solid suggestions, has been of equally great help. The author is indebted to the appropriate authorities of His Majesty's Government of Nepal for permission to study and use official archival materials.

MAHESH C. REGMI

July 16, 1974
Lazimpat
Kathmandu, Nepal

Chapter 1

THE KINGDOM OF NEPAL

Land and agriculture have played the leading part in Nepal's social, economic, and political life through the centuries. Almost 93 percent of Nepal's working population is employed in agriculture,[1] the highest percentage among the countries of South Asia. Trade, manufacturing, and other occupations are important in particular regions or among particular communities, but the predominant importance of land and agriculture in Nepal's economy is a reality which no observer of the Nepali scene can deny. Land has therefore traditionally represented the principal form of wealth, the principal symbol of social status, and the principal source of economic and political power. Ownership of land has meant control over a vital factor of production and therefore a position of prestige, affluence, and power.

SIZE AND LOCATION

To understand the reasons for the predominant importance of land in Nepal's economy, it will be appropriate to begin with a brief description of Nepal's size, location, and geographical features. The Kingdom of Nepal extends about 800 kilometers from east to west and about 160 kilometers from north to south. It is situated mainly along the southern slopes of the Himalayas, the highest chain of mountains in the world. Approximately one-third of the 2,400-kilometer Himalayan range lies in Nepal. The kingdom adjoins the Tibetan autonomous region of China in the north. In the east, south, and west, Nepal's boundaries touch those of India. In the northeast, the Kingdom of Nepal adjoins Sikkim. Nepal is therefore a landlocked country. The

---

[1] The 1961 national population census disclosed that Nepal had a total resident population of 9,412,996. Of these, 4,306,839 were economically active. This figure included 4,038,895 (93.7 percent) engaged in farming and related occupations. Central Bureau of Statistics, *Rashtriya Janaganana 2018 Ko Parinam* [Results of the 1961 national population census], (Kathmandu: the Bureau, 2026 [1969]), IV, 166–67, table 5.

nearest seaport, Calcutta, India, lies at a distance of about 400 kilometers. Because the country is elongated in the east-west direction, most areas are more accessible from India than from other parts of Nepal itself.

Nepal has a total surface area of 141,000 square kilometers. Compared with its giant neighbors in the south and the north, India and China, Nepal is indeed a tiny Himalayan kingdom. It would, however, be a mistake to regard Nepal as a small country. In area, Nepal is almost as large as Bangladesh. It is more than twice the size of Sri Lanka, and roughly three times that of Switzerland.

Geographic Divisions

Nepal has been likened to a giant staircase ascending from the low-lying Tarai plain to the culminating heights of the Himalayas.[2] The southern part of the kingdom consists of the Tarai, a narrow tract of level alluvial terrain that has been described as Nepal's modest share of the Ganges plain. Situated between the Indian frontier and the foothills through almost the entire length of the country, the Tarai is only about 300 meters above sea level and nowhere more than 45 kilometers in width. Eighteen of the 75 districts of Nepal are comprised in the Tarai region. These are Jhapa, Morang, Sunsari, Saptari, Siraha, Dhanusha, Mahottari, Sarlahi, Rautahat, Bara, and Parsa in the east; Nawal-Parasi, Rupandehi, Kapilavastu, in the west; and Banke, Bardiya, Kailali, and Kanchanpur in far-western Nepal. From the economic viewpoint, the Tarai is the most important region of Nepal. With its extensive tracts of cultivable land and forests, its relatively high man-land ratio, and its proximity to the markets of India, the Tarai has long contributed the major portion of Nepal's national income and revenue and provided opportunities for land reclamation and settlement. Indeed, there is evidence that the importance of this region as a source of revenue was well recognized by the rulers of Nepal even during the latter part of the eighteenth

---

[2]This section is based chiefly on the following sources: Pradyumna P. Karan et al., *Nepal: A Physical and Cultural Geography* (Lexington: University of Kentucky Press, 1960); Toni Hagen, *Nepal: The Kingdom in the Himalayas* (Berne: Kimmerley and Frey, 1961); and Harka Gurung, "The Land," in Pashupati Shunshere J. B. Rana and Kamal P. Malla, eds., *Nepal in Perspective* (Kathmandu: Center for Economic Development and Administration, 1973), pp. 25–33.

century.³ At present, the Tarai region contributes nearly 75 percent of the national revenue and nearly 60 percent of the gross domestic product.⁴

The Siwalik hills, the southernmost mountains of the Himalayan system, averaging 1,500 meters in altitude, rise straight from the plains of the Tarai without any foothills. Farther north, the Mahabharat mountains run from west to east across almost the entire country, parallel to but often merging directly into the Siwalik hills. At certain points, the Chure and Mahabharat ranges are separated by wide valleys whose topography is similar to that of the Tarai. Those valleys are therefore known as the inner Tarai. At two points, Dang and Chitaun, the inner Tarai region of Nepal directly adjoins the Indian frontier. The inner Tarai comprises the districts of Sindhuli and Udayapur in eastern Nepal, Makwanpur and Chitaun in central Nepal, and Dang and Surkhet in western Nepal.

Between the Mahabharat range and the main Himalaya mountains lie the midlands, a complex of hills and valleys some 60 to 100 kilometers in breadth and extending much of the length of the country, at elevations of 600 to 2,000 meters above sea level. The midlands region has been described as the heart of the country. It is divided into the following 45 districts: Taplejung, Panchthar, Ilam, Sankhuwa-Sabha, Terhathum, Dhankuta, Solukhumbu, Okhaldhunga, Khotang, Bhojpur, Dolakha, Ramechhap, Kabhrepalanchok, and Sindhupalchok in the east; Bhaktapur, Lalitpur, and Kathmandu in Kathmandu Valley; and Dhading, Nuwakot, Gorkha, Tanahu, Lamjung, Syangja, Kaski, Parbat, Gulmi, Argha-Khanchi, Palpa, Myagdi, Baglung, Rukum, Rolpa, Salyan, Pyuthan, Dailekh, Jajarkot, Tibrikot, Jumla, Bajhang, Bajura, Doti, Achham, Darchula, Baitadi, and Dandeldhura in western Nepal. Notwithstanding the importance of the Tarai region in Nepal's economy, the main currents of the kingdom's political and economic history have originated in the midlands. It was from Gorkha, a small principality situated in the central midlands, that the campaign of territorial conquest which culminated in the establishment of the modern Kingdom of Nepal was launched about the middle

---

³Mahesh C. Regmi, *A Study in Nepali Economic History, 1768–1846* (New Delhi: Manjusri Publishing House, 1971), pp. 9–10.
⁴Frederick H. Gaige, "The Role of the Tarai in Nepal's Economic Development," *Vasudha*, vol. XI, no. 7, Ashadh 2025 (June 1968), 57–58.

of the eighteenth century.[5]

The main Himalaya range towers up, abrupt and gigantic, some 80 kilometers north of the Mahabharat mountains. It is largely an arctic waste. The nature of this range can be realized from the fact that at least 250 peaks are more than 6,000 meters in altitude. No vegetation is possible in most of the Himalayan region: the landscape is wild and desolate, and no human habitation exists in the upper reaches. In western and central Nepal, some areas of the kingdom are situated north of the main Himalaya range. Six of Nepal's 75 districts—Rasuwa, Manang, Mustang, Dolpa, Mugu, and Humla—lie wholly in the trans-Himalayan region.

The Kingdom of Nepal thus embraces a striking diversity of terrain, from the lowlands of the Tarai to Sagarmatha (Everest), the highest peak of the world (8,848 meters). It is accordingly a distinctive feature of the kingdom that almost all the climatic zones of the earth are represented here, from tropical jungle in the Tarai to arctic desert wastes in the higher regions and in the arid zone of the Tibetan plateau.

If the alternating highlands and lowlands that characterize Nepal's terrain have made transport and communications between the northern and southern parts difficult, Nepal's intricate river system makes them even more so. Nepal has three river systems—those of the Karnali in the western region, the Gandaki in the central region, and the Koshi in the eastern region. With their numerous tributaries, these three rivers cover their drainage basins like the branches of a tree. The major rivers of Nepal originate in the Tibetan plateau and cut deep, narrow gorges and valleys through the Himalayas and other mountain ranges before sweeping down to the plains of northern India as tributaries of the Ganges.

Importance of Agriculture

This brief summary of Nepal's geographical features highlights the basic problems of its agricultural economy. Most of the surface area consists of forests, alpine and snow-clad terrain, and rivers, together with villages and towns, and hence is not available for agricultural use. In fact, only 1.98 million hectares—14.06 percent of the total

---

[5]Nepal's present ruling dynasty came from Gorkha, and, until quite recently, the Kingdom of Nepal was known as Gorkha Raj. Government of Nepal, "Adal Ko" [On disciplinary matters], *Muluki Ain* [Legal code], pt. V (Kathmandu: Gorkhapatra Press, 2012 [1955]), sec. 1, p. 1.

surface area—are actually under cultivation.⁶ The majority of Nepal's 11.5 million people⁷ depend on this limited area for their livelihood. Per capita availability of agricultural land approximates 0.2 hectare, against 0.4 hectare in India.⁸ The pressure of population is aggravated by the unequal distribution of the limited area of cultivated land. In the hill and mountainous regions live 63.6 percent of the people, although these regions comprise only 30 percent of the total cultivated area. On the other hand, the Tarai region contains 70 percent of the cultivated area and only 36.4 percent of the population.⁹ The density of population depends on agricultural productivity and the availability of employment opportunities. The Tarai region has an average density of 300 persons per square mile, but in the agriculturally richer eastern part the figure is 700. Population density in the mountainous region rarely exceeds 25 persons per square mile, but Kathmandu Valley, which covers 0.4 percent of the total area of the kingdom, accounts for 5 percent of the total population, with a density of more than 50,000 per square mile in Kathmandu town.¹⁰

The majority of the inhabitants are peasants; hence the Kingdom of Nepal is predominantly rural. Almost 97 percent of the people live in villages. There are nearly 29,000 villages,¹¹ but only 16 settlements with a population of 6,000 or more.¹² Most of the bigger towns are situated in Kathmandu Valley and the Tarai region. The most important of them are Kathmandu (150,402), Patan (59,040), and Bhadgaun (40,112) in Kathmandu Valley; Biratnagar (45,100), Nepalganj (23,523), Dharan (20,503), Bhairahawa (17,272), and Birganj (12,999) in the Tarai region; and Pokhara (20,611) in the midlands.¹³

---

⁶Ministry of Food and Agriculture, *Agricultural Statistics of Nepal* (Kathmandu: the Ministry, 1972), p. 1.
⁷This figure is taken from the 1971 national population census. *Nepal Statistical Bulletin*, IX, no. 1 (July 30, 1973), 5.
⁸Ministry of Food and Agriculture, *Farm Management Study in the Selected Regions of Nepal, 1968–69* (Kathmandu: the Ministry, 1971), p. 13. The figures relate to 1966.
⁹M. A. Zaman, *Evaluation of Land Reform in Nepal* (Kathmandu: Ministry of Land Reforms, 1973), pp. 3-4.
¹⁰Harka Gurung, "Geographic Setting," in Nepal Council of Applied Economic Research, *Nepal: A Profile* (Kathmandu: the Council, 1970), pp. 8-9. The figures are based on the 1961 national population census.
¹¹The actual number is 28,446. Harka Gurung, "Geographic Foundations of Nepal," *Himalayan Review*, special issue, 1968, p. 7.
¹²*Nepal Statistical Bulletin*, IX, no. 1 (July 30, 1973), 10.
¹³Ibid.

THE KINGDOM OF NEPAL
The Social Milieu

The Kingdom of Nepal has been a meeting ground for diverse peoples and cultures through the centuries. The dominant strains in Nepal's population are Caucasoid and Mongoloid, with varying degrees of admixture. Some of these ethnic groups were immigrants from the east as part of the westward movement of tribal peoples from southeastern Asia. Other groups originated in Tibet, whereas still others moved in from the Indian plains or eastward from the hill areas of the western Himalayas.[14]

A classification of Nepali society purely from the ethnic viewpoint would hardly be meaningful, however, in a socio-economic study. From the standpoint of landownership, Nepali society may be divided into two broad categories—those elements that belong to the central and western midlands and those that belong to other parts of the country. Nepali political history, as mentioned above, had its genesis in the central midlands, whose inhabitants dominated the social, political, and economic life of the country. Members of Nepal's political elite,[15] the bureaucracy, and the army have traditionally come from these regions. Communities belonging to the eastern hill regions, the Himalayan regions, and the Tarai played scarcely any role in politics, the administration, or the army. They were important to the newly established Gorkhali state solely because of the role of their inhabitants as peasants, porters, artisans, and taxpayers.

Nepal's political elite, therefore, has traditionally belonged to the central and western midlands. The midlands population broadly represented three different ethnic and cultural groups, each with its characteristic contribution to the political history of Nepal. Social and political leadership was provided by Brahmans and Chhetris, the descendants of early immigrants from northern India and members of

---

[14]Leo E. Rose, *Nepal: Strategy for Survival* (Bombay: Oxford University Press, 1971), p. 7; Dor Bahadur Bista, "The People," in Rana and Malla, *Nepal in Perspective*, p. 35.

[15]The term "political elite" is here used to mean a group within the political class "which comprises those individuals who actually exercise political power in a society at any given time." T. B. Bottomore, *Elites and Society* (Penguin Books, 1971). Bottomore uses the term "political class" to refer to "all those groups which exercise political power or influence, and are directly engaged in struggles for political leadership." The political elite, on the other hand, includes "members of the government and of the high administration, military leaders, and, in some cases, politically influential families of an aristocracy or royal house and leaders of powerful economic enterprises."

the local Khas community who had succeeded in elevating their caste and social status. The ruling dynasty of Gorkha, one of whose descendants now occupies the throne of Nepal, is said to be a branch of one of the Rajput families that once ruled Udaipur, in what is now the Indian state of Rajasthan. By the middle of the eighteenth century, indeed, the whole of the central and western midlands had come under the control of dynasties that claimed to have had their origin among various Rajput families in medieval India. These groups apparently brought under their control the chieftains of the tribes of this region, mostly Mongoloid groups of Magar or Gurung origin, and assumed political leadership. The local Magar and Gurung communities were then gradually assimilated into the new political structure, but at lower and middle echelons of the army[16] rather than as prospective claimants to political power. With regard to landownership also, these two groups—the political elites and the military groups—occupied the dominant position. Ascriptive landownership rights, which emerged through grants or temporary assignments of land, were limited to these groups for all practical purposes.

At the bottom came occupational and untouchable castes (e.g., Kami and Sarki) and certain Mongoloid groups, (e.g., Bhote, Majhi, Chepang, and Kumhal) which were denoted by the generic term Prajajat.[17] Members of these communities enjoyed no political rights and were not even admitted into the army. Their functions were limited to traditional occupations such as blacksmithing, leatherworking, and ferrying. These groups played a part in the process of territorial unification, and, later, that of administrative consolidation, through porterage and other unpaid services under the forced-labor system.

---

[16]In the main, troops traditionally were recruited from Khas, Magar, Gurung, and Thakuri communities. Naraharinath Yogi and Baburam Acharya, eds., *Rashtrapita Shri 5 Bada Maharaja Prithvi Narayan Shah Devako Dibya Upadesh* [Divine counsel of the Great King Prithvi Narayan Shah Dev, Father of the Nation] (2d rev. ed.; Kathmandu: Prithvi Jayanti Samaroha Samiti, 2010 [1953]), p. 23. See also Regmi, *A Study in Nepali Economic History*, pp. 10-11. The recruitment of Limbus in the army began only in 1860. His Majesty's Government, Ministry of Finance, Department of Land Revenue, Lagat Phant (Records Office), "Order to the Limbus of Pallokirat regarding Recruitment and Enslavement," Magh Sudi 9, 1917 (January 1861). All unpublished documents used in this study, unless otherwise stated, have been obtained from this source. Until 1903, the government of Nepal used lunar calendar dates in official documents. Conversion of these dates requires more specialized knowledge than the author possesses. Therefore only the equivalent Western calendar month and year will be found within the parentheses.

[17]Government of Nepal, "Jari Ko" [On abduction], *Muluki Ain*, pt. V (2012 [1955], secs. 35, 43, pp. 91-93.

They held lands generally under customary or communal forms of tenure, or else worked as tenants on the holdings of those groups that possessed rent-receiving rights in land by virtue of their ascriptive status. Slaves and bondsmen also belonged mostly to these groups. With the expansion of the Gorkhali empire, several communities in the eastern midlands, such as Danuwar, were automatically assimilated into this category.

This somewhat oversimplified classification of Nepali society is not necessarily a disjunctive one. Naturally, not every Brahman or Chhetri occupied a position of political power and influence. As their numbers increased, large segments of these communities spilled over to the lower and middle echelons of the army and the administration, often at the cost of Mongoloid groups such as the Magars and Gurungs. There were also numerous cases in which communities that were qualified to play political, military, or administrative roles by virtue of their ethnic origin remained content with a peasant's life. Such cases nevertheless do not disprove the main basis of the classification of Nepali society as presented above. Lack of opportunity should by no means be confused with ineligibility to play customary and traditional roles in the society.

The Historical Background

It may be relevant here to outline briefly the historical background of the process of political unification that led to the founding of the modern Kingdom of Nepal. Around the middle of the eighteenth century, the kingdom was divided into about sixty principalities. Each of the three towns of Kathmandu Valley—Kathmandu, Lalitpur, and Bhaktapur—was the capital of an independent kingdom. During 1768-69, Prithvi Narayan Shah, King of Gorkha, conquered these three kingdoms and made Kathmandu the capital of the modern Kingdom of Nepal. By the early years of the nineteenth century, this new kingdom extended over the whole of its present territory and even occupied large areas in the modern Indian states of Himachal Pradesh, Uttar Pradesh, and Bihar. It was reduced to its present size after a war with the British in 1814-16, except for the present districts of Banke, Bardiya, Kailali, and Kanchanpur, which were restored only in 1861, in appreciation of Nepal's helping the British quell the Indian rebellion of 1857.

The political history of the Kingdom of Nepal took a fateful turn in

1846 when political power passed from the Shah dynasty to the Rana family. For nearly nine years before this event, Nepal had been a victim of political instability caused by factions belonging to the royal family and the nobility. The confusion culminated in a massacre of leading members of the important political families in September 1846 and the flight or banishment of others. Jang Bahadur Rana,[18] a member of one of the less influential sections of the families that had followed the Shah dynasty from Gorkha to Kathmandu, was then appointed prime minister of Nepal. The Rana regime acquired an institutional character through a royal order promulgated in 1856 which decreed that succession to the office of prime minister should be based on seniority, first among Jang Bahadur Rana's brothers, and then among his sons and nephews.[19] The Rana political system was essentially a military despotism of the ruling faction within the Rana family over the king and the people. The government functioned as an instrument to carry out the personal wishes and interests of the Rana prime minister. Its main domestic preoccupation was the exploitation of the country's resources in order to enhance the personal wealth of the prime minister and his family.[20]

The Panchayat System

The Rana regime was overthrown in early 1951 by a popular movement that enjoyed the blessings of the king and the active support of the government of India. Nepal then opted for a parliamentary system. The first general elections were held in 1959. The Nepali Congress party won nearly two-thirds of the seats of the lower house and so formed the government. Eighteen months later, in December 1960, it was dismissed on charges of corruption, misuse of power, and mismanagement of economic affairs. The parliamentary form of government was then rejected as unsuitable to Nepal. The new polity that was subsequently introduced, known as the Panchayat system, envisioned a multi-tiered structure of popular bodies with the village Panchayat at the bottom and the national Panchayat, the national

---

[18]The title of Rana was actually conferred on Jang Bahadur by King Surendra in 1849. Satish Kumar, *Rana Polity in Nepal* (Bombay: Asia Publishing House, 1967), pp. 158–59. Until then the family was known as Kanwar.

[19]Ibid. pp. 159–60

[20]Bhuwan Lal Joshi and Leo E. Rose, *Democratic Innovations in Nepal: A Case Study of Political Acculturation* (Berkeley and Los Angeles: University of California Press, 1966), pp. 38–39.

legislature, at the apex. A system of representation of such class and professional groups as women, youths, workers, peasants, and former servicemen was introduced. The basic objective of the Panchayat system was to "promote the welfare of the people by establishing a social order which is just, dynamic, democratic, and free from exploitation by integrating and coordinating the interests of different classes and professions from a broad national viewpoint."[21] It was recognized that such arrangements were possible only through a partyless system "originating from the very base with the active cooperation of the entire people and embodying the principles of decentralization."[22]

Nepal has a unitary system of government. The central government is situated at Kathmandu. Until 1961, the kingdom was divided into 32 districts and about 15 feudatory principalities which had been left semiautonomous in the process of political unification. After the political changes of 1960, the feudatory principalities were abolished[23] and the kingdom was reorganized into 75 districts.[24] There is a district-level Panchayat, or elected Council, in each of these districts. At the local level, the kingdom has 3,856 village Panchayats and 16 town Panchayats.

RECENT SOCIAL AND ECONOMIC DEVELOPMENTS

One of the most significant gains of the political changes of 1950–51 was the infusion of the ideal of individual liberty and equality. The interim constitution, proclaimed in 1951, provided for equality before the law and equal protection of the law to all citizens without any discrimination on the basis of religion, caste, or sex.[25] In 1963, the government of Nepal promulgated a new legal code that abolished

[21] "First Amendment to the Constitution of Nepal," *Nepal Gazette*, vol. 16, no. 45 (Extraordinary), Magh 14, 2023 (January 27, 1967), art. 4.
[22] Ibid., art. 2.
[23] Ministry of Law, "Raja Rajauta Ain, 2017" [Rajya abolition act, 1961], *Nepal Gazette*, vol. 10, no. 30 (Extraordinary), Chaitra 27, 2017 (April 9, 1961).
[24] Ministry of Law and Justice, "Sthaniya Prashasan Adhyadesh, 2022" [Local administration ordinance, 1965], *Nepal Gazette*, vol. 15, no. 25 (Extraordinary), Poush 1, 2022 (December 16, 1965).
[25] Government of Nepal, "Nepal Antarim Shasan Vidhan" [Interim constitution of Nepal], *Nepal Gazette*, vol. 4, no. 14, Kartik 30, 2011 (November 15, 1954), arts. 15–16, p. 43. Restrictions on the recruitment of specified castes and communities in the army were abolished a few days after the overthrow of the Rana government on Falgun 20, 2007 (March 3, 1951). Grishma Bahadur Devkota, *Nepalko Rajnaitik Darpan* [Political mirror of Nepal] (Kathmandu: Keshav Chandra Gautam, 1960), pp. 83–84.

untouchability along with all other forms of social discrimination.[26] It is true, of course, that such social evils can hardly be eradicated through legislation alone, and the promulgation of the reform measures has by no means marked their complete disappearance from Nepali society. Even so, no Nepali is punished by the courts today if he marries a woman of higher caste. Moreover, no longer is "two-thirds of the time of the judges employed in the discussion of cases better fitted for the confessional, or the tribunal of public opinion, or some domestic court than for a King's Court of Justice."[27]

Another equally important outcome of the 1950–51 changes was the commitment to the cause of planned national economic development. To be sure, initial steps toward planning had been taken by the Rana regime on the eve of its overthrow, but the post-1951 efforts were undertaken in a more congenial climate of international assistance and cooperation. Indeed, it might be true to some extent to say that these efforts were partly aimed at achieving legitimacy for an increased share in such assistance and cooperation. The first plan period was started in September 1956 with the basic objectives of attaining national self-sufficiency and establishing a welfare state. Since then, the kingdom has seen two five-year plans and one three-year plan. Another five-year plan is scheduled to begin in 1975.

Slow Economic Growth

Notwithstanding two decades of planning, the pace of economic growth has remained slow. In fact, authoritative statistics indicate that there has been retrogression in crucial sectors of the nation's economy. According to a report on the national economic situation published by the National Planning Commission, the target was an increase in the gross national product of 4 percent each year during the plan period from 1970 to 75. However, the GNP increased by only 4 percent (at 1964–65 prices) over the period from 1970 to 1973, while the population increased by 6.2 percent.[28] The main reason for this slow progress was the failure to increase agricultural production as planned. The target of the five-year plan was an increase in food

[26]Government of Nepal, *Muluki Ain*, In *Nepal Gazette*, vol. 12, no. 44C (Extraordinary), Chaitra 30, 2019 (April 12, 1963).
[27]Brian H. Hodgson, "On the Law and Legal Practice of Nepal, as regards Familiar Intercourse between a Hindu and an Outcast," *Journal of the Royal Asiatic Society of Great Britain and Ireland*, I (1834), 47–48.
[28]*Gorkhapatra*, Aswin 17, 2030 (October 3, 1973).

production of 3 percent each year, but production actually declined by 5.4 percent during the 1970–73 period.[29] That decline has been attributed mainly to adverse weather conditions.[30] One would expect greater attention to the development of irrigation facilities in this situation, but the irrigated area has remained unchanged since 1970[31] at about 180,000 hectares,[32] or less than 10 percent of the total cultivated area.

As a result of the decline in gross national product,[33] per capita income, which had been estimated at Rs. 578 (at 1964–65 prices) in 1970–71, actually declined to Rs. 562 in 1972–73.[34] A per capita income of Rs. 562 is one of the lowest in the world. At the same time, it must be recognized that this is only an average figure and that large segments of the population are earning much less.[35] Such abstract statistics can hardly illustrate the actual condition of the Nepali people and the real economic problem of the nation. Official statistics indicate that nearly half of the farm families of Nepal belong to the "small" category, with holdings of less than 0.5 hectare each.[36] Their average income is Rs. 1,016 per year in the hills and Rs. 1,456 in the Tarai.[37] Each family in Nepal consists, on an average, of 5.3 persons;[38] hence

[29] Ibid.
[30] "Economic Survey Report, 1972–73," ibid., Ashadh 18, 2030 (July 2, 1973).
[31] "Mid-term Progress Report of Fourth Five-Year Plan," ibid., Falgun 17, 2029 (February 28, 1973).
[32] Zaman, *Evaluation of Land Reform in Nepal*, p. 4.
[33] This is by no means a new trend. According to an official report, "Gross Domestic Product for the year 1968–69 at current prices was estimated at Rs. 8,512 million. In terms of constant prices (1964/65 = 100), this indicated an increase by about 2.2 percent per annum, a marginal improvement on 2.0 percent population growth." Nepal Rashtra Bank, *Agricultural Credit Survey, Nepal* (Kathmandu: the Bank, 1972), I, 17. The claim of marginal improvement is belied by more recent statistics indicating that the rate of population growth is higher than 2.0 percent per annum.
[34] Statistics released by Central Bureau of Statistics, *Gorkhapatra*, Aswin 30, 2030 (October 16, 1973).
[35] According to a recent article by Pashupati Shumshere J. B. Rana, former director of the Center for Economic Development and Administration: "Everyone knows that the nation has been achieving economic development at a snail's pace. During the past decade, increase in the gross national product was offset by population growth, so that the rate of increase in per capita income has been zero. In these circumstances, if any group attains prosperity, it is self-evident that the rest of the population has become poorer. During the past two decades, 100 or 200 families have succeeded in strengthening their control over the main sources of the nation's power and prosperity." *Arati*, Falgun 25, 2029 (March 8, 1973).
[36] Ministry of Food and Agriculture, op. cit. (in n. 8 above), p. 14.
[37] Nepal Rashtra Bank, op. cit., II, 266.
[38] Central Bureau of Statistics, op. cit. (in n.1 above), I, 1, table 1.

the per capita income of about half of Nepal's population amounts to no more than Rs. 191 in the hill regions and Rs. 274 in the Tarai. Moreover, in about 10 percent of Nepal's farm population, holdings consist of less than 0.1 hectare;[39] this part of the population is virtually landless and so has a still lower per capita income.

Most peasant families in Nepal therefore live on the margin between subsistence and destitution. A recent agricultural-credit survey conducted by the central bank of Nepal notes that in the hill regions even farmers with "large" holdings of more than 1 hectare each often have to meet consumption needs through borrowing.[40] Once the spiral of increasing indebtedness has begun, the "only way out is a son's enlistment in the army, or the father's finding employment in India."[41] In fact, hundreds of thousands of Nepalis from the hill regions have been forced to seek employment in India or in the Indian and British armies.[42] The 1961 national population census showed that 328,470 persons in a total population of 9,412,996—or nearly 4 percent—were living in India and other countries of South and Southeast Asia for periods of six months or more. The problem of emigration was particularly acute in the rural areas of the hill regions. In the western hill regions, for instance, such emigrants accounted for nearly 8 percent of the population.[43] One study shows that approximately a million Nepalis belong to families that can claim at least one pensioner of the Indian or British government. Many Nepalis also benefit from remittances by the estimated half-million emigrants to India.[44]

[39] Figures based on reports of the 1961 national agricultural census.
[40] Nepal Rashtra Bank, II, 51.
[41] John T. Hitchcock, *The Magars of Banyan Hill* (New York: Holt, Rinehart and Winston, 1966), p. 18.
[42] Joshi and Rose, *Democratic Innovations in Nepal*, p. 9.
[43] *Central Bureau of Statistics*, op. cit., I, 32, 33, tables 12, 13. A recent study shows that 30.3 percent of households of all castes in Doti district, and 11.6 percent in Salyan district, had members currently employed in India or serving in the Indian army. Charles Mcdougal, *Village and Household Economy in Far-Western Nepal* (Kirtipur: Tribhuwan University, 1968), p. 60.
[44] Myron Weiner, "The Political Demography of Nepal," *Asian Survey*, vol. XII, no. 7 (July 1973). For local studies of the economic impact of military and other employment abroad see Lionel Caplan, *Land and Social Change in East Nepal: A Study of Hindu Tribal Relations* (Berkeley and Los Angeles: University of California Press, 1970), pp. 113-21; Mcdougal, op. cit., pp. 59-60; A. Patricia Caplan, *Priests and Cobblers: A Study of Social Change in a Hindu Village in Western Nepal* (San Francisco: Chandler Publishing Co., 1972), pp. 40-44. The hill regions export goods worth Rs. 13 million each year, whereas the value of their imports amounts to Rs. 48 million. The deficit is met wholly with income from remittances made by Nepali emigrants. *Gorkhapatra*, Poush 25, 2029

LAND AND ECONOMIC DEVELOPMENT

The social and economic policies that Nepal should pursue in order to rid itself of this poverty involve controversial issues which it would be out of place to discuss here. Nevertheless, hardly anyone would deny that the solution to the problem lies mainly in land and agriculture. It is now universally recognized that the "existence of a substantial agricultural surplus is a precondition for industrial development,"[45] and that "rising agricultural productivity supports and sustains industrial development in several important ways."[46] Rising agricultural productivity can be achieved only through "a general spread of the application of a modern technology which almost without exception is more labour-intensive."[47] In the opinion of Gunnar Myrdal, a prerequisite for this is "a land and tenancy reform which creates such a relationship between the tillers and the land as to make that possible, and which gives them incentives for investing such funds as they can dispose of or acquire, and above all their own labour, in order to increase the productivity of the land."[48]

Reforms in land and tenancy systems can be realistic and meaningful only if based on a proper understanding of such systems, and it is to the cause of such understanding that this study seeks to devote itself.

(January 8, 1973). For the best available account of the history of Nepali recruitment in the Indian and British armies see Rose, op. cit. (in n.14 above), pp. 132-34, 141-43, 181, 258.

[45] William H. Nicholls, "The Place of Agriculture in Economic Development," in Carl K. Eicher and Lawrence W. Witt, eds., *Agriculture in Economic Development* (reprint; Bombay: Vora & Co., 1970), p. 25.

[46] Ibid., p. 12.

[47] Gunnar Myrdal, *The Challenge of World Poverty* (Penguin Books, 1971), p. 126.

[48] Ibid.

Chapter 2

THE STATE AND THE LAND

The purpose of this study is to analyze how individuals and institutions acquire rights in agricultural lands in Nepal, and how those rights are divided between the owner and the actual cultivator. Almost no social scientist would deny today that the agrarian structure is one of the most important factors affecting economic development. Agrarian structure, or the institutional framework of agricultural production, however, is a comprehensive term. It includes, in addition to land tenure and tenancy, problems relating to agricultural credit and marketing, taxation, and services made available by government to the rural population.[1] This study is limited to only three of these aspects of agrarian structure: land tenure, or the legal or customary systems under which land is owned or occupied; land tenancy, or the system under which land is cultivated by tenants and the product is divided between landowner and tenant; and the burden imposed by the government on the landowner in the form of land taxation.

We may begin with the truism that in any society, systems of land tenure develop within the framework of its political philosophy and its general policies toward property in land.[2] Where the society is still in the primitive stage of economic development, land-tenure policy is based upon the custom that land belongs to the person who reclaims and cultivates it. The nature and extent of rights in the land in such a situation are governed by the need for survival and personal use. The concept of property rights in the land, divorced from the requirements of personal use, emerges only through the sovereign powers of government and is based on law and documentary evidence.[3]

[1] United Nations, *Land Reform: Defects in Agrarian Structure as Obstacles to Economic Development* (New York: U.N. Department of Economic Affairs, 1951), pp. 4–5.
[2] Kenneth H. Parsons, "The Tenure of Farms, Motivation, and Productivity," in *Science, Technology and Development*, vol. III, *Agriculture* (Washington: U.S. Government Printing Office, n.d.), p. 27.
[3] Kenneth H. Parsons, "Agrarian Reform Policy as a Field of Research," in *Agrarian Reform and Economic Growth in Developing Countries* (Washington: U.S. Government Printing Office, 1962), p. 18.

The *Raikar* System

In Nepal, land has traditionally been considered to be the property of the state. This system of state landlordism is known as *Raikar*.[4] There is considerable evidence to support the view that state ownership of the land is an institution that has been sanctified both by law and by tradition. Traditionally, agricultural lands under *Raikar* tenure were cultivated by private individuals, but within the limits required for subsistence and without the rights of alienation through sale or otherwise. Rights in *Raikar* lands thus comprised only the right to its use and its fruits.

Inasmuch as the state was the owner of all lands situated within its domain, it alone possessed the right of alienation through sale, mortgage, or bequest. The state used to grant *Raikar* lands, both waste and cultivated, to individuals as well as to religious and charitable institutions under generally freehold tenure. Often, it also sold or mortgaged *Raikar* lands to individuals. Such practices reinforce the theory of state ownership of the land in Nepal. Private rights in the land thus emerged solely through governmental initiative. The emergence of private rights in the land resulted in the creation of a number of secondary forms of land tenure. The nature of such rights depended primarily on two factors: the purpose of the relinquishment of its ownership rights by the state, and the character of the beneficiary. This leads us to a description of *Birta*, *Guthi*, and *Jagir* tenure as derivatives of the *Raikar* land-tenure system.

Birta

The term *Birta* is a corrupt form of the Sanskrit term *Vritti*, meaning livelihood. *Birta* therefore meant an assignment of income from the

---

[4]The term *Raikar* has never been legally defined. Traditionally, all state-owned lands were regarded as *Raikar*. Recent legislation has made a distinction between state and public lands. State lands have been defined as lands in the possession of the government for such purposes as roads, railways, and government offices, including waste land, forests, and rivers. Public lands, on the other hand, have been defined as lands used by the community for paths, sources of water, pastures, and the like, which are not owned by any individual or family and cannot be used for agricultural purposes. Ministry of Law and Justice, "Jagga Nap Janch Ain" [Land survey and measurement act], *Nepal Gazette*, vol. 12, no. 44A (Extraordinary), Chaitra 30, 2019 (April 12, 1963), sec. 2(e), (f). No question of taxation or individual ownership arises on either state or public lands. The connotation of *Raikar* has thus contracted to lands that are owned by individuals subject to payment of tax to the state.

land by the state in favor of individuals in order to provide them with a livelihood. In a society such as Nepal's, we generally find groups which, by virtue of religious tradition or their social and political function, cannot participate in economic pursuits. Their maintenance, generally at the cost of the agrarian class, is a primary responsibility of the state. Divestiture of ownership rights in the land through *Birta* grants in favor of priests, religious teachers, soldiers, and members of the nobility and the royal family was thus the pivot on which rested the social and political framework of the state. *Birta* ownership not only insured a stable and secure income to the beneficiary, but also symbolized high social and economic status. *Birta* was in fact regarded as a form of private property with a clearly defined right vis-à-vis the state.

Guthi

Birta rights did not, however, include protection from resumption or confiscation by the state. The power to grant implies the power to resume, and there have been many instances in the history of Nepal in which the state has nullified *Birta* grants on various pretexts. Protection from arbitrary governmental action was generally guaranteed only through the *Guthi* system, under which the state or *Birta* owners endowed lands for the establishment or maintenance of such religious and charitable institutions as temples, monasteries, schools, hospitals, orphanages, and poorhouses. *Guthi* is thus a form of institutional landownership, the religious and charitable aspects of which have given rise to special problems and characteristics in the fields of land tenure and taxation.

Jagir

Before 1951, it was a common practice in Nepal to assign the income of *Raikar* lands as emoluments of office to government employees and functionaries. Such assignments were known as *Jagir*, while *Raikar* lands not so assigned were called *Jagera*. The use of the term *Jagir*, which is of Persian origin, to denote land assignments to government employees and functionaries was originally confined to India. There is, however, evidence that the *Jagir* system as it evolved in Nepal acquired characteristics that differentiated it basically from the system followed in India. *Jagir* ownership in India did not necessarily imply the obligation to discharge specific functions. In fact, it was often the result of services rendered in the past, instead of a form of compensation for current services. In Nepal, on the other hand, *Jagir* land assignments were invariably made in consideration of current services, and land grants in appreciation of services rendered in the past were usually associated with the *Birta* system. *Jagirdars* consequently had more permanent rights in their land assignments in India than in Nepal. This perhaps explains the fact that when the *Jagir* system was abolished in India after 1947, compensation was paid to the expropriated *Jagirdars*. On the other hand, their counterparts in Nepal received no such consideration when the *Jagir* system was abolished in early 1952.

Birta and *Guthi* owners and *Jagirdars* acquired their rights through royal grants or assignments that made them lords and masters of the land and the peasant in every sense. These rights were the result of an act of alienation, whether temporary or permanent, by the state of its own rights. In the course of time, the development of a central state authority circumscribed this type of landownership rights in various ways, but their ascriptive nature was never in doubt. At the same time, the rights of *Birta* owners and *Jagirdars* in the land were not necessarily synonymous with property rights, which exist only where opportunities to use and occupy the land are made secure by law, and where these opportunities are transferable by lease, sale, or inheritance. From this viewpoint, only a few categories of *Birta* owners enjoyed full-fledged property rights in the land.

Rakam

Unlike *Birta*, *Guthi*, and *Jagir*, *Rakam* refers not to any particular category of land grants and assignments, but to *Raikar* lands, including those assigned as *Jagir*, and *Guthi* lands on which the cultivators were required to provide unpaid labor on a compulsory basis to meet governmental requirements. The right of the state to exact compulsory and unpaid labor from its subjects has been traditionally recognized in Nepal. When this obligation was commuted to a specific service to be rendered on a regular and inheritable basis by the inhabitants of a prescribed village or area, it was known as *Rakam*. Under the *Rakam* system, their services were assigned for the performance of specific functions designated by the government, and the lands being cultivated by them, irrespective of their previous tenurial status, were converted into *Rakam* tenure. *Rakam* tenure thus imposed obligations on the peasant in the form of both in-kind or cash payments and labor services. This system was limited to the hill region, particularly Kathmandu Valley.

The *Kipat* System

Raikar and its secondary forms do not, however, exhaust the list of systems of land tenure in Nepal. We have noted previously that the concept of statutory rights in the land emerges only through the sovereign powers of government and that in traditional societies landtenure policy is based upon the custom that land belongs to the person who reclaims it. In Nepal, although the concept of statutory rights in the land had developed long before the political unification of the kingdom during the latter part of the eighteenth century, there still existed areas and communities where traditional concepts of customary rights in the land persisted. Such rights were generally of a communal character and were known as *Kipat*. *Raikar* and *Kipat* are therefore based on diametrically opposed conceptions of the source of rights to use the land. The *Raikar* system and its secondary forms implied individual use of the land subject to the overriding rights of the state. Possession of land under these tenure forms was unrelated to the ethnic or communal origin of the landowner. In the *Kipat* form of land tenure, however, communal authority superseded any claim that the state might extend on grounds of internal sovereignty or state landlordism. A *Kipat* owner derived rights in *Kipat* lands by virtue of his membership in a particular ethnic group and their location in a particular area.

TABLE 1
AREA UNDER VARIOUS FORMS OF LAND TENURE, 1952

Form of tenure	Area (hectares)	Percentage of total area
Raikar	963,500	50.0
Birta	700,000 [a]	36.3
Guthi	40,000	2.0
Kipat	77,000	4.0
Jagir, Rakam, etc.	146,500	7.7
Total	1,927,000	100.0

Source: See chap. 2, n. 5.

[a] Inasmuch as a part of the 700,000 hectares of land under *Birta* tenure was used as *Guthi* by individuals, the total area under *Guthi* tenure may have approximated 4 percent.

In contradistinction to the *Raikar* system of land tenure and its derivatives, therefore, *Kipat* represented a communal form of tenure. Landownership under the *Kipat* system was limited to certain communities of Mongoloid origin, such as the Limbus, Rais, Danuwars, Sunuwars, and Tamangs, in the eastern and western hill areas of Nepal. Table 1, based on recent estimates, gives the area under the different forms of land tenure before 1950.[5]

INTERRELATIONSHIP OF DIFFERENT FORMS OF LAND TENURE

Nepal's land-tenure system is schematically represented in chart 1, from which it can be seen that the basic forms of land tenure are *Raikar* and *Kipat*. *Raikar* lands belong to the state, according to the theory of state landlordism, whereas *Kipat* lands belong to the community under a customary form of land tenure that was gradually merged into the state tenure system. *Raikar* land was known as *Birta* when it was alienated by the state in favor of individuals, and as *Jagera* when it was assigned as emoluments to government employees and functionaries. *Guthi* tenure originated from the alienation of *Jagera*, *Birta*, or *Kipat* lands by the state, or by private individuals, for religious and charitable purposes. Fiscal and tenurial concessions granted to cultivators of *Jagera*, *Guthi*, *Jagir*, and *Kipat* lands led to the emergence of *Rakam* tenure. Although *Raikar* was a reflection of the unlimited prerogative of an absolute government which identified landownership with sovereignty, its secondary forms were basically a response to the need to adapt the land system to different economic, political, social, religious, and administrative requirements. The *Birta* system thus helped to create a feudalistic class that gave social and political support to the rulers; the *Guthi* system contributed to the satisfaction of religious propensities of both the rulers and the common people; and the *Jagir* and *Rakam* systems enabled the government to support an administrative structure without the use of much cash in a situation where an exchange economy had not yet fully developed.

It would, of course, be misleading to assume that the different forms of land tenure traditionally prevalent in Nepal, and their interrelationships, as analyzed above, have remained static through the centuries. On the contrary, they have undergone recurrent changes in both form and substance under the impact of changing social, economic, and political conditions. Notwithstanding such changes, which will be

[5] Zaman, *Evaluation of Land Reform in Nepal*, p. 7.

Chart 1. Land-Tenure System in Nepal

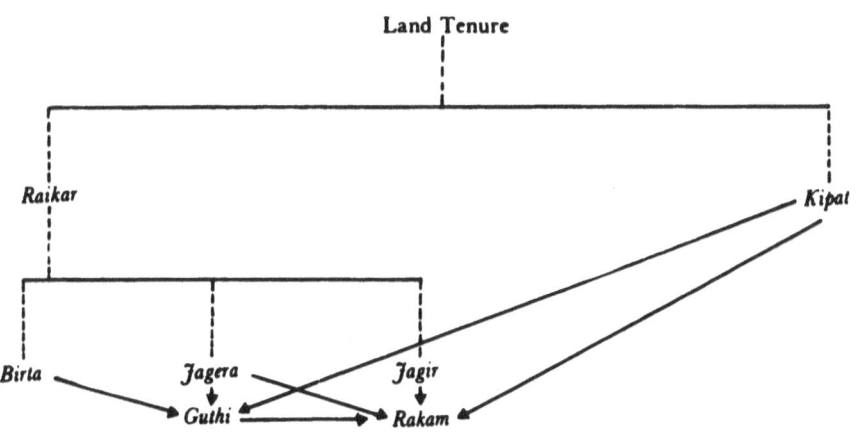

discussed in the appropriate chapters, the basic forms of land tenure in Nepal remained until 1951 more or less the same as they were at the time of the political unification of the country during the latter part of the eighteenth century. Thus they proved anachronistic in the changed circumstances of post-1951 Nepal. The *Birta* system limited the internal sovereign rights of the state, particularly its power to tax all forms of property within its domain. The system was a symbol of privileges which was antithetical to the egalitarian ideals ushered in by the 1950 revolution. The *Jagir* system symbolized the process whereby an oligarchic group was able to use its political power for economic advancement. Even the *Kipat* system, despite its origin in customary law, betrayed a spirit of narrow communalism. *Rakam* tenure, although advantageous to the government, conflicted with the general ban on forced labor proclaimed after the overthrow of the Rana regime. It is not surprising, therefore, that the *Birta*, *Jagir*, and *Rakam* systems should have been abolished during the post-1951 period. Moreover, legislation has already been enacted to abolish the *Kipat* system. Notwithstanding these abolition measures, a study of all the traditional forms of land tenure in Nepal is essential in order to provide a balanced perspective of the evolution of the land-tenure system as a whole, and, in addition, to assure a better understanding of recent land-reform measures.

Chapter 3

PRIVILEGED LANDOWNERSHIP: *BIRTA* TENURE

Oligarchic regimes, such as those that governed Nepal before 1951, have always depended on select classes in the society for the sustenance of their authority. Land grants to members of those classes assured them a stable income and ample leisure to engage in war, religion, or politics in the interests of the rulers. In Nepal, land grants by the state in favor of priests, religious teachers, soldiers, and members of the nobility and royal family accordingly constituted the foundation of social and political life during the pre-1951 period. Such grants led to the emergence of the *Birta* system. This system had an ancient origin in Nepal. Even before the mid-eighteenth century, when the country was divided into a number of petty principalities, the *Birta* system existed in more or less similar forms in such widely separated areas as Morang in the eastern Tarai,[1] Dullu in the northwest,[2] and Kathmandu Valley.[3] A common religious, social, and economic

---

[1]Shankar Man Rajvamshi, ed., *Puratattwa-Patrasangraha* [A collection of ancient documents] (Kathmandu: Department of Archeology and Culture, His Majesty's Government, 2018-19 [1961-62]), II, 12-13. This refers to a *Birta* grant made by King Kamadatta Sen of Vijayapur in eastern Nepal to a Brahman, Ramachandra Pandit, in the Vikrama year 1820 (1763).

[2]Naraharinath Yogi, *Itihas Prakash* [Light on history] Kathmandu: Itihas Prakash Mandal, 2012-13 [1955-56]), II (1), 49-52. This refers to a land grant made by King Prithvi Malla of Dullu to a Brahman in the Shaka year 1278 (1356). The inscription uses the term *Vritti* to denote the grant.

[3]Rajvamshi, op. cit., I, 24-25. This document refers to a *Kusha Birta* grant made by King Jaya Prakash Malla of Kathmandu to a Brahman, Laxmi Narayan Upadhyaya, in the Nepal year 880 (1760). However, the use of the term *Vritti* to denote tax-free land grants appears to have been unknown in Kathmandu Valley during the Licchavi period. Such grants were then known as *Agrahara*, and *Vritti* denoted the category of land assignments that we have described as *Jagir* in this study. Dhanabajra Bajracharya, *Licchavi Kalka Abhilekh* [Inscriptions of the Licchavi period] (Kathmandu: Institute of Nepal and Asian Studies, Tribhuwan University, Ashadh 2030 [June 1973]), p. 96. The use of the term *Birta* was not confined to Nepal. In several parts of India, the variant *Birt* was used to denote tax-free land grants. B. R. Misra, *Land Revenue Policy in the United Provinces* (Banaras: Nand Kishore and Bros. 1942), p. 205.

background contributed to a similarity of land-tenure forms notwithstanding political diversity.

Origin and Evolution of the *Birta* System

The *Birta* system owed its origin to the divestiture of ownership in the land by the state in favor of individuals. Private ownership of the land, which the system implied, did not constitute an original right, but was the result of a grant by the state. Mere possession, in the absence of documentary evidence, usually did not entitle an owner to retain landownership rights under *Birta* tenure.[4] Although *Birta* grants often took the form of assignments of revenue, so that the beneficiary was not entitled to cultivate the land himself, his unquestioned rights to increase rents, evict tenants, resume the land, or sell it under specified circumstances show that *Birta* constituted a form of private property.

Birta land grants were made primarily because religious, economic, and political considerations made it necessary for the state to provide means of subsistence or enrichment to certain individuals. The religious motivation of land grants to Brahmans, for instance, was one of the primary factors in the emergence of the *Birta* system in Nepal. In view of the importance of land in the national economy, the system was also utilized to extend the cultivated area and increase public revenues. Political considerations, too, played a large role in shaping the *Birta* system, for it was used both to enrich members of the ruling classes and to assure them of the support of vested interests with a stake in the preservation of their authority. The relative importance of these various factors has differed from time to time, depending upon contemporary social and political conditions.

Ancient Sanskrit texts advocated tax-exempt and inheritable land grants to learned Brahmans, teachers, and priests.[5] A *Birta* grant made by a king of Dullu in western Nepal as early as A.D. 1356 stated that any person who bequeathed land to Brahmans would dwell in heaven for 60,000 years, while anyone who confiscated land grants would become a worm living in human excrement for the same period.[6] Such injunc-

---

[4]This was the main legal basis on which lands used as *Birta* or *Guthi* were confiscated in 1806. The measure will be described in detail later in this chapter.

[5]R. Shama Sastry, *Kautilya's Arthasastra* (8th ed.; Mysore: Mysore Printing and Publishing House, 1967), p. 45.

[6]See n. 2 above. This belies the claim that the injunction was first given by King Jayasthiti Malla of Kathmandu in 1395. Daniel Wright, *History of Nepal* (reprint of 1877 ed.; Kathmandu: Nepal Antiquated Book Publishers, 1972), p. 187.

tions also are found in later grants.[7] In several cases, the grants also invoked the blessing of the recipient for the spiritual well-being of the donor, and of his relatives and successors as well.[8] Included in the category of religious *Birta* were those granted for the establishment of *Guthi*. The government appears to have made grants of this nature liberally. It would probably be erroneous, however, to regard all such grants as altruistic, for the recipients were usually permitted to appropriate the surplus income after discharging the functions stipulated under the *Guthi*.

Land being the most valuable natural resource in Nepal, governmental policy was directed to maximizing agricultural production and augmenting revenue from the land. The *Birta* system was often utilized as a tool for the implementation of such policies. In many cases, *Birta* grants were made in order to extend the cultivated area.[9] In the same way, *Birta* lands were granted for residential purposes with the objective of encouraging settlement.[10] *Raikar* lands were occasionally sold by the state to individuals as *Birta* in Kathmandu Valley during the pre-Gorkhali period.[11] In the hill regions, mortgages of *Raikar* lands,

[7]"Kush Birta Grant to Brahma Upadhyaya Adhikari and Haribamsha Adhikari," Ashadh Badi 4, 1874 (June 1817), in Mahesh C. Regmi, *Land Tenure and Taxation in Nepal*, (Berkeley and Los Angeles: University of California Press, 1963-68), II, 150-51.

[8]Naraharinath Yogi, *Itihas Prakash*, I, 89.

[9]"Order to Prajapati Padhya regarding Land Reclamation in Arun-Tista Region," Baisakh Sudi 10, 1862 (May 1805). During the early 1940s, regulations were enforced permitting any person who reclaimed waste land in the Tarai region to acquire it as *Birta* on payment of the capital value of the yield at 5 percent. Regmi, op. cit., II, 18-19. Obviously, the tax exemption and other privileges which the *Birta* grant insured were considered a sufficient inducement for the pioneer venture of reclaiming waste lands.

[10]"Any person who constructs a house with a tiled roof on waste *Raikar* lands outside urban areas and in the hill regions shall be granted the area within the line of the roof and 10 cubits in the front for use as a courtyard under *Birta* tenure." Government of Nepal, "Ghar Banaunya Ko" [On construction of houses], in Ministry of Law and Justice, *Shri 5 Surendra Bikram Shahdevaka Shasan Kalma Baneko Muluki Ain* [Legal code enacted during the reign of King Surendra Bikram Shah Dev] (Kathmandu: the Ministry, 2022 [1965]), sec. 1, p. 340. The provision was in force until 1963. Government of Nepal, "Ghar Banaune Ko" [On construction of houses], *Muluki Ain*, [Legal code] pt. III (Kathmandu: Gorkhapatra Press, 2009 [1952]), sec. 1, p. 71.

[11]See Rajvamshi, I, 13-17, for such land sales by King Jagajjaya Malla (1722-36) and King Jaya Prakash Malla (1736-68) of Kathmandu. Similar transactions in Lalitpur are recorded in articles by Rajvamshi: "Siddhinarasimha Mallaka Tadapatra Tamasukharu" [Palm-leaf bonds of Siddhinarasimha Malla], *Ancient Nepal*, July 1968, pp. 23-26; "Srinivasa Malla ra Yoganarendra Mallaka Tadapatra Tamasukharu" [Palm-leaf bonds of Srinivasa Malla and Yoganarendra Malla], ibid., October 1968, pp. 29-33; "Lalitpurka Mallarajaka Tadapatra Tamasukharu" [Palm-leaf bonds of the Malla kings of Lalitpur], ibid., July 1969, pp. 29-33; and "Yogaprakasha Mallaka Tamapatra, Tadapatra ra Tamasukharu" [Copper and palm-leaf inscriptions and bonds of Yogaprakasha Malla], ibid., October 1969, pp. 25-32.

which created a new type of *Birta* tenure, were more common.[12] Such sales and mortgages helped the rulers to meet extraordinary expenditures on a one-time basis, even though at the cost of a permanent source of revenue. The Shah and Rana rulers seldom resorted to this practice.

In a society where land constituted the predominant source of income, and landownership was synonymous with social status, the power to bestow or withhold favors in the form of *Birta* grants was of considerable significance in organizing the foundations of a new political authority and administration. Personal loyalty to the rulers was thus leavened with the prospect of material gain. In addition, the system insured that the nobility would remain loyal, for disloyalty was punishable by confiscation of property, including *Birta* lands.[13] The *Birta* system accordingly constituted the bedrock of the political and administrative system introduced after the political unification of Nepal. The Shah rulers, without any exception, made lavish *Birta* grants to the leading families of the nobility of the day. On several occasions, *Birta* grants were made in appreciation of assistance rendered during military campaigns. There are numerous examples to prove that *Birta* grants were made by the Shah rulers to reward victorious generals and to win over or reward those who supported their newly established authority.[14] During the last decades of the eighteenth century, the Shah rulers also granted *Birtas* to the chieftains and members of the nobility of some of the hill principalities, mainly in Jumla, Dailekh, Doti, and Baglung districts, which were annexed in the process of political unification.[15] In the majority of cases, such

---

[12]"Orders regarding Confirmation of Bandha Lands Granted by Rajas of Tanahu and Lamjung," Ashadh Sudi 2, 1853 (June 1796). During 1795 and 1832–37, many of these mortgages were revalued and the excess area was converted into *Raikar*. "Regulations regarding Reduction in Bandha Holdings in Western Hill Region," Aswin Sudi 15, 1852 (October 1795); "Order regarding Revaluation of Bandha Lands in Western Hill Region, Shrawan Sudi 8, 1893 (August 1836).

[13]"The government shall confiscate the lands of any person who, during war with any kingdom, goes over to the enemy and gets such lands reconfirmed. Punishment shall be awarded to him at the discretion of the prime minister. This law, enacted by King Prithvi Narayan Shah in 1768, is herein retained." Government of Nepal, "Kagaj Janch Ko" [On official documents], *Muluki Ain*, pt. I (Kathmandu: Gorkhapatra Press, 2012 [1955]), sec. 8, p. 52.

[14]Naraharinath Yogi, I, 14. The reference is to a *Birta* grant made by King Pratap Simha (1775–78) in 1777 to General Abhiman Simha Basnet for his successful military campaigns in the Pallokirat region.

[15]"Order regarding Halbandi Birta of Bishnu Shahi," Bhadra 14, 2005 (August 30, 1948), in Regmi, II, 31–32.

favors were conferred because the nobility of the conquered principalities had defected to the Gorkhalis and rendered active assistance in their military campaigns. Where the chieftains refrained from fighting to the bitter end, they often retained their principalities on an autonomous, feudatory basis.[16] The obvious aim was to extend the overlordship of the Gorkha dynasty without alienating the support of the existing chieftains and nobility.

Birta Grants during the Rana Period

The emergence of the Rana regime in 1846 heralded a new phase in the history of the *Birta* system in Nepal. The composition of the nobility underwent a fundamental change when several of its members were massacred or banished in 1846. The new regime followed a policy of enriching the new nobility through liberal *Birta* grants. Moreover, the Rana family itself constituted an extensive class which was similarly enriched. The *Birta* system was exploited lavishly to serve these twin purposes.

Several factors explain why the Rana rulers were able to exploit the *Birta* system for their personal ends. Political power was combined with the unlimited greed of successive incumbents who had not benefited from their predecessor's accumulations because of the absence of a system of succession by primogeniture. Indeed, frequently, Rana prime ministers were in relatively straitened circumstances on the eve of their accession. Such a situation continued for more than a century. Although frictions, often sanguinary, were common within the Rana family itself, and usually resulted in the confiscation of the *Birta* holdings of the victims, this seldom meant that the confiscated lands were removed from the possession of the family as a whole. Moreover, the Rana rulers not only possessed large areas of lands as *Birtas* themselves, but also made liberal bequests to their relatives and favorites.

The Nature of the *Birta*-owning Class

Birta landownership was thus necessarily of an exclusive character.

---

[16] The Raja of Bajura was among those who were granted such status. He had rendered valuable assistance during Gorkha's wars with Achham, Doti, and Jumla. "Confirmation of Bajura as Feudatory State," Shrawan Sudi 15, 1848 (August 1791).

The religious, political, and other factors described above insured that favors bestowed by the state in the form of *Birta* grants were restricted to a few select classes in the community. Indeed, with regard to both religion and politics, *Birta* grants tended to be concentrated for the most part among Brahmans, Chhetris, and other classes of Indo-Aryan origin to the exclusion of aboriginal groups of Mongoloid origin such as Gurungs, Magars, Limbus, and Tamangs. The Newar community in Kathmandu Valley appears to have been an exception. Even though denied top positions in both the army and the civil administration, Newars were nevertheless outstandingly successful in court life and in acquiring positions in the middle echelons of the civil service, particularly during the Rana period. Members of that community were therefore closer to the rulers than those of the Mongoloid communities, and, as a result, received *Birta* grants. In particular, Brahmans constituted a powerful *Birta*-owning class in Nepal. Religious considerations made their *Birta* holdings not only fairly secure but also steadily expansive.

Birta lands, however, were generally transferable; hence the *Birta* system did not create a stable and exclusive landed aristocracy. Although the right to sell *Birta* lands was probably detrimental to the interests of the *Birta*-owning class, it was considered to be a form of privilege without which *Birta*-ownership was not meaningful in the full sense of the term. The exercise of that privilege meant that *Birta* lands often went into the hands of moneyed people who had little in common with the original recipients. Various methods were applied by the government, as well as by *Birta* owners themselves, to prevent the transfer of *Birta* lands. Certain grants specified that transfers could be made only with official permission.[17] Members of the royal and Rana families and royal priests were thus prohibited from transferring their lands without such permission.[18] *Birta* owners often sought to forestall attempts by their successors to transfer lands by assigning them as *Guthi* and allocating a small portion of the income for some religious or charitable purpose.[19]

[17]"Bakas Birta Grant to Colonel Pushpa Shamsher," Falgun 23, 2002 (March 7, 1946).

[18]Government of Nepal, *Madhesh Malko Sawal* [Revenue regulations for the Tarai districts] (Kathmandu: Gorkhapatra Press, n.d.), sec. 32, p. 17.

[19]The Legal Code took note of *Guthi* endowments made by landowners "only with objective of insuring that their descendants do not sell the lands." Government of Nepal, "Guthi Ko" [On Guthi], *Muluki Ain*, pt. III (2012 [1955]), sec. 4(2), p. 2. See also chap. 4 below.

The *Birta* system was therefore founded on archaic social, religious, economic, and political conditions and was preserved by governments that were unmoved by ideals of equality and the welfare of the common man. Outdated ideas of religion and caste sanctity, as well as the stratification of castes and classes within the community, created an atmosphere congenial to the growth of the *Birta* system. The tendency in the sphere of public finance to follow the line of least resistance and not to arouse antagonism to political authority by seeking to reform traditional institutions and privileges, together with neglect of problems of national development in general, obviated any interest in the abolition of the *Birta* system. The oligarchic regimes that fostered the *Birta* system depended, in turn, on the support of the privileged *Birta*-owning class, so that the interests of this class in keeping the *Birta* system intact coincided with those of the rulers and made all suggestion of *Birta* reform an anathema. It was not surprising, therefore, that the practice of making *Birta* grants was discontinued after the downfall of the Rana regime in 1951.

Vicissitudes of *Birta* Landownership

Birta landownership has had a checkered history in Nepal. The emergence of a new political authority was always followed by a change in the composition of the *Birta*-owning class.[20] Few grants made by the Malla kings, or even by the Shah kings before 1846, were extant in 1950. Even those that were probably owed their continued existence to subsequent confirmation. Additional evidence of this is provided by the *Birta*-abolition measures that were adopted after the downfall of the Rana regime.

After the political unification of Nepal, *Birta* lands granted by former rulers were confiscated when any new territory was subjugated by conquest rather than by surrender. Such confiscations were seldom of a general character, for elements who had supported the conquerors

---

[20] Developments during 1837–40 clearly illustrate how political upheavals affected the *Birta* system. The downfall of Prime Minister Bhimsen Thapa in 1837 resulted in the confiscation of the *Birta* lands of all members of the Thapa family. But the new prime minister, Ran Jung Pande, himself fell into royal disfavor after three years. *Birta* lands owned by members of the Pande family were then confiscated in 1842. Fortune again smiled upon the Thapas when Mathbar Singh Thapa, a nephew of Bhimsen Thapa, became prime minister in April 1843. The new prime minister forthwith took steps to restore the confiscated *Birta* lands of the Thapa family. He, too, fell from power after a few months, and his lands were confiscated. Regmi, II, 91.

during the struggle were naturally exempted. Often the victor had to pacify particular groups or areas by refraining from confiscation, or perhaps by subsequent restoration of confiscated *Birta* grants. Measures were initiated in 1787 to resume lands being utilized as *Birta* or *Guthi* without valid documentary evidence of title. For this purpose, both *Birta* and *Guthi* grants were scrutinized, and those that had not been made in the name of the reigning king were confiscated. Military requirements stepped up the pace of such measures during 1805-6. The basic features of measures undertaken during those years for the scrutiny of *Birta* and *Guthi* grants in different parts of the country may be summarized as follows. All land grants made by former kings, and by their queens and crown princes, were confirmed, provided the holders had accepted Kathmandu's suzerainty and had not been displaced. But the area in excess of the figure mentioned in the grant was confiscated. Land grants made without royal authority by officials deputed from Kathmandu were abolished. In case documentary evidence of title was not available, and the adjoining landowners had no knowledge of either the donor or the beneficiary, the lands were confiscated. Even when documentary evidence was not available, lands were not confiscated if the adjoining landowners took an oath that the grant was authentic.[21]

The primary objective of these measures was to detect cases in which newly reclaimed lands were being utilized without the payment of taxes. It would therefore be incorrect to regard them as *Birta*-confiscation moves. Inasmuch as *Birta* lands could be obtained only through royal grants, it would be inappropriate to use the term to denote lands reclaimed and cultivated without official permission. The regulations did not affect *Birta* owners with valid titles. Even when documentary evidence was not available, *Birta* owners were able to retain their lands if they stated under oath that these had been acquired through valid means. If several *Birta* owners were unable to make such an oath, and hence lost their lands, or had no alternative but to forge inscriptions to justify their possession, this could only mean that the official measures were directed not against *Birtas* as such, but against the use of lands without the payment of taxes.[22]

[21]"Land Survey Regulations," separate regulations for different regions promulgated on different dates during 1862-63 (A.D. 1805-6), in Regmi, *A Study in Nepali Economic History*, pp. 46-48.

[22]The policy of resuming invalid tax-free land grants was followed by the East India Company government also in the adjoining areas of Bihar, Bengal, and Orissa in India after 1782. Ram Narayan Sinha, *Bihar Tenantry (1783-1833)* (Bombay: People's

In September 1846, Jang Bahadur became prime minister and thus laid the foundation of Rana rule in Nepal. Apparently in order to mobilize support for his newly established authority, particularly from the Brahman community, he announced that "tranquillity [had] never prevailed in the palace" since *Birta* and *Guthi* lands had been confiscated in 1805-6. In an effort to gain popularity by exploiting the grievances of the dispossessed landowners, he decreed:

> The *Birta* and *Guthi* lands confiscated in 1806 have been assigned to the army. If now they are taken away from the army and restored to the original owners, the army will cease to exist. If the army does not exist, our enemies will be powerful and the religion of the Hindus may not be safe. Arrangements should therefore be made in such a way that the confiscated *Birta* and *Guthi* lands are restored, while also maintaining the army, so as to safeguard the religion of the Hindus.[23]

Arrangements were therefore made to grant waste tracts in exchange for the confiscated ones,[24] and to provide the beneficiaries with funds to reclaim lands,[25] but these orders were not satisfactorily implemented.[26] Thirty-six years later, in 1882, Prime Minister Ranoddip Singh pointed out that most of the recipients had not been able to

---

Publishing House, 1968), pp. 122-43. The existence of a large number of tax-free holdings of doubtful validity in some parts of Bihar even after the implementation of this policy shows that it was not effectively enforced. Francis Buchanan (Hamilton), *An Account of the District of Purnea in 1809-10* (Patna: Bihar and Orissa Research Society, 1928), pp. 447-50. The general principles followed in both countries to determine the validity of tax-free land grants were more or less similar, but procedures of implementation in Nepal were more authoritarian.

[23] For a detailed account of the restoration program, see Regmi, *Land Tenure and Taxation in Nepal*, II, pp. 89-91.

[24] "Birta Restoration Regulations," Aswin Badi 5, 1905 (September 1848), secs. 1-2.

[25] Chittaranjan Nepali, *Janaral Bhimsen Thapa ra Tatkalin Nepal* [General Bhimsen Thapa and contemporary Nepal] Kathmandu: Nepal Samskritik Sangh, 2013 [1956]), pp. 283-84.

[26] Jang Bahadur himself subsequently enacted legislation decreeing that lands and other property that had been "unjustly" confiscated by former kings and ministers need not be restored or compensated, on the ground that "those who have committed unjust acts will themselves account for their sins at the court of God" (Law Ministry Records, "Rajkaj Ko Ain" [State affairs act], sec. 1). This legislation, however, did not specifically invalidate the restoration decree, and there is evidence that several expropriated *Birta* owners actually obtained lands as compensation. One reason for the slack implementation of the *Birta* restoration program was the scarcity of waste lands. The problem was so acute that in 1858 some Brahman *Birta* owners of Thimi applied for permission to divert some local streams and reclaim the lands situated on the old beds for agricultural purposes, to compensate their expropriated *Birta*. "Order regarding Reclamation of Riverine Lands in Bhaktapur," Magh Sudi 3, 1914 (January 1858).

reclaim the lands allotted to them. He therefore decreed the grant of cultivated lands in exchange for the confiscated areas, so that "both giving and receiving should have some meaning."[27]

During the early years of his rule, Jang Bahadur enacted legislation decreeing that no prime minister or other member of the Rana family should accept grants of cultivated areas in the old territories of the kingdom as *Birta*.[28] The obvious intention of this measure was to prevent the misuse of political power by members of the Rana family for personal enrichment at the expense of the public exchequer, thereby enhancing the prime minister's role and influence in the Rana political elite. For several reasons, however, the restriction remained ineffective. It did not prevent the grant of waste or forest lands in the old territories as *Birta* to the prime minister and other members of the Rana family.[29] In fact, it is possible that this was an indirect way of legitimizing Jang Bahadur's acquisition of the far-western Tarai region, comprising the present districts of Banke, Bardiya, Kailali, and Kanchanpur, as the *Birta* of the Rana family.[30] In any case, this limitation remained partially effective only during approximately the first fifteen years of Jang Bahadur's rule. Thereafter, there is evidence that he acquired cultivated areas as *Birta* on various pretexts.[31] Similarly, Prime Minister Ranoddip Singh acquired, as *Birta*, lands that had been confiscated from "those who had attempted to assassinate him."[32] Later Rana prime ministers, notably Bir

---

[27] Regmi, II, 160–61.
[28] Law Ministry Records, "Rajkaj Ko Ain," sec. 2.
[29] Ibid, sec. 3.
[30] "Sarbakar-Akar-Sarbanga-Mafi Bitalab Birta Grant to Prime Minister Jang Bahadur," Aswin Sudi 6, 1917 (October 1860). For a full translation of this document see Regmi, II, 153–54, opp. C.
[31] For instance, on Poush Sudi 5, 1918 (January 1862), several villages were granted to Prime Minister Jang Bahadur as *Birta* "in appreciation of your services in escorting His Majesty [King Surendra] during his pilgrimage to Gaosainthan." Occasionally, Jang Bahadur obtained *Birta* lands against a monetary payment to the royal treasury. In 1874, for instance, he acquired approximately 250 *bighas* of land in Sarlahi district as *Birta* on payment of Rs. 125,000 in Indian currency. "Order regarding Birta Land Grant to Prime Minister Jang Bahadur in Sarlahi District," Falgun Sudi 13, 1930 (March 1874).
[32] The royal order to Prime Minister Ranoddip Singh stated: "The late [King Surendra] had granted 15,000 *bighas* of lands in the Tarai to Her Highness Haripriya Devi [wife of Prime Minister Ranoddip Singh] for use as *Guthi* and *Birta* in appreciation of her services in looking after us [King Prithvi Bir Bikram] while we were yet Crown Prince. You have now offered to use these lands to compensate the Brahmans whose *Birta* lands had been confiscated in 1806. However, since His late Majesty had already granted these lands to you, we hereby confirm the grant. Although the law

Shamsher, ignored all legal constraints in acquiring *Birta* lands for themselves and for the other members of the Rana family.[33] As a result, that family was the largest *Birta*-owning class in Nepal when Rana rule ended in 1951.

These developments highlight the regressive role played by the Rana regime in creating a new class of landed interests and enriching its own members. With this end in view, a radical departure from the old policy of confiscating *Birta* lands lacking documentary evidence of title was initiated. The Rana government decreed that whatever lands had been obtained during the reign of former kings on any condition should be confirmed in accordance with the grant, if any, or else on the basis of possession as confirmed by owners of adjoining holdings.[34]

The Rana rulers were, in fact, faced with a dilemma. They wanted to preserve the sanctity of the *Birta* system, while at the same time confiscating the *Birta* lands of persons other than their relatives and favorites. The solution that they adopted was to screen *Birta* grants on the basis of the terms and conditions mentioned therein, with the purpose of disclosing defects in titles and thus resuming *Birta* lands as *Raikar*.[35] For instance, legislation was enacted denying the right of inheritance on all grants that did not specifically make this provision.[36]

prohibits the vizier and his brothers and sons from accepting grants of lands other than forests in the old territories of the kingdom as *Birta*, we hereby grant the following [cultivated] lands to you, since such lands had been granted as *Birta* to the later Prime Minister Jang Bahadur also. Moreover, the lands which are now being granted to you as *Birta* were confiscated from those who attempted to assassinate you." "Order regarding Birta Land Grant to Prime Minister Ranoddip Singh," Ashadh Sudi 1, 1940 (June 1883). Violation of the law by Jang Bahadur thus set a precedent that was followed by his successors for their own benefit. One can say that these prime ministers at least realized that they were violating the law.

[33]"Bakas Birta Grant to Prime Minister Bir Shamsher," Poush Sudi 5, 1946 (January 1890). This document provided that lands yielding an income of Rs. 20,000 in Indian currency in Saptari and Rautahat districts were granted as *Birta* to Prime Minister Bir Shamsher. There is no reference to the limitations imposed by the State Affairs Act.

[34]Government of Nepal, "Jagga Michne Ko" [On encroachment on land], *Muluki Ain*, pt. III (2009 [1952]), sec. 1, p. 41.

[35]This seems to have been the objective of the survey and compilation of fresh *Birta* records by Prime Minister Bir Shamsher (1855-1901) in Kathmandu Valley, Palpa, and elsewhere.

[36]"[*Birta* lands] may be used according to the terms mentioned in the grant, if these have been in actual possession. In the case of *Birta* grants which permit inheritance, alienation shall be permitted only if the grants contain a specific provision to this effect. Otherwise, alienation shall not be permitted, and the lands may be used only according to the terms mentioned in the grant." Government of Nepal, "Jagga Jamin Goshwara Ko" [On miscellaneous land matters], *Muluki Ain*, pt. III (2009 [1952]), secs. 1, 1A, p. 61.

Owing mainly to the emphasis on legality, *Birta* rights remained more or less secure from arbitrary encroachment and confiscation throughout the period of Rana rule, so long as those rights did not directly clash with the political or economic interests of the Ranas. In the course of time, the Ranas became the largest *Birta*-owning family in Nepal, and they hesitated to take any action that might ultimately undermine the stability or sanctity of the system to their own obvious disadvantage.

Privileges and Obligations of *Birta* Landowners

Under the *Birta* system, in its traditional form, peasants worked on behalf of the *Birta* owners in conditions over which the government exercised no control. Police and judicial functions were discharged by the *Birta* owners,[37] and every local inhabitant was under obligation to provide unpaid labor services to them.[38] Exempt from the regular land tax due to the government, *Birta* owners were entitled to appropriate not only agricultural rents but also revenue from nonagricultural sources such as customs and market duties, judicial fines, and escheats.[39] The beneficiary of a *Birta* land grant was therefore not merely a landowner: in many respects he resembled the lord of a manor in England during the Middle Ages. Vested with the proprietorship of an estate, *Birta* owners enjoyed a miscellany of conventional rights and the proceeds of numerous personal servitudes and exactions. As long as they remained politically loyal and were not excessively oppressive, the government had no direct concern with the peasantry. Secure from official interference in the exercise of their rights, *Birta* owners owed allegiance only to the king, an allegiance occasionally manifested when a new king was crowned, or the royal princesses were

---

[37] *Birta* owners could adjudicate only in cases involving a maximum amount of Rs. 100 with a maximum fine of Rs. 25. They did not have the authority to imprison. Government of Nepal, "Jagirdar Birta Walle Jhagada Herda Ko" [On judicial authority of Jagir and Birta owners], *Muluki Ain*, pt. I (2012 [1955]), secs. 1-5, pp. 151-53.

[38] The Legal Code prescribed that unpaid labor should be exacted only if the *Birta* owner had authority to do so under the appropriate grant. Government of Nepal, "Jhara Khetala Ko" [On unpaid labor], *Muluki Ain*, pt. III (2009 [1952]), sec. 1, p. 91. However, the majority of *Birta* grants permitted the beneficiary to exact such labor. "Chhap Birta Land of Sahadatta Upadhyaya," Bhaktapur Birta Records, 1953 (1896).

[39] *Revenue Regulations for the Tarai Districts*, sec. 195, p. 77; sec. 393, p. 168.

married, or during war and other emergencies.[40] *Birta* grants, in fact, meant a virtual abdication by the state of its internal sovereign authority.

This should not create the impression that *Birta* ownership was allodial in character, however, for the government retained several substantial rights on the lands it granted as *Birta*. For instance, it retained the right to confiscate *Birta* lands if the owner was guilty of treason or other offense.[41] Moreover, *Birta* could be acquired for governmental purposes in exercise of the state's right of eminent domain, subject, however, to the payment of compensation.[42]

In many cases, the government of Nepal extended its control over *Birta* lands by incorporating specific conditions governing their use. Some *Birta* grants were thus valid only for the lifetime of the recipient, whereas others imposed restrictions on transfer, subdivision, and inheritance. Occasionally, *Birta* grants were made for specific purposes, with the result that the beneficiary was prevented from using them for other purposes. There were also cases in which *Birta* grants were made conditional upon the performance of specific services, generally of a religious or philanthropic character, and so were liable to be confiscated if the services were discontinued. Legislation enacted during the Rana period prescribed that the terms and conditions laid down in *Birta* grants should be followed to the letter. *Birta* lands that were not granted specifically on an inheritable basis were therefore usually treated as valid only for the beneficiary's lifetime and also as nontransferable. Even when the grants provided the right of inheritance, this did not necessarily secure the right of transfer.[43]

In Kathmandu Valley, the tax-exempt character of *Birta* land did not outlive the Gorkhali conquests. In 1772, King Prithvi Narayan Shah imposed a tax, known as *Pota*, on certain categories of *Birta*

[40] Regmi, II, 10–12, 29–30.

[41] In 1768 King Prithvi Narayan Shah (1768–75) enacted legislation according to which *Birta* lands could not be confiscated unless the owner had committed an offense. Government of Nepal, "Kagaj Janch Ko" [On official documents], *Muluki Ain*, pt. I (2012 [1955]), sec. 9, p. 52, and "Jagga Jamin Goshwara Ko" [On miscellaneous land matters], ibid., pt. III (2009 [1952]), sec. 1, p. 61.

[42] Ibid., sec. 5, p. 62; Government of Nepal, "Jagga Jamin Ko" [On land matters], *Muluki Sawal* [Administrative regulations] (Kathmandu: Gorkhapatra Press, 2010 [1953], sec. 16, pp. 135–36. Compensation for *Birta* lands acquired by the government was paid in cash or other lands were given in exchange. When compensation was paid in cash, it amounted to the capital value of the *Birta* income at 4 percent in Kathmandu Valley and 6 percent elsewhere.

[43] For a detailed account of the different categories of *Birta* grants, see Regmi, II, 28–45.

lands in this region.⁴⁴ The government of Nepal attempted in subsequent years to extend the *Pota* tax system to the hill region as well. This policy was primarily intended "to provide owners with documentary evidence of title and thus to avoid litigation, rather than to maximize government revenue."⁴⁵ Accordingly, the rates were fixed at a comparatively low level. Thanks to this policy, the government was able to utilize potential sources of revenue while at the same time appearing to respect the sanctity of *Birta* grants. Many *Birta* owners were apparently satisfied, because the registration of their tax-exempt *Birta* land as *Pota Birta* enabled them to safeguard their titles even in the absence of documentary evidence. The government, however, admitted in 1947 that not much progress had been achieved in the implementation of the policy.⁴⁶

During the Rana regime, two other taxable categories of *Birta* lands emerged—*Chhap* and *Tiruwa*. *Chhap Birtas* were generally granted for the maintenance of retired civil or military officials and so were noninheritable. Because the objective of the tax was obviously to insure the maintenance of records for facilitating resumption of the land on the death of the beneficiary, the rate was quite nominal. *Tiruwa Birta* grants, on the other hand, were made with the aim of encouraging the reclamation of waste lands in the Tarai through concessional rates of taxation. The rate of the tax on *Birta* lands of this category was roughly half of the level prevailing on *Raikar* lands.⁴⁷ Tax exemption thus no longer remained a characteristic feature of *Birta* ownership, although not all categories of *Birta* lands were taxable.

The expansion of state authority over *Birta* lands was paralleled by a trend toward gradual encroachment on the privileges of *Birta* landowners. During the first decade of the twentieth century, the government reorganized the entire judicial system of the country and established courts at the district level. This reduced the judicial powers of *Birta* owners, because the government was considered to be a more impartial dispenser of justice. Moreover, in 1907, the government, for the first time, enacted legislation seeking to regulate rents paid by tenants to *Birta* owners and to provide for the security of tenancy

⁴⁴Regmi, *A Study in Nepali Economic History*, p. 61.
⁴⁵Law Ministry Records, "Pota Tax Order," Marga 1, 1995 (November 16, 1938).
⁴⁶Law Ministry Records, "Pota Birta Regulations," Shrawan 23, 2007 (August 7, 1950). For a detailed account of *Pota* tax measures during the Rana period see Regmi, *Land Tenure and Taxation in Nepal*, II, 50–52.
⁴⁷Ibid., pp. 32–34, 43–44.

rights.⁴⁸ There is no evidence that, until then, the government exercised any of its police functions (the term being used in a wide sense to include the regulation of the relationship between the *Birta* owner and his tenant) on *Birta* lands.

Obligations were as integral a part of the *Birta* system as privileges. Some *Birta* grants made it obligatory for the beneficiaries to supply men and material during war or other emergencies.⁴⁹ This obligation was manifested in a more general form during the Nepal-Tibet war of 1855-56. On the plea that existing funds in the government treasury were inadequate to meet the expenses of the war, which was being waged to "protect the *Birta, Guthi,* and *Kipat* land of the people and maintain the sword of Gorkha aloft," the government imposed a levy on income from *Birta* and other lands.⁵⁰ Similarly, in 1882 the government decreed that, in the case of certain categories of *Birta* lands:

> If war breaks out in any year, the recipients of such *Birta* lands as well as persons who purchase them shall not be permitted to appropriate the income accruing therefrom, as this shall be utilized for military purposes. They may appropriate such income only after the war ends.⁵¹

This meant that the cost of military operations was to be realized from the *Birta* owners. But there is no evidence that this right was ever actually exercised by the government.

Although *Birta* ownership thus involved both privileges and obligations, the former tended to outweigh the latter. Presumably, the social and political power that the *Birta*-owning class was able to wield almost throughout the course of Nepal's post-1768 history made it possible to evade obligations with impunity. On the other hand, the oligarchic nature of the regime, with its vested interest in the *Birta* system, tended to emphasize the privileges attached to it. This was particularly evident during the Rana regime. According to one study:

---

⁴⁸Government of Nepal, "Jagga Pajani Ko" [On land evictions], *Muluki Ain,* pt. III (2009 [1952]), sec. 20, pp. 33-38.

⁴⁹Regmi, II, 10-12.

⁵⁰Foreign Ministry (Jaisi Kotha) Records, "Imposition of Levy on Birta and Other Landowners," Baisakh Sudi 1, 1912 (April 1855).

⁵¹"Birta Restoration Arrangements Order," Bhadra 1942 (September 1885). These obligations were imposed on *Birta* owners whose lands had been confiscated in 1806 and restored after 1846.

With the rise of the Ranas and the shifting of the foreign policy of the country in favor of the British, a long period of military inactivity and internal tranquillity ensued. The obligations, like supply of men and material during war, fell into disuse. In addition, the larger part of the feudal nobility created by Prithvi Narayan Shah was either purged or reduced to such a state of political insignificance that it was not considered politically expedient to make use of their liabilities. A new *Birta*-owning class came into prominence, but because it was composed for the most part of the new Rana rulers, their relatives, and their favorites, *Birta* ownership meant more a privilege than an obligation.[52]

The privileges conferred by *Birta* ownership were thus more regular, tangible, and effective than the obligations that it entailed. The gradual erosion of *Birta* obligations, combined with the expansion of government control over and regulation of *Birta* ownership, resulted in a fundamental change in the *Birta* system. The system now gradually evolved into a form of land tenure. With his police and judicial authority truncated, his authority over his tenants regulated by law, and his privilege of tax exemption undermined, the *Birta* owner lapsed from his traditional status approximating that of a territorial prince to that of an ordinary landowner subject to the authority of a multi-tiered administrative hierarchy.

Birta AND *Raikar*

The nature of the evolution undergone by the *Birta* system may be further clarified by a comparative analysis with the *Raikar* system of land tenure. Originally, *Raikar* implied a direct relationship between the state and the cultivator, who did not possess the right to appoint tenants to cultivate his holding, or to sell it. In contrast, *Birta* represented private property rights in the land, and *Birta* owners usually enjoyed full rights to possess, occupy, hold, transfer, mortgage, subdivide, and bequeath their lands. In the course of time, individual rights on *Raikar* lands too emerged as a form of property,[53] with the result that rent-receiving rights no longer remained a characteristic feature of *Birta* land. Irrespective of the original character of *Raikar* as state landownership, and of *Birta* as private ownership, the interplay of economic forces gradually brought them sufficiently close to each

---

[52] Mahesh C. Regmi, *Some Aspects of Land Reform in Nepal* (Kathmandu: the author, 1960), p. 9.
[53] This development will be examined in chapter 10.

other to eliminate to a significant extent the distinctive characteristics of each as regards possession, use, and transfer. Even so, when some categories of *Birta* were taxed, the government was careful to insure that the level of taxation was lower than that on *Raikar* land. *Birta* was therefore characterized by exemption, partial or complete, from the normal taxation on *Raikar* land. Because this meant a higher income on *Birta* land as compared to *Raikar* land, higher land values for *Birta* were inevitable.

The attachment to the "ownership" rights that *Birta* insured was not a mere sentiment. Such ownership protected the *Birta* owner from governmental acquisition without compensation, unlike that of *Raikar*. *Birta* ownership implied security of possession also in the sense that whereas *Raikar* land could be assigned as *Birta*, *Rakam*, or *Jagir*, *Birta* land suffered no such disability. *Birta* was therefore regarded as a form of private property in land, which had a clearly defined value and right vis-à-vis the state and which insured a stable and secure income. It meant land that people could call their own. It therefore symbolized wealth and, more important, social status. In contradistinction, *Raikar* provided neither security nor property rights in the real sense of the term.

Privileged Landownership

The *Birta* system undoubtedly served the social, economic, and political needs of the ruling classes of Nepal during the period before 1951. It was a form of privileged landownership that enabled them to exploit the land resources of the nation for their personal advantage. From the viewpoint of the nation, therefore, the *Birta* system was synonymous with inequality and exploitation.

Birta grants, being usually tax exempt, caused considerable loss of revenue to the government,[54] so much so that the high proportion of *Birta* land to the total cultivated area in some districts made it impossible to meet local administrative expenses through local revenue.[55] Moreover, in the absence of tax liability, *Birta* owners often found it possible to maintain large areas as waste or forest lands. This meant

---

[54] The extent of this loss can be appreciated from the fact that in 1957–58 the area of cultivated land under *Birta* tenure was estimated at 1.67 million acres, or 28.2 percent of the total cultivated area at that time. *Nepal Gazette*, vol. 7, no. 15 (Extraordinary), Chaitra 29, 2014 (April 11, 1958), p. 98.

[55] Land Reform Commission, "Report on Land Tenure Conditions in Western Nepal," mimeographed (Kathmandu: the Commission, 2010 [1953]), p. 18.

considerable wastage of national resources, particularly in a situation where the incidence of landlessness was high and ubiquitous. The system also led to the concentration of landownership rights in the hands of a privileged minority. It is true, of course, that social and economic inequality was a characteristic feature of the entire landholding system. The *Birta* system, however, was one of the worst manifestations of this inequality. The obnoxiousness of the system stemmed mainly from the association of tax exemption with inequality of ownership. The existence of large *Birta* landowners holding millions of acres of land without any tax liability presented a sharp contrast to the poverty of the majority of the agrarian population.

Landownership under the *Birta* system was inconsistent with the social, political, and economic ideals that the nation adopted after the downfall of the Rana regime in early 1951. According to the directive principles of state policy contained in the interim constitution which was promulgated soon thereafter:

> The government shall make all possible efforts to promote the welfare of the people by creating and fostering a social system which effectively insures social, economic, and political justice in institutions relating to the national life. In particular, the government shall insure the equal right of all citizens to adequate means of livelihood and distribute the material resources of the community in a manner best suited to the public welfare. It shall also introduce an economic system which prevents the concentration of wealth and means of production in a manner detrimental to the public interest.[56]

These directive principles were, of course, meant only as general policy guidelines, but it hardly needs any elaboration to show that they are quite inconsistent with the exclusive privileges and inequality associated with *Birta* landownership in Nepal. Their eventual abolition was, therefore, never in doubt during the post-1951 period, although the exigencies of the political situation precluded prompt measures toward this end. The reasons for the delay are not difficult to understand. *Birta* landownership was limited to influential groups in the society. Consequently, opposition to its abolition was quite strong and articulate. Nor was the government itself quite clear in its mind about

---

[56]Government of Nepal, "Nepal Antarim Shasan Vidhan" [Interim constitution of Nepal], *Nepal Gazette*, vol. 4, no. 14, Kartik 30, 2011 (November 15, 1954), arts. 4–5, p. 41.

the implications and modalities of *Birta* abolition. It decided in principle to abolish the *Birta* system and directed *Birta* owners to furnish particulars of their holdings in October 1951.[57] Simultaneously, it imposed a ban on the sale and mortgage of *Birta* holdings in excess of 25 *ropanis* in the hill regions and 25 *bighas* in the Tarai.[58] It thus created the impression that only large *Birta* holdings would be abolished, thereby accentuating opposition to the measure. The death knell of this first phase of efforts to abolish the *Birta* system was sounded in January 1958 when the government lifted the ban on sale and mortgage with the remark that the "collection of statistics of *Birta* holdings has not so far been completed and people have been harassed by such restrictions."[59]

Significantly, the statement made no reference to the goal of *Birta* abolition, for governmental attention had been directed, instead, to the introduction of a taxation system for all categories of *Birta* lands.[60] The government succeeded in introducing such a system in April 1958,[61] although the rates of taxation were quite nominal as compared with those on *Raikar* lands. In justifying the measure, an official report declared,[62] "It is self evident that the state possesses sovereign authority over all lands within its domain. It is not reasonable to retain a system which involves the private use of the produce of the land without any payment to the state." An attempt was made in 1958 to raise the taxation rates to the level then prevailing on *Raikar* land. Yet the tax differential between *Raikar* and *Birta* lands would have remained, for the measure also sought to increase taxation rates on

[57] *Nepal Gazette*, vol. 1, no. 9, Aswin 15, 2008 (October 1, 1951).
[58] Ibid., vol. 1, no. 21, Poush 16, 2008 (December 31, 1951).
[59] Ibid., vol. 7, no. 40, Magh 7, 2014 (January 20, 1958). In September 1955 a royal proclamation decreed the imposition of progressive taxes on *Birta* incomes as an interim measure pending the completion of a *Birta*-abolition program. The measure was never implemented. His Majesty's Government of Nepal, *Shri 5 Maharajadhiraj Bata Bakseka Ghoshana, Bhashan ra Sandesh Haru* [Proclamations, speeches, and messages of His Majesty] (Kathmandu: Department of Publicity and Broadcasting, 2019 [1962]), I, 35-39.
[60] According to the first five-year plan (1956-61): "The question of *Birta* lands has been agitating the public mind. There is sentiment in favor of the abolition of *Birta* holdings with compensation to present owners and, pending such action, for payment of land taxes by the *Birta Walas* [holders]." Government of Nepal, *Draft Five-Year Plan: A Synopsis* (Kathmandu: the Government, 1956), pp. 33-34.
[61] Ministry of Finance, "Arthik Ain, 2014" [Finance act, 1957-58], *Nepal Gazette*, vol. 7, no. 15 (Extraordinary), Chaitra 29, 2014 (April 11, 1958), secs. 3-5, pp. 74-75.
[62] *Nepal Gazette*, vol. 7, no. 15 (Extraordinary), Chaitra 29, 2014 (April 11, 1958), pp. 84-85.

Raikar land by 100 percent.⁶³ The entire program was abandoned,⁶⁴ because of opposition from *Birta* owners.

Notwithstanding the emphasis laid on taxation rather than on abolition, a number of steps were taken after 1951 to abolish some of the traditional privileges of *Birta* owners. In February 1957, all individual rights on *Birta* forests and waste lands were nationalized without compensation.⁶⁵ Five months later, in July, landowners, including *Birta* owners, were prohibited from exacting unpaid labor and payments other than agricultural rents from their tenants.⁶⁶ Similarly, in November 1958, revenues from liquor, hides and skins, and other sources being appropriated by *Birta* owners were resumed by the state.⁶⁷ In April 1959, legislation was enacted to abolish all special privileges relating to the use of forced and unpaid labor.⁶⁸ These measures appear to have been primarily aimed at such ulterior objectives as forest protection, fiscal reform, and amelioration of the condition of the peasant rather than at the abolition of the *Birta* system itself, but they certainly facilitated its eventual abolition. At the very least, they helped to reduce the amount of compensation that the government undertook to pay when the *Birta* system was finally abolished in 1959.

The goal of *Birta* abolition was revived when a popular government was installed after general elections in May 1959. As an interim measure, the new government made certain changes in the *Birta* taxation system that had been introduced in 1958. For this purpose, *Birta* lands were classified as A and B. Class A *Birta* land meant all

---

⁶³Ministry of Law and Parliamentary Affairs, "Kar Lagaune Ain, 2015" [Taxation act, 1958], ibid., vol. 9, no. 19 (Extraordinary), Poush 1, 2016 (December 15, 1959).

⁶⁴Ministry of Law, Justice, and Parliamentary Affairs, "Arthik (Samshodhan) Ain, 2015" [Finance (amendment) act, 1958], sec. 2, and "Arthik Ain, 2015" [Finance act, 1958], sec. 4 and schedule 1, ibid., vol. 9, no. 1 (Extraordinary), Baisakh 10, 2026 (April 22, 1959), pp. 23-27.

⁶⁵Ministry of Law and Parliamentary Affairs, "Niji Ban Jangal Rashtriya Karan Ain, 2013" [Nationalization of private forests act, 1957], ibid., vol. 6, no. 39, Magh 22, 2013 (February 5, 1957).

⁶⁶Ministry of Law and Parliamentary Affairs, "Bhumi Sambandhi Ain, 2014" [Lands act, 1957], ibid., vol. 7, no. 5 (Extraordinary), Shrawan 22, 2014 (August 18, 1957).

⁶⁷Ministry of Law and Parliamentary Affairs, "Birtawalle Birtama Rakam (Bheti Charsa Adi) Lagai Lina Khana Napaune Ain, 2015" [Birta levies abolition act, 1958], ibid., vol. 8, no. 19A (Extraordinary), Marga 8, 2015 (December 3, 1958).

⁶⁸Ministry of Law and Parliamentary Affairs, "Muluki Ain Jhara Khetalako Mahal (Samshodhan) Ain, 2015" [Legal code, law on unpaid labor (amendment) act, 1958], ibid., vol. 9, no. 1 (Extraordinary), Baisakh 10, 2016 (April 22, 1959).

Birta lands on which the recipient could collect and appropriate only the prescribed land revenue or an equivalent amount, irrespective of the mode of grant or acquisition. Such lands belonged mostly to members of the Rana family. All other forms of *Birta* land were classified as B. In other words, where the income of the *Birta* owner was limited to an amount roughly equivalent to the land tax on adjoining *Raikar* lands, the land was classified as A. If, on the other hand, the owner was appropriating rents in cash or in kind, or if he was using his *Birta* lands for personal residence or cultivation, the land was classified as B. On Class A *Birta* lands, a tax equal to the amount of such revenue was imposed, thus absorbing their entire income and, in effect, abolishing them without compensation. On Class B *Birta* lands, a tax amounting to 50 percent of the amount of tax on adjoining *Raikar* holdings was imposed.[69]

Against the background of these measures, the abolition program that followed in December 1959 was somewhat anti-climactic, for it contained no new element beyond the formal conversion of the term *Birta* into *Raikar* and payment of compensation to the expropriated Class A *Birta* owners. According to the 1959 *Birta* Abolition Act:

> The *Birta* system existing in the Kingdom of Nepal has been terminated and all *Birta* lands have been abolished and converted into *Raikar*. Landownership rights and privileges previously possessed by *Birta* owners on such *Birta* lands shall *ipso facto* lapse. All laws, regulations, orders, or other documents providing for the emergence or continuation of ownership rights and powers on *Birta* land in favor of any individual have been repealed or nullified.[70]

The program provided for the "nationalization" of Class A *Birta* lands and their registration as *Raikar* in the name of the tenant. The tax imposed on Class A *Birta* lands amounted, as before, to the total revenue being appropriated by the owners of such nationalized lands. Arrangements were then made to compensate them for their loss of income at the following rates:[71]

[69] Ministry of Law, "Arthik Ain, 2016" [Finance act, 1959], ibid., vol. 9, no. 19 [Extraordinary, Poush 1, 2016 (December 15, 1959), secs. 2, 5, pp. 235–236.

[70] Ministry of Law, "Birta Unmulan Ain, 2016" [Birta abolition act, 1959], ibid., vol. 9, no. 19 (Extraordinary), Poush 1, 2016 (December 15, 1959), sec. 3.

[71] Ibid., schedule.

Net annual income (Rupees)	Amount of compensation (Rupees)
500	5,000
1,000	7,500
3,000	9,500
6,000	11,000
10,000 or more	12,000

The maximum amount of compensation payable to a Class A *Birta* owner, irrespective of the total annual income being appropriated by him, was, as indicated, Rs. 12,000. Because waste lands did not yield any income to the *Birta* owner, these were nationalized without compensation.

The 1959 abolition act permitted the owners of Class B *Birta* lands to retain their lands subject to conversion into *Raikar* and payment of taxes at rates prevailing on adjoining *Raikar* lands. *Birta* lands of this category were therefore simply taxed and the grants were not abolished. Taxes had been imposed on all categories of *Birta* lands in 1958, however, and the 1959 act made little substantial change in the existing situation. The act only prescribed the taxation of Class B *Birta* lands at *Raikar* rates, instead of the nominal rates effective since 1958.

The political change of December 15, 1960, when the elected government was dismissed and replaced by a royal government, temporarily deflected the course of the implementation of the 1959 *Birta* Abolition Act. A few weeks after this change, a royal proclamation confirmed the goal of abolishing the *Birta* system, but stressed that efforts would be made to "profit from past experience" and adopt a "clear and scientific policy" in this regard.[72] Soon afterwards, in February 1961, a royal commission was formed to submit recommendations in the fields of taxation and *Birta* abolition.[73] The commission arrived at the conclusion that "the practical aspect of the *Birta*-abolition program is to make the *Birta* owner pay a reasonable tax to the state."[74] It therefore recommended that all *Birta* grants acquired by members of the Rana family, except *Birta* lands purchased by them, should be confiscated, subject to compensation in the form of 5 to 50 *bighas* of waste land on a taxable basis. On the other hand, the commission suggested the taxation of other categories of *Birta* lands at 50

---

[72] Ibid., vol. 10, no. 20 (Extraordinary), Poush 22, 2017 (January 5, 1961), p. 4.

[73] His Majesty's Government, *Shahi Kar Ayog Ko Report* [Report of the Royal Taxation Commission] (Kathmandu: Department of Publicity and Broadcasting, 2018 [1961]), p. 2.

[74] Ibid., pp. 18–19.

percent of the rates prevailing on adjoining *Raikar* holdings in all parts of the country except Kathmandu Valley, where it proposed specific rates ranging from Rs. 1.25 to Rs. 2.00 per *ropani*.[75] The government accepted the latter recommendation and prescribed differential rates of taxation for *Birta* lands as compared with *Raikar*. These arrangements, however, remained operative only for a few months in 1962.[76] In September 1962, the rates of *Birta* taxation were brought into line with those prevailing on *Raikar* lands in all parts of the country,[77] thereby complying with the provisions of the 1959 *Birta* Abolition Act both in letter and in spirit.

The *Birta*-abolition program introduced in 1959 has been justified on both political and economic grounds. According to an official statement made in 1960:

> A system under which some people had to pay taxes, while others were fully or partially exempt, even though cultivating or renting lands of similar quality in the same area, was not consistent with the democratic ideals of the changed times. A state of inequality in which some people helped the government by paying land taxes while others enjoyed rights without making any payment constituted an injustice to the majority of the people.[78]

Explaining the economic implications of the measure, the same statement noted:

> When the *Birta* system emerged, population was lower than at present. Land was available in abundance. No adverse consequences ensued even when large areas were granted as *Birta* to any person. Moreover, under the Rana regime, the government did nothing for national development. An insignificant percentage of whatever revenue was collected was spent, and the balance was appropriated for private benefit. Since the administration was in the hands of a feudal lord, he paid attention only to the enrichment of himself, his family, and his sycophants. The situation has changed now. Democracy has been introduced in the country, and it is time when we should work for the benefit of the community. Population is increasing daily and we have therefore to attain development. Development, however, requires a strong financial system.[79]

---

[75] Ibid., pp. 21-22.
[76] *Nepal Gazette*, vol. 11, no. 40 (Extraordinary), Magh 24, 2018 (February 6, 1962).
[77] Ibid., vol. 12, no. 17 (Extraordinary), Aswin 5, 2019 (September 21, 1962).
[78] His Majesty's Government of Nepal, *Bhumi Sudhar Ke Ho?* [What is land reform?], (Kathmandu: Department of Publicity and Broadcasting, 2017 [1960]), p. 10.
[79] Ibid., pp. 1-2.

The abolition program was criticized for failing to improve the condition of the peasantry. Its critics maintained that the program should have provided for security of tenancy rights, a fair share of the produce of the land for the cultivator, and the elimination of absentee landlordism.[80] Another line of criticism pointed out that although the 1959 abolition act had eliminated Class A *Birta* owners, who belonged mostly to the Rana family, it sought to mobilize "capitalist" support for the government by permitting Class B *Birta* owners to retain their lands.[81] Such criticism seems misdirected, because the act was framed only to abolish the *Birta* system and impose taxes on the lands concerned. It was never intended as a land-reform program. The sole objective of the government was to model the land-tenure system of the country on the *Raikar* pattern in order to widen the land-tax base.[82] The program was thus essentially fiscal in character.[83] The criticism in question has stemmed primarily from a refusal to recognize that *Birta* abolition was intended only to "create an atmosphere congenial to land reform" as a "preliminary step" toward "more effective measures which will have to be taken for improving the condition of the peasantry."[84] *Birta* abolition thus constituted a definite step ahead in the formulation and execution of land-reform programs, rather than a land-reform program in itself.

[80] See *Rashtravani*, Aswin 19, 2016 (October 5, 1959).
[81] Pushpa Lal Shrestha, "Birta Unmulan" [Birta abolition], *Navayug*, Bhadra 31, 2017 (September 19, 1960).
[82] Birta Abolition Act, 1959, preamble.
[83] His Majesty's Government, op. cit. (in n. 78 above), p. 5.
[84] National Planning Council, *Trivarshiya Yojana, 2019-22* [Three-year plan, 1962-65] (Kathmandu: the Council, 2019 [1962]), p. 70.

Chapter 4

INSTITUTIONAL LANDOWNERSHIP: *GUTHI* TENURE

In the preceding chapter we saw how the state made land grants to individuals under *Birta* tenure. Similar grants, when made for use by religious or charitable institutions, led to the emergence of *Guthi* landownership. Whereas the *Birta* system created a privileged class of individuals who gave social and political support to the regime, the *Guthi* system helped to satisfy the religious propensities of both the rulers and the common people.

Endowments of land for religious and charitable purposes, which the *Guthi* system denotes, are by no means confined to Nepal. *Guthi*, in this sense, is virtually synonymous with the *Debutter* land tenure of Hindus in India,[1] the *waqf* system of Muslim communities in India[2] and the Middle East countries,[3] and the tenure of church and monastic lands in medieval Europe.[4] The origin of such land endowments is probably as old as formal religion and settled agriculture. In all of these systems, surplus agricultural production, combined with religious factors, made the satisfaction of altruistic motives possible through the endowment of land.[5] It might therefore be correct to regard the origin and development of each of these systems as basically autochthonous in character. There is evidence, nevertheless, that the *Guthi* system, as it

[1] Noshirvan H. Jhabvala, *Principles of Hindu Law* 7th ed.; (Bombay: C. Jamnadas and Co., 1964), pp. 124-27.
[2] Karuna Mukerji, *Land Reforms* (Calcutta: H. Chatterjee and Co., 1952), p. 69.
[3] Gabriel Baer, *A History of Landownership in Modern Egypt, 1800-1950* (London: Oxford University Press, 1962), pp. 147-85; Ann K. S. Lambton, *Landlord and Peasant in Persia* (London: Oxford University Press, 1953), pp. 230-37.
[4] H. D. Hazeltine, "Mortmain," *Encyclopaedia of the Social Sciences*, XI, 40-49; H. E. Workman, "Monasticism," ibid., X, 584-90.
[5] A British anthropologist has provided a case study of the way in which surplus agricultural production has resulted in increased expenditure for religious purposes among the Sherpas in Solukhumbu. The introduction of the potato in that area during the mid-nineteenth century led to the sudden development of a surplus in food supplies. This surplus, over a period of fifty to eighty years, made possible the construction of new temples, monasteries, and other religious monuments. Christoph von Fürer-Haimendorf, *The Sherpas of Nepal* (Calcutta: Oxford Book Co., 1963), pp. 10-11.

exists in Nepal at the present time, has been strongly influenced by the *Gosthi* system followed by the Shakya, Licchavi, and other communities in the adjoining areas of northern India during the early centuries of the Christian era.[6] The Licchavi rulers, during whose period the *Guthi* system appears to have attained a fairly advanced stage of development in Nepal, were originally immigrants from northern India.[7] The term *Guthi* itself is a corrupt form of the Sanskrit *Gosthi* used in inscriptions in both Nepal and India during that period.[8]

In both Nepal and India, the term *Gosthi* or *Guthi* was originally used to denote an association of persons responsible for the management of religious and philanthropic land endowments, not the endowments themselves.[9] The use of this term to denote the lands endowed, rather than the body formed to supervise the functions to be discharged with the income, probably started only after the Gorkhali conquests.[10] It was also after the conquests that religious and charitable land endowments in most parts of the country came to be known as *Guthi*.[11]

[6] Atindra Nath Bose, *Social and Rural Economy of Northern India* (Calcutta: Firma K. L. Mukhopadhyay, 1961), I, 81-82, 89-90. The Pali equivalent of this term, *Gothi*, was also used in India.

[7] Hit Narayan Jha, *The Licchavis* (Varanasi: Chowkhamba Sanskrit Series Office, 1970), p. 107.

[8] The earliest recorded endowment of land in Nepal for religious purposes was made by the Licchavi King Manadeva for the temple of Changunarayan in Kathmadu, A.D. 464. Dhanabajra Bajracharya, *Licchavi Kalka Abhilekh* [Inscriptions of the Licchavi period] Kathmandu: Institute of Nepal and Asian Studies, 2030 [1973]), p. 13. The term *Guthi* first occurs in its original Sanskrit form of *Gosthi* in an inscription installed by Dhruvasangha, a government official, in the Pashupatinath temple area in Kathmandu in 533. Ibid., p. 115. An inscription installed by the Licchavi King Shivadeva and his minister, Amshuvarma, at Lele village, now in Lalitpur district of Kathmandu Valley, in 604 shows the extent of the development that the *Guthi* system had attained in Kathmandu Valley during the Licchavi period. It refers to the reconfirmation of a number of land endowments made by former kings and other individuals in the village. Ibid., pp. 282-89.

[9] Bose, op. cit., p. 82; Bajracharya, op. cit., p. 115. During the Malla period (1480-1768) also, lands endowed for religious and charitable purposes were entrusted to a "Gosthi Jana," or board of trustees. Rajvamshi, *Puratattwa-Patrasangraha*, I, 9. The Newari variations of this term are "Guthi Jana" (ibid., pp. 18-19) or "Guthi Loka" (Bhola Nath Poudyal, "Yaksheshwara Mandira" [The temple of Yaksheshwara], *Purnima*, 5, Baisakh 2022 [April 1965], p. 19).

[10] Soon after the conquest of Kathmandu in 1768, King Prithvi Narayan Shah made a "Guth" land endowment for the Gorakhnath temple in Kathmandu. Naraharinath Yogi, *Itihas Prakash*, II, bk. 3, 287.

[11] In Garhwal, which remained under Gorkhali rule from 1803 to 1816, "The term 'Gunth' by which all assignments of land made by religious establishments are now designated [dates] only from the times of the Gurkhas, the older names by which such endowments were known being the ordinary Hindu words Shankalap and Bishenprit." E. K. Pauw, *Report on the Tenth Settlement of the Garhwal District* (Allahabad: North Western Provinces and Oudh Government Press, 1896), p. 39.

Traces of the ancient practice of using the term *Guthi* to denote a corporate body formed to discharge social, cultural, or religious functions, rather than the lands endowed for financing these functions, can still be found in the customs of the Newar community in Kathmandu Valley. Among the Newars, the term *Guthi* is used to denote an organization based on caste or kinship, or, occasionally, on geographical propinquity, which insures the continued observances of social and religious customs and ceremonies of the community. The term *Guthi*, in this sense, is primarily used to denote a social institution that determines the rights and obligations of a Newar vis-à-vis his community. It is obvious that such an institution has no relationship with the land-tenure system. A *Guthi* organization of this type may acquire and hold land and other forms of property, which then automatically come under the *Guthi* land-tenure system. Nevertheless, the organization is not based on ownership of land as such,[12] and thus lies outside the scope of the present study.

Form and Nature of *Guthi* Endowments

Recent legislation has defined the term *Guthi* to mean an endowment made by any philanthropist with religious or philanthropic motives for the performance of any regular or ceremonial religious function or festival of any monastery or deity, or the construction, maintenance, or operation of temples, resthouses, roadside shelters, wells, tanks, ponds, waterspouts, arrangements for the supply of drinking water, roads, bathing ghats, bridges, shelters under trees, libraries, schools,

---

[12]Gopal Singh Nepali, *The Newars* (Bombay: United Asia Publications, 1965). pp. 191-97. A British anthropologist observes: "Among Newars there is an ubiquitous form of a voluntary association known as a *Guthi*. These are common interest groups with restricted recruitment. All Newar males must belong to a *Sanam Guthi* and all members of a single *Guthi* of this type must belong to the same caste. A *Sanam Guthi* is a kind of funeral society basically. Each *Guthi* has a senior member and an organizing committee. Each *Guthi* requires an annual cash subscription from its members, and an entrance fee from new members. In addition to the obligation of turning out for the funerals of fellow members, each individual member has the privilege of attending the annual feast paid for out of the funds. And he may in some cases borrow money at favorable rates of interest, or no interest at all, from the *Guthi* funds. Wealthy *Guthis* may own land and considerable property, the income of which is used for these feasts and loans." Colin Rosser, "The Newar Caste System," in Christoph von Fürer-Haimendorf, ed., *Caste and Kin in Nepal, India and Ceylon* (Bombay: Asia Publishing House, 1966), pp. 96-97; see also pp. 110-20. For additional information on the *Guthi* system as practiced by the Newar community of Kathmandu Valley see U. N. Sinha, "The Genesis of Political Institutions in Nepal," in R. S. Varma, ed., *Cultural Heritage of Nepal* (Allahabad: Kitab Mahal, 1972), pp. 86-90, and R. S. Pandey, "Nepalese Society during the Malla and Early Shah Period," ibid., p. 145.

dispensaries, hospitals, and the like.¹³ The term *Guthi* therefore has a connotation wider than is suggested by its use in the context of land tenure, for endowments under the *Guthi* system can be made in other forms of property as well. *Guthi* endowments have traditionally been made also in the form of revenues from different sources¹⁴ and cash investments.¹⁵ Nevertheless, the majority of existing *Guthi* endowments are in the form of land because of the predominant importance of land as a form of property and a source of income. *Guthi* endowments in the form of land had several advantages that other forms of endowment lacked. Endowments in land facilitated the collection of rents in the form of commodities required for the performance of the prescribed *Guthi* functions and utilizing the unpaid services of the cultivators. In view of these advantages of *Guthi* endowments in land, even *Guthis* established with cash endowments occasionally invested their funds in land purchases.¹⁶

The *Guthi* system, from the point of view of the present study, is concerned with the endowment of lands for the performance of religious and charitable functions. In other words, to be a part of the *Guthi* system, it is not enough that lands should merely be endowed for specific purposes. The religious or charitable nature of such purpose constitutes the criterion for determining whether or not the endowments fall within the ambit of the *Guthi* system in the sense of the term we are using. *Guthi* endowments have, at times, been made also for such purposes as the supply of subsidized food to the military,¹⁷ provision for major expenses of the royal household,¹⁸ maintenance of

---

[13] Ministry of Law and Justice, "Guthi Samsthan Ain, 2029" [Guthi Corporation act, 1972], *Nepal Rajapatra*, vol. 22, no. 30A (Extraordinary), Aswin 5, 2029 [September 21, 1972], sec. 2 (e). (*Nepal Gazette* was renamed *Nepal Rajapatra* early in 1967.)

[14] Naraharinath Yogi, II, bk. 2, 43. According to this document, every household at Chhinasim in Jumla district was ordered in 1822 to supply one *pathi* of grains for religious ceremonies at the temple of Chandannath. Similarly, in 1840, King Rajendra assigned a sum of Rs. 75 each year from the proceeds of judicial fines to the temple of Tripurasundari in Tibrikot. Ibid., I, 11.

[15] Prime Minister Chandra Shamsher (1901-28) created a *Guthi* endowment with Rs. 2.1 million in Indian currency, utilizing the income to sell rice to the military at subsidized prices. Law Ministry Records, "Sainik Samartha Chandrodaya Samstha Regulations," Kartik 12, 1983 (October 29, 1926). He made a similar endowment also to finance a sanatorium in Kathmandu. Law Ministry Records, "Tokha Sanatorium Regulations," Kartik 25, 1992 (November 10, 1935).

[16] Law Ministry Records, "Sainik Samartha Chandrodaya Samstha Regulations."

[17] Ibid.

[18] Foreign Ministry (Jaisi Kotha) Records, "Administrative Regulations of the Government of Nepal," Falgun Badi 4, 1849 (February 1793), sec. 11. For a full translation of this document see Regmi, *A Study in Nepali Economic History*, pp. 209-11.

irrigation channels,[19] and payment of salaries to mechanics employed in government arsenals.[20] Such *Guthi* endowments resulted from the backward state of the fiscal and administrative systems. Instead of making budget allocations every year for secular purposes such as those described above, the government found it simpler to utilize the *Guthi* system, which was traditionally used to finance religious and charitable endowments. It seems appropriate, however, to exclude secular *Guthi* endowments from the scope of the present study. Inasmuch as no motives of religion or charity are involved in these endowments, resumption by the donor does not constitute an encroachment upon religious tradition. Permanence and irrevocability, two essential characteristics of *Guthi* land-tenure, are thus absent.

To sum up, the religious and charitable aspects of the *Guthi* system, and its basis in the endowment of land, are the primary elements determining its present connotation as a form of land tenure utilized for the establishment of temples, monasteries, orphanages, charity kitchens, and other similar institutions. *Guthi* is thus a form of institutional land tenure, the religious and charitable aspects of which have given rise to special problems and characteristics in the fields of land tenure and taxation.

Objectives of *Guthi* Land Endowments

Guthi land endowments were made primarily with the objective of acquiring religious merit. Gifts of land per se earned religious merit for the donor. According to traditional Hindu belief, "he who makes a gift of land remains in heaven for 60,000 years."[21] Such gifts took on increased importance when made for religious or charitable purposes through the *Guthi* system. The 1854 legal code, explaining the spiritual

---

[19] Guthi Lagat Janch Office, "Guthi Land Endowment for Maintenance of Irrigation Channel in Bhaktapur," Marga 14, 2000 (November 29, 1943).

[20] "Royal Order to the Subbas and Other Officials of Bara and Parsa Districts," Bhadra Sudi 11, 1850 (September 1793). Similarly, King Siddhinarasimha Malla (1620–61) is said to have assigned *Guthi* lands to carpenters whom he had employed to build temples and palaces in Lalitpur. Wright, *History of Nepal*, p. 234.

[21] This is mentioned in a grant of land made by King Prithvi Malla of Dullu to a Brahman in 1415 Vikrama (1358). Naraharinath Yogi, I (1), 69–70. Land grants made under *Birta* tenure in recent times, instead, stress the sin involved in confiscating land grants: "Whosoever confiscates land granted by himself or by others shall, in his next life, become a worm living in human excrement for 60,000 years." See "Kush Birta Grant to Brahma Upadhyaya and Harivamsha Adhikari," Ashadh Badi 4, 1874 (June 1817), in Regmi, *Land Tenure and Taxation in Nepal*, II, 150–51.

motivation behind *Guthi* land endowments, states:

> Religious acts (such as *Guthi* land endowments) make the country prosperous and ward off diseases and epidemics. Famine is averted and the country becomes beautiful. Local artisans and craftsmen develop their skills, and poor people are able to maintain themselves by earning wages. In case any person makes a *Sadavarta*[22] endowment, his family obtains spiritual deliverance for seven generations.[23]

Indeed, it was a popular belief that religious acts prevented drought and famine and brought prosperity to the country.[24]

Guthi land endowments were sometimes made to propitiate local deities or pacify evil spirits. Such endowments appear to have been made mostly in the northern areas of the country, where belief in shamanistic practices is widespread. The following endowments made in Jajarkot during the early eighteenth century may be regarded as typical:

> In former times a goddess emerged [on this land] and started harassing the local inhabitants. The Raja then endowed lands as *Guthi*, constructed a shrine, and initiated religious ceremonies. People thereupon felt relieved.
>
> In former times, the Raja granted this land to a Brahman, but later confiscated it. Grieved at this, the Brahman committed suicide on the land. He became an evil spirit and began to harass the Raja, who therefore endowed the land as *Guthi*, constructed a shrine there, and initiated religious ceremonies. The Raja then felt relieved.[25]

At times, *Guthi* endowments were made for the deity of the donor's choice to insure the fulfillment of a personal wish. For example, King Surendra (1847–81) made a *Guthi* endowment for a temple in Mahottari district, wishing "a long life, luster, and valor" to his

---

[22]*Sadavarta* means a *Guthi* endowment made for supplying raw or cooked food to poor people, travelers, mendicants, and the like.

[23]Government of Nepal, "Datta Guthi" [On Guthi endowments], in Ministry of Law and Justice, *Shri 5 Surendra... Muluki Ain*, sec. 1, p. 9.

[24]In Tibrikot, for example, "Lamas had been conducting religious functions at the local monastery. This brought rain, made the country prosperous, and provided succor to us. In 1842, no lama came to the monastery, so that its lands remained uncultivated. This dislocated religious functions there and led to drought and famine." Naraharinath Yogi, II, bk. 2, 221.

[25]*Regmi Research Series*, year 5, no. 6 (June 1, 1973), pp. 112–18.

grandson, later King Prithvi Bir Bikram (1881-1912).[26] Similarly, Commander in Chief Dhir Shamsher endowed lands as *Guthi* on the eve of his departure for the front to insure victory in the 1855-56 Nepal-Tibet war.[27] The desire to obtain divine assistance through *Guthi* land endowments for success in war was not confined to individuals. During the 1792-93 Nepal-China war, *Guthi* land endowments were made by the government itself to Brahmans for performing mystic rites to ward off the Chinese invasion.[28]

Acts of religion and charity have traditionally been interpreted in a broad sense in Nepal. *Guthi* land endowments in the name of religion have been made also for such purposes as grazing the sacred bulls of the Pashupatinath temple in Kathmandu and for feeding sacred monkeys in the temple area.[29] Such endowments reflect the religious sentiment attached to the protection and maintenance of every form of life, particularly of animals associated in any manner with the gods. However, the major types of religious endowments made by the state or by individuals include basic religious functions or specific offerings or rituals at temples and monasteries and the financing of festivals. *Guthi* land endowments were made also for the maintenance of resthouses and roadside shelters at places of pilgrimage, or along main

---

[26] "Guthi Land Grant to Gulab Das Bairagi," Magh 1945 (January 1889). Royal orders confirming such grants were usually issued several years later.

[27] "Guthi Land Endowment by Commander in Chief Dhir Shamsher at Sipakot," Poush 24, 1960 (January 8, 1904). One private *Guthi* endowment at the temple of Taleju in Bhaktapur provides for a daily offering of betel leaves to the goddess, apparently in fulfilment of a personal vow. Guthi Lagat Janch Office, "Guthi Land Endowment for Offering of Betel Leaf at Taleju Temple in Bhaktapur," Falgun 23, 1990 (March 7, 1934). After electric power was introduced in Kathmandu in 1911, several such *Guthi* land endowments were made for the electrification of temples. Guthi Lagat Office, "Guthi Land Endowment for Electric Supply at Maitidevi Temple in Kathmandu," Baisakh 21, 1991 (May 3, 1934). Often endowments were made for the playing of specified musical instruments at temples. Pashupati Goshwara Office, "Guthi Land Endowment of Mod Nath Upadhayaya," Magh 5, 1998 (January 18, 1942).

[28] Bhaktapur Guthi Records, "Guthi Land of Shubham Devi Brahmani," 1953 (1896).

[29] Pashupati Amalkot Kachahari Office, "Guthi Land Acquisition for Gauchar Airport," Ashadh 1,2019 (July 16, 1962). This document records that 250 *ropanis* of land were endowed for the maintenance of the bulls by King Rana Bahadur Shah. In 1816, an additional 750 *ropanis* were granted for this purpose, "Land Grants for the Maintenance of Bulls at Deopatan, Kathmandu," Ashadh Badi 12, 1873 (July 1816). Thirty-six *ropanis* of land were endowed in one case in Kathmandu for feeding corn to the monkeys of Pashupatinath temple (Guthi Lagat Janch Office, "Guthi Land Endowment for Feeding Monkeys at Pashupatinath Temple in Kathmandu," Ashadh 24, 1973 (July 8, 1916).

pilgrimage routes, where drinking water, food, and lodging were supplied to pilgrims and travelers.[30] Many endowments have been made in different parts of the country for the establishment and maintenance of charity kitchens, poorhouses, orphanages, schools, and hostels.[31] In 1914, the Rana government established two separate *Guthi* institutions to look after destitute orphans and disburse cash allowances to widows, aged persons, and children belonging to the families of high-ranking civil and military officers who were not in a position to take advantage of existing *Guthi* facilities.[32]

Not all *Guthi* land endowments in Nepal have been made with religious or charitable intent. Security from confiscation by the state and seizure by creditors, and a ban on the revocation of the endowment, are essential attributes of the *Guthi* system. Landowners have often taken advantage of these attributes to fulfill objectives quite remote from considerations of religion and charity. Throughout Nepal's history, whenever any new territory was subjugated by conquest, the general practice appears to have been to confiscate lands granted by former rulers. Almost without exception, political upheavals and changes in the balance of power among rival political factions led to large-scale confiscation of the *Birta* lands of the losers. But if *Birta* lands were endowed as *Guthi*, religious susceptibilities generally prevented the state from confiscating them.[33] Moreover, lands endowed

[30]"Guthi Land Endowment for Gargeshwar Mahadev Temple in Rising, West No. 4 District," Poush Sudi 14, 1890 (January 1834); "Guthi Land Endowments for Temple and Resthouse in Mahottari District," Baisakh Badi 14, 1891 (April 1834); Law Ministry Records, "Administrative Arrangements regarding Pindeshwar Monastery in Morang District," Bhadra 15, 1993 (August 31, 1936).

[31]"Guthi Land Endowments for Orphanages and Poorhouses in Tarai District," Ashadh 28, 1969 (July 12, 1912); "Guthi Land Endowment for Sanskrit School and Hostel at Gangasagar," Janakpur, Baisakh Badi 10, 1941 (May 1884); Government of Nepal, "Guthi Bare Ko" [On Guthi matters], *Muluki Sawal* [Administrative regulations], 2010 [1953], sec. 10, pp. 196–97; Law Ministry Records, "Ridi Sadavarta Regulations," 1992 (1935).

[32]Law Ministry Records, "Benevolent and Charitable Society Regulations," Chaitra 24, 1970 (April 6, 1914), preamble and secs. 1, 7.

[33]For instance, King Prithvi Narayan Shah confiscated the property of the local nobility when he conquered Lalitpur in 1768, but confirmed the "acts of charity performed by one of them on the night before their capture." Wright, *History of Nepal*, p. 232. Similarly, the entire property of Prime Minister Bhimsen Thapa was confiscated when he fell from power in 1837, but evidently lands endowed by him as *Guthi* were spared. Regmi, *Land Tenure and Taxation in Nepal*, IV, 13. It was obviously in continuance of this tradition of exempting *Guthi* land endowments from any penalties inflicted on persons held guilty of treason or other crimes that the 1867 legal code prescribed: "In case any person has made *Guthi* land endowments to feed poor people and mendicants, or to perform regular and ceremonial religious functions (at temples),

as *Guthi* could not be attached by creditors in settlement of debts. Of course, endowment of land as *Guthi* was not regarded as valid if the donor owed arrears of payment to the government or to private creditors. Once this condition was fulfilled, however, and lands were endowed as *Guthi* by a person who had no such debts outstanding, these were immune from seizure or foreclosure in consideration of any debts he might incur subsequently.[34] Finally, lands endowed as *Guthi* could not be sold or otherwise transferred. The nonsalable character of *Guthi* was a factor that made the *Guthi* system popular among different classes of people in Nepal. Because *Guthi* lands could not be sold, landowners often endowed their *Birta* lands as *Guthi*. A small portion of the income accruing from the lands thus endowed was then utilized for religious and charitable purposes, and the balance was appropriated by the donor's family. Landowners could thus legally prevent their heirs from alienating landed property by endowing it as *Guthi*. In this manner, the religious character of the *Guthi* system was exploited to safeguard familial interests.[35] Far from discouraging *Guthi* endowments of this nature, the government actually granted them legal validity.

---

and in case he himself or his descendants are convicted of murder or treason, he shall be sentenced to capital punishment for murder, or his property shall be confiscated if appropriate, or, if he is convicted of rape, punishment shall be inflicted according to law. But [lands endowed by him as *Guthi*] shall not be confiscated, and the prescribed religious functions shall be performed in the customary manner." Government of Nepal, "Datta Guthi" [On Guthi endowments], in Ministry of Law and Justice, *Shri 5 Surendra... Muluki Ain*, sec. 2, p. 10.

[34]"In case any person who has no arrears of payment due to the government or loans repayable to other individuals has purchased lands with his wealth and endowed such lands, or his own *Birta* lands, as *Guthi*, and in case he subsequently accumulates such arrears of payment or loans, neither the government nor his creditors shall seize the lands endowed as *Guthi*. The arrears of payment or loans shall be recovered from other property. In case he has no other property, such arrears or loans shall be converted into unsecured loans." Ibid., sec. 18, p. 14.

[35]Such practices are not confined to Nepal. Classical Muslim law, for example, views the endowment of income from property in favor of certain relatives as a charitable action. In Egypt, "A special type of *waqf* intended to maintain the status of rich and honoured families took the form of an endowment by the head of the family of a parcel of land, the income from which was devoted to maintaining a travellers' guest house." Baer, op. cit. (in n. 3 above), pp. 153, 161. In India, according to the 1913 Mussalman Wakf Validating Act, "It shall be lawful for any person professing the Mussalman faith to create a Wakf for the maintenance and support wholly or partially of his family, children or descendants, and also for his own maintenance and support during his life-time or of the payment of his debts provided that the ultimate benefit is expressly or impliedly reserved for the poor or for any other purpose recognized by the Mussalman law as a religious, pious or charitable purpose of a permanent character." Noshirvan H. Jhabvala, *Principles of Mahomedan Law* (8th ed., reprint; Bombay: C. Jamnadas and Co., 1964), p. 108.

Legislation enacted in 1886 recognized that such endowments were made "only with the objective of preventing one's heirs from selling or otherwise alienating lands."[36] *Guthi* endowments of this category are still legally valid, although current law does not expressly refer to this motive.[37]

Familial interests were often served through *Guthi* endowments even when the donor did not have this specific objective in mind. Legislation enacted in 1854 provided that descendants of persons who had endowed lands as *Guthi* with religious or philanthropic motives were entitled to get free food and clothing from the *Guthi* endowment if they "are of evil temperament, and addicted to gambling or the use of narcotics, and have no occupation, and are thus unable to earn their livelihood."[38]

Religion and charity, and also security and protection of landed property, constituted the primary objectives of *Guthi* land endowments in Nepal. The existing land-tenure and taxation systems provided an appropriate setting for these subjective motivations. The *Guthi* land-endowment system was sustained by a feudalistic land-tenure system such as *Birta*, which permitted the unlimited concentration of landownership rights in the hands of select groups in the society. Influential persons were able to obtain large *Birta* grants from the government; endowment of a part of these lands as *Guthi* contributed to both religious edification and social prestige. The state being more preoccupied with the need to maintain social stability and religious tradition than with such egalitarian ideals as the welfare of the peasantry, it too made liberal land endowments under the *Guthi* system.

Since the downfall of the Rana regime in 1951, however, the state practice of making land endowments for temples or other religious and charitable institutions has become obsolete. Among private

---

[36] Law Ministry Records, "Guthi Ko" [On Guthi], *Muluki Ain* [Legal code], 1886 ed., sec. 24. For instance, in one case involving a Buddhist monastery in Solukhumbu district, "All the land around Phaphlu [village] belongs to close cousins and their families, having been purchased by the grandfather of the present owners. It was this worthy genetleman who forty years ago founded this monastery as an act of merit and endowed all members of the community with basic food supplies in perpetuity." David Snellgrove, *Buddhist Himalaya* (Oxford: Bruno Cassirer, 1957), p. 217. The founder thus derived the dual satisfaction of earning religious merit by donating land to the monastery and of insuring economic security for his descendants.

[37] Ministry of Law and Justice, "Guthi Ko" [On Guthi], *Muluki Ain* (Kathmandu: Gorkhapatra Press, 2020 [1963], sec. 3 (2), p. 112.

[38] Government of Nepal, "Datta Guthi" [On Guthi endowments] in Ministry of Law and Justice, *Shri 5 Surendra... Muluki Ain*, sec. 10, pp. 12–13.

individuals, apprehensions of arbitrary confiscation of landed property for political reasons no longer persist. Moreover, growing contacts with the outside world and with materialist values and attitudes have made the *Guthi* land-endowment system somewhat out of step with the times. Finally, recent land-reform measures can scarcely be expected to promote *Guthi* land endowments, since land has become less desirable as a form of property than in former times and ceilings have been imposed on landholdings. From the viewpoint of the state, land endowments for particular religious and charitable institutions are of less importance in its campaign of social welfare than the maximization of revenue from the land to finance developmental activities. Consequently, *Guthi* land endowments are no longer an important aspect of state and individual conduct, as they were during the eighteenth and nineteenth centuries.

Area and Location of *Guthi* Land Endowments

Recent official estimates indicate that 40,000 hectares of a total cultivated area of 1,927,000 hectares were under *Guthi* tenure in 1950. A part of the 700,000 hectares under *Birta* tenure at that time was also being used as *Guthi*.[39] Approximately 4 percent of the total cultivated area was thus under *Guthi* tenure at the end of the Rana regime.

Information about the total area under *Guthi* land tenure in different periods of Nepal's history is not available, but it appears correct to presume that it underwent an unprecedented expansion after the foundation of the Kingdom of Nepal by King Prithvi Narayan Shah in 1768. We do not intend to suggest that the royal dynasties displaced in different parts of Nepal after 1768 were less concerned with religion than the Shah and Rana rulers. But it is indisputable that the latter were in possession of far greater resources in the form of lands and revenues than any of their predecessors, most of whom were petty chieftains. Moreover, the government considered itself directly responsible for the maintenance of existing temples, monasteries, and other religious and charitable institutions. It therefore made munificent land endowments under the *Guthi* system on its own initiative.[40]

---

[39] Zaman, *Evaluation of Land Reform in Nepal*, p. 7.

[40] Regulations promulgated in 1806 show that a special officer was appointed for ritual donations and other religious affairs at the royal palace and that his duties included the supervision of religious endowments. He was thus directed: "In case traditional *Guthi* functions have been dislocated anywhere because of [administrative] confusion, report the matter to us and make arrangements for the endowment of lands

Private endowments too were made in large numbers, particularly for financing specific rituals at temples. The Shah and Rana rulers seldom imposed any restriction on the endowment of lands as *Guthi*. On the contrary, they made liberal land grants to private individuals for *Guthi* endowments. Any person could approach the government and make a request for a grant of *Raikar* land for endowment as *Guthi*.[41] Dynastic stability during the past two centuries was possibly another factor contributing to the steady proliferation of *Guthi* land endowments in Nepal.

Statistics regarding the distribution of *Guthi* lands in different districts are not available. The majority of existing *Guthi* endowments, however, as well as some of the richest, appear to be concentrated in Kathmandu Valley and the eastern and central Tarai districts of Bara, Parsa, Rautahat, Sarlahi, Dhanusha, Mahottari, Siraha, Saptari, Morang, and Sunsari. Kathmandu Valley is the site of renowned Hindu temples and Buddhist shrines that have benefited from the liberal *Guthi* land endowments made by kings and commoners alike throughout several centuries. In addition, Kathmandu Valley accommodated the capitals of the Malla kings, who were great temple-builders. Although not notable as builders themselves, the Shah rulers excelled in making *Guthi* land endowments for the upkeep of these temples. The central and eastern Tarai was once the domain of kings of the Sen dynasty, a branch of which styled itself "Lord of the Hindus." The Sen kings founded temples and monasteries which even today are among the richest *Guthi* owners in Nepal. In addition, certain areas of great religious sanctity are located in the central Tarai. Janakpur, in Dhanusha district, is said to have been the birthplace of Sita, famed in the Ramayana. Several temples there are consecrated to Rama and other personalities connected with the epic, and they too own extensive *Guthi* lands in this region.[42]

---

as *Guthi* so as to insure that religious functions are performed without any interruption." "Regulations in the Name of Panditraj Ranganath," Shrawan Sudi 7, 1863 (July 1806). Local authorities too were often instructed to report to the government if no land endowments had been made for any temple. "Royal Order to the Amalis and Dwares of Patan," Shrawan Badi 3, 1874 (July 1817).

[41] Government of Nepal, "Datta Guthi," in Ministry of Law and Justice, *Shri 5 Surendra... Muluki Ain*, sec. 1, p. 9; Ministry of Law and Justice, "Guthi Ko," *Muluki Ain* (2020 [1963]), sec. 1, p. 112.

[42] For a brief description of religious places and monasteries in this region see Janak Lal Sharma, "Chitwandekhi Janakpur-sammaka Kehi Puratattwik Sthal" [Some archeological sites from Chitaun to Janakpur], *Ancient Nepal*, January 1968, pp. 1–10, and "Varahakshetra ra Anya Kehi Sthal" [Barahakshetra and some other sites], ibid., July 1968, pp. 27–35.

Categories of *Guthi* Land Endowments

Guthi land endowments were made by all classes of people in Nepal, from members of the ruling family to the ordinary landowner. Such endowments were traditionally classified on the basis of their authorship. A distinction was made between *Raj Guthi*, endowments made by members of ruling families,[43] and *Duniya Guthi*, those made by private individuals on lands on which they enjoyed the rights of transfer and bequest.

State endowment of *Raikar* lands as *Guthi* was subject to certain restrictions. Only waste or unclaimed *Jagera* lands could be endowed as *Guthi*. The endowment of *Jagir* lands was specifically prohibited.[44] During the nineteenth and early twentieth centuries, the rulers of Nepal faced a shortage of cultivated lands available for endowment as *Guthi*; hence a large number of *Guthi* endowments were made from waste lands. Even members of the royal family often had to make *Guthi* land endowments from their own private landholdings.[45] At times, the shortage of cultivated lands under *Jagera* tenure created such difficulties that the law was deliberately violated in order to convert *Jagir* land into *Guthi*.[46]

The emergence of a rentier class on *Raikar* lands (which we shall consider in chapter 10) enabled not only the state but private individuals as well to endow rent-receiving rights on *Raikar* lands as *Guthi*. Such endowments did not concern the state, and the land continued to be registered as *Raikar* in the official tax-assessment records. Private rent-receiving rights on *Raikar* lands did not emerge until the early twentieth century. Therefore, the vast majority of existing *Duniya Guthi* endowments were made on *Birta* lands. Moreover, the use of *Raikar* lands for endowment as *Guthi* entailed risks, because, up to 1961, no compensation was paid when such lands were acquired by the government. Where *Guthi* tenure emerged from the endowment of *Birta* lands, the income accruing therefrom to the *Guthi* was determined

---

[43] According to the 1870 edition of the legal code, *Raj Guthi* denoted *Guthi* endowments made by King Drabya Shah (1559–70), prince of the ruling dynasty of Lamjung who founded the Kingdom of Gorkha in 1559, and his successors, and by the chieftains of principalities annexed by Gorkha during the eighteenth and nineteenth centuries. Law Ministry Records, "Guthi Ko" [On Guthi], *Muluki Ain*, 1870 ed., sec. 34, p. 20.

[44] Government of Nepal, "Guthi Ko", *Muluki Ain*, pt. III (Kathmandu: Gorkhapatra Press, 2009 [1952], sec. 10. p. 4. This provision was repealed in 1963.

[45] "Guthi Land Endowment by Her Majesty the Third Queen," Baisakh 10, 1986 (April 22, 1929); Naraharinath Yogi, II (2), 61

[46] Regmi, *Land Tenure and Taxation in Nepal*, IV, 33.

by the nature of the original *Birta* grant, as were the other terms and conditions of the endowment. For instance, lifetime *Birta* lands could not be endowed as *Guthi*, for the owner had no right to endow on a permanent and irrevocable basis lands that would revert to the state after his death. *Duniya Guthi* endowments were legally valid only if the owner did not owe arrears of payment to the state or to other individuals at the time of the endowment.

Classification of *Guthi* endowments on the basis of their authorship has lost all significance today, for not all existing *Raj Guthis* have been endowed by members of the royal family. At present, *Raj Guthis* include lands which, though originally endowed by private individuals, were subsequently acquired by the government as a result of confiscation, the extinction of the donor's family, or voluntary surrender by the donor or his successors. Such conversion of *Duniya Guthis* into *Raj Guthis* was possible because of the generally accepted principle that *Guthi* endowments are permanent and irrevocable, and that any violation of the religious and charitable functions prescribed therein constitutes an encroachment upon religion. The state therefore assumed the obligation of insuring that these functions were not disrupted under any circumstances. If *Duniya Guthi* holders committed treason, their *Guthi* lands were taken away from them and granted to the nearest relative. In the absence of such relatives, the *Guthi* was taken under state management. The role of the state as protector of the *Guthi* system is further highlighted by the obligation it assumed in taking over the management of *Guthis* left unclaimed as a result of the extinction of the donor's family or, in the case of endowments made through a ritual gift with the intent of religious merit, of the beneficiary's family.[47] According to recent legislation, the Guthi Corporation is empowered to take up the management of any *Duniya Guthi* if the majority of its owners make a request to that effect.[48]

The exigencies of administration and management, and not the nature of authorship, thus constituted the criterion differentiating *Raj Guthis* from *Duniya Guthis*. *Raj Guthis* were, therefore, redefined as *Guthis* under the jurisdiction of His Majesty's Government, or those for which it made the necessary administrative arrangements.[49] In 1964 the management and control of *Raj Guthis* were placed under

---

[47]Ibid., pp. 22-23.
[48]Guthi Corporation Act, 1972, sec. 19.
[49]Ministry of Law and Justice, "Guthi Samsthan Ain, 2021" [Guthi Corporation act, 1964], sec. 2 (g), *Nepal Gazette*, vol. 14, no. 15, Aswin 17, 2021 (October 2, 1964).

an autonomous body known as the Guthi Corporation. All rights and liabilities of the government in respect to *Raj Guthis* were then delegated to that body.[50]

Amanat AND *Chhut Guthis*

On the basis of the administrative arrangements made to ensure the regular discharge of the prescribed *Guthi* functions, *Raj Guthi* endowments were classified as *Amanat* and *Chhut*. Under the *Amanat* system, *Guthi* functions are discharged under the direct control and supervision of the government. *Raj Guthis* which had been assigned to private individuals on a lifetime or inheritable basis then came to be known as *Chhut*. During the Rana regime, *Raj Guthis* with large surpluses were assigned on a *Chhut* basis to relatives and favorities, thereby enabling them to appropriate a part or the whole of the surplus income. There were also cases, however, in which *Chhut Guthi* assignees were required to deposit such surplus income with the government on payment of a nominal fee. The essential characteristic of a *Chhut Guthi* was thus private management, irrespective of the method used for disposing of the surplus income. As a result of the emergence of the two sub-categories of *Amanat* and *Chhut*, the term *Raj Guthi* was used to denote several degrees of governmental control and supervision, from mere registration on payment of a nominal annual fee to full-fledged governmental operation and management.

The *Chhut Guthi* system represented a compromise between individual ownership and full-fledged state control of *Guthi* land endowments. It reconciled individual control and operation with the nominal administrative authority of the state. The system enabled the state to enlarge the ambit of the *Raj Guthi* system without at the same time undertaking the onerous responsibility of operating deficit *Guthis*, or those with small surpluses. Even in the case of *Guthi* endowments with large surpluses, the state was able, under the *Chhut Guthi* system, to absorb a part or, at times, even the whole of the surplus income without simultaneously undertaking managerial responsibilities.[51]

Although the *Chhut Guthi* system relieved the government of its administrative responsibilities, such a system of private management of public institutions for individual benefit was somewhat out of step with the social ideals ushered in after the downfall of the Rana

[50] Ibid., sec. 12.
[51] Regmi, IV, 24–27.

regime. The Government of Nepal therefore enacted legislation in September 1972 to abolish *Chhut Guthi* endowments for *Amanat* operation and management. However, deficit *Guthis*, or those with small surpluses, may be handed back to the erstwhile assignees for management and operation during a term of five years at a time under the supervision, control, and guidance of the Guthi Corporation. But in no circumstances will the managers be permitted to appropriate the surplus income, which will accrue to the corporation.[52]

Recent Changes in the *Raj Guthi* Landholding System

Under the 1972 Guthi Corporation Act, persons holding *Raj Guthi* lands have been divided into two broad categories: those who pay rents to the Guthi Corporation wholly or partly in kind, and those who pay rents in cash. In the rural areas of Kathmandu Valley and other parts of the hill region, all rights of *Raj Guthi* landholders of the first category will be taken over by the Guthi Corporation on payment of compensation. However, the actual cultivator, who has been elevated to the status of a protected tenant, is responsible for the payment of such compensation. In the urban areas of Kathmandu Valley and other parts of hill regions, on the other hand, *Raj Guthi* landholders will not be expropriated in this manner even if they may have been paying rents in kind to the Guthi Corporation. Rather, they have been permitted to retain two-thirds of the *Raj Guthi* holding, the balance of one-third being registered in the name of the actual cultivator without any consideration. Landholding rights on *Raj Guthi* lands of this category in urban areas will be salable.[53]

A different policy has been applied in those areas where rents on *Raj Guthi* lands were payable in cash. The status of *Raj Guthi* landholders of this category has been recognized as the same as that of owners of *Raikar* lands. They will accordingly be permitted to make payments to the Guthi Corporation at the tax-assessment rates prevailing on *Raikar* lands, sell their *Raj Guthi* lands, or appoint tenants to cultivate these lands.[54] The result is that, for all practical purposes, the distinction between *Raikar* lands and *Raj Guthi* lands of this category has disappeared.

Although it is too early to assess the impact of these reforms in *Raj*

---

[52] Guthi Corporation Act, 1972, secs. 15 (2), 18, 20.
[53] Ibid., sec. 25.
[54] Ibid., sec. 29.

Guthi landownership, they appear to have certain negative trends that should not be overlooked. The policy of abolishing private ownership rights if revenue was being paid in kind, and of retaining them if payments were being made in cash, may have been dictated by practical considerations of implementation. Nevertheless, the distinction is quite arbitrary and contrary to universally accepted principles of equity. Nor is it clear why the actual cultivator should be asked to shoulder the burden of compensation payable to the expropriated *Raj Guthi* landowners. Such investment on his part in tenancy rights that are not salable, and hence have no value as property, means that the *Raj Guthi* cultivator is being called upon to pay for something that his counterpart on *Raikar* lands,[55] and on *Raj Guthi* lands of other categories, is entitled to receive without undergoing a comparable sacrifice.

The 1972 Guthi Corporation Act also defines the powers and functions of the Guthi Corporation as the supreme custodian and manager of *Raj Guthi* lands. The corporation has been permitted to cultivate certain categories of *Raj Guthi* lands itself, subject to a ceiling of 1,500 *bighas*, or else appoint tenants on a permanent basis to do so.[56] Similarly, the corporation has been permitted to reclaim waste *Raj Guthi* lands itself, or have this done through tenants without prejudice to its ownership rights in such lands. It is only when neither alternative is possible that the corporation may relinquish its ownership rights in waste *Raj Guthi* lands and permit private individuals to reclaim them in the capacity of landowners. One wonders, however, to what extent the corporation's expertise in managing and operating religious and charitable endowments will help it to undertake entrepreneurial ventures of this nature in the field of agricultural development.

General Characteristics of *Guthi* Landownership

In the foregoing sections, we have briefly traced the origin of the

[55] Ministry of Law and Justice, "Bhumi Sambandhi Ain, 2021" [Lands act, 1964], sec. 25, *Nepal Gazette*, vol. 14, no. 18 (Extraordinary), Marga 1, 2021 (November 16, 1964). "Any person who has been cultivating in the capacity of a tenant land belonging to any landowner shall acquire tenancy rights therein. In case any person gives away his land for cultivation to another person and in case the latter grows the main annual crop on such land in the capacity of a tenant at least once, he shall ipso facto become a tenant enjoying rights in such land."

[56] Guthi Corporation Act, 1972, secs. 24–26. The Guthi Corporation announced in 1974 that it had decided to start cultivation on 1,500 *bighas* of land under these arrangements. *Gorkhapatra*, Chaitra 29, 2030 (April 11, 1974).

Guthi system and enumerated its main categories. We shall now examine the general characteristics of *Guthi* as a form of institutional landownership. These tenurial characteristics may be defined as permanence and irrevocability of *Guthi* land endowments, relinquishment of individual title to the lands endowed, a ban on alienation, and tax exemption.

Guthi land endowments, once made, cannot be revoked. The dislocation of the prescribed functions, which the resumption of the endowed lands would involve, is prohibited by law [57] and the offender is prosecuted by the state itself.[58] Permanence and irrevocability present no problems in the case of *Raj Guthi* land endowments, which are operated under governmental control and supervision, but the private character of *Duniya Guthi* endowments makes it difficult to detect instances of dislocation of their functions. Complaints from persons affected by such dislocation are the only basis for governmental action. In order to insure that *Guthi* land endowments of both *Raj Guthi* and *Duniya Guthi* categories are not revoked, provisions have been made for relinquishment of individual title to the land endowed and a ban on the sale of *Guthi* lands.

Guthi landownership emerges as a result of the alienation of rent-receiving rights for the performance of religious and charitable functions. *Guthi* endowments therefore involve a relinquishment of individual title to the property endowed with religious or charitable motives. Relinquishment of title is complete and unqualified in the case of *Guthi* land endowments made through a formal ritual gift with the intent of acquiring religious merit. In such instances, the donors or heirs are not permitted to resume possession of the endowed lands, or of the management of the *Guthi*, under any circumstances. The lands are held by the grantee and his successors according to current property and inheritance laws. The only right enjoyed by the donor or his successors is that of replacing a beneficiary who violates the performance of the prescribed functions by a relative. When a *Guthi* endowment has been made through a simple endowment and not through a formal ritual gift, the donor and his successors are permitted to inherit the endowed lands and appropriate the surplus income. The endowed lands are not bequeathed outside the donor's family, hence

---

[57] Ministry of Law and Justice, "Guthi Ko" [On Guthi], *Muluki Ain* (Kathmandu: the Ministry, 2020 [1963], sec. 2, p. 112.

[58] Ministry of Law and Justice, 'Adalati Bandobast Ko" [On judicial procedure], ibid., sec. 22, p. 12.

relinquishment of title is effective only in preventing resumption and use of the income for purposes other than those mentioned in the deed of endowment.[59]

Until 1886, the sale of *Guthi* lands was permitted only if the proceeds were meant for the purchase of other lands of at least equal yield. In other words, the motive behind the sale determined the validity of the transaction. If the proceeds were misappropriated, the transaction was nullified, and the original land endowment was restored.[60] This concession was apparently abused by *Guthi* managers. Moreover, there was hardly any way in which the government could ascertain how the proceeds of the sale of *Guthi* lands were actually used. In 1886, therefore, the law was amended to prescribe that *Guthi* lands should not be sold or mortgaged in any manner.[61] This provision is still in force. *Guthi* cannot be alienated even if the buyer stipulates that he will perform the functions mentioned in the prescribed deed of endowment. However, there is no restriction on the temporary alienation of the right to appropriate surplus income through mortgage.[62]

Before 1951, it was the usual practice to remit taxes when *Raikar* land was endowed as *Guthi* with official approval. At present, the government of Nepal has not assumed any powers to grant such remission.[63] However, certain categories of *Birta* lands used as *Guthi* have been provisionally exempted from taxation. These include *Birta* lands endowed as Guthi by the government, lands similarly endowed by individuals but subsequently taken over for governmental management for any reason, and *Birta* lands endowed as *Guthi* with official permission.[64] These tax-exempt categories did not include *Birta* lands endowed as *Guthi* by individuals without official permission or knowledge. Such lands were converted into *Raikar* and taxed at normal

[59] Ministry of Law and Justice, "Guthi Ko," ibid., secs. 3, 5, pp. 112–13.
[60] Government of Nepal, "Datta Guthi," in *Shri 5 Surendra...Muluki Ain*, sec. 16, p. 13.
[61] Law Ministry Records, "Guthi Ko," *Muluki Ain*, 1886 ed., sec. 4.
[62] Ministry of Law and Justice, "Guthi Ko," *Muluki Ain* (2020 [1963], sec. 3, p. 112.
[63] The 1960 Land-Taxation Act had empowered the government to remit, in whole or in part, taxes on lands utilized for hospitals, temples, resthouses, roadside shelters, public schools, orphanages, and other religious and charitable institutions. Ministry of Law, "Jagga Kar Ain, 2017" [Land Taxation Act, 1960], *Nepal Gazette*, vol. 10, no. 3 (Extraordinary), Jestha 2, 2017 (May 15, 1960), sec. 12 (1). This law was, however, repealed on March 23, 1966. Ministry of Law and Justice, "Khareji ra Samshodhan Ain, 2022" [Repeal and amendment act, 1965], ibid., vol. 15, no. 36 (Extraordinary), Chaitra 10, 2022 (March 23, 1966).
[64] Birta Abolition Act, 1959, op. cit. (in chap. 3, n. 70), sec. 11.

Raikar rates. According to an official clarification:

> *Birta* lands endowed as *Guthi* have been retained as usual, since the government does not intend to disrupt the religious system. So far as private *Guthi* endowments made without governmental permission are concerned, they may continue to be operated as before; the government does not interfere in such matters. How can it know what anybody has done privately without its permission?[65]

As *Guthi* endowments are permanent and irrevocable, we might assume that the area under this form of land tenure in Nepal has been growing at a steady pace. Nevertheless, the religious character of *Guthi* land endowments has never hindered the state from exercising its right of eminent domain. Before 1961, the law contained provisions enabling the government to acquire *Guthi* lands. When *Duniya Guthi* lands, which enjoyed a status similar to *Birta*, were acquired for such purposes, compensation was paid in cash according to the value of land, or other land of equal yield was given in exchange. The second method of compensation was more common, for it insured that the prescribed *Guthi* functions were not disrupted. However, land-acquisition legislation enacted in 1961 gives no consideration to the tenure status of the land proposed to be acquired.[66] Moreover, no provision has been made to grant other lands in exchange for acquired *Guthi* lands.[67] As a result of these measures, a progressive depletion of the area under *Guthi* tenure seems inevitable in the future.

Guthi AND THE STATE

Usually, the rulers of Nepal did not interfere in the social and religious life of the people. During the campaign of political unification in the latter part of the eighteenth and early nineteenth centuries, existing *Guthi* endowments in conquered territories were confirmed

[65] His Majesty's Government of Nepal, *Bhumi Sudhar Ke Ho?* [What is land reform?] (Kathmandu: Department of Publicity and Broadcasting, 2017 [1960]), p. 10.

[66] Ministry of Law, Justice, and Parliamentary Affairs, "Jagga Prapti Ain, 2018" [Land acquisition act, 1961], *Nepal Gazette*, vol. 11, no. 48 (Extraordinary), Bhadra 9,2018 (August 25, 1961), secs. 2-3; Ministry of Law and Justice, "Rajamarga (Nirman Byabastha) Ain, 2021" [Highways (construction arrangements) act, 1964], ibid., vol. 14, no. 15 (Extraordinary), Aswin 17, 2021 (October 2, 1964), secs. 2-5.

[67] Ministry of Law and Justice, "Kshatipurti Ain, 2019" [Compensation act, 1963], ibid., vol. 12, no. 44B (Extraordinary), Chaitra 30, 2019 (April 12, 1963), secs. 3-4. Under this law, property acquired by the government is paid for in cash or in bonds.

by military commanders and local officials pending formal approval from Kathmandu.[68] The policy customarily followed was to confirm *Guthi* endowments formally made by the displaced rulers and confiscate lands being used as *Guthi* without such authority. In accordance with that policy, the government "scrutinized the signature" on *Guthi* land endowments made by the displaced Malla kings in Kathmandu Valley,[69] "abolished those that were to be abolished, and confirmed those that were to be confirmed."[70]

In chapter 3, we referred to the measures taken by the government of Nepal during the period after political unification to discover and confiscate lands being used as *Birta* and *Guthi* without proper authority. Occasionally, even *Birta* and *Guthi* lands granted under the seal of kings other than those belonging to the donor's dynasty were confiscated. Such measures inevitably disrupted existing *Guthi* institutions, even though the land endowments that financed them were irregular. (A possible explanation for this apparently irreligious policy may be found in the legal view that all lands belonged to the state and therefore could not be alienated except under the seal of the reigning king.) The government therefore discouraged the endowment of lands as *Guthi* by officials acting on their own inititive. Regulations promulgated for Kathmandu Valley in 1799 stipulated that "in case any official has granted *Birta* lands as *Guthi* without royal permission, he shall be fined with an amount four times the value of the land. If it is necessary to offer lands for gods and goddesses, we shall do so. If it is necessary to confiscate such lands, we shall do so. Let such matters be represented to us."[71]

The Shah rulers also did not hesitate to confiscate *Guthis* in cases involving violation of stipulated religious or charitable functions and sale of *Guthi* lands.[72] It would have been more consistent with religious traditions in such cases to punish the guilty persons and make arrangements to continue the prescribed *Guthi* functions. Apparently, the government wanted to take advantage of lapses on the part of *Guthi*

[68]Naraharinath Yogi, II, bk. 2, 54-55. This document refers to *Guthi* endowments made for a temple in Jumla which had been retained by local military commanders during the conquest of this region by Gorkha and were formally confirmed by the government in 1824.

[69]Ibid., p. 291.

[70]"Confirmation of Guthi Lands of Chandeshwari Temple in Banepa," Bhadra Badi 6, 1861 (August 1804).

[71]"Land Administration Regulations for Kathmandu Valley," Aswin Badi 5, 1856 (September 1799), sec. 18.

[72]"Judicial Regulations for Morang District," Jestha Sudi 14, 1861 (June 1804).

functionaries to extend the area of land under state control, while nominally professing to respect the sanctity of *Guthi* land endowments. Considerable areas of *Guthi* lands must have been confiscated on such legalistic pretexts, for one is struck by the virtual nonexistence of *Guthi* land endowments made by the various royal dynasties that ruled different parts of Nepal before its unification. A few endowments made by the Malla kings in Kathmandu Valley are still extant, but their number and volume seem small when we note that this dynasty ruled a comparatively prosperous and advanced part of the country for more than four centuries, and, moreover, was well known for the construction of temples and the performance of religious acts.

Jang Bahadur, who became prime minister of Nepal in September 1846, posed as a staunch defender of religious traditions and institutions, particularly the *Guthi* system. He declared:

> Foolish kings and evil-minded ministers who damage temples, resthouses, roadside shelters, bridges, water spouts, tanks, roads, wells, gardens, etc., constructed by others, or who confiscate *Guthis* endowed by others, block their way to heaven and pave their way to hell. Incapable of tolerating the religious merit acquired by good people, they act against the public interest. Such people will sink in sin.[73]

He therefore initiated measures to restore the *Birta* and *Guthi* lands that had been confiscated in 1806, as was described in chapter 3.

The restoration of confiscated *Guthi* lands was not the only measure undertaken by Jang Bahadur to entrench the sanctity of the *Guthi* system. He also decreed that if any person disrupted the prescribed religious or charitable functions, the *Guthi* should be taken over for state management:

> Nobody shall confiscate *Guthi* lands even if the person who endowed them or his descendants commit any crime punishable by death, life imprisonment, loss of caste or confiscation of property. In such cases, their relatives may operate the *Guthi* and appropriate the surplus income. If no relative exists, the *Guthi* shall be operated by the state.[74]

This meant a departure from the old policy of confiscating *Guthi* lands held by such offenders. These provisions are still in force in much the same form,[75] and have effectively prevented the depletion

---

[73]Government of Nepal, "Datta Guthi," in *Shri 5 Surendra...Muluki Ain*, sec. 1, pp. 9–10.
[74]Law Ministry Records, "Guthi Ko," *Muluki Ain*, 1870 ed., sec. 4, p. 2.
[75]Ministry of Law and Justice, "Guthi Ko," *Muluki Ain* (2020 [1963]), sec. 2, p. 112.

of the area under *Guthi* land tenure through governmental action.

Critique of the *Guthi* System

The foregoing analysis shows that, according to both law and popular conception, *Guthi* is a system under which lands are endowed for religious and charitable purposes. It is primarily intended to be a manifestation of "the desire to please the gods." However, it is to a human agency that the cultivation of *Guthi* lands, collection of rents, and discharge of the prescribed religious and charitable functions must be entrusted. The revenue collector and the temple manager are therefore essential components of the *Guthi* system, and it is to them rather than to the gods that the cultivator owes primary allegiance. Aided by such circumstances as rising prices and growing government control over *Guthi* endowments, the revenue collector and the temple manager have been successful, in many cases, in gradually garnering for themselves the major share of income from *Guthi* lands. The system of *Guthi* landownership has, in fact, degenerated to one under which a small portion of the total agricultural produce is devoted to purposes that not infrequently are of dubious religious and charitable significance. The system evolved in an age when society desired stability rather than growth. It was the product of a situation in which privileged classes in the society utilized economic resources for nonmaterial objectives to earn "religious" merit for themselves. The system permits the use of surplus agricultural production for such purposes as the regular performance of mystic rites at a temple or the feeding of monkeys. It attaches more importance to custom and tradition in the sphere of religion and charity than to the material needs and egalitarian aspirations of the society.

Moreover, *Guthi* lands yield no revenue to the state. Whereas *Birta* and other tax-exempt categories of land tenure have been brought within the ambit of the *Raikar* system, religious sentiment has hampered the extension of this policy to *Guthi* landownership. There can certainly be no objection to any act of beneficence to religious or charitable institutions. Such endowments should not, however, obstruct the mobilization of resources for nation-building activities. In particular, it may be pointed out that the tax exemption provided to owners of *Birta* lands endowed as *Guthi* with governmental approval "until alternative arrangements are made to operate the *Guthi* according to custom and tradition" is difficult to justify. Such exemption can be justified only if the *Guthi* has no surplus income and the tax has to be paid from funds reserved for the prescribed religious or charitable functions. This is seldom the case, and owners of such *Guthi* lands appropriate the surplus income even while the state relinquishes tax revenue. There is no reason why these owners should be placed in a special category and permitted to enjoy a tax-free income merely because a part of the income from their land is being used for religious or charitable functions. Nor is there any evidence that such taxation would dislocate *Guthi* functions. There have been very few complaints that the imposition of taxes on the *Birta* lands endowed as *Guthi* without government approval has had this result.

Finally, the *Guthi* land-tenure system does not create favorable conditions for insuring that land is put to its best physical or ecological use. In several cases, lands that might be better suited for the cultivation of more valuable crops are being used to grow paddy, or even flowers, because the original deed of endowment prescribed assessment in these forms. The situation is even worse in the case of *Guthi* lands suitable for nonagricultural purposes. Under the existing *Guthi* landholding system, no one is in a position to insure that *Guthi* lands are put to the most economical use, or that agricultural production is maximized. Regular payment of the prescribed assessment in the prescribed form is all that the system requires. *Guthi* landownership, in fact, has the worst features of absentee landlordism. The Guthi Corporation is interested only in revenue and is not at all concerned with the actual processes of agricultural production. What it takes from the land is not reinvested in the form of seeds, fertilizers, and insecticides. It is the largest landowner in Nepal, with extensive areas of agricultural lands in different parts of the country under its control. But this has not brought any of the advantages of large-scale operation or investment. The corporation is less interested in maintaining the fertility of the soil, or in increasing agricultural production, than in holding wealth in a secure form. This accumulation of wealth, however, has not led to productive investment.

The post-1951 period has witnessed the abolition of the *Birta* and *Jagir* systems. The *Guthi* system has been left basically untouched, mainly because of traditional religious considerations. An idealized conception of the system, without regard for its social and economic ramifications, has retarded an objective evaluation of its contribution to religion and charity. It is true, of course, that changes have been introduced in the administration of *Raj Guthi* endowments in recent years. The formation of the Guthi Corporation in 1964, and the abolition of the *Chhut Guthi* system in 1972, are major reforms that will go a long way toward improving the working of *Raj Guthi* institutions. Nevertheless, the institutional character of *Guthi* landownership remains intact.

Chapter 5

THE LAND-ASSIGNMENT SYSTEM: *JAGIR* TENURE

The form of land tenure known as *Jagir* came into being when revenues on lands were assigned as emoluments to government employees and functionaries.[1] Lands on which the state retained its right to collect and appropriate the revenue were known as *Jagera*, and the totality of *Jagir* and *Jagera* lands constituted the area owned by the state under *Raikar* tenure.

The *Jagir* system appears to have been borrowed from India before the political unification of Nepal during the latter part of the eighteenth century.[2] In Nepal, however, the system gradually acquired a distinct character. The term *Jagir*, in India, "covered a medley of grants for maintenance, appreciation, or remuneration created for reasons of political expediency or exigencies of administration."[3] In India, *Jagir* ownership did not necessarily imply the obligation to discharge specific functions and was often the result of services rendered in the past. In Nepal, on the other hand, land grants made in appreciation of services rendered in the past were associated with the *Birta* system,

---

[1] "Jagir is really a compound of two Persian words and should strictly be, though is most often not, spelt *Jai-Gir*. Literally, it means [one] holding or occupying a place." Irfan Habib, *The Agrarian System of Mughal India* (Bombay: Asia Publishing House, 1963), p. 256. According to Habib, the term was used to denote "a tract of land which kings grant to *Mansabdars* and [persons] of that kind, that they might take its revenue from cultivation, whatever it be." He adds that *Jagir* as a technical term in this sense came into use in India in the fifteenth century.

[2] According to a Nepali antiquary: "Toward the middle of the eighteenth century, the chieftains of principalities in the hill regions and the Tarai assigned lands to their employees, from top-ranking officials to orderlies, instead of paying them cash salaries." Baburam Acharya, "Nepalko Bhumi Byabastha" [Nepal's land system] (unpublished). No documentary evidence is available of any such grant in the hill regions. For a *Jagir* land grant made by King Bisantar Sen of Vijayapur in eastern Nepal in 1751, before the Gorkhali conquest, see Rajvamshi, *Puratattwa-Patrasangraha* II, 9. This grant, however, appears to be more in the nature of the modern *Birta*. The term *Jagir* was thus employed in the kingdom of Vijayapur in the same sense in which it was used in India.

[3] G. D. Patel, *The Land Problems of the Reorganized Bombay State* (Bombay: N. M. Tripathi [Private], 1957), p. 199.

whereas *Jagir* lands usually were assigned in consideration of current services.

Objectives of *Jagir* Land Assignments

The evolution of the *Jagir* system in Nepal was influenced mainly by fiscal, administrative, and political circumstances. These included the preponderantly nonmonetized and noncentralized character of the fiscal system, the need to finance a fast-growing administrative and military establishment during the period after political unification, and the ubiquitous yearning for landownership and privilege in an agrarian society.

We shall first examine the fiscal problems that the government of Nepal attempted to solve through *Jagir* land assignments during the period following the political unification of the country. Over a large part of the hill region and Kathmandu Valley, the land tax was assessed in kind. Collection of revenue in this form, however, would have created manifold problems, such as the construction of storage facilities in different parts of the country and quick sales in the absence of transport and communication facilities. Consequently, although the flow of income from land-tax collections was checked at different points, the financial liabilities of the government remained intact. Instead of assuming the burden of land-tax collections directly, therefore, the government mitigated such liabilities to some extent by assigning lands to its employees as their emoluments.[4] All that the government was required to do under this system was to prepare land records and, later, lists of tax assessments, leaving the more difficult task of collection and utilization to the *Jagirdar*. Even when land and other revenues were assessed in cash, such assignments made it unnecessary for the government to maintain a permanent machinery for revenue collection. In other words, the *Jagirdar*, in addition to the functions pertaining to his office, also indirectly acted as a collection agent on behalf of the government.

After 1768, the increased administrative and military requirements of the rapidly growing empire lent an added significance to the *Jagir*

[4]According to one study: "To carry produce to the centre and then back, in order that the King's representatives on the spot should have their share of the produce, the share which they need for their support, is so wasteful as to be absurd. It is vastly easier to allow the local lords to take their share on the way, so that it is only the residue, after they have taken what is due to them, which comes to the centre." John Hicks, *A Theory of Economic History* (London: Oxford University Press, 1969), pp. 17-18.

land-assignment system. Territorial expansion was achieved through military conquests for which troops were recruited in large numbers. In the absence of a broad-based money economy and a centralized public-finance system, the government was in no position to pay cash salaries to its troops. Military employees were therefore recompensed for their services through land assignments under the *Jagir* system.[5] In fact, considering the lack of a broad-based money economy and public-finance system, the requirements of a large-scale administrative and military machinery could scarcely have been fulfilled without recourse to the *Jagir* system. Because cultivable lands were abundant, it was much more sensible to assign lands rather than to pay emoluments in cash. Legislation prescribing the assignment of lands in preference to cash salaries as the emoluments of government employees was enacted in early 1793.[6] Particularly after 1804, when the government of Nepal resumed its westward thrust in the Jamuna-Sutlej region (now in Himachal Pradesh and Punjab, India), military recruitment grew to such a scale that it was limited only by the area of agricultural lands available for assignment as *Jagir*. Steps were therefore taken during the early nineteenth century to reclaim waste lands and confiscate large areas of agricultural lands that were being utilized as *Birta*, *Guthi*, or *Kipat* without proper authorization.[7] This led to an unprecedented enlargement of the area covered by the *Jagir* land-tenure system.

Fiscal and administrative exigencies alone do not explain the importance acquired by the *Jagir* land-tenure system in Nepal during the period following the political unification of the country. Of perhaps equal importance was the opportunity that the *Jagir* system provided to members of the nobility as well as the martial castes and communities for deriving economic benefit from territorial expansion. Prithvi

[5]The French scholar Levi observed: "The ingenious system of the annual '*Jagirs*' permits the Gurkhas to compensate the shortage of metallic currency. Each year at the *Pajani* the king as absolute proprietor of the land bestows on the servants he employs or maintains, a fief the extent and value of which naturally vary with the importance of the obligations. On the expiry of the year the fief returns to the king, who again disposes it according to his wishes. These fiefs bear the Persian name of '*Jagirs*' and the privileged are called '*Jagirdars*.'" Sylvain Levi, *Le Nepal* (Paris: Ernest Leroux, 1905-8).

[6]Foreign Ministry [Jaisi Kotha] Records, "Administrative Regulations of the Government of Nepal," Falgun Badi 4, 1849 (February 1793), sec. 12.

[7]For a detailed study of these developments see Regmi, *A Study in Nepali Economic History*, pp. 37-54. An account of how land determined the strength of the Nepali army during the early history of modern Nepal is given in Ludwig F. Stiller, *The Rise of the House of Gorkha* (New Delhi: Manjusri Publishing House, 1973), pp. 277-94.

Narayan Shah's conquests led to a heavy influx of these people from the western hills, particularly Gorkha, to Kathmandu Valley. The granting of *Jagir* lands to such of them as received appointments in the government and the army was an important factor contributing to the stability and organization of the newly established regime. Without the *Jagir* system, it would have been virtually impossible for the government to distribute rewards to its nobility and military personnel, who, although hardy of spirit, were bereft of sources of income other than what their small holdings in the hill regions afforded. *Birta* grants also provided an equal opportunity for economic advancement, but the *Jagir* system served the needs of the government better because it was tied directly to service. It is against this background that the following directive of Prithvi Narayan Shah acquires meaning: "It is of utmost importance that the soldiers required by the king should be provided with lands and homesteads, so that they may remain free from worries about their family and bear a stout heart."[8] The *Jagir* system thus constituted a mechanism through which government service was utilized to acquire landed wealth.

OTHER USES OF THE *Jagir* SYSTEM

For the government, the *Jagir* system served other purposes as well. For instance, *Jagir* grants occasionally involved the obligation to supply troops,[9] weapons,[10] or military supplies[11] whenever required. Lands were often granted as *Jagir* to promote the resettlement of strategic areas and organize them as military bases.[12] Such grants were

[8] Naraharinath Yogi and Baburam Acharya eds., *Rashtrapita Shri 5 Bada Maharaja Prithvi Narayan Shahdevako Divya Upadesh* [Divine Counsel of the Great King Prithvi Narayan Shah Dev, Father of the Nation] (2d rev. ed.; Kathmandu: Prithvi Jayanti Samaroha Samiti, 2010 [1953]), p. 23.

[9] In 1834, a royal order appointing Jan Shah as Chautara, or minister, mentioned the lands assigned to him as *Jagir* and directed him to utilize these lands for equipping 46 persons with muskets and to have one cannon ready for use. Naraharinath Yogi, *Itihas Prakash*, II (3), 415–16.

[10] "Jagir Land Grant to Ran Singh Adhikari for Supply of Arrows," Bhadra Sudi 30, 1850 (September 1793).

[11] "Jagir Land Grant to Inhabitants of Kitini for Supply of Charcoal and Other Materials to Gunpowder Factory," Aswin Badi 13, 1854 (September 1797).

[12] In 1804, *Jagir* land grants were made in Makwanpur to several families and the *Jagirdars* were instructed to reclaim waste lands; promote settlement; repair and maintain forts; collect information about "the southern areas" (i.e., British India); procure food grains, cannon, and ammunition to meet military requirements; and equip troops with bows and arrows, train them, and gradually increase their number. "Jagir Grant to Ghanshyam Bania and His Brothers in Makwanpur," 1861 (1804).

important particularly before the emergence of the Rana regime, when security against military aggression and territorial expansion were prime objectives of official policy.

During that period, the *Jagir* system was occasionally also utilized to promote land reclamation and resettlement. Although cultivable lands may have been abundant, large areas were still waste and uncultivated during the nineteenth century. *Jagirdars* naturally preferred assignments of lands which had already been reclaimed and cultivated. As a result of the growing number of civil and military personnel to whom lands had to be assigned as *Jagir*, there was a shortage of cultivated lands. But there is no evidence that that shortage constituted any limitation to the proliferation of *Jagir* land grants. In many cases, waste lands were granted as *Jagir*, and *Jagirdars* were under obligation to reclaim them and appropriate rents thereon.[13] The government thus solved simultaneously the problems of compensating its employees and promoting land reclamation and settlement. Indeed, *Jagir* land grants were often made with the specific objective of encouraging land reclamation,[14] and tax exemptions were provided to the recipient to make the assignment more attractive financially.[15]

Birta AND *Jagir*

Jagir assignments, like *Birta* grants, entitled the beneficiaries to appropriate agricultural rents and other income from the lands covered by the assignment, but there existed basic differences between these two forms of landownership. In its ultimate form, the *Jagir* system implied a mere assignment of land revenue. Unlike *Birta* owners, therefore, *Jagirdars* generally did not enjoy the right to resume land for personal residence or cultivation. Whereas *Birta* landownership rights were usually inheritable and transferable, *Jagir* rights were limited to the individual use of the assignee so long as he remained in the service of the government. The *Jagirdar* was permitted to sell or mortgage rents on his *Jagir* lands, but such trans-

---

A similar grant in the same area required the *Jagirdars* to "maintain only one route through the Churia hills, whichever is the worst one," and to close others by planting cane and thorny bushes. "Jagir Grant to Jagannath Khatri and Others in Makwanpur" Baisakh Sudi 4, 1861 (May 1804).

[13] "Jagir Grant to Chautariyas Bidur Shah and Sher Bahadur Shah," Kartik Badi 7, 1856 (October 1799).

[14] "Jagir Grant to Nizamat Shah," 1842 (1785).

[15] "Jagir Grant to Meghavarna Khawas," Poush Badi 6, 1849 (December 1792).

actions had no effect on his *Jagir* rights as such. In other words, whereas *Birta* constituted a form of private property, *Jagir* was a temporary assignment intended to compensate the *Jagirdar* for the services currently rendered by him to the state. Moreover, *Jagir* land assignments were terminable at the discretion of the government. No alienation of its ownership rights in the land by the state was involved in *Jagir*, in contradistinction to *Birta*. Under the law, "*Raikar* land belongs to the government, even when it is assigned as *Jagir*."[16]

Jagir Privileges and Incomes

At this point, it would be useful to examine the form into which the *Jagir* system evolved in Nepal by the beginning of the present century. The privileges to which *Birta* grants entitled the recipients were described in chapter 3. These privileges were also generally enjoyed in the same form by *Jagirdars*. *Jagir* assignments, whenever the area covered by them so warranted, included not only land taxes but also customs and market duties, forest revenues, judicial fines, and escheat property.[17] The gradual centralization of the administrative and judicial systems made it possible for the government to resume most of these nonagricultural sources of revenue, leaving the *Jagirdar* with only rents from the agricultural lands and homesteads assigned to him. It is important to remember that, until the early years of the twentieth century, such rent-receiving rights were limited to *Birta* and *Jagir* lands. As will be explained further in chapter 10, these rights had not yet evolved on *Raikar* lands.

The assignments of land as *Jagir* did not automatically entitle *Jagirdars* to collect rents from the cultivators. For this, they received annually documents known as *Tirja* which specified the form and level of rent payments. The figure mentioned in the *Tirja* conformed to that indicated in the tax-assessment records. Nevertheless, there were

[16] Government of Nepal, "Balika Jhagada Ko" [On rent disputes], *Muluki Ain*, pt. III (Kathmandu: Gorkhapatra Press 2009 [1952]), sec. 20, p. 57.

[17] "Jagir Grant to Jagannath Khatri and Others in Makwanpur," Baisakh Sudi 4, 1861 (May 1804). Whereas *Jagir* land assignments covered entire villages or divisions, *Jagirdars* exacted payment in the form not only of agricultural commodities but also of forest, mineral, or cottage-industry products, animals, and so on. A royal prince who had been assigned lands in the Chharkabhot area of Dolpa district in 1799 obtained falcons, partridges, horses, sheep, blankets, carpets, and miscellaneous other produce of the Himalayan region. "Order regarding Supply of Commodities from Jagir Lands of Chautaria Ran Udyot Shah in Pokhara, Chharka, and Other Areas," Kartik Badi 30, 1856 (November 1799).

certain circumstances in which the nature and level of the payments indicated in the *Tirja* were not adhered to. Where assessments were in kind, existing regulations prescribed that cultivators should grow suitable crops according to the availability of irrigation facilities, irrespective of the actual form of the revenue assessment. *Jagirdars* were thus required to receive payments in the form of crops actually cultivated and not to insist on payments in the form of paddy as prescribed in the *Tirja*.[18]

Ordinarily, a higher income was enjoyed by the *Jagirdar* than that indicated in the *Tirja*. In Kathmandu Valley, *Jagir* assignments were made by commuting cash salaries into paddy at Rs. 2.22 per *muri*.[19] A *Jagirdar* who was entitled to emoluments amounting to Rs. 55.50 received a *Jagir* land assignment that fetched him a rent of 25 *muris* of paddy. But the actual value of paddy was much higher than Rs. 2.22 per *muri*, and, moreover, continued to increase. In 1950, on the eve of the downfall of the Rana regime, 25 *muris* of paddy was worth approximately Rs. 750 in the Kathmandu market. In other words, the *Jagirdar*'s recorded income was Rs. 55.50, but the static figure used for calculating the value of his *Jagir* rents and the rising price of paddy made it possible for him to appropriate an income nearly 15 times higher. This was the case, of course, only in areas where land-tax assessments were in kind.

Nevertheless, the *Jagirdar*'s prospects were not as rosy as these figures would appear to indicate. There is evidence that the *Jagir* system did not always provide the *Jagirdar* with a stable and dependable income. In the event of crop failure, he was required to give appropriate remissions to the cultivator.[20] Indeed, the *Jagirdar*'s income might disappear altogether if the lands assigned to him sustained permanent damage and hence remained uncultivated.[21]

---

[18]"Order to Mohinaike Bandobast Office regarding Rents on Jagir Lands," Baisakh 30, 1979 (May 13, 1922): "Peasants grow paddy even on lands situated on a high level, devoid of irrigation facilities, and dependent upon rainfall, on the plea that the *Tirja* prescribes payment of rents [to *Jagirdars*] in paddy, instead of growing crops suited to the soil. As a result, crops often fail in the event of inadequate rainfall, so that both the landlord and the peasant sustain losses. From 1922, therefore, suitable crops such as maize, millet, and dry paddy [*Ghaiya*] shall be grown [on such lands]. *Jagirdars*, on their part, shall accept payments in the form of crops actually cultivated. They shall not insist on payment in paddy even if the *Tirja* so prescribes."

[19]Law Ministry Records, "Kampu Tirja Office Regulations," 1992 (1935), sec. 8.

[20]Government of Nepal, op. cit. (in n. 16 above), secs. 8–9, pp. 55–56.

[21]Law Ministry Records, "Jagir Administration Regulations," Jestha 29, 1961 (June 11, 1904).

Nor was he permitted to benefit from the reclamation of waste lands situated within his holding. At times, it was possible for a *Jagirdar* to receive assignments of damaged or even nonexistent lands that had been incorporated into the records through clerical error. However, the *Jagirdar* was not entitled to claim compensation from the government for the resultant losses to himself.[22] At most, he was permitted to relinquish the *Jagir* assignment and demand its replacement by a cash salary if he had not already collected rents in full for two years.[23] He was not even permitted to recoup his losses during bad years with the increased production during good years, for the figure mentioned in the *Tirja* represented the maximum amount of rents that he could collect from the cultivator in any year. The difficulties faced by *Jagirdars* can be imagined when we remember that the lands assigned to them might be situated at a distance of several days' journey and difficult of access. For the *Jagirdar*, the acceptance of land assignments under the *Jagir* system was therefore an uncertain gamble. If he was lucky or influential, he could appropriate an income several times higher than the salary pertaining to his position. Ordinarily, however, he could never be certain about the size of his income, or, in fact, whether he would receive any income at all. This explains why *Jagirdars* at times voluntarily offered to have their land assignments replaced by cash salaries.

Furthermore, *Jagir* land assignments did not provide the *Jagirdar* with a regular income throughout the year. Agricultural rents were paid only once or twice in the year, and it required considerable financial prudence on the *Jagirdar*'s part to meet his expenses month by month until the next payment fell due. Initially, the government appears to have attempted to overcome this difficulty by prescribing that the cultivator should supply the *Jagirdar* with loans that would be adjusted later to the *Jagir* rents.[24] It is doubtful, however, whether most cultivators were in a position to make such advance payments before crops were harvested, when payment was due in any case. That this system failed to accomplish its objectives is clear from the arrangements made during the Rana period to provide *Jagirdars* with loans from the government against the security of their *Tirja* certificates.[25]

[22] Ibid.
[23] Government of Nepal, "Bali Talab Bare Ko" [On salaries], *Muluki Sawal* [Administrative regulations] (Kathmandu: Gorkhapatra Press, 2010 [1953], sec. 12, p. 63.
[24] Regmi, *A Study in Nepali Economic History*, p. 98.
[25] Law Ministry Records, "Kampu Tirja Office Regulations," sec. 49.

THE LAND-ASSIGNMENT SYSTEM

The *Jagir* System and the Peasant

From the viewpoint of the cultivator, the assignment of land as *Jagir* meant the replacement of the authority of the state by that of the *Jagirdar*. The *Jagir* system not only exposed the cultivator to the vagaries of an individual rent-receiver who had little interest in the land and was intent only on making the most of the assignment while it remained in his possession, but also subjected him to higher exaction than would have been the case had the land continued under *Raikar* tenure.

After the beginning of the twentieth century, the government of Nepal initiated measures to build up a centralized public-finance system. Accordingly, it commuted the in-kind land-tax assessments of the hill regions into cash for purposes of collection. The rates at which in-kind tax assessments were commuted into cash were fixed on a long-term basis in 1910. Even when the prices of agricultural commodities increased subsequently, the commutation rates remained static. The result was that the real burden of land taxation on the cultivator fell in the same proportion as prices went up. The impact of this development on the fiscal obligations of owners of *Raikar* lands will be examined in detail in chapter 8. For the purpose of the present analysis, it may be sufficient to stress that the profit yielded by the difference between the official value of the land tax and its actual value in the market accrued only to cultivators on *Jagera* lands. On *Jagir* lands, the commutation system was not introduced, because the government was not responsible for collection; *Jagirdars* continued to collect rents in kind. *Raikar* cultivators were thus under obligation to make payment at a lower level than their counterparts on *Jagir* lands. Consequently, a cultivator on *Raikar* lands faced a sudden loss of both his status and his earnings in the event that his lands were assigned as *Jagir*.

An example will help to make these developments clearer. Suppose there were two cultivators, A and B, each cultivating one *ropani* of *Raikar* land and paying an in-kind tax of two *muris* of paddy. Subsequently, A's land was assigned to a *Jagirdar*, whereas B's land was retained under *Raikar* tenure. A continued to pay two *muris* of paddy to his *Jagirdar* landlord, but B met his tax obligation by paying Rs. 8 (the commuted value of two *muris* of paddy), to the government. In 1920, the market value of the two *muris* of paddy paid by A to his landlord was about Rs. 11.86, but B was still paying only Rs. 8.00.

The introduction of a commutation system on *Raikar* land therefore diminished the earnings of the *Jagir* cultivator vis-a-vis his *Raikar* counterpart.

Let us now suppose that B's *Raikar* land too was subsequently assigned as *Jagir*. Although he had been paying a tax of only Rs. 8.00 on his *Raikar* land previously, he was now obliged to pay the original in-kind assessment of two *muris* of paddy to the *Jagirdar*, worth Rs. 11.86 in the market. The assignment of his Raikar land as *Jagir* thus caused an annual loss of Rs. 3.86 to B. This loss increased in the same proportion as the price of paddy went up in the market. In 1950, when this price was Rs. 30 per *muri*, it amounted to as much as Rs. 52.

Ownership rights in *Jagera* lands that had not been assigned as *Jagir* therefore involved risk and uncertainty. Apparently unwilling to antagonize the growing class of *Jagera* landowners, the Government of Nepal promulgated regulations in 1904 prohibiting the assignment of *Jagera* lands as *Jagir*.[26] The result was that expansion in the area under *Jagir* tenure was no longer possible at the expense of *Jagera*, and *Jagera* landowners remained secure in both status and earnings. *Jagir* holdings that were temporarily vacant as a result of the death or dismissal of the *Jagirdar* were then placed under a separate category for subsequent reassignment as *Jagir*.

Collection of *Jagir* Rents

The hardships that cultivators suffered under the *Jagir* land-tenure system stemmed also from the methods employed for the collection of rents. We have noted above that *Jagirdars* were entitled to appropriate rents generally on the basis of *Tirja* certificates issued every year in their favor. *Tirja* certificates were negotiable, and *Jagirdars* appear to have preferred to exchange them for cash rather than visit the cultivator and collect rents in kind. Intermediaries called *Dhokres* made it their business to purchase *Tirja* certificates from *Jagirdars* and collect the rents from cultivators. There was no restriction on the price at which any *Tirja*, irrespective of its face value, might be sold to *Dhokres*, and failure on the part of the latter to make full collections could not give rise to any claim against the *Jagirdar* concerned unless he had undertaken liability to that effect in writing. *Dhokres* were not entitled, however, to demand payments from cultivators in kind. The government may have been willing to compel the cultivator to part

[26] Law Ministry Records, "Jagir Administration Regulations," 1904.

with his gains for feeding the *Jagirdar*, but not for swelling the profits of the *Dhokres*. *Dhokres* were therefore expected to accept the value of the rent in cash at local prices at the time of the presentation of the *Tirja*.[27]

Dhokres resorted to extortive practices, and the peasantry suffered hardships as a result. Thus, in Salyan district in 1833: "Persons who purchase the *Tirja* from *Jagirdars* do not allow the cultivators even three or four days' time. They demand payment even before the prescribed date. Several cultivators have therefore vacated their lands, which have consequently remained uncultivated."[28] On the other hand, the cultivator suffered also when *Dhokres* deliberately delayed collection in an attempt to cash the *Tirja* at high prices. In Palpa district in 1923, for example, "*Jagirdars* sell their *Tirja* at low rates to *Dhokres*, who go to the cultivators in June or July and make collections at high prices. This causes hardship to the cultivators, since food grains cannot be transported to the market because of the rainy season."[29] This meant that *Jagirdars* sold their *Tirja* at low rates, whereas the *Dhokre* who purchased it visited the village during the off season and collected the rent at high prices. This practice yielded higher profits to the *Dhokre*, but *Jagirdars* did not receive the entire collection actually made from cultivators. It also created difficulties for the cultivators, because food grains were generally scarce during the months of June and July.

Critique of the *Jagir* System

The *Jagir* land-assignment system fulfilled several political and administrative exigencies of the government during Nepal's phase of territorial expansion and consolidation in the late eighteenth and early nineteenth centuries. The system made it possible for the government to recompense its employees and functionaries for their services without direct payments in cash. It thus resolved most problems of land administration and revenue collection, and also enabled the government to maintain a larger civil and military establishment than its monetary revenues warranted.

[27] Government of Nepal, "Bali Bikri Ko" [On sale of rents], in Ministry of Law and Justice, *Shri 5 Surendra...Muluki Ain*, sec. 3, p. 50.
[28] "Order regarding Collection of Jagir Rents in Salyan," Kartik Badi 3, 1890 (November 1833).
[29] "Abolition of Jagir Lands in Palpa," Ashadh 3, 1980 (July 16, 1923).

Nevertheless, in the course of time, the *Jagir* system outlived its utility and tended to inhibit the growth of a monetized public-finance system. It was basically a product of an undeveloped monetary and public-finance system in which land was the main resource available to the government and the administrative machinery was not adequately organized to collect land revenue directly. No government anxious to develop a centralized system of administration could tolerate a situation in which the major part of the revenue from the most important resource available to it, the land, was spent before it reached the treasury. Statistics of the land revenue directly collected and appropriated by the government during 1852–53 illustrate the nature and extent of the problem. In that year, out of a total land-revenue assessment of Rs. 2.1 million in the hill regions, including Kathmandu Valley, less than one percent actually reached the government treasury; the balance had all been assigned as *Jagir*.[30]

Moreover, the *Jagir* system created a form of land tenure that had adverse repercussions on agricultural development. The *Jagirdar* possessed neither the capacity nor the inclination to develop the lands assigned to him. *Jagir* lands were often assigned in distant and widely separated areas, with the result that he was usually unable personally to supervise the management of his lands. Because of the uncertainty of his tenure, his sole interest lay in exacting the maximum gain from the lands assigned to him as *Jagir* so long as these remained in his possession.

Jagir Policy during the Rana Period

A trend toward the resumption of *Jagir* lands as *Jagera* and the replacement of *Jagir* land assignments by cash salaries started early after the establishment of Rana rule in Nepal. In order to explain this trend, it is necessary to describe the basic goals and objectives of Rana rule.

The paramount goal of the Rana political system was to keep effective control over the civil and military administration in the hands of the Rana family. This required a highly centralized administration.[31] But an administrative machinery composed for the most part of landowning *Jagirdars* who were virtually autonomous feudal lords within their assignments was an obstacle to centralization. A

---

[30] "Revenue and Expenditure of the Government of Nepal," 1909 (1852–53).
[31] Joshi and Rose, *Democratic Innovations in Nepal*, pp. 36–38.

system that gave government employees a feudalistic status without any obligations to the government in their capacity as landlords obviously did not fit into the conception of a centralized administrative machinery. The new set-up called for employees who regarded government employment as a career and not as a mere steppingstone to *Jagir* privileges.

The incompatibility of the *Jagir* system with the need for a centralized administrative machinery was not the only factor that initiated a trend toward its abolition after the establishment of Rana rule. Another equally important factor was the change in the objectives of government policies subsequent to this development. The Rana government functioned as nothing more than an instrument to exploit the country's resources in order to enhance the personal wealth of the Rana prime minister and his family. No distinction was made between the personal treasury of the Rana ruler and the treasury of the government; any government revenue in excess of administrative expenses was pocketed by the Rana ruler as private income.[32] The *Jagir* system did not serve these interests of the Rana government, for *Jagir* assignments reduced revenue and thus the prime minister's profits.

It is true, of course, that the abolition of *Jagir* land assignments did not mean a net saving to the government, for employees still had to be recompensed for their services through cash salaries. More effective control of the land, however, and enhancement of taxes through periodic revision of revenue settlements eventually increased the revenue to a figure that would never have been attained had the *Jagir* system been allowed to persist in the form that had prevailed before the establishment of Rana rule. During the entire period of Rana rule, from 1846 to 1951, the total amount collected by the government as land revenue in the hill regions, including Kathmandu Valley, increased approximately 200-fold. No doubt, the cultivated area also underwent considerable expansion during this period, but the part played by the official policy of reducing the area under *Jagir* tenure was by no means insignificant.

In accordance with this policy, Prime Minister Chandra Shamsher (1901–29) reorganized the land-tax collection system in the hill

[32]"Before the formation of the interim government [in February 1951] the surplus national income left after meeting the expenses of government was considered to be the personal property of the Rana prime minister. There was no clear division between the state treasury and his personal treasury." Government of Nepal, "2008 Salko Bajet-Baktavya" [Budget statement for the year 1951–52], *Nepal Gazette*, vol. 1, n. 26, Magh 21, 2008 (February 3, 1952), p. 26. See also Joshi and Rose, p. 39.

regions, with the result that the importance of *Jagirdars* as revenue-collection agents declined. *Jagir* land assignments were progressively replaced by cash salaries,[33] and the policy of witholding cash salaries so long as *Raikar* lands were available for assignment as *Jagir* was abandoned. Nevertheless, extensive areas of agricultural lands were simultaneously assigned as *Jagir* to the leading members of the Rana family, so that it is difficult to claim that the policies mentioned above actually resulted in a decline in the area under *Jagir* land tenure. Rana policy, at least in the beginning, led merely to a change in the composition of the *Jagir* landholding class.

Not until the early 1920s was action initiated to abolish the *Jagir* land-assignment system entirely in selected districts. In 1923, *Jagir* lands were fully abolished in several midland districts, including Palpa,[34] Salyan,[35] and Bandipur.[36] A step that had more far-reaching effects was taken in 1928, when the government decreed:

> No land shall henceforth be assigned in the midlands region, except in Sindhupalchok, Kabhrepalanchok, Dhading, Nuwakot, Kathmandu, Lalitpur, and Bhaktapur. So far as existing assignments are concerned, *Jagirdars* may have their *Jagirs* replaced by cash salaries, even though the law provides that emoluments shall not be paid in cash as long as lands are available for assignment as *Jagir*. In case *Jagirdars* are not willing to have their *Jagirs* replaced by cash salaries in this manner, no action need be taken for the present, but vacant *Jagir* holdings shall not be reassigned as *Jagir*.[37]

Subsequently, in 1935, orders were issued prohibiting the assignment of lands as *Jagir* in Sindhupalchok, Kabhrepalanchok, Dhading, Nuwakot, and Bhaktapur. Unirrigated lands in Kathmandu and Lalitpur were similarly prohibited from being assigned as *Jagir*.[38] The result was that only rice lands in Kathmandu and Lalitpur remained available for new *Jagir* land assignments. Moreover, unirrigated *Jagir* lands of *Jagirdars* who had expressed their un-

---

[33] Perceval Landon, *Nepal* (London: Constable and Co., 1928), II, 206.

[34] "Abolition of Jagir Lands in Palpa," Ashadh 3, 1980 (July 15, 1923).

[35] Government of Nepal, "Salyan Malko Sawal, 1991" [Salyan revenue regulations, 1934], sec. 108 (1), *Nepal Kanun Patrika*, year 4, no. 9, Chaitra 2018 (March-April 1962), p. 118.

[36] Law Ministry Records, "Bandipur Malko Sawal, 1991" [Bandipur revenue regulations, 1934], sec. 108.

[37] "Abolition of Jagir Lands in Hill Districts," Jestha 11, 1985 (May 24, 1928).

[38] Law Ministry Records, "Kampu Tirja Office Regulations, 1935," secs. 4, 71.

willingness to accept cash salaries were converted into *Raikar* during the extensive revenue-settlement operations that were conducted in a number of hill districts between 1933 and 1948.[39]

It is noteworthy that rice lands in Kathmandu and Lalitpur were still available for assignment as *Jagir*. This was perhaps due to the government's desire to retain some scope for the exploitation of the *Jagir* system in the interests of its favorites, albeit in a greatly restricted area. Nevertheless, it must be conceded that the abolition measures described above did not discriminate in favor of members of the ruling family or their favorites. Indeed, the *Jagir* lands of several top-ranking Ranas were affected by these measures,[40] which, therefore, should be regarded as a genuine attempt to simplify the land-tenure and taxation system in Nepal.

The Rana regime thus followed a double-edged policy in respect to the *Jagir* land-tenure system. Its interest in increasing cash payments into the treasury and reforming the administration conflicted with the assignment of land as *Jagir*. Nevertheless, because such assignments constituted a privilege which the Ranas and their favorites were reluctant to relinquish, the regime was unwilling to abolish the system altogether. *Jagir* land assignments therefore were made on an increasingly selective basis, and the *Jagir* system occupied a much less important position in Nepal's land system toward the end of the Rana regime than it had in 1846. But though the fiscal and administrative factors responsible for the emergence and growth of the *Jagir* land-assignment system had disappeared several decades earlier, political reasons delayed its abolition until after the downfall of the Rana regime. *Jagir* land assignments, when made on a selective basis, provided the opportunity for a new type of privilege that the Rana regime could hardly be expected to ignore. A system that had been utilized by Prithvi Narayan Shah and his successors to lay the foundation of the kingdom and expand its size therefore degenerated into a regressive and obnoxious system of oligarchic privilege at the hands of the Rana rulers.

Abolition of the *Jagir* System

It was inevitable that the *Jagir* system should not outlive the end of the Rana regime. In October 1951, the government of Nepal resumed

[39] Ibid., addendum of Bhadra 9, 2002 (August 24, 1946).
[40] Ibid.

all assignments of *Raikar* land as *Jagir* and imposed taxes on them at current rates. It also directed payment of cash salaries to all government employees according to prescribed pay scales.[41] This marked the end of the *Jagir* system of landownership in Nepal. There is no evidence that the government encountered much opposition in this task. Most of the leading members of the Rana family, who were the main beneficiaries of *Jagir* assignments, resigned from their posts in the government and the army after the downfall of the Rana regime; as a result, their *Jagir* land assignments automatically reverted to the government. Those *Jagir* assignees who remained were too few and demoralized to offer any opposition to this measure. But though the abolition of the *Jagir* land-assignment system made it possible for the government to increase its revenue from the land, administrative difficulties hindered the extension of the land-tax system to the abolished *Jagir* lands with immediate effect.[42]

The *Birta* and *Jagir* systems had made it possible for classes that wielded social and political authority in the society to use their power for strengthening their economic position through the ownership of land, which enabled them to squeeze a surplus out of the peasantry. The abolition of these systems represented the disappearance of the feudal lord from the agrarian scene. It meant "separating a large section of the ruling class from direct ties with the land"[43] and thus marked "the change from a tenure system where social and political aspects are dominant features to one where the social and political attributes have become separated."[44]

[41]*Nepal Gazette*, vol. 1, no. 12, Kartik 12, 2008 (October, 1951).
[42]Some *Jagir* lands were still being used without paying taxes in 1964. Ibid., vol. 14, no. 5A (Extraordinary), Ashadh 23, 2021 (July 6, 1964), p. 48.
[43]Barrington Moore, Jr., *Social Origins of Dictatorship and Democracy* (Penguin Books, 1967), p. 279.
[44]Peter Dorner, *Land Reform and Economic Development* (Penguin Books, 1972), p. 76.

Chapter 6

COMMUNAL LANDOWNERSHIP: *KIPAT* TENURE

The *Birta, Jagir,* and *Guthi* systems, which were the subjects of the preceding chapters, emerged from grants made by the state. Landownership rights under these tenure forms stemmed from the statutory authority and were based on documentary evidence. They had no reference to the ethnic or communal origin of the landowner, nor to the location of the land in any particular geographical area. They reverted to the state if the owner died without leaving an heir, or relinquished his lands for any reason. In the *Kipat* form of landownership, on the other hand, the communal authority superseded any claim the state might extend on grounds of internal sovereignty or state landlordism. Rights under *Kipat* tenure emerged not because of a royal grant, but because the owner, as a member of a particular ethnic community, was in customary occupation of lands situated in a particular geographical area. *Kipat* was thus a form of communal landownership, under which "each person has a right to exclusive use of a particular piece of land, but where his rights to dispose of the land are restricted on the theory that the land belongs to the chief or to the tribe."[1]

The *Kipat* system may have been a relic of the customary form of land control which communities of Mongoloid or autochthonous tribal origin established in areas occupied by them before the immigration of racial groups of Indo-Aryan origin.[2] The general view is

[1] W. Arthur Lewis, *The Theory of Economic Growth*, (London: George Allen and Unwin, 1963), p. 121.

[2] Such customary forms of communal land control are by no means confined to Nepal. A similar system, which has been described as "a non-Aryan commune," has existed among the Munda community of Chhotanagpur in India. Suresh Singh, "The Munda Land System and Revenue Reforms in Chhotanagpur during 1869–1908," and J. C. Jha, "History of Land Revenue in Chhotanagpur," in Ram Sharan Sharma, ed., *Land Revenue in India* (Delhi: Motilal Banarsidass, 1971), pp. 80–107. Communal forms of land tenure in various parts of the world are noted in Gerard Clauson, *Communal Land Tenure* (Rome: FAO, 1953), pp. 6–25, and United Nations, *Land Reform* (New York: U.N. Department of Economic Affairs, 1951), pp. 4–5.

that racial groups of Caucasian origin, which are the most important numerically, socially, and politically in much of Nepal, immigrated from northern India.[3] The newcomers acquired landownership rights under a statutory form of landownership, such as *Birta* or *Jagir*, whereas the Mongoloid or autochthonous communities retained their customary occupation of lands under a form of ownership that eventually came to be known as *Kipat*. Prominent among the *Kipat*-owning communities of Nepal were the Limbus of Pallokirat, a term traditionally used to denote the present districts of Ilam, Dhankuta, Panchthar, Terhathum, Taplejung, and Sankhuwa-Sabha. Other *Kipat*-owning communities, which included Rai, Majhiya, Bhote, Yakha, Tamang, Hayu, Chepang, Baramu, Danuwar, Sunuwar, Kumhal, Pahari, Thami, Sherpa, Majhi, and Lepcha, were scattered throughout the eastern and western midlands.

Communal Characteristics of *Kipat* Landownership

These *Kipat*-owning communities came under varying degrees of Indo-Aryan political and economic control in the course of time. The characteristics of *Kipat* as a form of communal landownership were deeply influenced by such control, and it is therefore difficult to describe a standard pattern of *Kipat* landownership rights and privileges. We shall therefore commence with an analysis of these rights and privileges as enjoyed by the Limbu *Kipat* owners of Pallokirat, and then note variations prevalent among other *Kipat*-owning communities elsewhere in the hill regions of Nepal.

Kinship, geographical location, and customary occupation were the main characteristics of *Kipat* landownership. A *Kipat* owner derived his rights by virtue of his membership in a particular ethnic group. Thus, under the *Kipat* system "each segment of a dispersed patrilineal clan was associated with a particular territory and individual rights to land were established on the basis of membership in such local descent group."[4] So long as agnatic links were remembered and traced, a member of a local clan segment, even if living away from the territory of the group, could exercise his rights to a plot of land.[5] There were also a number of Limbus who were not members of *Kipat*-owning

---

[3] Joshi and Rose, *Democratic Innovations in Nepal*, p. 10.
[4] Lionel Caplan, "Some Political Consequences of State Land Policy in East Nepal," *Man*, 2, no. 1 (March 1967), 107–8.
[5] Lionel Caplan, *Land and Social Change in East Nepal* p. 28.

kin groups and so possessed no *Kipat* landownership rights.⁶ The exclusive character of *Kipat* landownership in relation to specific ethnic groups was manifested in practical form in the nonsalability of land to members of other groups. In other words, *Kipat* land generally could not be sold outside the community. There was, however, no restriction on alienation within the group itself. *Kipat* land alienated by a Limbu to another Limbu would still retain its communal character, but not when transferred to a Tamang.

In addition to kinship, the communal character of *Kipat* landownership was based on geographical location. For instance, the geographical boundaries within which the Limbus of Pallokirat were permitted to retain the lands in their customary occupation under *Kipat* tenure were specifically demarcated as lying between the Arun and Mechi rivers in the eastern hill region of Nepal, although the area situated within these boundaries was not entirely under *Kipat* tenure.⁷

Customary occupation by the community was yet another characteristic of *Kipat* landownership. *Raikar* land could not be converted into *Kipat* simply on the ground that it had come into the possession of members of a *Kipat*-owning community. In Pallokirat, only such lands were traditionally recognized as *Kipat* as had been under this form of landownership during the time of the Sen kings, before the Gorkhali conquest of that region in 1774.⁸ In all cases, the *Kipat* holdings of Limbus were confirmed only on the ground that possession had been continuous "from the time of your ancestors."⁹

The communal nature of *Kipat* landownership, and its basis primarily in ethnic affinity, appears to indicate its origin in the occupation of particular areas by members of particular ethnic groups. Such customary rights as these settlers acquired in the land on account of settlement and occupation were of necessity exclusive to the community, for primitive tribal organization was hardly conducive to intertribal cooperation in this enterprise. Nor did the need for such cooperation arise, because of the abundant supply of land. Land was therefore held on a customary and communal basis, under what later

---

⁶Ibid., p. 45.

⁷"Confirmation of Traditional Rights and Obligations of Limbus in the Area Situated between the Arun and Mechi Rivers," Ashadh Badi 13, 1883 (June 1826).

⁸"Order regarding Restoration of Kipat Lands in Pallokirat," Poush Sudi 8, 1945 (December 1888).

⁹Rajvamshi, *Puratattwa-Patrasangraha*, II, 38.

came to be known as the *Kipat* System.[10]

Traditionally, *Kipat* rights were recognized not only on cultivated lands, but also on waste and forest lands. It would be logical, therefore, to assume that at some stage there had been an apportionment of the existing area among members of the concerned community to enable each to possess not only cultivated lands but also waste lands and forests as *Kipat*. *Kipat* rights therefore emerged not as a result of actual reclamation by voluntary individual effort, but rather through apportionment of the available area to each member of the community at a particular time. We do not know the actual basis on which such apportionment was made. It may be assumed, however, that the criterion was not the requirements of each family at the time, for in that case ownership in waste lands under *Kipat* tenure would have been out of the question. Accordingly, the apportionment led to *Kipat* rights on lands which it was neither possible nor necessary to use or reclaim immediately.

The communal character of *Kipat* landownership did not mean that land was actually cultivated on a communal basis. *Kipat* land, in fact, was owned and cultivated by individuals, but only subject to "the reversionary rights of the community."[11] This meant that if any member of the *Kipat*-owning community ceased to exercise his right to own and cultivate his ancestral plot of land, the right to determine the nature and extent of its use by others was enjoyed not by him, nor by the state as on *Raikar* lands, but by the community. Such vacant lands were then reallotted to a suitable applicant within the community by the headman in his capacity of representative of the community. Village headmen exercise a similar right in respect also to vacant *Raikar* holdings, but in such cases the ethnic status of the applicant is not a factor that governs reallotment.

---

[10] Occasionally, the government of Nepal has "granted" *Kipat* lands to particular communities in the hill regions for the performance of specified duties. King Prithvi Naryan Shah, for instance, made a grant of *Kipat* lands to members of the Tamang community in Nagarkot and elsewhere in the eastern part of Kathmandu Valley. "Confirmation of Kipat Lands in Nagarkot and Other Villages," Poush Sudi 4, 1857 (January 1801). These cases appear to have led some writers to believe that the system of *Kipat* landownership owes its origin to state grants. Baburam Acharya, *Nepalko Samkshipta Vrittanta* [A concise account of Nepal], (Kathmandu: Pramod Shamsher and Nir Bikram "Pyasi," 2022 [1966]), p. 147. This theory of the origin of the *Kipat* system does not appear to be tenable. It ignores the fact that *Kipat* landownership is of communal and customary origin and that such systems are by no means confined to Nepal.

[11] Clauson, *Communal Land Tenure*, p. 5.

Individual cultivation of *Kipat* lands led to systems of demarcation of boundaries and registration of title on an inheritable and subdivisible basis without reference to the communal rights in the land. The result was a disintegration of the communal character of this system.[12] Indeed, for all practical purposes, *Kipat* ownership ultimately developed into a system of freehold ownership like *Birta*. The communal character of the system was limited to nonalienability outside the community and the reversionary rights of the community in the event of the temporary absence or the extinction of the *Kipat* owner's family.

Kipat AND *Raikar*

The communal origin of *Kipat* tenure led to the emergence of a number of characteristics that differentiated it from *Raikar* tenure. On *Raikar* lands, the state immediately exercises its right of foreclosure in the event of tax delinquency. On *Kipat* lands, on the other hand, a number of safeguards were provided to insure that the rights of the community were not violated through individual delinquency. It was only when the community failed to protect these rights by assuming liability for the arrears that the state exercised its right of foreclosure.[13] Furthermore, *Kipat* owners did not lose their land ownership rights even if they vacated their holdings temporarily. During their absence, their *Kipat* lands were held in trust by the headman on payment of the taxes due thereon.[14] In contradistinction, *Raikar* land holdings vacated in this way revert immediately to the state.

It is in respect to taxation, however, that the distinction between *Raikar* and *Kipat* landownership is more obvious. Generally, taxes are assessed on *Raikar* lands and homesteads on the basis of the area or approximate size. The amount of tax paid by a *Raikar* landowner thus varies in proportion to the area of land owned by him. On the other hand, taxes on *Kipat* lands were assessed on homesteads only, leaving rice lands wholly tax-exempt.[15] The incidence of taxation on *Kipat* holdings therefore varied in inverse ratio to the size. In other words, it was proportionately heavier on poor *Kipat*-owners, and lighter on those who possessed extensive *Kipat* lands. This did not mean that the

---

[12] United Nations, *Land Reform*, p. 29.
[13] Regmi, *Land Tenure and Taxation in Nepal*, III (1965), pp. 111–12.
[14] Ibid., p. 109.
[15] Ibid., pp. 105–7.

incidence of taxation was invariably heavier on *Kipat* than on *Raikar* land, for a *Kipat* holding might be large enough to warrant higher taxation under *Raikar* tenure. At the same time, progressive fragmentation of *Kipat* holdings might result, and had probably resulted in many cases, in a situation in which tax liability on *Kipat* lands would decrease in the event of their conversion into *Raikar*.

These communal characteristics of the *Kipat* system of landownership show a basic conflict between it and the *Raikar* system of state landlordism.[16] An attempt was therefore made to effect a compromise between the customary rights and local autonomy of *Kipat*-owning communities and the authority of the state through statutory confirmation of *Kipat* rights. In other words, royal orders were issued to formalize those rights.[17] The result was that *Kipat* landownership rights came to be regarded as based on documentary evidence in the same manner as *Birta* landownership rights.

Kipat Policy in Pallokirat

During the period after political unification, the land-tenure policy of the Government of Nepal was aimed primarily at maximizing the area of lands under state control for grant as *Birta* or *Jagir*.[18] In the light of this objective, *Kipat* landownership presented a different problem. *Kipat* owners controlled large areas of agricultural lands, both waste and cultivated, that were not available for *Birta* or *Jagir* grants. The problem would have been less intractable had there existed a system of taxing *Kipat* lands. Rice lands under *Kipat* tenure were generally tax-exempt, and *Kipat* owners paid a tax only on their homesteads. The *Kipat* landownership system thus deprived the government of resources in the form of both land and revenue.

Nor was this all. The *Kipat* system also prevented the government from establishing effective administrative control over the whole of its territory. The problem was particularly acute in the Pallokirat region, which had been incorporated into the Kingdom of Nepal in 1774. Kathmandu considered it more expedient to bring the region under its general suzerainty than to annex the territory outright.

---

[16] Kenneth H. Parsons, "Agrarian Reform Policy as a Field of Research," in *Agrarian Reform and Economic Growth in Developing Countries* (Washington: U.S. Department of Agriculture, 1962), p. 20.

[17] Rajvamshi, II, 43.

[18] Regmi, *A Study in Nepali Economic History*, pp. 37–54.

It therefore recognized the authority of the local Limbu chiefs and guaranteed the security of their traditional rights and privileges. By the terms of a royal proclamation issued in 1774 immediately after the conquest of Pallokirat, the Limbu chiefs were permitted to "enjoy the land from generation to generation, as long as it remains in existence." The proclamation added: "In case we confiscate your lands, may our ancestral gods destroy our kingdom."[19] These guarantees were reiterated during successive regimes, even though the specific privileges and obligations attached to *Kipat* landownership underwent divergent interpretations and recurrent vicissitudes.

In fact, the government of Nepal followed an ambivalent policy toward the *Kipat* system of landownership in Pallokirat. No doubt, it desired to extend state control over *Kipat* lands, but it also had to recognize the strategic location of Pallokirat in the Nepal-Tibet-Sikkim trijunction. Moreover, the Limbus were a turbulent community that long remained unreconciled to Gorkhali occupation and rule. *Kipat* policy was therefore largely guided by the objective of gradually reducing the area under this form of land tenure, subject to considerations of political expediency.[20] As an official report stated in 1883: "Pallokirat is a border area which has been administered since early times through a conciliatory policy. If the customs and traditions of the Limbus are violated, they will leave the country and the government will be harmed."[21] The conciliatory policy, in effect, consisted of a series of measures designed to reduce the area under *Kipat* landownership and bring *Kipat* lands within the ambit of the *Raikar* land-taxation system. The appointment of Limbu headmen and the official confirmation of their traditional religious and other customs were made subject to the surrender of *Kipat* lands under *Raikar* tenure. In addition, the *Kipat* system was occasionally encroached upon, but in such a way that the issues were too minor to create widespread and organized opposition, or the resultant losses to Limbu *Kipat* owners were compensated by privileges of a minor character. At times, existing privileges were withdrawn, to be restored later when the Limbus surrendered land and other privileges in return.[22] Moreover, even when *Kipat* holdings were confirmed through royal order, the area and boundaries were seldom specified, and the documents merely

---

[19]"Royal Order to the Limbus of Pallokirat, 1774," in Regmi, III, 151–52.
[20]Caplan, *Land and Social Change in East Nepal*, pp. 55–60.
[21]"Order regarding Tiruwa Subbas in Pallokirat," Aswin 1940 (September 1883).
[22]Regmi, III, 123–25.

mentioned "lands being cultivated from the time of your ancestors." It was therefore fairly easy for local *Raikar* landholders or overzealous officials to charge *Kipat* owners with having encroached upon *Raikar* lands, so that statutory confirmation did not necessarily guarantee the security of *Kipat* landownership rights. Indeed, the *Kipat* system in Pallokirat, on the eve of the downfall of the Rana regime, bore little resemblance to the traditional customs and privileges of the Limbu community as originally guaranteed in 1774. A taxation system, accompanied by practices desgined to bring about the progressive reduction of the area under *Kipat* tenure, had been built into the structure of the traditional *Kipat* system in this region.

Loss of *Kipat* Landownership Rights

In its efforts to bring progressively larger areas of *Kipat* lands in Pallokirat under state control, the government of Nepal was helped to a great extent by the trend toward the immigration and settlement of non-Limbu communities. Given primitive methods of cultivation, immigration helped to strike a better balance between available land and labor resources. Accordingly, even before the Gorkhali conquest of Pallokirat, non-Limbus had been settling there at the invitation of the Limbus themselves. The scale of such immigration appears to have increased after the conquest. A mass exodus of the defeated Limbus into India resulted in *Birta* grants of the vacated *Kipat* lands to non-Limbu communities. Most of the Limbu fugitives eventually returned and the government issued orders restoring their landownership rights, but not all such non-Limbu settlers could be dislodged. The government of Nepal also followed the policy of encouraging non-Limbu immigration into Pallokirat in order to break the Limbu hegemony over landownership. In particular, it refused to recognize *Kipat* landownership rights in waste lands within traditional *Kipat* holdings and permitted non-Limbus to reclaim such lands under *Raikar* tenure.[23]

Originally, no restriction appears to have existed on the right of Limbu *Kipat* owners to sell their *Kipat* lands to non-Limbus. In fact, there is evidence that such transactions were frequent, with the result that Limbus had already become out-numbered by non-Limbu settlers and their descendants in several areas of Pallokirat by the latter part of the nineteenth century. The Limbus resented the growing encroachment on their traditional *Kipat* landownership rights, and at

[23]Regmi, *A Study in Nepali Economic History*, pp. 51–53.

the same time non-Limbus felt that their rights over the lands they controlled were insecure. In this struggle for land, the government generally sided with the non-Limbus. In May 1886, legislation was enacted prescribing that all *Kipat* lands that had been or might be sold or otherwise transferred to non-Limbus would be converted into *Raikar*. The Limbus therefore remained in control of only such *Kipat* lands and homesteads as they were actually using at the time.[24]

This policy seems to have resulted in a considerable depletion in the area under *Kipat* landownership in Pallokirat. Limbu *Kipat* owners therefore succeeded in obtaining a partial reversal of the policy during the period from 1901 to 1903, when a series of orders were issued imposing a complete ban on the sale of cultivated *Kipat* lands. Limbus were still permitted to alienate waste or unirrigated *Kipat* lands to non-Limbus for use as rice fields. Because the ban on the sale of cultivated lands was not retroactive, the result was that all *Kipat* lands sold to non-Limbus in the past irreversibly passed under *Raikar* tenure.[25] Only approximately one-third of the total cultivated area in Pallokirat remained under *Kipat* tenure by the end of the Rana period.[26]

This figure does not represent the area in the actual possession of Limbu *Kipat* owners in Pallokirat, however, for the ban on the alienation of cultivated *Kipat* lands did not affect possessory mortgages. Even before the imposition of the ban, non-Limbus in Pallokirat appear to have acquired large areas of *Kipat* lands through such mortgage; after the enactment of this measure, it was the only way whereby they could bring *Kipat* lands under their control.[27] Under the system of possessory mortgage, non-Limbus supplied loans to Limbu *Kipat* owners and, pending repayment, assumed the rights of usufruct on the mortgaged lands, both as security and in payment of interest. The temporary loss of *Kipat* landownership rights through possessory mortgages had proceeded to such an extent that in one area of Ilam district approximately 70 percent of lands possessed by Limbus were under mortgage in 1964-65.[28] Possessory mortgage was thus the

---

[24] Regmi, *Land Tenure and Taxation in Nepal*, III, 95-97.

[25] Ibid., p. 98.

[26] In Ilam, only 39.7 percent of rice lands was under *Kipat* tenure in 1965. Caplan, *Land and Social Change in East Nepal*, p. 56.

[27] Ibid., p. 112. "Because *Raikar* lands are in short supply, their costs are prohibitive, and most non-Limbus, to remain economically viable, must rely on maintaining their access to *Kipat* lands by means of possessory mortgages."

[28] Ibid., p. 111.

primary factor contributing to landlessness among the Limbus, notwithstanding the fact that their ownership rights on mortgaged *Kipat* lands were theoretically intact.

Originally, mortgages on *Kipat* lands were valid only during the lifetime of the Limbu mortgagor. After his death, the creditor could no longer retain possession of the land as security for the loan, although he was entitled to recover his loan from the estate of the deceased person.[29] Such a system was of disadvantage to non-Limbu settlers in Pallokirat. The law was subsequently amended to provide that in case relatives of the Limbu debtor failed to redeem the mortgage after his death, the creditor should be permitted to cultivate the mortgaged holding subject to the payment of the tax due thereon.[30] This, on the other hand, resulted in the progressive loss of *Kipat* lands to non-Limbus. Finally, in 1948, such special legislation relating to *Kipat* land mortgages was replaced by the general law on mortgages, according to which possessory mortgages might be redeemed by the mortgagor or his heirs at any time, except when the deed of mortgage stipulated a specific time limit.[31] The rights of non-Limbus who had acquired *Kipat* lands on mortgage were thus extremely insecure, as the Limbu debtor could repay the loan and take back the lands at any time. Such insecurity of tenure had adverse effects on the productivity of land and the conservation of soil and forest resources in Pallokirat, because the non-Limbu mortgagee naturally sought to extract as much benefit as possible from the land while it remained in his possession.

[29] Government of Nepal, "Jagga Jamin Ko" [On land], in *Shri 5 Surendra...Muluki Ain*, sec. 23, p. 24. "In case any person has given a loan to a *Kipat* owner and has acquired his *Kipat* land on possessory or other mortgage, and in case the borrower dies or absconds, and the land is allotted [by local headmen] to another person, who has been making the payment due on such lands, the creditor shall not be permitted to claim possession thereof. His loan shall be recovered from the borrower or his heirs, or else converted into a personal loan." In 1888, several non-Limbu moneylenders in Pallokirat demanded that such vacant *Kipat* holdings should be allotted to relatives of the dead or absconding *Kipat* owner on condition that they repay the loan, or else the creditor himself should be permitted to use the land subject to the payment of taxes. "Report of the Sadar Dafdarkhana Office regarding Mortgages on *Kipat* Lands," Marga Sudi 10, 1945 (November, 1888). The government stipulated that local headmen could reallot the vacant holding to another person only if the relatives of the dead or absconding person, or the creditor, defaulted in the payment of taxes. "Order regarding Eviction on Kipat Lands in Pallokirat," Poush Sudi 2, 1945 (December 1888).

[30] Government of Nepal, "Jagga Pajani Ko" [On land evictions], *Muluki Ain* [Legal code], pt. III (Kathmandu: Gorkhapatra Press, 1992 [1935]), sec. 19, p. 25.

[31] Government of Nepal, "Sahu Asami Ko" (On creditors and debtors), *Muluki Ain*, pt. III, (Kathmandu: Gorkhapatra Press, 2009 [1952]), sec. 12, pp. 113–14.

As a result of population growth, which led to the subdivision and fragmentation of holdings, as well as loss of *Kipat* lands through possessory mortgages or outright sale, the Limbu community of Pallokirat appears to have been faced with the problem of land shortage even before the middle of the nineteenth century. This initiated a trend toward emigration,[32] which the government attempted to check by offering to resettle the Limbus on forest lands or in the Tarai regions, but apparently not with effective results.[33] Similarly, the people of Ilam complained in 1913 that formerly a considerable area of land was waste, while the number of Limbus was small, but more recently the number of Limbus had been increasing, while the land remained the same.[34] Although subdivision and fragmentation of holdings is a nationwide problem, it assumed a new dimension under the *Kipat* system, where tax liability did not decrease in proportion to the reduced size of the holding.

Other *Kipat*-owning Communities

The defects of the *Kipat* landownership system, from the viewpoint of the government, were identical both in Pallokirat and elsewhere. The official policy of gradually converting *Kipat* lands into *Raikar* was also similar in both cases. The only difference consisted in the measures applied to implement this policy and the extent of the resistance offered by the victims.

We have noted previously that royal charters were issued from time to time to confirm customary landownership rights under the *Kipat* system both in Pallokirat and elsewhere. Whereas in Pallokirat such rights were confirmed for the Limbu community as a whole within the traditional boundaries of Pallokirat, elsewhere individual *Kipat*

---

[32] "Royal Order to the Limbus of Pallokirat," Ashadh 11, 1891 (June 25, 1834). This order stated that Limbus were leaving their *Kipat* lands because of harassment by moneylenders and oppression by government officials. It therefore declared a moratorium on the repayment of moneylenders' loans "for eight or ten years" and a three-year remission on homestead taxes. These concessions appear to have had little effect. In 1896, the government again noted that "no other part of the country suffers so much from emigration as Pallokirat. "Notification regarding Emigration from Pallokirat," Shrawan Badi 3, 1953 (August 1896).

[33] "If you do not possess sufficient land, clear forests and settle thereon. If, even then, you do not get sufficient land, settle in the forest areas of Morang. Do not emigrate to India on any account". "Order to the Limbus of Pallokirat regarding Land Reclamation," Baisakh Sudi 5, 1956 (April 1899).

[34] Government of Nepal, "Order regarding Kipat Land in Ilam and Dasmajhiya," *Nepal Kanun Patrika*, 4, no. 7, Magh 2018 (January-February 1962), 59.

owners alone were beneficiaries. Royal orders confirming *Kipat* rights on ancestral lands usually were issued only when it was necessary to impress labor services from *Kipat* owners, or when it appeared that lack of tenurial security was leading to depopulation.[35] Where such factors were nonexistent, *Kipat* owners were too ignorant and complacent to demand statutory protection of their customary *Kipat* landownership rights. The government, on its part, was reluctant to make unnecessary commitments that would only circumscribe its fiscal and administrative authority. Several *Kipat* holdings, therefore, remained without documentary evidence of title. The general policy, however, was to confirm lands as *Kipat* even in the absence of such evidence, on condition that the owner had remained in unchallenged possession.[36] Only in 1963 was legislation enacted prescribing that *Kipat* lands lacking documentary evidence of title should be treated as *Raikar*.[37]

Several measures were taken from time to time to encroach gradually upon the customary rights of *Kipat*-owning communities outside Pallokirat, such as the imposition of ceilings on *Kipat* holdings, the impressment of unpaid-labor services on a compulsory basis, and taxation. The policy of imposing ceilings was first introduced in 1791 in the eastern hill regions, but only for *Kipat* holdings that had not been confirmed through royal order.[38] No such distinction was observed while imposing ceilings on *Kipat* holding in both the eastern and the western hill regions during 1806[39]

---

[35] "Order to Kipat-owning Chepangs in Pinda (West No. 1), 1847," *Regmi Research Series*, year 2, no. 2, February 1, 1970, p. 46.

[36] "Land Administration Regulations for Kathmandu Valley," Aswin Badi 5, 1856 (September 1799), sec. 9. "If any *Kipat* holding has customarily been so used, it shall be confirmed even without documentary evidence if possession has not been challenged by anyone." This policy received country-wide application when it was incorporated in the legal code. Law Ministry Records, "Jagga Jamin Goshwara Ko" [On miscellaneous land matters], *Muluki Ain*, 1870 ed., sec. 21; Government of Nepal, "Jagga Jamin Goshwara Ko" sec. 3, pp. 61–62, and "Jagga Pajani Ko," sec. 1, p. 27, in *Muluki Ain*, pt. III (2009 [1952]).

[37] Ministry of Law and Justice, "Jagga Pajani Ko," *Muluki Ain* (Kathmandu: the Ministry, 2020 [1963]), sec. 1, p. 119.

[38] "Purbiya Kshetrako Jagga Janch Ko Akhtiyari Lalmohar" [Royal order regarding land surveys in eastern Nepal], Shrawan Sudi 2, 1848 (July 1791), in Chittaranjan Nepali, *Shri 5 Rana Bahadur Shah* [King Rana Bahadur Shah] (Kathmandu: Mrs. Mary Rajbhandari, 2020 [1963]), pp. 115–16.

[39] "Order regarding Redistribution of Birta, Kipat and Other Lands in the Solukhumbu Region," Jestha Sudi 6, 1862 (May 1805). In the western hill regions also, the *Kipat* holdings of the Darai, Kumhal, Majhi, Baramu, Chepang, Ghale, Bhote, Pahari, Rohani, and other communities had been similarly redistributed in 1805–6. Reference

and 1936.⁴⁰ The result was that large areas of lands owned by different communities under *Kipat* tenure were irrevocably converted into *Raikar* tenure on a taxable basis.

Kipat owners of communities other than Limbu were also under obligation to provide unpaid-labor services to the state on a compulsory basis. Their *Kipat* lands were, in fact, traditionally treated as *Seba Birta*,⁴¹ that is, *Birta* lands granted for the performance of specific services to the state. Confirmation was granted to such lands subject to the imposition of ceilings in the course of periodic revenue-settlement operations and scrutiny of land grants if their owners had been providing labor services, even if the lands had not been confirmed through royal order previously.⁴²

Finally, *Kipat* owners of non-Limbu communities were subjected to higher taxes than their counterparts in Pallokirat. Their rice lands were usually tax exempt.⁴³ On *Pakho* lands and homesteads, however, taxes were imposed in addition to miscellaneous other payments.⁴⁴ Occasionally, the tax on rice lands of these categories of *Kipat* was imposed in the form of half of the crop, thereby obliterating all distinction between *Kipat* and *Raikar*.⁴⁵

---

to these measures is contained in "Land Survey Regulations for Trishuli-Pyuthan Region," Kartik Sudi 1, 1893 (October 1836).

⁴⁰"In the regions situated west of Sanga and Sindhu and west of the Dudhkosi river, reconfirm the allotments made [in 1805] after reducing the area of *Kipat* holdings. Make allotments from the *Kipat* lands of Hayus, Danuwars, Paharis, Chepangs, and Thamis at the prescribed rates, and confiscate the surplus area." "Land Survey Regulations for Eastern Hill Regions," Kartik Sudi 1, 1893 (October 1836), sec. 2.

⁴¹"Reallot the *Kipat-Seba Birta* lands of subjects who provide labor and other services (*Doko-Boko*), according to the prescribed rates and assign the surplus area [as *Jagir*] to the army." "Land Survey Regulations for Eastern Hill Regions," Jestha Sudi 9, 1862 (June 1806), sec. 8.

⁴²Regulations enforced in Doti, Achham, and other districts in 1908 provided that "*Kipat* lands lacking documentary evidence of title and not involving unpaid labor obligations shall be converted into *Raikar*." Law Ministry Records, "Revenue Regulations for Doti and Achham Districts," Jestha 28, 1965 (June 10, 1908).

⁴³"Register of Kipat Holdings of Putwars in Changu and Other Villages," 1950 (1893). There are also references to "rice lands used as *Kipat* without paying any tax (*Mahsul*)" by Bhotes, Murmis, Hayus, Chepangs, Baramus, Danuwars, Kumhals, and others in the hill regions. "Land Survey Regulations for Bhimdhunga and Other Areas," Kartik Sudi 1, 1893 (October 1836), sec. 2.

⁴⁴"Confirmation of Kipat Holdings of Majhis in Gajurighat," Jestha Sudi 14, 1862 (June 1805). The Majhi *Kipat* owners of this village paid Rs. 40 as *Mahsul*, Rs. 4 as *Darshan-Bhet*, and 6 annas as *Jalkar* tax.

⁴⁵"Confirmation of Kipat Holding of Ramnarsing Mijhar," Bhadra Badi 5, 1865 (August 1808). This *Kipat* owner was directed to reclaim waste lands within his *Kipat* holdings and pay rents thereon at a rate amounting to half of the produce after a three-year exemption period.

Legislation banning the sale of *Kipat* lands was promulgated at an earlier date for other *Kipat*-owning communities than for the Limbus.[46] In Kathmandu Valley, the sale of *Kipat* lands was declared an offense in 1799.[47] Such a ban appears to have existed in other parts of the country also, but *Kipat* owners circumvented it by relinquishing their lands to outsiders without mentioning any monetary transaction.[48] In any case, the ban appears to have gradually become inoperative. There is evidence that mortgages too were common.[49] In the absence of strong pressures from *Kipat*-owning communities for strict enforcement of the ban, the government apparently saw no reason to interfere in such transactions. In the course of time, the sale of *Kipat* land began to be openly admitted in official documents.[50]

The history of the *Kipat* system of landownership in Majhkirat, a region with a predominantly Rai population, situated west of Pallokirat between the Arun and Dudhkosi rivers, presents a good example of how traditional rights and privileges were infringed when the commu-

[46] This was done presumably to check large-scale transfers. The Sherpa community of Solukhumbu appears to have been a major beneficiary of such transfers. "All Sherpas share the tradition of having immigrated from Tibet." Christoph von Fürer-Haimendorf, *The Sherpas of Nepal* (Calcutta: Oxford Book Co., 1964), p. 18. One source maintains that the ancestors of the Sherpas of Solukhumbu originally came from a district called Salmo Gang in eastern Tibet. Dipak Chaudhari, "German Research on Sherpas," *Rising Nepal*, March 23, 1973. These immigrants appear to have acquired agricultural and pasture lands in Solukhumbu through purchase. This may be the reason why their *Kipat* holdings are at times described as *Kinuwa* (i.e., purchased) in Nepali official records. "Orders regarding Reconfirmation of Kinuwa Kipat Lands of Sherpas in Solukhumbu," Kartik Badi 7 and Marga Sudi 3, 1886 (October-November 1829). In the course of time, these holdings were treated on the same basis as other categories of *Kipat* lands, particularly in matters relating to revenue assessment and collection. "Order regarding Revenue Assessment on Kipat Holdings of Fendo Lama of Junbesi," Magh Badi 5, 1909 (January 1854).

[47] "Land Administration Regulations for Kathmandu Valley," Aswin Badi 5, 1856 (September 1799).

[48] "Confirmation of Lands Alienated by Kipat Owners in Thulochitre," Marga Sudi 9, 1890 (December 1833). Similarly, at Gajurighat, a *Kipat* owner "relinquished" his waste *Kipat* land to one Indrabir Thapa for reclamation as rice land. "Confirmation of Lands Alienated by Bahabal Mijhar Majhi to Indrabir Thapa in Gajurighat," Shrawan Sudi 10, 1920 (August 1863).

[49] "Judicial Regulations," separate regulations promulgated on Marga Badi 2, 1866 (December 1809), for areas east of the Dudhkoshi river and for the Daraundi-Kali and Bheri-Kali regions.

[50] "In West No. 3 district, *Kipat* lands on which the owners are under obligation to provide porterage services have been sold and purchased. But since [the new owners] belong to distant places, urgent governmental work has been dislocated." "Order regarding Appointment of Katuwal in Bandipur," Marga 2, 2007 (November 17, 1950).

nity proved too weak to defend them, or when strategic considerations did not deflect official policy. In 1773, when this region came under Gorkhali control, Kathmandu promised the Rais of Majhkirat "security of life and property" and "succor in all matters," although their communal autonomy was not recognized.[51] In subsequent years the Rais were subjected to various policies that affected their *Kipat* landownership rights. Chief among these policies was the nonrecognition of *Kipat* rights on waste lands which they reclaimed within the boundaries of their *Kipat* holdings. Finally, in 1910, the government of Nepal promulgated orders converting all *Kipat* lands in Majhkirat into *Raikar*. Inasmuch as their rice lands were no longer tax exempt, the Rais apparently saw no point in continuing under a system of homestead taxation that was more burdensome than on *Raikar* lands. During 1940-41, therefore, the government abolished the differential rates of taxation on *Kipat* homesteads in Majhkirat, in effect converting them into *Raikar* tenure.[52]

Critique of the *Kipat* System

The system of *Kipat* landownership, in the form it assumed by the middle of the twentieth century, contained a number of defects from the viewpoints of social cohesion, national finance, and economic development. It had been envisaged as a system of local autonomy for the Limbu community of Pallokirat after its incorporation into the Kingdom of Nepal in 1774. The Limbus were long able to preserve this autonomy in substantial respects. Because it had an ethnic and not a geographical basis, the growing non-Limbu population of Pallokirat could not directly participate in it. Pallokirat was thus divided into two social segments, Limbu and non-Limbu.

From the viewpoint of the government, the *Kipat* system of landownership in Pallokirat was unsatisfactory because it reduced revenue from the land. *Kipat* owners paid a fixed sum of money as tax, irrespective of the area of rice or other land in their possession; therefore revenue would increase if *Kipat* lands were converted into *Raikar*. In Ilam district, for instance, 39 percent of all rice lands was under *Kipat* tenure in 1964-65, but *Kipat* owners contributed only 10.6 percent of the total land revenue.[53]

[51] "Royal Order to the Rais of Majhkirat," Shrawan 1830 (August 1773) in Regmi, III, 151.
[52] Ibid., pp. 89-91.
[53] Caplan, *Land and Social Change in East Nepal*, p. 59.

The drawbacks of the *Kipat* system from the standpoint of economic development are more obvious. The nonalienable character of *Kipat* lands in Pallokirat has made temporary occupation under possessory mortgage a chronic and ubiquitous problem. The right of Limbu *Kipat* owners to redeem their mortgaged *Kipat* lands whenever they can has made the tenure of non-Limbu creditors extremely precarious. Such tenurial insecurity discourages efforts to improve the land and raise its productivity. There is evidence that it has had disastrous results on the productivity of land and the conservation of soil and forest resources in Pallokirat.[54]

ABOLITION OF THE *Kipat* SYSTEM

The end of the Rana regime in 1951 fundamentally altered the foundations of the communal character of the *Kipat* system of landownership. Communal privilege, regressive taxation, and tenurial insecurity, which were characteristic features of this system, conflicted with the need for social and economic change. A form of landownership that benefited only one section of the local population inevitably blocked intercommunal integration; and, at a time when the national goal was to accelerate the pace of all-round social and economic development, insistence on the traditional rights of any particular community without reference to the national interest was an anachronism. The post-1951 regime enjoyed considerable political support among the non-Limbu population of Pallokirat, whose interests could hardly be ignored for the sake of entrenching the traditional rights of the Limbu community. Moreover, government policy no longer functioned under the traditional constraint of having to follow a "conciliatory" policy toward the Limbus because of the strategic location of Pallokirat.

The new approach to *Kipat* policy was initiated by a royal order issued in December 1951, which called on the Limbus to comply with the provisions of all existing orders and regulations for the time being, and gave assurances that fresh orders would eventually be promulgated in consultation with both Limbus and non-Limbus. The reason given by the royal order for this decision was that "people belonging to other communities too have settled in Pallokirat and [it is desirable that] no community should be affected adversely."[55]

---

[54] Krishna Prasad Bhandari, "Pallokirat Ko Jagga" [Land in Pallokirat], *Samyukta Prayas*, Bhadra 15, 2016 (August 30, 1959).

[55] "Royal Order to the Limbus of Pallokirat, 1951," in Regmi, III, 152.

This policy received a temporary setback in early 1961 when the government of Nepal, obviously in an attempt to persuade the Limbu community to accept the newly created Panchayat system, confirmed their "traditional rights and privileges" and called on them to engage themselves in development activities "with the active cooperation of Panchayats."[56] It must have been poor consolation for the Limbus to realize that the term "traditional" in the new order also embodied the encroachments that the *Kipat* system had undergone in the past, and that their repeated demands for a reversion to the system originally guaranteed in 1774 had been spurned.

The 1961 reconfirmation of the "traditional customs and privileges" of the Limbu *Kipat* owners of Pallokirat proved to be only a policy aberration dictated by the exigencies of the political situation. Legislation was finally enacted in October 1968 prescribing that "*Kipat* lands may be alienated in the same manner as *Raikar* lands."[57] All tenurial distinctions between *Kipat* and *Raikar* have thus been obliterated.

Kipat owners belonging to other communities too have met with the same fate as the Limbus. The immediate effect of the 1951 political change was the obsolescence of the labor obligations that had been imposed on their *Kipat* lands. The imposition of such obligations had constituted a basis for the reconfirmation of these *Kipat* lands, so that their obsolescence paved the way for taxation. In early 1961 the government decreed the abolition of several categories of *Kipat* lands on which labor services had been imposed.[58] Legislation enacted in 1963 abolished all forced-labor obligations,[59] including those imposed on *Kipat* owners, and prescribed the assessment of taxes on *Kipat* lands at the rates applicable on *Raikar* lands.

All categories of *Kipat* lands throughout the country have thus legally been brought within the ambit of the *Raikar* taxation system. The actual enforcement of this measure depends upon cadastral surveys and the compilation of land-tax assessment records, which are stated to be already under way.

[56] "Royal Order to the Limbu Kipat Owners of Pallokirat, 1961," ibid., p. 153.
[57] Ministry of Law and Justice, "Bhumi Sambandhi (Dosro Samshodhan) Ain, 2025" [Lands (second amendment) act, 1968], *Nepal Gazette*, vol. 18, no. 21 (Extraordinary), Kartik 9, 2025 (October 25, 1968), sec. 3.
[58] Regmi, III, 129.
[59] Ministry of Law and Justice, "Jyala Majuri Ko" [On wages], *Muluki Ain* (Kathmandu: the Ministry, 2020 [1963], sec. 1, p. 105.

Chapter 7

JIMIDARI LANDOWNERSHIP

Under the *Birta* and *Jagir* forms of landownership, a landowner acquired his rights through a royal grant or assignment which made him lord and master of the land and its inhabitants. These rights were the result of an act of permanent or temporary alienation by the state of its own rights, often its entire internal sovereign authority. In the course of time, the rights of landowners of these categories were circumscribed by the extension of the central state authority in various ways, but the essentially ascriptive nature of these rights remained intact.

Another category of property rights in the land emerged when individuals employed by the government to collect land and other taxes at the village level succeeded in acquiring lands and in entrenching their authority in such a manner that it gradually assumed the form of property. This development was confined to the Tarai districts of Nepal, and the second category of landownership rights that comes within the purview of our study belongs to these revenue-collection functionaries, known as *Jimidars*. This chapter will first describe the origin of the *Jimidari* system and analyze the role of *Jimidars* as landowners, and then will examine recent measures aimed at abolishing the *Jimidari* system.

HISTORICAL BACKGROUND OF THE *Jimidari* SYSTEM

Before the emergence of the modern Kingdom of Nepal, most of the districts now comprised in it constituted independent principalities. Their administrative structure seems to have been fairly rudimentary, consisting of a central political authority superimposed upon a traditional hierarchy of local functionaries who collected taxes, allotted waste lands for reclamation, and administered justice.[1] In the hill districts, including Kathmandu Valley, these functions

[1] For a brief account of local revenue functionaries during the pre-Gorkhali period see Regmi, *A Study in Nepali Economic History*, pp. 33-35.

were traditionally discharged by village headmen and functionaries, who were generally chosen from among the "most substantial landowners of the village," and who "chiefly represent[ed] the community."[2] In the Tarai, on the other hand, the *Parganna*, which comprised a number of villages, was the basic unit of land administration. A functionary, called the *Chaudhari*, was appointed from among local landowners to collect the revenue. There were also numerous other functionaries, both at *Parganna* and village level, to assist in the collection of revenue and promote land reclamation and resettlement.

The Gorkhali rulers continued to utilize the services of these local functionaries during the period after political unification. But because the new kingdom encompassed a large area, it became necessary to create a district-level authority between the village and the center. This new authority, at various times in different parts of the country, was composed of military commanders, revenue contractors, or civil administrators.[3] The scope of administrative functions was limited essentially to defense, law and order, and revenue collection, and there was no need initially to create parallel layers of general and revenue administration at the district level. Only during the 1860s were general administrative functions separated from those relating to revenue collection, and revenue offices established at the district level, in both the hill districts and the Tarai.

Except in Kathmandu Valley, these district revenue offices were saddled with a number of functions not related to revenue administration, such as supervision of hospitals and dispensaries, and maintenance of the state elephants. Moreover, they functioned as government treasuries and registration offices. Some of this burden was removed with the development of banking facilities and the expansion of government departments connected with forests, agricultural development, cooperatives, and the like after 1951.[4] In recent years, the government of Nepal has been following the policy of making district revenue offices responsible solely for the collection of land taxes, leaving other functions relating to land, such as maintenance of land registers, registration of real-estate transactions and land-reform operations, to be performed by newly created land administration

---

[2] Brian H. Hodgson, "Some Account of the Systems of Law and Police as Recognized in the State of Nepal," *Journal of the Royal Asiatic Society of Great Britain and Ireland*, I (1834), 274-75.

[3] Regmi, pp. 124-41, 173-78.

[4] Regmi, *Land Tenure and Taxation in Nepal*, I, 123-26.

offices.⁵ This policy is being enforced gradually, and it has so far covered 18 of the 75 districts. Revenue offices still function as government treasuries where banks have not been established.

Formerly, district revenue offices collected land taxes directly from landowners in Kathmandu Valley alone. Elsewhere, the offices functioned only as repositories of the proceeds of tax collection by nonofficial local functionaries, who may be broadly designated as *Jimidars* in the Tarai and *Talukdars* in the hill region.⁶ The *Jimidari* system in the Tarai emerged during 1861–62, when the revenue administration system was reorganized with the objective of extending its base to the village.⁷ The *Talukdari* system was similarly reorganized in the hill districts between 1820 and 1837.⁸ *Jimidars* and *Talukdars* thus functioned as intermediaries between individual landowners and the official revenue administrative machinery at the district level.

Despite phonetic similarity, the *Jimidar* of the Nepal Tarai should not be confused with the *Zamindar* of adjoining areas in India. The term *Jimidar* is obviously derived from the Arabic term *Jimmadar*, or functionary,⁹ whereas the Indian term *Zamindar* is of Persian origin and means a landowner.¹⁰ During the eighteenth century there were *Zamindars* both in India and in the Tarai regions of Nepal. The term was used to denote landlords whose rights "extended over lands occupied by a number of persons"—that is, the population of a village or township.¹¹ In 1793, *Zamindars* in several parts of northern India

⁵Ministry of Law and Justice, "Bhumi Prashasan Ain, 2024" [Land administration act, 1967], *Nepal Gazette*, vol. 17, no. 29A (Extraordinary), Kartik 6, 2024 (October 23, 1967). Until May 1970, Land Administration Offices were responsible for land-tax collection also. Separate offices were thereafter created to discharge this function. "Notification of the Ministry of Finance," *Nepal Gazette*, vol. 20, no. 3, Baisakh 21, 2027 (May 4, 1970), and vol. 22, no. 44, Falgun 8, 2029 (February 19, 1973).

⁶Regmi, I, 126–34.

⁷"Revenue Regulations for Eastern Tarai Districts." Separate regulations promulgated on Marga Badi 6, 1918 (November 1861), for Morang and other districts in the eastern Tarai.

⁸Regmi, *A Study in Nepali Economic History*, pp. 176–78.

⁹H. H. Wilson, *Glossary of Judicial and Revenue Terms* (2ed.; Delhi: Munshiram Manoharlal, 1968), p. 567. Wilson defines *Zimmadar* as "A trustee, a person in charge," and adds: "in eastern Bengal it is applied especially to the holder of an under-tenure or portion of a *Zamindari*, paying revenue either to government direct, or to a *Zamindar*: it also applies to a *Zamindar* who is authorized to collect, on behalf of government, the payments of properties in the vicinity of his own: these dependent *Taluks*, or estates, are designated his *Zimma*, in distinction from his own, or *Vij*."

¹⁰Ibid., pp. 562–63.

¹¹Irfan Habib, *The Agrarian System of Mughal India* (Bombay: Asia Publishing House, 1963), p. 140.

were recognized as landlords with inheritable and transferable rights, and the revenue payable by them to the government was fixed on a permanent basis.[12] In the Tarai region of Nepal, on the other hand, the government preferred to allot taxable lands to individual cultivators,[13] thereby adopting a system which resembled the *ryotwari* system[14] in non-*Zamindari* areas in India and assigned no place to *Zamindars* in the collection of revenue. As their emoluments, the *Jimidars* of the Tarai districts of Nepal were assigned lands under *Jirayat* tenure,[15] as well as a percentage of the revenue collected by them.[16] Unlike the *Zamindars* of India, they were not given ownership rights in the lands under their jurisdiction.

The institution of the *Talukdar* in the hill districts was similar in several respects to that of *Jimidars* in the Tarai. Like the *Jimidar*, the *Talukdar* was a village-level functionary who collected taxes from the people and transmitted the proceeds to the district revenue office.[17]

[12]B. H. Baden-Powell, *Land Revenue and Tenure in British India* (Oxford: Clarendon Press, 1913), p. 157; Narendra Krishna Sinha, *The Economic History of Bengal* (Calcutta: Firma K. L. Mukhopadhyay, 1962), II, 147-82; Ram Narayan Sinha, *Bihar Tenantry, 1783-1833* (Bombay: People's Publishing House, 1968), pp. 61-78.

[13]Regmi, pp. 91-93.

[14]For a brief description of the *ryotwari* system in India, see Baden-Powell, pp. 125-26. Wilson (op. cit., p. 433) defines the term as "according to or with *Raiyats*, familiarly applied to the revenue settlement which is made by the government officers with each actual cultivator of the soil for a given term, usually a twelvemonth, at a stipulated money rent, without the intervention of a third party." The *ryotwari* system was first introduced in Madras, India, during 1820-27. Romesh Dutt, *The Economic History of India* (Delhi: Publications Division, Ministry of Information and Broadcasting, Government of India, 1963), I, 105-17.

[15]In the eastern Tarai districts, regulations promulgated in 1861 stipulated that cultivated lands, if available, fetching an income equal to 5 percent of the total tax assessment on the area under his jurisdiction, should be assigned to the *Jimidar* as his *Jirayat*. "Revenue Regulations for Eastern Tarai Districts" (1861), sec. 58. In the western Tarai, on the other hand, waste lands yielding an income equal to 10 percent of the total tax assessment were thus assigned. "Butaul Revenue Regulations," Marga Badi, 1918 (November 1861), sec. 17. In subsequent years, the correlation between the amount of tax assessment and the area of lands assigned to *Jimidars* as *Jirayat* disappeared. There is reason to believe that *Jimidars* expanded their *Jirayat* holdings at the expense of the ordinary landholders notwithstanding a legal ban on such practices. "Revenue Regulations for Eastern Tarai Districts" (1861), sec. 35; Government of Nepal, *Madhesh Malko Sawal* [Revenue regulations for the Tarai districts] (Kathmandu: Gorkhapatra Press, n.d.), sec. 71.

[16]Government of Nepal, *Madhesh Malko Sawal*, sec. 19. This commission amounted to about 2 percent of the amount actually collected. Regmi, *Land Tenure and Taxation in Nepal*, I, 132. The practice of paying such commissions in addition to *Jirayat* land assignments seems to have been introduced comparatively recently, for no reference to it is available in the 1861 "Revenue Regulations for Eastern Tarai Districts."

[17]Regmi, I, 128-31.

But there the similarity ended. The *Talukdar* in the hill districts was not able to attain the status of a landowner in the same way as the *Jimidar* in the Tarai. A *Talukdar* was expected to function primarily as a tax-collecting functionary, not as a source of agricultural finance or as an agricultural entrepreneur. *Talukdari* holdings were not salable, at least after 1911,[18] and did not contain agricultural lands attached to them for personal cultivation, like the *Jirayat* lands of *Jimidars*; hence *Talukdari* rights did not constitute a form of property. The scope for capital investment in *Talukdari* holdings was thus virtually nonexistent.

Origin of the *Jimidari* System

As indicated above, there were *Jimidars* in the Tarai regions of Nepal even before the installation of the Rana regime, but the term appears to have applied to large nonworking landlords. The function of tax collection was entrusted to selected *Jimidars* at the village level concurrently with the existing *Chaudharis* at the *Parganna* level as part and parcel of the reform measures introduced by Jang Bahadur (1846–77), the first Rana prime minister of Nepal. The objective of this measure appears to have been to tighten land-tax collection arrangements while simultaneously creating a rural aristocracy capable of injecting capital investment and entrepreneurial ability into the field of agriculture. In 1861, comprehensive regulations were promulgated outlining the basic framework of the *Jimidari* system, within which entrepreneurial ability and initiative could be utilized for the extension of the cultivated area in the eastern Tarai districts. These regulations provided that any individual could offer to reclaim virgin waste or forest lands which were situated at a distance of more than a day's walk from existing settlements and which peasants were unable to reclaim through their own labor and resources. If his offer was accepted, he was permitted to procure settlers from India, or else divert cultivators from *Birta* lands. He was granted tax exemption for ten years and one-tenth of the total reclaimed area as his *Birta*. Waste lands for which no settlers were available were then given to him as his *Jirayat*. For cultivating his *Jirayat* lands, a *Jimidar* was permitted to appropriate the unpaid services of one ox-team, or at least one plowhand, from every settler family each year. His rights

[18]Law Ministry Records, "Sindhupalchok Revenue Regulations," 1991 (1934), sec. 99.

to the entire reclaimed area were inheritable and secure from arbitrary eviction, and from confiscation even if he committed an offense against the state. The settlers were given allotments free of taxes for five years. The *Jimidar* was under obligation to supply the credit needed by them for maintenance as well as for cultivation, on payment of interest.[19] These arrangements, with some modifications, were subsequently extended to the western and far-western Tarai regions also.[20] Similarly, in the inner Tarai, local well-to-do persons were offered "official status, emoluments, and the right to exact unpaid labor" if they undertook to reclaim waste lands fetching a revenue of at least Rs. 100 per year.[21] The success of these policies can be measured by the fact that in 1892 one *Jimidar* alone in Kailali-Kanchanpur district was able to reclaim as many as 1,200 *bighas* with *ryots* "from across the borders." Even more significant, he voluntarily relinquished tax exemption during the fifth year on the ground that registration of the *ryots* in the tax-assessment records would encourage them to keep the reclaimed lands under their permanent occupation.[22]

Because the low density of population was the biggest hurdle in promoting land reclamation in the Tarai, the Rana government initially encouraged immigration from India. Efforts were made also to attract settlers from the hill districts, but the pressure on cultivated land there had not yet become critical and hillsmen could not easily be persuaded to take up land allotments in the hot, humid, and malarial Tarai.[23] Greater emphasis was therefore placed on the policy of providing facilities and concessions that would be sufficiently attractive to prospective Indian immigrants. Any Indian who moved into Nepali territory along with his family was given a free allotment of agricultural land in addition to a homesite and free supplies of building material for constructing a hut. Once he was settled in Nepal along with his

[19]"Revenue Regulations for Eastern Tarai Districts" (1861), sec. 68; "Regulations regarding land Reclamation in the Eastern Tarai Districts," Magh Badi 3, 1921 (January 1865).

[20]"Order regarding Registration of Newly Reclaimed Lands in Kailali and Kanchanpur," Baisakh Badi 3, 1953 (April 1896).

[21]"Order regarding Land Reclamation in the Chisapani-Gadhi Region, Aswin Badi 4, 1949 (September 1892).

[22]"Order regarding Registration of Newly Reclaimed Lands in Kailali and Kanchanpur" (1896).

[23]Frederick H. Gaige, "The Role of the Tarai in Nepal's Economic Development," *Vasudha*, XI, no. 7 (Ashadh 2025 [June 1968]), 55.

family, he could be appointed as a *Jimidar*.[24] Available evidence suggests that these facilities were utilized on a considerable scale, thereby accelerating the pace of agricultural development in the Tarai. Only during the 1920s was a ban imposed on the purchase of land and *Jimidari* holdings in the Tarai by Indians,[25] possibly because of the growing influx of hillsmen and the need to counteract the cumulative effect of unrestricted immigration in the past on the ethnic composition of the population. No ban, however, was imposed on immigration.[26]

Jimidari Rights as a Form of Property

We shall now turn to the chief functions and responsibilities of *Jimidars*, the rights and privileges that were granted to insure the efficient discharge of these functions and responsibilities, and the gradual evolution of these rights and privileges as a form of property. The chief function of the *Jimidar* was to collect land taxes from the inhabitants of the villages under his jurisdiction and to transmit the proceeds to the district revenue office.[27] The essence of the system was his personal liability for revenue collections. Should the *Jimidar* be unable to complete such collections and transmit the proceeds to

---

[24]"Revenue Regulations for Eastern Tarai Districts" (1861), secs. 23, 42, 68. These facilities and concessions offered by the government of Nepal must have appeared attractive to prospective immigrants from the adjoining Indian provinces. In Bihar and Bengal, the 1793 permanent settlement had made it impossible for ordinary peasants to acquire ownership rights in the lands they tilled. R. N. Sinha, *Bihar Tenantry*, pp. 94–96; N. K. Sinha, *Economic History of Bengal*, pp. 169–73. Similarly, in the United Provinces, the majority of the peasants were tenants who had "no protection whatever against eviction or enhancement [of rents]." B. R. Misra, *Land Revenue Policy in the United Provinces* (Banaras: Nand Kishore and Bros., 1942), pp. 157–59; see also Jagadish Raj, *The Mutiny and Biritsh Land Policy in North India*, 1856-68 (Bombay: Asia Publishing House, 1965), pp. 164–68.

[25]Government of Nepal, "Adal Ko" [On disciplinary matters], *Muluki Ain* [Legal code], pt. V (Kathmandu: Gorkhapatra Press, 2012 [1955]), sec. 20, pp. 7–8.

[26]Ibid., sec. 20(1), p. 7. "In case *Chuni* [i.e., tax-paying] *ryots* from a foreign country come to live here on a permanent basis and reclaim lands here as *ryots* of the government of Nepal, they shall be allowed to reclaim lands and have these registered on a taxable basis in their names. Persons who have taken up the responsibility of reclaiming lands may also make land allotments to them for purposes of reclamation. Such [immigrant] *ryots* may acquire additional cultivated lands on a taxable basis after five years. However, they shall not be permitted to utilize this status to attain the position of a *Jimidar* or *Talukdar*."

[27]Government of Nepal, *Madhesh Jilla Jillako Jimidar Patuwarika Naunko Sawal* [Regulations for Jimidars and Patuwaris in the Tarai districts] (Kathmandu: Gorkhapatra Press, 2012 [1955]), secs. 3, 11, pp. 2–8.

the district revenue office by May 13 each year, the shortfall was made up by auctioning his *Jimidari* lands.[28] The personal liability of the *Jimidar* for the full collection of the tax assessed in the area under his jurisdiction remained unaffected even when cultivators vacated their holdings. The *Jimidar* was required to find another cultivator to occupy such holdings. Otherwise, he was compelled either to pay the tax due on the vacant holdings himself, or to relinquish his entire *Jimidari*.[29]

The *Jimidar* not only provided insurance to the government for revenue collections—he also functioned as a source of agricultural finance. He was required to make available seeds, bullocks, and other agricultural resources "as far as possible" to peasants who lacked them.[30] In many instances, new *Jimidaris* were created when individuals undertook to open up waste lands for reclamation and settlement, stipulating that they would procure settlers and supply loans to them both for maintenance and for agricultural operations.[31]

The benefits that accrued from *Jimidaris* more than compensated the risks involved in undertaking personal liability for revenue collections. The *Jimidar* not only appropriated a small percentage of the total collections, but also cultivated his *Jirayat* lands as his personal demesne. He was allowed to cultivate them either personally or through tenants, but the latter were not entitled to tenancy rights on such lands. Usually, *Jirayat* lands were farmed directly by the *Jimidar*, and every local household was under obligation to make one ox-team or at least a plowhand available to the *Jimidar* every year without payment for this purpose.[32] It scarcely needs to be mentioned that this was the statutory minimum of unpaid labor that the *Jimidar* could exact from local landowners; there was seldom any check on whether he actually utilized more.

The *Jimidari* system thus involved financial investment and entreprenurial risk. To create new *Jimidaris* on waste lands had meant bearing a heavy capital expenditure in procuring settlers, building huts

[28] Government of Nepal, *Madhesh Malko Sawal*, sec. 18, pp. 9–11.
[29] Government of Nepal, *Madhesh Jilla Jillako Jimidar Patuwarika Naunko Sawal*, secs. 3–11, pp. 2–8. For a detailed account of the tax collection procedure under the *Jimidari* system in the Tarai districts see Regmi, I, 146–49.
[30] "Revenue Regulations for Eastern Tarai Districts" (1861), secs. 31–32; Government of Nepal, *Madhesh Jilla Jillako Jimidar Patuwarika Naunko Sawal*, sec. 29, p. 17.
[31] "Order regarding Registration of Newly Reclaimed Lands in Kailali and Kanchanpur," Baisakh Badi 3, 1953 (April 1896).
[32] Government of Nepal, *Madhesh Jilla Jillako Jimidar Patuwarika Naunko Sawal*, secs. 23–24, p. 14.

for them, and providing for their maintenance, as well as for purchasing seeds, bullocks, and agricultural implements. There was thus little prospect of any net gain to the *Jimidar* for at least two or three years—longer if crops were damaged by floods, hailstorms, or pests, or if the settlers were lured away by rival *Jimidars*. For prospective *Jimidars* to invest their labor and capital in such an undertaking, there had to be assurance that they would not lose their entire investment if they wanted to relinquish their *Jimidari* for any reason. Moreover, some way had to be found to make it possible for them to share their risks and obligation with others if they so desired. These problems were solved in part by permitting the sale and fragmentation of *Jimidaris*.[33]

The rights of the *Jimidar* to collect land and other taxes from the inhabitants of the area under his jurisdiction could thus be inherited, subdivided, sold, mortgaged, and fragmented like any other form of property. In addition, the *Jimidar* was owner of the taxable *Jirayat* lands allotted to him as part of his remunerations. A *Jimidar* was not merely a revenue-collection functionary, but the owner of rights in the land that were as effective and tangible as those of *Birta* owners.

Ukhada LANDOWNERSHIP

The position of the *Jimidar* as landowner was more prominent under a special form of the system, known as *Ukhada*, which existed in the districts of Nawal-Parasi, Rupandehi, and Kapilavastu. The chief characteristic of the *Ukhada* system was that landownership rights were vested in the *Jimidar*, who collected rents from the registered landholders in cash. The difference between these cash rents and the tax payable to the state constituted the *Jimidar*'s profit.[34] During the

[33]Government of Nepal, *Madhesh Malko Sawal*, secs. 27, 27a, 27b, pp. 15–16. In Butaul district, fragmentation of *Jimidari* holdings was reported in 1949 to have proceeded to such an extent that in some cases there were as many as 35 or 36 *Jimidars* in one village. Hridaya Nath Sharma, "Industrial Survey of Butaul District," mimeographed (Kathmandu: Department of Industrial and Commercial Intelligence, n. d. [1949]), p. 27. It appears that *Jimidari* rights had become salable as early as 1885. "Order regarding Transfer of Jimidari Holding of Prag Tharu in Khajahani," Poush Badi 8, 1942 (December 1885).

[34]Gobind Prasad Lohani, *Nepalma Bhumi-Sambandhama Sudhar Tarf Bhayeko Gativighi ra Ajasammako Upalabdhi* [Developments in the field of land reform in Nepal and the achievements made so far] (Kathmandu: Department of Publicity, Ministry of Publicity and Broadcasting, 2023 [1966]), p. 18; Tek Bahadur Panthi, *Hamro Arthik Samasya* [Our economic problem] (Kapilavastu: Bishnumaya Devi Panthi, 2019 [1962]), pp. 42–44.

early 1930s, when agricultural prices slumped and land-tax delinquency was therefore widespread, the government of Nepal initiated measures to control rents and guarantee tenurial security on *Ukhada* lands in an attempt to stabilize the agrarian population. These measures provided that *Jimidars* should collect rents in cash only at rates fixed by the local administration with the approval of Kathmandu.[35] Eviction of landholders occupying *Ukhada* lands, the appointment of new tenants, and the resumption of *Ukhada* lands by *Jimidars* were similarly permitted only with the approval of the government.[36] Landholders occupying *Ukhada* lands were consequently in a privileged position compared with their counterparts on other categories of *Jimidari* lands. Their position was rendered further secure by the exemption granted to them from providing unpaid labor to the *Jimidar*.[37] These advantages were, however, partly offset by the denial of the right of transfer.[38]

Why did *Jimidars* in these western Tarai districts grant such favorable terms to landholders occupying waste lands? If one is to believe the official view in this regard, they did so "for their own benefit."[39] Waste and forest lands in those districts were registered in the names of *Jimidars* on a taxable basis. In order to lessen their tax liability, *Jimidars* gave such lands to cultivators on relatively favorable terms, which eventually assumed the form of the *Ukhada* system. The *Ukhada* system thus constituted a via media between full-fledged *Jimidari* landownership and tenancy. Rents not being payable in kind, the tenant was able to profit by rising prices. The system was therefore different from tenancy in the form prevalent elsewhere in the country. The *Jimidar*, on the other hand, was assured nominal ownership of the land and a small margin of profit. In the form it ultimately assumed, the *Ukhada* system represented an uneasy compromise thrust upon these two classes by the government in an effort to minimize tax delinquency and stabilize the agrarian population. The system lost its usefulness during the post-1940 period because of rising prices and increasing profitability of land, and was thereafter

[35] Law Ministry Records, "Order regarding Rents on Ukhada Lands," Jestha 23, 1989 (June 5, 1932).
[36] Government of Nepal, *Madhesh Malko Sawal*, secs. 357–58, p. 158.
[37] Law Ministry Records, "Order to the Jimidars and Patuwaris of Butaul District," 1978 (1921).
[38] Tek Bahadur Panthi, "Ukhada Byabastha Bare Ek Adhyayan" [A study of the Ukhada system], *Naya Samaj*, Shrawan 17, 2020 (August 1, 1963).
[39] Law Ministry Records, "Order to the *Jimidars* and *Patuwaris* of Butaul District" (1921).

characterized by deteriorating landlord-peasant relations.[40]

Critique of the *Jimidari* System

The *Jimidari* system fulfilled several needs of nineteenth-century Nepal. It facilitated revenue collection and the supply of agricultural credit. It created a class of people whose interests lay in the promotion of land reclamation and settlement and hence coincided with those of the state. Moreover, the *Jimidari* system permitted the accumulation of the agricultural surplus in the hands of those who could be expected to use at least a portion of it for the development of additional lands. For the government, it was of considerable importance that *Jimidars*, rather than impecunious peasants, were responsible for tax payment, because even in bad years, *Jimidars* could draw on their other property and reserves to fulfill their fiscal obligations.

These advantages of the *Jimidari* system presuppose the existence of a situation in which land values and prices of agricultural commodities are low. When the density of population is low in relation to the cultivable area, land values tend to be low and land-tax delinquency to be high. In nineteenth-century Nepal, tax delinquency was further encouraged by the fact that, owing to the low density of population and the lack of clear property rights, land had hardly any exchange value. In such a situation, crops rather than the land on which they were grown provided the security for payment of taxes. One study notes, while explaining the reasons for the introduction of the *Jimidari* system in the Tarai region during 1860–61, that in former times it was always a difficult task to collect rents from the cultivators, "who usually held lands for fixed periods, and evaded the payment of rent by escaping into British territory immediately after reaping the harvest."[41] Eventually, occupancy rights in the land evolved in the form of property, as will be taken up at length in chapter 10, and the growth of population, both through natural factors and immigration, caused a scarcity of cultivated lands in or around settlements. Land became, therefore, a form of property of greater value than the arrears of one or two years' taxes. The threat of auction became a more or less effective deterrent to tax delinquency, and the services rendered by *Jimidars* as insurers of revenue collection became virtually superfluous.

[40] Panthi, "Ukhada Byabastha Bare Ek Adhyayan."
[41] Padma Jung Rana, *Life of Maharaja Sir Jung Bahadur of Nepal* (Allahabad: the author, 1909), p. 254.

As previously noted, many *Jimidaris* were created through the execution of reclamation and settlement schemes financed by prospective *Jimidars*, and in such cases lands were granted to them under *Jirayat* tenure. Such opportunities for entrepreneurial ability became progressively rare when cultivable lands of favorable location were reclaimed and transport facilities were not developed sufficiently to open up new areas. The maximum contribution that now could be wrested from *Jimidars* was the reclamation of waste lands contained inside their own holdings, either personally or through *ryots*. *Jimidars* were therefore directed:

> Provide maintenance and credit facilities for the reclamation and cultivation of vacant holdings. Allot such holdings to hillsmen, *Birta* cultivators, landless peasants, local peasants who possess plows and plowhands, and nonresident cultivators. If cultivators of these categories are not available, reclaim or cultivate the holdings yourself. Otherwise, you shall be held personally liable for the taxes due on them.[42]

Moreover, if the *Jimidar* did not undertake tax liability for holdings that had remained waste for any reason, he could be removed and another responsible person who offered to undertake such liability could be appointed as *Jimidar*, if available.[43] Rising land value, however, made it possible for *Jimidars* to shoulder the tax liability on such waste lands in expectation of higher capital gains in the future. Similarly, the role of the *Jimidar* as a source of finance for agricultural development degenerated to that of a usurious moneylender, who generally constituted the sole source of finance in the agricultural community.

As a result of these developments, the *Jimidar* only combined the functions of tax collector, rent receiver, and moneylender, and did not fulfill those of an agricultural entrepreneur. This triple role conferred on him a number of political and economic powers that made it possible for him to exploit the peasantry in various ways. As a rule, *Jimidars* left their *ryots* with barely the means to exist throughout the year, so that the latter remained in perennial indebtedness. This set off a vicious circle which, to say the least, led to the exploitation of the peasantry and retarded agrarian prosperity. Certainly, there is no

---

[42]Government of Nepal, *Madhesh Jilla Jillako Jimidar Patuwarika Naunko Sawal*, sec. 30, pp. 17–18.

[43]Government of Nepal, *Madhesh Malko Sawal*, sec. 159, pp. 65–66.

evidence that the *Jimidar* fulfilled the role expected of him: to remain "true and honest, not to cause losses to the government, and not to harass landowners."[44] It is possible that he acted according to the law in "maintaining local landowners with his own funds, if so necessary, and providing seeds to those who are in need."[45] Nevertheless, these obligations gave him an opportunity for usurious moneylending.

Jimidars were appointed directly by the central government on the recommendation of the local administrators;[46] hence the authority of *Jimidars* as a class depended on sanction from the central government. It was perhaps due to more than a desire to demonstrate its power that Kathmandu assumed the power to appoint these village-level functionaries. Apparently this arrangement provided a reasonable guarantee that *Jimidars* would not align themselves too closely with local interests in opposition to those of the central government and the land magnates of the Rana aristocracy. As *Jimidari* rights gradually acquired the distinctive character of property, the *Jimidar* class came to have more in common with the landowning aristocracy than with the common peasantry. For all practical purposes, therefore, the functionaries who had been appointed as a medium of control by the landowning aristocracy became themselves a part of that aristocracy.

We have mentioned before that the *Jimidar* was gradually able to attain the triple role of tax collector, rent receiver, and moneylender in the village. This economic and administrative function of the *Jimidar* was buttressed by his political role in representing the interests of the landowning aristocracy vis-á-vis the peasantry. *Jimidars* naturally used this vast concentration of economic, administrative, and political power for their own economic benefit during the period of Rana rule.

Revenue regulations provide insights into the various questionable practices adopted by *Jimidars* to increase their landholdings and

---

[44] Government of Nepal, *Madhesh Jilla Jillako Jimidar Patuwarika Naunko Sawal*, preamble, p. 1.

[45] Government of Nepal, *Madhesh Malko Sawal*, sec. 28, p. 16.

[46] The 1861 "Revenue Regulations for Eastern Tarai Districts" (sec. 42) empowered local authorities to appoint *Jimidars*. However, regulations promulgated for the far-western Tarai districts in 1890 show that this authority was subsequently taken over by Kathmandu. "Kailali-Kanchanpur Revenue Regulations," 1947 (1890), cited in "Order regarding Appointment of *Jimidars* in Kailali and Kanchanpur, Kartik Badi 2, 1954 (October 1897). Subsequently, local authorities were empowered to appoint *Jimidars* only if the total tax assessment on the *Jimidari* holding did not exceed Rs. 5,000 in Indian currency. On holdings with a total tax assessment exceeding Rs. 15,000 in Indian currency, the appointment of *Jimidars* required the sanction of the prime minister. Government of Nepal, *Madhesh Malko Sawal*, sec. 26, pp. 13–14.

augment their income. A common practice was to refuse to accept payment of taxes, or to withhold receipts,[47] with the apparent intention of penalizing landowners for default. The regulations prohibit the exaction of fees while recording land transfers,[48] thereby implying the existence of such a practice. There were also complaints that *Jimidars* often exacted extra amounts when receiving land-tax payments from landowners.[49] Moreover, as tax collector, the *Jimidar* was responsible for the maintenance of land records and the registration of land transfers.[50] A frequent complaint was that the records were so confused that it was not possible to identify individual holdings.[51] The confusion was apparently deliberate, for *Jimidars* often took advantage of it to claim lands as their own and force the cultivators to pay rents to them in the capacity of tenants. In Kailali district, for example, according to an official source, rents on approximately 22,000 *bighas* of lands out of a total area of 71,865 were being fraudulently appropriated by *Jimidars*.[52] Confused land records also made it possible for *Jimidars* to transfer landholdings fraudulently. In Bardiya district, several holdings that belonged to *ryots* in 1910 had passed to *Jimidars* by 1947, and there was evidence that not all such transfers had been made in a lawful manner.[53] *Jimidars* were able to use various devious means to increase their holdings at the expense of the peasantry. Moreover, whereas 52,000 *bighas* had belonged to individual landowners and 24,000 *bighas* to *Jimidars* in 1910, the situation was reversed in 1951.[54] According to another source, *Jimidars* were able also to augment their holdings by retaining possession of lands left vacant or relinquished by cultivators for any reason.[55] The law permitted them to do so only in the event no prospective settler was

[47] *Madhesh Malko Sawal*, sec. 68, p. 31.
[48] Ibid., sec. 16(8), p. 9.
[49] Land Reform Commission, "Report on Land Tenure Conditions in Saptari, Mahottari, and Sarlahi," typescript (Kathmandu: the Commission, 2010 [1953]).
[50] Government of Nepal, *Madhesh Jilla Jillako Jimidar Patuwarika Naunko Sawal*, secs. 1–2, pp. 1–2.
[51] Nepali Congress, *Kisanharuko Nimti Nepali Congressle Ke Garyo?* [What has the Nepali Congress done for the peasants?] (Kathmandu: Nepali Congress, n.d.), p. 23.
[52] "Notification of the Ministry of Food and Land Administration," *Nepal Gazette*, Jestha 6, 2009 (May 19, 1952). The total area of 71,865 *bighas* contained in holdings has been given on the basis of the National Agricultural Census Report for 1961. The figure must have been much lower in 1952.
[53] Nepali Congress, op. cit., pp. 12–13.
[54] Ibid., p. 19.
[55] Madan Bahadur Pradhan; "Butaul Jillako Bhumi Samasya" [Land problems of Butaul district], *Kisan*, vol. 1, nos. 2–3 (n.d. [1962?]).

available, but it was perhaps hardly reasonable to expect *Jimidars* to comply faithfully with such a self-denying restriction.

The findings of an official survey of two revenue subdivisions in Morang district in 1948 show the extent to which the *Jimidari* system had become synonymous with inequality. Of the local families, 23.1 percent possessed holdings of less than one *bigha* each, but some *Jimidars* each owned as much as 20,000 to 22,000 *bighas* and employed 450 to 500 plowhands and cowherds.[56] There is no reason to believe that this trend was confined to Morang district.

Role of the Government

In resorting to such malpractices and underhand methods to augment his income, the *Jimidar* was only following in the footsteps of the government. Notwithstanding his numerous obligations and responsibilities, he received a remuneration amounting to only about 4 percent of the total amount collected and deposited with the local revenue office. It is true, of course, that he was also assigned *Jirayat* lands in partial compensation for his services. *Jirayat* lands were taxable, however, and the profits that the *Jimidar* derived from them were almost the same as those that an ordinary landowner obtained from his holding. The ownership of taxable lands was hardly a special privilege conferred on *Jimidars*.

The Rana government was, in fact, faced with a major difficulty when it reorganized the *Jimidari* system in the Tarai districts. The creation of such an agency at the village level was essential for both revenue collection and administration, but it was a difficult task to extract enough money directly from the peasantry to remunerate the *Jimidars* adequately. The Rana government therefore resorted to the practice commonly followed under these conditions in preindustrial societies;[57] it gave sufficient power and authority to the *Jimidar* to squeeze the peasantry, and itself capitalized on these gains of the *Jimidar* to maximize its revenue.

The methods employed by the government to garner the greatest possible revenue from *Jimidari* holdings were ingenious, although often also crude. A common practice was to overstate the area of holdings. The area of one holding in Palhi-Majhkhand, for instance,

[56]Thir Bahadur Raimajhi, "Saptari ra Biratnagar Ko Audyogik Survey Report" [Industrial survey report of Saptari and Biratnagar], unpublished (Kathmandu: Department of Industrial and Commercial Intelligence, 2006 [1949]), pp. 10–11.

[57]Barrington Moore, Jr., *Social Origins of Dictatorship and Democracy* (Penguin Books, 1967), p. 172.

was recorded as 241 *bighas* in 1895, 321 *bighas* in 1908, and 324 *bighas* in 1921. Inasmuch as the holding did not contain any waste land, this discrepancy was due either to deliberate overstatement or the use of incorrect units of measurement.[58] Indeed, the measuring chain was variously 8.25 or 8.50 cubits long instead of the prescribed 9 cubits, "because the settlement officers are responsible to the government and therefore want to please it"[59] by increasing revenue assessment. Discrepancies between the registered area and the actual area of taxable holdings were very common, and even nonexistent holdings frequently were recorded in the tax-assessment registers.[60] Nevertheless, there was no remission in the revenue when these discrepancies were detected.

Both good and bad lands often were included in the same holding,[61] so that the *Jimidar* was compelled to utilize part of the income from the good land to compensate for the loss that he sustained on the bad. *Jimidars* were not permitted to sell only bad lands, while retaining good lands.[62] Moreover, many *Jimidari* holdings in the Tarai included large area of lands in nonagricultural categories, such as roads and ponds, on which taxes were assessed as on cultivated lands. In Sheoraj and Khajahani in the western Tarai, only in 1932 did the government grant remissions on this account, admitting that the inclusion of ponds in the taxable area involved hardships for the people.[63] Similarly, in 1948, tax remissions were granted in Saptari district for lands covered by roads, bridges, ponds, wells, irrigation canals, and homesteads, and for nonexistent holdings and the discrepancy between the actual area and the registered area.[64] But in most parts of the country the

[58] Land Reform Commission, "Report on Land Tenure Conditions in the Western Tarai," mimeographed (Kathmandu: the Commission, 2010 [1953]), pp. 23-24.

[59] Ibid., p. 10.

[60] Law Ministry Records, "Survey Regulations for Morang District," 1970 (1913), sec. 20. Similarly, in the western Tarai, "There are many cases in which nonexistent lands have been included in *Jimidari* holdings, in addition to forests, tanks, ponds, etc. *Jimidars* pay the taxes due on such area by exploiting the peasantry." Nepali Congress, op. cit. (in n. 51 above), p. 24.

[61] Government of Nepal, *Madhesh Malko Sawal*, sec. 159, pp. 65-66.

[62] Ibid., sec. 27, p. 15.

[63] Law Ministry Records, "Tax Assessment Order for Sheoraj and Khajahani," 1989 (1932).

[64] Law Ministry Records, "Tax Assessment Order for Saptari and Udayapur," 2006 (1949). Regulations promulgated in 1861 had prohibited the measurement of ponds, mounds, uncultivated tracts, paths, etc., for purposes of tax assessment. "Survey Regulations for Eastern Tarai Districts," (1861), sec. 5. It is obvious that these regulations were never effectively enforced.

inequities of the land-tax assessment system consequent to such questionable practices continued. A clear exposition of the *Jimidar*'s case is contained in the following report submitted to an official land-reform commission in 1953:

> Suppose there is a plot of 100 *bighas* of waste or forest land in some place. Suppose again that the government is somehow able to find out five persons to reclaim it. One of them is enterprising and possesses some capital. The government then tells him: Take 50 *bighas* as your *Jirayat* holding, and allot the remaining area to the other four persons. You will be under obligation to pay land tax not only on your *Jirayat* lands, but also on the lands allotted to these persons. If they are unable to cultivate their allotments, you will be under obligation to do so yourself. If any of the allottees vacates his land, you will have to cultivate it yourself, but only until another person comes forward to take it up. For these services, you will be paid remuneration amounting to 3.8 percent of the total amount of land tax collected.[65]

Explaining the role of the *Jimidar* as landowner and moneylender, the same report states:

> *Jimidars* keep plowhands for cultivating their *Jirayat* lands. They have to give interest-free loans to these hands at rates ranging from Rs.300 to Rs. 1,000 each. Since agricultural labor is scarce, the amount of loans is necessarily high. *Jimidars* have also to pay monthly wages in kind to these plowhands. Their farming operations are generally profitable even after meeting all these expenses, but often there are losses.[66]

Nevertheless, the profits obviously outweighed any losses *Jimidars* might have had to incur in the course of their operations. At all events, the *Jimidari* system gradually became more a tool utilized by the Rana regime to squeeze surplus agricultural production from the peasantry than an institution aimed at fostering agricultural growth. The modus operandi of this exploitation was fairly simple: the *Jimidar* squeezed the peasantry, and in turn he was squeezed by the government.[67]

---

[65] Land Reform Commission, op. cit. (in n. 58 above), p. 8.

[66] Ibid., pp. 4–5.

[67] An example of such squeeze is provided by the manner in which *Jimidars* were often harassed and, at times, even tortured in an attempt to insure full collections. Often they were imprisoned for petty amounts of arrears. "Complaint of Jimidar Jhoti Khan of Rautahat," Shrawan Badi 9, 1922 (July 1865). In some western Tarai districts, land taxes were collected from *Jimidars* with the help of peons who were entitled to exact from them food and money until payment was completed. People sought appointment as peons without any remuneration, or on very low salaries, as they expected to be compensated for their labor through these exactions. "Order regarding Hawala Exactions in Banke District," Kartik Badi 11, 1854 (November 1897).

Still, the pickings left to him were substantial enough to insure the sustenance of a class that contributed little to the agricultural economy. In terms of the "ratio between services rendered and the surplus taken from the peasants,"[68] the *Jimidari* system had become parasitic even as early as the beginning of the twentieth century, if not sooner. How isolated it had become from the mainstream of rural life in the Tarai became evident in 1946, when a conference of *Jimidars* convened by the Rana government in Kathmandu limited its demands to such matters as a simpler procedure for the supply of timber for constructing irrigation projects and permission to retain on deposit a maximum amount of Rs. 1,000 from the proceeds of revenue collections.[69] The problems of the peasantry were, obviously, quite outside the range of their vision and interests.

Abolition of *Jimidari* Landownership

During the period immediately following the 1951 political changes in Nepal, conflicts between *Jimidars* and peasants erupted in several districts of the Tarai, and the demand for the abolition of the *Jimidari* system gradually gained momentum. In 1953, an official land-reform commission advocated the abolition of the system on the ground that it had become a "symbol of immoral exploitation." It suggested that the function of land-tax collection should be taken over by the government, and that *Jimidars* should be permitted to retain the ownership of their *Jirayat* lands. These recommendations were not implemented at that time, because the government felt that it would be inadvisable to abolish the *Jimidari* system without providing for alternative sources of agricultural credit.[70]

The question of *Jimidari* abolition was taken up after about a decade as part of a comprehensive program of land reform. The 1964 Lands Act contained provisions for the abolition of the *Jimidari* system.[71] In those districts where this measure has been enforced, land taxes are now

---

[68] Moore, *Social Origins of Dictatorship and Democracy*, p. 471.

[69] Bal Chandra Sharma, *Nepal ko Aitihasik Ruprekha* [An outline of the history of Nepal] (Banaras: Krishna Kumari, 2008 [1951]), p. 374.

[70] Land Reform Commission, "Reports of the Land Reform Commission," mimeographed (Kathmandu: the Commission, 2010 [1953]), pp. 5, 40-41.

[71] Ministry of Law and Justice, "Bhumi Sambandhi Ain, 2021" [Lands act, 1964], *Nepal Gazette*, vol. 14, no. 18 (Extraordinary), Marga 1, 2021 (November 16, 1964), chap. II, secs. 3-6. This law relates only to *Jimidari* holdings on *Raikar* lands. Similar provisions for the abolition of the *Jimidari* system on *Raj Guthi* lands are contained in the 1972 Guthi Corporation Act, chap. 4, secs. 21-23.

collected by local Panchayats. Nevertheless, *Jimidars* have been allowed to retain the ownership of the taxable *Jirayat* lands assigned to them as part of their emoluments. They have thus been able to preserve their status as landowners, but without the power and authority that characterized the *Jimidari* system in the past. Legislation to abolish *Ukhada* landownership rights in Nawal-Parasi, Rupandehi, and Kapilavastu districts was enacted in the same year.[72] The lands were registered in the name of the actual cultivators, who were then under obligation to pay compensation to the erstwhile *Ukhada* owners at a rate amounting to ten times the land tax. This meant a maximum payment of between Rs. 270 and Rs. 510 per *bigha*, which is considerably below the current prices of agricultural lands in these districts.

With the abolition of *Jimidari* landownership, feudalistic forms of land control have been almost completely eradicated in Nepal. Individual ownership of land is now possible only under the *Raikar* and *Guthi* systems. The evolution of property rights in these categories of land forms the subject matter of the next part of our study.

[72] Ministry of Law and Justice, "Ukhada Sambandhi Ain, 2021" [Ukhada land-tenure act, 1964], *Nepal Gazette*, vol. 14, no. 15 (Extraordinary), Aswin 17, 2021 (October 2, 1964). The act was amended in 1965. Ibid., vol. 15, no. 11 (Extraordinary), Ashadh 30, 2022 (July 14, 1965).

Chapter 8

RAIKAR LAND TAXATION

Although the abolition of *Birta*, *Jagir*, *Kipat*, and *Jimidari* forms of landownership had to wait until after 1951, certain trends that appeared as early as the latter part of the nineteenth century upgraded the status of peasants cultivating *Raikar* lands to that of rent-receiving landowners. These newly emerged rent-receiving rights on *Raikar* lands were more or less identical to the ascriptive rights attached to *Birta* and *Jagir* landownership; hence their impact on the agrarian structure seems to have been profound. Before analyzing the process of this recent change in Nepali agrarian society, we shall make an attempt in chapters 8 and 9 to study the main contributory factors—the progressive reduction in the fiscal burden of peasants cultivating *Raikar* lands, and the gradual dilution of their unpaid labor obligations.

In chapter 2, *Raikar* was defined as a form of state landlordism. Under this system, the state holds *Raikar* lands directly under its ownership and appropriates revenues from such lands for its own use. We shall now examine the form and level of payments due to the state from peasants who cultivated *Raikar* lands. The diversity of geographical conditions in the Kingdom of Nepal has had a profound effect on economic conditions and institutions, including agriculture and land taxation, so we shall deal separately with the Tarai region, the central and eastern hill regions including Kathmandu Valley, and the far-western hill region. We shall start with an account of official policies in the field of *Raikar* land taxation during the period from political unification to the mid-nineteenth century before analyzing trends and developments during both the Rana period (1846–1951) and the subsequent two decades (1951–73).

It should be explained at the very outset that, traditionally, taxes are not imposed on agricultural lands in Nepal until a few years after they are brought under the plow. The obvious intention of such exemption is to compensate the peasant for the initial overhead costs and risks. This practice was begun by King Ram Shah (1606–36) of Gorkha, who decreed that no taxes should be collected on newly reclaimed lands for three years.[1] The period was subsequently extended to five years.[2] However, there is evidence that this rule was not uniformly applicable to all parts of the country. In mountainous regions, where there was keen competition for the available cultivable land, the period of exemption was shorter than in the Tarai. In several hill districts in the northwestern regions, for instance, taxes on newly reclaimed lands were exempted for only three years.[3] On the other hand, tax exemption on such lands was granted for the full five-year period in the Tarai districts.[4] Current legislation prescribes a four-year period of initial tax exemption, but only if virgin or riverine lands, or those covered by bushes, are reclaimed.[5]

Pre-Rana Systems of Land Taxation

The system of land taxation in the Tarai, particularly in the eastern region, was modeled on the Mughal revenue system in India.[6] Under that system, taxes were assessed in cash per unit of area at different rates for different crops.[7] However, the Mughal system was followed only to the extent of using the nature of the crop and the area sown as the basis of tax assessment; there is no evidence that in the Tarai the assessment was made at the same rates and on the same crops as those of the Mughals.

[1] Ministry of Law and Justice, *Shri 5 Surendra... Muluki Ain*, p. 699, app. A.
[2] "Jagga Jamin Ko" [On land matters], ibid., sec. 3, p. 19–20.
[3] In Dullu and Dailekh, for instance, revenue-collection arrangements made in 1881 prescribed a three-year period of tax exemption if virgin lands were brought under the plow. "Order regarding Revenue Collection in Dullu and Dailekh," Marga Badi 5, 1938 (November 1881).
[4] "Revenue Regulations for Eastern Tarai Districts," 1918 (1861), sec. 68.
[5] Ministry of Law and Justice, "Jagga Abad Garne Ko" [On land reclamation], *Muluki Ain* [Legal code] (Kathmandu: the Ministry, 2020 [1963]), sec. 5, pp. 116–17. During the 1930s, legislation was enacted fixing this period at a maximum of ten years if forest lands were reclaimed in areas allotted by the government for this purpose in the districts of Banke, Bardiya, Kailali, and Kanchanpur in the far-western Tarai region and Morang in the eastern Tarai region. Government of Nepal, "Jagga Birhaune Ko" [On land reclamation], *Muluki Ain*, pt. III (Kathmandu: Gorkhapatra Press, 1992 [1935]), sec. 5.
[6] Francis Buchanan (Hamilton), who visited Nepal during 1802–3, observed that "the Mogul system of finance had been completely introduced" in the eastern Tarai region. *An Account of the Kingdom of Nepal, and of the Territories Annexed to This Dominion by House of Gorkha* (reprint; New Delhi: Manjusri Publishing House, 1972), p. 150.
[7] Ibid., pp. 153–54. The crop-assessment system was followed not only in Morang but also in Bara and elsewhere in the eastern Tarai region. "Order regarding Land-Tax Assessment Rates in Different Pargannas of Bara District," Bhadra Badi 12, 1848

Roughly, the land-tax assessment system in the eastern Tarai operated as follows during the pre-Rana period. After lands were reclaimed and the prescribed period of tax exemption ended, taxes were assessed according to the number of ox teams employed to cultivate each holding.[8] The rates of taxation were progressively increased during a prescribed number of years. The land was thereafter measured and taxes were assessed at different rates for different crops for each unit of area.[9] There were also cases, however, in which tax assessments on newly reclaimed lands were fixed according to the area from the very beginning,[10] possibly because their productivity was more than the average, or because they were favorably located.

A different system was followed in the inner and western Tarai, where Mughal fiscal systems do not appear to have been introduced at any time. In those areas, tax assessments were generally based on the number of ox teams maintained by each peasant, irrespective of the actual area tilled. It is possible that large areas in these regions were not sufficiently populated to justify the cost and effort involved in land-measurement operations.[11]

Land-Tax Assessment System in the Midlands

An analysis of the land-tax assessment system in the midlands,

(August 1791). The system was known as *zabti* in Mughal India. According to one source, "Under the *zabti* system, the land under cultivation of different crops was actually measured for purposes of assessment. To it was then applied a schedule of rates [i.e., *zabti*] prepared on the basis of average yield per unit of land for each crop. Concessions were made to the assessee on the basis of the actual state of productivity of his land at any given time. One-third of the total produce thus assessed was regarded as the share of the state and this share was commuted into cash on the basis of average prices for different crops prevalent in the area. The total amount of revenue thus estimated on the basis of average yields and average prices provided the basis for the formation of average revenue rates per unit of area for different qualities of soil and for different crops." Sulekh Chandra Gupta, *Agrarian Relations and Early British Rule in India* (Bombay: Asia Publishing House, 1963), p. 14.

[8]The system of assessing taxes on land on the basis of the number of ox teams used to cultivate each holding was followed with some variations in India also, where "a stated charge was made on each plough and team, the unit of a productive power, and the owner of the team was free to cultivate as much land as he could and in whatever way he chose." Sir Richard Burn, ed., *Cambridge History of India* (Delhi: S. Chand & Co., 1957), III, 457.

[9]"Order regarding Land-Tax Assessment Rates in Morang," Shrawan Badi 2, 1862 (July 1805).

[10]"Order regarding Land Reclamation in Dostiya, Bara District," Jestha Badi 2, 1864 (May 1807).

[11]This description of pre-Rana systems of land-tax assessment in different regions is based on Regmi, *A Study in Nepali Economic History*, pp. 80–89, 178–85.

including Kathmandu Valley, must be preceded by a note on the system followed for classifying agricultural lands. Traditionally, lands of this category have been classified as *Khet* and *Pakho*. *Khet* are lands in river valleys and terraces that can retain water for sufficiently long periods to grow rice and wheat. *Pakho* are lands situated on high terrain that are incapable of retaining water, so that only such crops as maize, millet, and dry rice can be grown.[12]

Khet lands have always been considered more profitable than *Pakho* in Nepal. Possession of *Khet* lands enabled landowners to collect rents in the form of rice, the staple diet of well-to-do Nepalis. Rents on *Khet* lands were high, generally approximating 50 to 75 percent of the total rice crop. In order to insure that peasants should be able to pay such high rents, *Khet* lands were usually allotted only to peasants who resided in the village where these were situated. Peasants were thus under obligation to cultivate both *Khet* and *Pakho* lands. In other words, the bulk of the rice produced on *Khet* lands went to the landowner, whereas *Pakho* lands yielded maize, millet, and so on for the peasants' subsistence.

Because *Pakho* lands had a low revenue potential compared to *Khet* lands, the government paid greater attention to the land-tax assessment system on agricultural lands of the latter category. Attention was paid not only to the area of every plot, but also to the texture of its soil, the availability of irrigation facilities, the climate, and productivity. In contrast, *Pakho* lands were generally not even measured. Revenue settlements on such lands usually meant only an enumeration of households and a rough estimation of the size of the holding.[13] An additional reason why *Pakho* lands were seldom measured or graded was that in the majority of cases they were situated in difficult terrain.[14]

For the purpose of tax assessment without measurement, *Pakho* lands were classified on the basis of whether they possessed a homestead or not. A plot of unmeasured *Pakho* land without a homestead was subject to a nominal cash payment based roughly on the estimated

---

[12] The term *Khet* is obviously a corrupt form of the Sanskrit *Kshetra*. *Pakho* appears to have been derived from the Persian *bakhs*, meaning unirrigated land. Ann K. S. Lambton, *Landlord and Peasant in Persia* (London: Oxford University Press, 1953), p. 424.

[13] Regmi, *Land Tenure and Taxation in Nepal*, I, 154-55.

[14] For instance, in some hill areas of Makwanpur district, "the gradient is so steep that a peasant has to catch hold of a bush with one hand, use a spade with the other, and plant seeds with his mouth." Law Ministry Records, "Makwanpur Assessment Order," Bhadra 16, 2003 (September 1, 1946).

area.[15] If the plot contained a homestead, *Pakho* holdings were classified according to the number of ox teams required to plow them. A holding that could be plowed by one ox team in one day was classified as *Hale*; half of that was *Pate*; a holding that was too small to be plowed with oxen and had to be dug with a spade was a *Kodale*.[16] Taxes on *Hale*, *Pate*, and *Kodale* holdings were generally in cash and were characterized by lack of uniformity.[17]

The nature and level of taxes on *Khet* lands were governed mainly by the tenurial policy of the government. During the nineteenth century, agricultural lands in the midlands rarely contributed revenue to the public exchequer, but consisted for the most part of *Birta*, *Jagir*, or *Guthi* grants. Accordingly, the form and amount of payments that the peasant was obligated to make depended primarily on the consumption requirements of *Birta* owners, *Jagirdars*, and *Guthiyars*.[18] In the central and eastern midlands, including Kathmandu Valley, taxes on *Khet* lands were usually collected under the *Adhiya* system, under which the cultivator paid half of the paddy crop as tax, retaining the balance for himself.[19] This system helped the government to avoid complicated methods of tax assessment and remission and eliminated the need to measure the land. From the standpoint of the cultivator, it contained a built-in mechanism to enable him to escape

[15]Such a plot of *Pakho* land, cultivated by a nonresident peasant, was called *Fadke*. Harilal, *Pahad Mal Bishaya* [Revenue offices in the hill regions] (Kathmandu: Nepali Bhasha Prakashini Samiti, 2008 [1951]), p. 187.

[16]Ibid., pp. 186-87. According to another view, to which reference has also been made by Harilal p. 6): "Maize lands or lands situated on the hill-side, are divided into three kinds, namely 'hal,' 'patay,' and 'kodalay.' *Hal* is the area cultivated by a tenant with a pair or pairs of bullocks. This pays one Nepali rupee only for the whole area thus cultivated. A tenant owning only one bullock and with the help of another bullock borrowed from his neighbor is a *Patay* tenant and pays three-fourths of a Nepali rupee. The *Kodalay* tenant uses the spade only and pays half a Nepali rupee as rent for his land." Perceval Landon, *Nepal*, (London: Constable and Co., 1928), II, 206. The system of assessing land taxes after classifying holdings as *Hale* and *Pate* appears to have been introduced in Kailali and other districts of the far-western Tarai region on lands reclaimed by settlers from the hill regions. "Order regarding Land Reclamation in Kailali District," Kartik Badi 12, 1954 (November 1897).

[17]Regmi, I, 85-87.

[18]Ibid., III, 17-18.

[19]Regmi, *A Study in Nepali Economic History*, pp. 84-86. The crop-sharing system was prevalent in India both during the Hindu and Mughal periods. See Radha Kumud Mookerji, "Indian Land-System," in Government of Bengal, *Report of the Land Revenue Commission, Bengal* (Alipore: Bengal Government Press, 1940), II, 159; Irfan Habib, *The Agrarian System of Mughal India* (Bombay: Asia Publishing House, 1963), pp. 197-98; B. H. Baden-Powell, *Land Revenue and Tenure in British India* (Oxford: Clarendon Press, 1913), pp. 35-36.

the adverse effects of occasional crop failure. It also protected him from the costs and risks involved in marketing his produce. In the Karnali region, which included Jumla, Humla, Dullu, Dailekh, Doti, Bajura, and Bajhang, tax assessments on *Khet* lands appear to have been traditionally in cash. The reason may have been that trade, rather than agriculture, was the main occupation of the majority of the inhabitants of these areas because of adverse climatic and terrain factors. There is also evidence that the economy of these areas had been monetized to a considerable extent even during the eighteenth century.[20]

To sum up, taxes were collected in kind on the basis of half of the produce in most of the midlands areas during the period after political unification, whereas in the far-western hill region the Gorkhali rulers retained the traditional system of cash assessments. In the eastern Tarai, taxes were assessed in cash according to the area and the type of crop sown, and in the inner and western Tarai the assessment was generally based on the number of ox teams owned by each cultivator.

Factors Contributing to Change

These traditional systems of land-tax assessment in the different regions of the country underwent a number of changes during the late eighteenth and early nineteenth centuries, mainly for fiscal and administrative reasons. In the eastern Tarai, the land-tax assessment system was reorganized in 1793 in an attempt to establish uniform rates of taxation in each revenue division. The existing system of assessing taxes on the basis of area separately for different crops was retained, but greater importance was now given to the length of time during which lands had been under cultivation and to the relative importance of different crops in each revenue division. The highest rate of tax was levied on lands growing tobacco in Mahottari, paddy in Saptari, and sugar cane in Morang.[21] In the inner and western Tarai, the practice of land measurement was gradually introduced whenever it did not have an adverse impact on the current volume of revenue collection.

Changes in the land-tax assessment system during the post-unification period were more significant in the central and eastern hill regions.

[20] Regmi, pp. 21–22, 30.
[21] "Confirmation of 1793 Tax-Assessment Rates in Mahottari," Kartik Sudi 10, 1866 (November 1809); "Order regarding Land-Tax Assessment Rates in Pakari, Saptari District," Jestha Badi 13, 1865 (May 1808); "Order regarding Land-Tax Assessment Rates in Fattaharipur, Morang District," Marga Badi 1, 1865 (November 1808).

Notwithstanding its simplicity, the *Adhiya* system was disadvantageous to *Jagir* land assignees because it fixed their income from the land at half of the produce and thus prevented them from taking advantage of competition among prospective tenants to raise rents. This difficulty led to the introduction of the *Kut* system, under which the cultivator usually paid a stipulated sum in cash or quantity of produce.[22] *Kut* assessment rates bore no relationship to actual productivity, nor was there any limit beyond which they could not be raised. *Jagir* assignees often utilized the opportunities created by the introduction of the *Kut* system to raise rents to exorbitant levels. As for the government, it issued orders from time to time permitting *Jagir* assignees to increase rents "according to the capacity of the land" and evict tenants who refused to pay the increased amount.[23]

The *Kut* assessment system suffered from one major defect from the viewpoint of the government. Because *Kut* rents were fixed at a specific figure, and not in a percentage of the actual produce, the government was constantly faced with the problem of determining the veracity of claims for remission on account of floods, washouts, and other mishaps. This difficulty was solved by fixing *Kut* assessment rates on a contractual basis; that is, by stipulating full payment even when crops were damaged by natural calamities. *Kut* rent assessments of this category usually were in cash. This system was introduced during the 1830s in several hill regions where transport and communication difficulties made it difficult to collect rents in kind and to dispose of claims for remission.[24]

The gradual introduction of the *Kut* system in various forms had far-reaching effects on the nature and level of land taxation in the central and eastern midlands. Whereas under the *Adhiya* system half of the produce represented the maximum payable as rent, under the *Kut* system it represented the minimum. The level of *Kut* rents was determined not by what the land yielded, but by what the landlord could squeeze from the cultivator. Frequently, *Kut* rents reflected the scarcity value of agricultural lands because of favorable location or other circumstances for which the *Adhiya* system had provided no scope. Available evidence suggests that under the *Kut* system, rates of in-kind rents reached an average of 75 percent of the rice crop. Often

[22] Regmi, pp. 86–89.
[23] Ibid., pp. 179–84.
[24] "Order regarding Land Allotments on Kut Basis in Majhkirat," Baisakh Badi 8, 1890 (April 1833); "Allotment of Jagir Lands on Kut-Thek Basis to Nahar Thapa," Bhadra Sudi 1, 1890 (August 1833).

they were so high that no person was willing to bear the burden, so that land remained uncultivated.[25]

The cumulative effect of these developments was to make the rent-assessment system followed in the central and eastern hill regions highly complex. Assessments under the *Kut* system could be either in cash or in kind. At times, those assessments could also be on a contractual basis, so that remissions were not allowed in the event of crop failure. To add to this confusion, some holdings continued to pay rents under the *Adhiya* system and the government occasionally made fresh land allotments on the *Adhiya* basis.

THE RANA PERIOD

Important changes occurred in the land-tax assessment system after the middle of the nineteenth century as a result of various developments in the political and administrative fields. These developments included the emergence of the Rana regime, the gradual decline in *Jagir* land assignments, and the monetization of payments on the land. Rana land-taxation policy aimed at reaching an objective basis of land-tax assessment where this was lacking, establishing a correlation between tax-assessment rates and productivity, insuring uniform rates wherever possible, and gradually monetizing the land-tax assessment system.

Soon after the emergence of the Rana regime, the policy of permitting *Jagirdars* to take advantage of competition among the peasantry and raise rents was reversed. In general, the existing level of taxation was retained when revenue settlements were revised during the years 1854–68. Legislation was enacted prescribing that no cultivator should be evicted from his lands and homesteads so long as he made the payments due from him according to the tax-assessment records compiled in the course of these settlements. Increase of rents on any ground whatsoever, other than default in payment of rents, was

---

[25] For Instance, at Chiti in Lamjung district, competition among prospective tenants forced up rents to 100.25 *muris* of paddy on a plot of 232 *muris* of land. The bidder was unable to pay the rent and so vacated the land, which then remained uncultivated for several years. The rent was subsequently reduced to 92.25 *muris* of paddy. The report adds: "There are many cases in Lamjung in which lands have remained uncultivated because of exorbitant *Kut* rents." "Order regarding Kut Rents in Lamjung," Magh Badi 12, 1921 (January 1865); "Allotment of Waste Jagir Holding to Nahar Singh Rana and Others in Tanahu," Ashadh Sudi, 1902 (June 1846).

prohibited until the revenue settlement was again revised.[26] Competitive bidding for rents was permitted only on newly reclaimed lands that were being cultivated by nonresident cultivators. But even though the Rana government made an attempt to check arbitrary increases in agricultural rents in this manner, it did nothing to alleviate the hardships created by such increases in the past. The reason was that all arbitrary increases by *Jagirdars* in the past were now incorporated into the regular tax assessment. Nor was this all. No attempt was made to formulate objective criteria to correlate the level of tax assessments with productivity. Whenever it was necessary to fix tax assessments, as on newly reclaimed lands, the Rana government followed the seemingly equitable policy of doing so at specific rates on the basis of the rate prevailing on adjoining lands. Even when fresh *Jagera* lands were assigned as *Jagir*, income from such lands was calculated on the same basis. Accordingly, rents on *Jagera* lands that had been assigned as *Jagir* were increased if the rate prevailing on the adjoining holding was higher. This policy insured that the highest rate prevailing in any area determined the level of rents. It also marked the abolition of the *Adhiya* system for all practical purposes. *Adhiya* rent assessments were now retained only in circumstances where it appeared that any increase in rents would remove the land from cultivation.[27]

GRADING OF AGRICULTURAL LANDS

In an earlier section, we saw that the gradual introduction of the *Kut* system on *Khet* lands in the hill districts put an end to the correlation between actual yields and the amount of tax assessment that had been achieved through the *Adhiya* system. One of the most significant aspects of Rana land-taxation policy was the evolution of formulas intended to reestablish this correlation. In the process, the Ranas imparted to the land-tax assessment system a degree of sophistication that it had never known previously. This objective was accomplished

[26]Government of Nepal, "Mohi Talsing Ko" [On tenants and landlords], in Ministry of Law and Justice, *Shri 5 Surendra... Muluki Ain*, sec. 25, pp. 43-44.

[27]"Order to Bakyauta Tahasil Offices in Kathmandu Valley," Baisakh Badi 13, 1954 (April 1897). Revenue regulations for hill districts, promulgated in 1934, provided that "In case assessments on any plot of land have been made on *Adhiya* basis, collection shall henceforth be made on *Kut* basis according to the amount actually collected or the rate prevailing on adjoining holdings, whichever is higher. The land shall be measured for this purpose, if so necessary." Law Ministry Records, "Sindhupalchok Revenue Regulations," 1991 (1934), sec. 44.

through the wider application of the traditional system of dividing agricultural lands into the four grades of *Abal, Doyam, Sim,* and *Chahar*.[28] Standard formulas for the grading of agricultural lands as *Abal, Doyam, Sim,* and *Chahar* appear to have been devised for the first time only during revenue settlements at Sankhu in Kathmandu district in 1919.[29] There were different formulas for *Khet* and *Pakho* lands. The grade of *Khet* lands was determined on the basis of such criteria as the physical properties of soil, its capacity to retain water, the availability of irrigation facilities, and the estimated productivity per unit of area:

On *Abal* lands, the entire plot can be irrigated by means of irrigation channels or otherwise, and water once used stays on the land for three or four days. The soil is good and moist and the yield is at least 3.5 *muris* per *ropani*, either with two crops or one paddy crop.

On *Doyam* lands, only three-fourths of the plot can be irrigated by means of irrigation channels or otherwise, and water once used stays on the land for two or three days. The soil is good and moist, although the level of the land may be somewhat high. The yield is less than 3.5 *muris* but more than 2.5 *muris* per *ropani*, either with two crops or one paddy crop.

On *Sim* lands, half of the plot can be irrigated by means of irrigation channels or otherwise, and water once used stays on the land for only one day. The soil is fertile, even though sandy to some extent. The yield is less than 2.5 *muris* but more than 1.75 *muris* per *ropani*, either with two crops or one paddy crop.

Very little land can be irrigated on *Chahar* lands or the entire plot is dependent upon rainfall. The land is dry, sandy, or stony, and water does not stay on it. There is only one crop in the year, and the yield is less than 1.75 *muris* per *ropani*.[30]

[28]This system of gradation appears to have been used in Kathmandu Valley at least since the time of King Jayasthiti Malla (1382-95). Devi Prasad Lamsal, ed., *Bhasha Vamshavali* (Genealogy in the vernacular language) (Kathmandu: Nepal Rashtriya Pustakalaya, Department of Archaeology, 2023 [1966]), II, 38. In the hill regions, the terms *Abal, Doyam, Sim,* and *Chahar* applied to various categories of the peasantry rather than to the land tilled by them. Colonel Kirkpatrick, *An Account of the Kingdom of Nepaul* (reprint; New Delhi: Manjusri Publishing House, 1969), p. 101. In 1854, legislation was enacted providing for the grading of agricultural lands in the hill regions under this system. "Jagga Jamin Ko" (On land matters), in Ministry of Law and Justice, *Shri 5 Surendra...Muluki Ain*, sec. 40, p. 28. Outside of Kathmandu Valley, however, it appears to have been introduced for the first time in Ilam, Jumla, Dullu, and Dailekh districts during the revenue settlements of 1890-91. "Orders regarding Land Surveys," separate orders for Jumla, Dullu, and Dailekh (Marga Sudi, 1947) [December 1890], and Ilam (Falgun Badi 3, 1947) [February 1891].

[29]Law Ministry Records, "Sankhu Survey Regulations," Marga 30, 1976 (December 14, 1919).

[30]Ibid.

In 1934 these formulas were applied to newly cultivated *Khet* lands in other parts of Kathmandu Valley and also to all hill districts where land-tax assessments were wholly or partly in kind. They were later extended to a number of hill districts where land-tax assessments were in cash, including Ilam, Chhathum, Bajhang, Baitadi, Gorkha, Kunchha, and Pokhara.[31]

The grading system mentioned above was applied to *Pakho* lands also at Sankhu in 1919. Lands that contained good and moist soil with a minimum yield of 1.25 *muri* of maize, dry rice, or millet per *ropani* were graded as *Abal*. If the yield did not exceed 0.75 *muri* per *ropani*, the land was graded as *Doyam*. Lands with sandy or gravelly soils were graded as *Sim* if the yield was 0.5 *muri* and as *Chahar* if it was less.[32] This system was later extended to the whole of Kathmandu Valley except Bhaktapur in respect to newly reclaimed holdings only, and tax-assessment rates thereon were standardized at 2 to 7 *pathis* of maize payable in cash at R. 0.50 to Rs. 1.75 per *ropani*.[33] Bhaktapur was the only area where *Pakho* lands were measured and graded into the two categories of *Hale-Pakho* and *Kodale-Pakho*, and tax-assessment rates were fixed in kind but were payable in cash at R. 0.98 and R. 0.52 per *ropani* respectively.[34]

The grading system devised by the Rana government does not appear, however, to have been overly effective in correlating tax assessments with actual productivity. It tended to be rigid over a period of time, ignoring recurrent physical changes in the land or alterations in the cropping pattern. Little attention was paid to scientific studies of soils and yields. The settlement officer, consequently, had a wide degree of latitude within which to exercise his discretion. Moreover, revenue settlements even in adjoining areas were often held several decades apart, so that there was a striking lack of uniformity in grading from district to district. Finally, there was little justification in attempting to grade agricultural lands in the fertile and accessible region of Kathmandu Valley on the same basis as those in the poorer agricultural areas of the hill regions. A grading system that failed to take into account such factors as location and altitude in a country like Nepal could hardly be expected to provide a

---

[31] Regmi, *Land Tenure and Taxation in Nepal*, I, 57–58.
[32] Law Ministry Records, "Sankhu Survey Regulations," 1976 (1919).
[33] Law Ministry Records, "Kathmandu Revenue Regulations," Shrawan 28, 1991 (August 12, 1934), sec. 40.
[34] Law Ministry Records, "Regulations for Talukdars in Bhaktapur," 1995 (1938), sec. 4.

satisfactory basis for an equitable land-tax assessment system.

TAX ASSESSMENTS ON *Khet* LANDS

The tax-assessment system on *Khet* lands that the Rana government gradually evolved in the revenue divisions of the hill region is set forth in chart 2. As this chart shows, tax assessments on *Khet* lands were either in kind or in cash. In-kind assessments were those made under the *Adhiya* and *Kut* systems. Assessments in cash, which contained no provision for remission in the event of crop failure or permanent damage to the lands through floods or landslides, were a result of the revenue arrangements made directly between the government and village headmen after the 1820s. Such contractual arrangements were occasionally made also for individual holdings in several districts, including those comprising Kathmandu Valley. These districts accordingly had tax assessments in both cash and kind. Simple cash assessments, on which remissions were permitted, were introduced in Pokhara and elsewhere in the western hill region in the course of reforms undertaken by the Rana government during the 1930s to simplify the system, but in the Karnali region they dated back to the period preceding the conquest of this area by the Gorkhalis.

Chart 2. Forms of Tax Assessment on *Khet* Lands in the Midland Region.

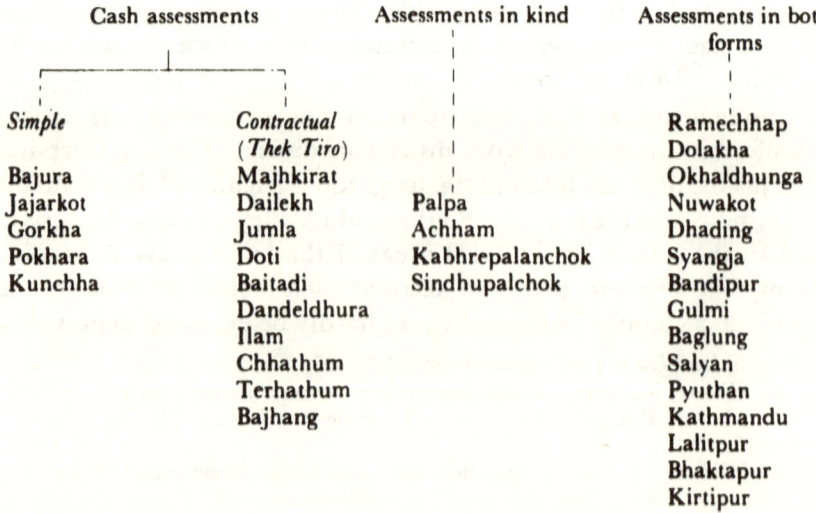

Cash assessments		Assessments in kind	Assessments in both forms
Simple	*Contractual* (*Thek Tiro*)		Ramechhap
			Dolakha
Bajura	Majhkirat		Okhaldhunga
Jajarkot	Dailekh	Palpa	Nuwakot
Gorkha	Jumla	Achham	Dhading
Pokhara	Doti	Kabhrepalanchok	Syangja
Kunchha	Baitadi	Sindhupalchok	Bandipur
	Dandeldhura		Gulmi
	Ilam		Baglung
	Chhathum		Salyan
	Terhathum		Pyuthan
	Bajhang		Kathmandu
			Lalitpur
			Bhaktapur
			Kirtipur

Tax assessments that were wholly or partly in kind generally assumed the form of paddy or wheat, or both. Two levies in cash were usually paid along with this in-kind assessment—*Ghiukhane* and *Chardam Theki*. The name *Ghiukhane* implies a tax on the dairy products of the farm; *Chardam Theki* probably represented a fee for confirmation of the peasants' right in the land every year. There were also a large number of cases, particularly in the revenue divisions of Kathmandu Valley, in which additional payments were due on *Khet* lands in the form of such commodities as straw, fuel wood, soybeans, curd, oil, brown sugar, brooms, and vegetables. In these revenue divisions, rice or semimilled paddy was occasionally payable instead of paddy. The tax-assessment system in Kathmandu Valley proved also to be very complex in that, although *Khet* lands by definition grow only such wet crops as paddy and wheat, assessments were occasionally made in the form of maize, millet, and other dry crops. In some instances a fixed levy in cash was payable in addition to paddy and the *Ghiukhane* levy. Indeed, the land-tax assessment system on *Khet* lands in the hill districts, particularly in Kathmandu, was characterized by a bewildering lack of uniformity at the end of the Rana period.[35]

Efforts toward Simplicity and Uniformity

The lack of uniformity in tax-assessment systems in the hill regions was further aggravated by the fact that there existed no definite rules regarding rates on newly reclaimed lands. The problem did not arise so long as taxes were collected at the rate of half of the gross produce, but the gradual obsolescence of that system made it necessary for the government to adopt an objective basis for tax-assessments on lands of this category. During the period from 1920 to 1934, at least three measures were adopted in this field on an experimental basis in specified districts or regions. During the early 1920s, regulations were promulgated according to which taxes on newly reclaimed and certain other categories of lands were fixed at one-sixth of the gross produce after a four-year exemption period.[36] These regulations are significant because the transition from one-half of the gross produce to one-sixth as the upper limit of land-tax assessment was rather abrupt. Obviously for this reason, the regulations do not seem to have been widely

---

[35] Regmi, I, 92–97, 102–05.
[36] Law Ministry Records, "Kathmandu Valley Survey Order," 1980 (1923), sec. 33.

applied. References to this system are found as recently as 1950,[37] but seldom do tax assessments appear to correspond to anything like one-sixth of the gross produce.

In 1934, therefore, the government prescribed specific tax-assessment rates for newly reclaimed lands in all midland districts, including Kathmandu Valley, where tax-assessments were mostly in kind.[38] These rates are shown in table 2. The importance attached to general geographical and economic conditions in determining the level of in-kind assessments is well illustrated by the difference between rates in Kathmandu Valley and those in the midlands. The estimated productivity per *ropani* of *Khet* land of *Abal* grade was identical at 3.5 *muris* of paddy in both cases, but the total assessment in Kathmandu was approximately 15 percent higher. Moreover, notwithstanding these uniform rates, actual payments were not uniform, because in-kind assessments were converted into cash for purposes of tax collection at different rates in different areas.

TABLE 2

TAX-ASSESSMENT RATES ON NEWLY RECLAIMED LANDS, 1934

Grade of land	Kathmandu Valley			Hill Districts	
	Paddy	Wheat	Ghiukhane	Paddy	Ghiukhane
	(*Pathis*)			(*Pathis*)	
Abal	16	3	R. 0.12	14	R. 0.08
Doyam	13	2	0.12	11	0.08
Sim	9	2	0.12	7	0.08
Chahar	6	–	0.12	5	0.08

Source: See chap. 8. n. 38.

The rates mentioned above were not applicable to districts where assessments were traditionally in cash. In those districts, newly reclaimed lands were assessed at rates prevalent on adjacent holdings.[39] This system not only enabled the government to fix tax-assessment

[37] Law Ministry Records, "Kathmandu Assessment Order," Aswin 8, 2007 (September 24, 1950).

[38] Law Ministry Records, "Sindhupalchok Revenue Regulations," 1991 (1934), sec. 40.

[39] Law Ministry Records, "Chhathum Survey Regulations," 1991 (1934), sec. 35. "For assessing taxes on newly reclaimed agricultural lands, a survey shall be conducted first according to local customs and traditions and tax-assessment rates shall then be determined on the basis of those prevailing on adjoining holdings." See also Government of Nepal, "Jagga Jamin Goshwara Ko" [On miscellaneous land matters], *Muluki Ain*, pt. III (Kathmandu: Gorkhapatra Press, 2009 [1952]), sec. 7, pp. 62–63.

rates at a level accepted by the local agricultural community, but also insured a certain degree of uniformity. Even then, difficulties arose because the rates at which taxes were collected on adjacent holdings were frequently themselves unequal and arbitrary.[40] The government seems to have taken note of these difficulties as early as 1901,[41] but the reconfirmation of the same system in regulations promulgated in 1934[42] appears to indicate that it was unable to explore any alternative means to standardize tax-assessment rates on newly reclaimed lands in districts where taxes were assessed and collected exclusively in cash.

COLLECTIONS IN CASH

Rana land-taxation policy was influenced to a considerable extent by the decline in the importance of *Jagir* land assignments during the early decades of the twentieth century. When any land was withdrawn from *Jagir* and converted into *Raikar*, the government was obliged to make arrangements for the collection of taxes thereon, a function that previously had been discharged by the *Jagirdar* himself for his own benefit. A change in the tenurial status of the land therefore also necessitated a change in the form of revenue collection. A government that was in the process of being modernized could not meet its requirements through in-kind revenue as individual *Jagirdars* had done. Arrangements were therefore made to collect taxes on *Raikar* lands in the hill districts, including Kathmandu, in cash where such taxes had previously been assessed and collected in kind. It should be noted that during the early 1840s, such factors as the desire of some *Jagirdars* to collect rents in cash rather than in the form of food grains, generally because of the difficulties of transportation, had led the government to prescribe collections of even *Jagir* revenue in cash.[43] The system of land-tax collection in cash, imposed on an in-kind tax-assessment system, rendered the system as a whole unduly complicated. An example may be cited to illustrate the nature of this complication. On newly cultivated *Khet* lands in Kathmandu, the official records listed the particulars of assessment as 16.3 *pathis* of paddy, 3.0 *pathis* of wheat, and R. 0.12 in cash per *ropani*, whereas actual collection was made in cash, for a total of Rs. 4.28.[44] It would have been much

[40] Law Ministry Records, "Sankhu Survey Regulations," 1976 (1919), sec. 9.
[41] "Report of the Majhkirat Janch Tahasil Office," 1958 (1901).
[42] Law Ministry Records, "Chhathum Survey Regulations," 1991 (1934).
[43] Regmi, *A Study in Nepali Economic History*, pp. 180–81.
[44] Regmi, *Land Tenure and Taxation in Nepal*, I, 107.

simpler to record the assessment in the form in which it was actually collected.

After 1933, the government initiated steps to abolish the in-kind assessment system in the hill regions, but this reform was introduced only in Pokhara, Kunchha, Jajarkot, and Gorkha by the end of the Rana regime in 1951.[45] Even while making arrangements for the collection of land tax in cash, however, the government was reluctant to abolish the in-kind tax-assessment system, at least in the beginning. One reason for this reluctance was the realization that payment in cash would create difficulties for peasants in the interior hill areas where market facilities were not always available. In the hill areas outside Kathmandu Valley, therefore, regulations prescribed that "people who want to pay land taxes in kind shall not be compelled to make payments in cash."[46] On the other hand, in Kathmandu Valley, where such facilities were more easily available, the government directed that "collections shall not be made in kind even if landowners so desire."[47] The rising prices of agricultural produce eventually made in-kind payments unprofitable everywhere. Yet another reason why the in-kind assessment system was retained was that the government reserved the right to make in-kind collections when needed to meet famine and other emergencies.[48]

Conversion Rates

In order that in-kind rent assessments might be paid in cash, it was necessary to fix conversion rates on an official basis. In the beginning, these rates were fixed every year in each district. This practice led to delay in collections, because the government was unable to fix rates well in advance of the date when payments were due, or to publicize them adequately. In 1910, therefore, the conversion rates were fixed on a long-term basis.[49] They were revised only twice, in 1934[50] and

---

[45]Ibid., p. 95.

[46]Law Ministry Records, "Sindhupalchok Revenue Regulations," 1991 (1934), sec. 31.

[47]Law Ministry Records, "Regulations for Talukdars in Bhaktapur," 1995 (1938), sec. 16.

[48]"Notification of the Department of Forests and Land Revenue," *Nepal Gazette*, vol. 2, no. 19, Poush 15, 2009 (December 29, 1952).

[49]Law Ministry Records, "Notification regarding Conversion Rates for In-Kind Land-Tax Assessments," 1967 (1910).

[50]Law Ministry Records, "Sindhupalchok Revenue Regulations," 1991 (1934), sec. 29.

1962,[51] before the commutation system itself was finally abolished in the hill districts in 1963[52] and in Kathmandu Valley in 1966.[53]

The conversion rates were fixed separately for each revenue division, and, in a few cases, for groups of villages, because prices of agricultural produce varied in different parts of the country. In other words, they reflected the level of such prices in each area or district at the time when they were determined. The conversion rate was thus 5 *pathis* of paddy per rupee in Kathmandu Valley, 10 *pathis* in Gorkha, and as much as 16 *pathis* in Achham. The highest rate, one *muri* of paddy per rupee, was fixed for Dolakha town. Conversion rates were similarly fixed also for other food grains and agricultural, dairy, forest, and cottage-industry products that were components of the land tax on *Khet* lands.[54]

The commutation of in-kind tax-assessments in the hill regions, including Kathmandu Valley, fully monetized the land-tax system on *Raikar* lands in all parts of the country. Inasmuch as the conversion rates remained more or less unchanged for about half a century, from 1910 to 1962, it mattered little to the ordinary *Raikar* landowner whether the tax he was paying had been assessed in cash or was a commuted form of an in-kind assessment.

The *Bijan* System

The lack of an objective basis of tax-assessment was conspicuous on *Pakho* lands in the hill regions, where the *Hale* system was generally prevalent. In the absence of measurement, the approximate estimations of size that the *Hale* system necessitated were seldom uniform. The subjective nature of the classification created additional complications. For example, in Chhathum, Dhankuta district, "Some *Hale* holdings contain more land than others, while in some cases a *Kodale* holding is larger than a *Hale*. Moreover, since the area of such holdings has not been determined, it is difficult to determine the veracity of complaints of encroachment upon adjoining holdings."[55] In view of

---

[51] *Nepal Gazette*, vol. 12, no. 17 (Extraordinary), Aswin 5, 2019 (September 21, 1962), pp. 6–7.

[52] Ibid., vol. 13, no. 10 (Extraordinary), Shrawan 32, 2020 (August 16, 1963).

[54] Regmi, I, 197–200, app. G.

[55] Law Ministry Records, "Chhathum Survey Regulations," 1995 (1938), sec. 17. According to a report from the western hill region, "A *Hale* pays a tax of Rs. 1.04 only but actually possesses ten to twelve *bighas* of land. He personally cultivates as much as he can and gives away the rest on rent. The same is true with regard to *Pates* and *Kodales* as well." Land Reform Commission, "Report on Land Tenure Conditions in the Western Hill Districts," mimeographed (Kathmandu: the Commission, 2010 [1953]), p. 1.

these defects of the *Hale* system, the government attempted to replace it gradually by the *Bijan* system, under which taxes on *Pakho* lands were assessed on the basis of the estimated quantity of seed maize needed for sowing. Because of administrative difficulties, this reform was implemented in only fifteen of the thirty revenue divisions in this region during the period from 1933 to 1948.[56] The *Bijan* system constituted an attempt to develop the tax-assessment system on *Pakho* lands on a more objective basis than that provided by the *Hale* system. Nevertheless, the subjective element was not altogether absent in *Bijan* tax assessment, for the ascertainment of the actual quantity of seed expected to be needed for sowing left considerable scope for the individual discretion of the settlement officer.

Reference to the practice of estimating the size of holdings on the basis of the quantity of seed needed for sowing is found also during the eighteenth century,[57] but it was first utilized as the basis of tax assessment only during the last decade of the nineteenth century, in Bajura[58] and Dandeldhura.[59] When the system was extended to other areas after 1933, the existing classification of *Pakho* holdings as *Hale* and *Kodale* was retained for purposes of *Bijan* tax assessment. Higher rates of *Bijan* tax were imposed on *Hale* holdings than on *Kodale* holdings per unit of seed estimated to be needed for sowing, obviously on the assumption that productivity and tax-paying capacity improve with size. In the eastern hill districts of Sindhupalchok, Kabhrepalanchok,[60] Dolakha, and Ramechhap,[61] an attempt was made to establish a more accurate correlation between tax assessment and productivity by prescribing lower rates in mountainous areas than in river valleys. In Bajura, Dandeldhura, Bajhang, and Baitadi districts, however, holdings were graded into different categories for purposes of *Bijan* tax-assessment,[62] although the criteria used for such grading are not clear.

The tax rates imposed under the *Bijan* system in Bajura and Dandel-

[56]Regmi, I, 87–91. In Ilam district, a proposal to introduce the *Bijan* system in 1937 was abandoned in the face of strong public opposition. Arrangements initiated in November 1950 to introduce the system in Nuwakot and Dhading were stalled by the political disturbances that occurred soon thereafter.

[57]"Land Grant to Paramanand Bhatta and Others on Kut Tenure," Magh Sudi 6, 1846 (January 1790).

[58]"Tax-Assessment Register for Bajura," 1953 (1896).

[59]"Tax-Assessment Register for Dadeldhura," 1953 (1896).

[60]"Tax-Assessment Registers for Sindhupalchok and Kabhrepalanchok," 2005 (1948).

[61]"Tax-Assessment Registers for Dolakha and Ramechhap," 2004 (1947).

[62]Regmi, I, 78–88.

dhura districts during the last decade of the nineteenth century varied in different areas, ranging from R. 0.18 to R. 0.37 per *pathi* of seed in Bajura, and from R. 0.12 to R. 0.30 in Dandeldhura. The rates imposed after 1933, however, in some eastern and western hill areas insured full uniformity at the district level. They ranged from R. 0.32 to Rs. 1.12 per *pathi* of seed in the eastern hills, and from R. 0.20 to R. 0.72 in the western. These rates appear to have been fixed on the basis of the existing aggregate assessment in the district under the *Hale* system. The *Bijan* system thus resulted in a consolidation of all existing taxes and levies on *Pakho* lands and homesteads.[63]

The *Bijan* system was not introduced in Kathmandu Valley. In that region, the *Hale* system was used only in the outlying areas. Terrain conditions being more favorable than elsewhere in the hill regions, the normal practice was to measure *Pakho* lands in the same manner as *Khet* lands and to assess taxes on the basis of the area. The form and level of tax assessments varied considerably. In Kathmandu, Lalitpur, and Kirtipur, tax assessment in the form of maize or millet was the most common. Taxes were payable also in the form of paddy in some cases, even though *Pakho* lands are supposed to have no irrigation facilities and hence are not suitable for the cultivation of rice. Often tax assessments assumed the form of a fixed sum in cash for the entire holding, without reference to the rate per unit of area. Indeed, tax systems on *Pakho* lands in Kathmandu Valley were much more varied than in the hill districts. Most of the cultivated area in this region was at one time under *Jagir* tenure, and the numerous cesses and levies exacted by *Jagirdars* were all included in the land tax when the lands were resumed by the state.[64]

Although the Rana government was unable to abolish the *Hale* system in all districts of the midlands region, it made an attempt at least to bring about uniformity in tax-assessment rates based on that system. This policy was first implemented in Ilam district in 1912, when the rates on *Hale*, *Pate*, and *Kodale* holdings were standardized at Rs. 2.50, Rs. 2.00, and Rs. 1.50 respectively. The rates were calculated by dividing the total amount of revenue collected on *Pakho* lands and homesteads through various taxes and levies by the existing number of holdings.[65] A similar measure was introduced in Sankhu in

[63] Ibid.
[64] Ibid., pp. 98-103.
[65] A reference to this reform measure in Ilam district is contained in Law Ministry Records, "Sankhu Tax-Assessment Order," 1979 (1922). The 1912 rates were reconfirmed during the 1937 revenue settlement in Ilam district. Law Ministry Records, "Ilam Tax-Assessment Order," 1994 (1937).

Kathmandu Valley in 1921, when the rates were fixed at Rs. 2.00, Rs. 1.50, and R. 1.00 for *Hale*, *Pate*, and *Kodale* holdings respectively.[66] These rates appear to have been made applicable in subsequent years to other areas also in Kathmandu Valley where *Pakho* lands had not been measured.[67] In 1934, another step was taken to introduce uniform tax-assessment rates under the *Hale* system, when holdings created through subdivision and fragmentation in the hill regions were made liable to pay R. 1.00, R. 0.75, and R. 0.50 for *Hale*, *Pate*, and *Kodale* respectively.[68]

Land-Tax Assessments in the Tarai

The crop-assessment system traditionally followed in the Tarai suffered from a number of defects, foremost among which was the opportunity it provided to the cultivator to deliberately downgrade his land by cultivating a low-tax crop. Pointing out the defects of this system, regulations promulgated for Morang district in 1913 stated:

> Previously, agricultural lands were classified according to the type of crop grown and taxes were assessed separately for each crop. The tax-assessment records were therefore very complicated. No consideration was paid to productivity, with the result that crops on which taxes were lower were grown even on lands that were suitable for the cultivation of more valuable crops. Such a practice was harmful both to the government and the people.[69]

This criticism did not note yet another defect of the crop-assessment system—the failure to make adjustments in tax-assessment rates if and when crops paying low rates were replaced by those paying higher

---

[66] Law Ministry Records, "Sankhu Tax-Assessment Order," 1979 (1922).

[67] Regmi, I, 98.

[68] Law Ministry Records, "Sindhupalchok Revenue Regulations," 1991 (1934), sec. 126(3). The rates were fixed at a lower level for subdivided and fragmented holdings on the ground that only the number of fragments, and not the total taxable area, had increased.

[69] Law Ministry Records, "Morang Survey Regulations," Marga 5, 1970 (November 20, 1913), sec. 27. Traditionally, the land tax in the Tarai districts was not a single item of payment, but comprised a multitude of cesses and levies. During the period from 1849 to 1857, several cesses and levies were abolished and the remaining ones were consolidated into a single payment. "Order regarding Abolition and Consolidation of Cesses and Levies on Lands in Tarai Districts," 1914 (1857); "Survey Regulations for Eastern Tarai Districts," 1918 (1861), sec. 8.

ones.[70] Indeed, the system was not based on actual productivity but on an ad hoc consideration of the nature and importance of the crop customarily grown on it at the time of the revenue settlement. The crop-assessment system was therefore gradually discarded in the Tarai districts after 1909. Nevertheless, assessments made under this system were retained on particular holdings or villages in Bara, Parsa, Sarlahi, Jhapa, and other districts,[71] although it is difficult to explain why.

After 1909, the nature of the crop grown was used as the basis for tax assessment in the eastern Tarai districts under a new system. Agricultural lands were first classified into the two categories of *Dhanahar* and *Bhith* for purposes of tax assessment, primarily according to the nature of the crops grown. *Dhanahar* thus meant lands on which such crops as rice, sugar cane, tobacco, jute, and oilseeds could be grown. *Bhith* included uncultivated and pasture lands, and lands suitable for the cultivation of maize, lentils, and the like.[72] The *Dhanahar-Bhith* system used in the eastern Tarai was thus roughly similar to the *Khet-Pakho* system of the hill districts.

Dhanahar lands were usually graded as *Abal*, *Doyam*, *Sim*, and *Chahar* in most areas of the eastern Tarai. On *Bhith* lands, however, this system of grading was followed only in the revenue divisions of Morang, Jhapa, Siraha, and Hanumannagar.[73] Notwithstanding the fact that agricultural lands are usually graded as *Abal*, *Doyam*, *Sim*, and *Chahar* in the hill regions also, the grading formulas adopted in the Tarai were more complex. They attached equal importance to such pragmatic considerations as land values, salability, location, and the nature of the crops that could be grown, along with physical factors such as terrain and the availability of irrigation facilities. In Bara, Parsa, Rautahat, and Sarlahi revenue divisions, for example, according to regulations promulgated in 1909, *Dhanahar* lands of *Abal* grade were defined as follows:

> At least three-fourths of the village enjoys irrigation facilities. The terrain is level, so that water once released stays for fifteen or twenty days. At least two-thirds of the total area is cultivable, and yields exceed

[70] In order to insure that revenue did not decline, peasants were not permitted, according to regulations promulgated in 1861, to replace high-tax crops by low-tax ones, except when the land was damaged. "Survey Regulations for Eastern Tarai Districts" (1861), sec. 17. But the system was not flexible enough to provide for improvements in productivity.

[71] Regmi, I, 107-08.

[72] Law Ministry Records, "Morang Survey Regulations," 1970 (1913), sec. 27.

[73] Regmi, I, 109-10.

40 maunds of paddy or 35 maunds of other crops throughout the year. Railway transport facilities are available,[74] so as to insure the quick disposal of agricultural produce and compensate occasional damage because of drought. At least three-fourths of the total cultivated area can be sold at a price exceeding Rs. 60 per *bigha*. Even if irrigation facilities are not available, such crops as tobacco, opium, castor beans, and vegetables can be grown, so that the total return is not less than what the land would have fetched had it been under paddy.[75]

This system of grading was not introduced throughout the Tarai region. In several areas of Mahottari district, for instance, *Dhanahar* lands were not graded at all. In the western Tarai, grading of agricultural lands for purposes of tax assessment appears to have been limited to the revenue divisions of Sheoraj, Khajahani, and Palhi-Majhkhand.[76] In the revenue division of Kailali-Kanchanpur, land-tax assessments were based on whether lands were owned by "common" or "respectable" people, with higher rates for the former.[77] Such a policy may have been adopted in order to attract "respectable" settlers to this area, which was once notorious for its malaria and for the shelter it provided to runaway slaves and criminals. In the inner Tarai, classification or grading of agricultural lands was the exception rather than the rule. For instance, a uniform rate of Rs. 1.25 per *bigha* was charged in Makwanpur irrespective of the class or grade of the land. A system of grading was introduced, and land-tax assessment rates were revised accordingly, only in 1946.[78]

Classification of agricultural lands as *Dhanahar* and *Bhith*, and their grading as *Abal*, *Doyam*, *Sim*, and *Chahar*, were not the only way whereby the government attempted to establish a correlation between estimated productivity and tax assessments in the Tarai region. In some eastern Tarai districts, the tax-assessment system was further refined by recognizing three east-west zones. The northernmost

---

[74] The reference is to railway facilities in India for the export of Nepal's foodgrains. In 1907, the Indian railway network was extended to Raxaul, which adjoins Parsa district in Nepal. Prakash C. Lohani, "Industrial Policy: The Problem Child of History and Planning in Nepal," in Pashupati Shumshere J. B. Rana and Kamal P. Malla, eds., *Nepal in Perspective* (Kathmandu: Center for Economic Development and Administration, 1973), p. 204.

[75] Law Ministry Records, "Survey Regulations for Bara, Parsa, Rautahat, and Sarlahi," Marga 28, 1966 (December 13, 1909).

[76] Regmi, I, 111-12.

[77] Kumarichok (Audit Office) Records, "Tax-Assessment Registers for Kailali and Kanchanpur," 1983 (1926).

[78] Law Ministry Records, "Makwanpur Tax-Assessment Order," 2003 (1946).

strip of the eastern Tarai region, along the point where it met the foothills of the Churia range, was recognized as the *Sir* zone, and the southern most strip, adjoining India, as the *Bhatha* zone. The intermediate strip was then recognized as the *Majh* zone.[79] Tax-assessment rates were lowest in the *Sir* zone on account of such circumstances as the depredations of wild animals, and progressively higher in the *Majh* and *Bhatha* zones, but usually *Majh* and *Bhatha* were treated on an equal footing for tax-assessment purposes.[80] A similar consideration governed the distinction made for purposes of tax assessment in Dang-Deukhuri and elsewhere in the inner Tarai region between lands situated in the hill zone and those in the plains zone.[81]

The level of tax assessments fixed in the Tarai districts after 1909 were thus based on several considerations of an empirical nature, such as the general economic condition of the district, transport and communication facilities, climate and other geographical features, and, not least important, the aggregate amount of taxation previously collected. Due consideration also was paid to local public opinion. As regulations promulgated for Morang district in 1913 stated:

> Previously, tax-assessment rates were fixed before settlement operations were started, with the result that the rates became exorbitant for some and low for others. Settlement officers shall now recommend, in consultation with local government officials, prominent persons, landowners, and *Jimidars*, such rates as will not cause loss to the government, nor hardship to the people. The assessments shall then be fixed as approved by the government.[82]

The system was therefore substantially the same as that followed in the adjoining areas of British India during the latter half of the nineteenth century.[83]

[79] Landon, *Nepal*, II, 207.

[80] "Survey Regulations for Eastern Tarai Districts," Marga Badi 6, 1918 (November 1861); Regmi, I, 109.

[81] Law Ministry Records, "Dang-Deukhuri Tax-Assessment Order," 1970 (1913).

[82] Law Ministry Records, "Morang Survey Regulations," 1970 (1913), sec. 28.

[83] For instance, in the adjoining United Provinces, the settlement officer was required to take the following factors into consideration for ascertaining the net produce of the land for purposes of tax assessment: "(i) The return of the cultivated and cultivable area of the village, of irrigated land and the different kinds of soils; (ii) the past experience of settlement officers and collectors, and the price realized, if the village was brought to sale; (iii) the gross rentals of the village under settlements as compared with other villages in the same tract; (iv) the character of the people, style of cultivation, possibility of improvements and the state of market for the produce; lastly, (v) the opinion of the *Pargana* officers and the estimate of the neighbouring *Zamindars*." B. R. Misra, *Land Revenue Policy in the United Provinces* (Banaras: Nand Kishore and Bros., 1942), p. 76.

The Rana government was reluctant to take any step that might directly alienate the peasantry. It therefore seldom made drastic changes in the existing level of tax assessments. For instance, during a revenue settlement in Bardiya district in 1949 it declared that the sole aim of revenue settlements was to "benefit the people and tax the land according to its productivity" and not to increase the revenue.[84] Similarly, in Saptari district in the same year: "The existing situation would justify an increase in land-tax assessment rates. But such a measure will create hardships for the people and it has therefore been decided not to make any increase in existing rates."[85] At times, the government even refused to sanction the increases recommended by settlement officers.[86] Revenue settlements often meant nothing more than the apportionment of the aggregate revenue in each division among the existing households, so that the burden on the peasantry remained unchanged.

Nevertheless, the Rana government was not averse to increasing revenue from the land whenever this could be done without arousing too much public protest or opposition. Indeed, it appears to have occasionally resorted to, or at least condoned, various questionable practices in order to maximize revenue, even while maintaining tax-assessment rates at relatively low levels. In chapter 7, we have already referred to the manner in which taxes were extorted from *Jimidars* even on nonexistent lands. Settlement officers often tended to upgrade lands, although downgrading was not permitted in the course of subsequent settlements.[87] The result in such cases was that the landowner was compelled to pay a higher tax than was actually justified by the productivity of his land. No remission was granted if any holding was found in the course of subsequent revenue settlements to contain less than the area actually recorded. On the other hand, the government did not hesitate to increase the assessment if the actual area was found to be in excess of the recorded area. Regulations relating to tax assessment on *Pakho* holdings specifically prescribed that "existing

---

[84]Law Ministry Records, "Tax-Assessment Order for Bardiya," 2006 (1949).

[85]Law Ministry Records, "Tax-Assessment Order for Saptari and Udayapur," 2006 (1949).

[86]In 1940, for instance, settlement officers recommended an increase in the total tax assessment in Makwanpur district to Rs. 3,705.96, but the government contented itself with Rs. 2,390.90. Law Ministry Records, "Tax-Assessment Order for Makwanpur," 1997 (1940).

[87]Law Ministry Records, "Bardiya Survey Regulations," Kartik 19, 2003 (November 4, 1946), sec. 21.

taxes shall on no account be reduced."[88]

Efforts to increase land revenue through higher rates of land taxation were limited for the most part to the Tarai. The reasons for such a policy are not difficult to understand. Particularly after the mid-nineteenth century, the importance of the Tarai in the economy of Nepal, which was already considerable, was augmented by such factors as the development of railway facilities in the adjoining areas of India, the increase in the volume of exports of agricultural commodities, including such cash crops as jute, and the tenurial reforms that made property rights in the land more secure. The Rana government could scarcely be expected to relinquish the financial benefits of these developments. In contrast, the revenue potential of the midlands remained more or less static and was governed mainly by demographic factors.

Land-Tax Rates in 1951

At the end of the Rana period, land-tax rates in the midlands were at times as low as R. 0.32 per *ropani* of rice land in Bajhang, whereas the highest rate, fixed in Gorkha district in 1938, was Rs. 3.00.[89] The rates were higher in Kathmandu, and highest in Bhaktapur district, where they amounted to Rs. 6.62, Rs. 4.65, Rs. 3.10, and Rs. 1.74 per *ropani* of rice lands of *Abal, Doyam, Sim,* and *Chahar* grades respectively. In the Tarai districts, the rates ranged from about R. 0.75 per *bigha* in a few cases in Sheoraj district to Rs. 15.00 in some areas of Mahottari district. In the inner Tarai districts, the rate seldom went above Rs. 7.97 per *bigha*; the lowest rate was about Rs. 1.58 (and, at least in a few cases in Surkhet, it was as low as R. 0.44). Inasmuch as recent land-tax measures in the Tarai region are based on the existing level of tax assessments, as we shall describe in detail in the next section, it appears necessary to give the figures of land-tax assessments on *Dhanahar* lands most commonly followed in some revenue divisions of the Tarai at the end of the Rana period. These data are shown in table 3.

Rice lands in Kathmandu Valley were the most heavily taxed in the kingdom, followed by the hill region and the Tarai, in that order. On the basis of the rate charged on rice land of *Abal* grade in Bhaktapur, Rs. 6.62 per *ropani*, the amount payable per *bigha* in the Tarai would exceed Rs. 87.00, whereas the highest rate charged in the agriculturally

[88] Law Ministry Records, "Sindhupalchok Revenue Regulations," 1934, sec. 101 (1).
[89] This section is based on Regmi, I, 85–122.

TABLE 3
LAND-TAX RATES IN THE TARAI AND INNER TARAI DISTRICTS
(PER *bigha* OF *Dhanahar* LAND)

Region and district	Grade of land			
	Abal Rs.	Doyam Rs.	Sim Rs.	Chahar Rs.
Eastern Tarai				
Morang	9.00	8.00	6.00	4.50
Jhapa	9.09	8.09	6.09	4.59
Siraha	11.44	10.26	9.51	6.00
Mahottari	15.00	14.25	13.50	—
Parsa	10.50	9.75	8.75	—
Rautahat	11.25	9.75	8.75	—
Western Tarai				
Sheoraj	9.28	9.03	8.28	5.43
Khajahani	10.59	9.34	9.09	8.09
Kailali	8.25	7.12	5.25	·3.75
Kanchanpur	7.50	6.50	4.50	3.00

Note: Land taxes in the Tarai districts, and in several areas of the inner Tarai and hill districts, formerly were assessed and collected in Indian currency. In 1956, the government of Nepal started making collections in Nepali currency. Existing assessments were subsequently converted into Nepali currency at the rate of Indian Rs. 100 to Nepali Rs. 150. The figures given in the table are in Nepali rupees calculated at that rate. Mahesh C. Regmi, *Land Tenure and Taxation in Nepal* (Berkeley and Los Angeles: University of California Press, 1963-68), I, 191-92, app. E.

rich district of Mahottari in the eastern Tarai was Rs. 15.00. Even the lowest grade of *Khet* lands in the poor hill district of Gorkha paid as much as Rs. 1.20 per *ropani*, or Rs. 15.90 per *bigha*. Accordingly, the main thrust of recent reform measures has been toward country-wide uniformity with regard to both grading of lands and tax assessment.

STANDARDIZATION OF GRADING FORMULAS

In 1963, the government of Nepal enacted legislation standardizing the formulas for the grading of taxable lands throughout the country. The traditional categories of *Dhanahar* or *Khet* and *Bhith* or *Pakho* were retained, and *Dhanahar* or *Khet* lands were divided into the four grades of *Abal, Doyam, Sim,* and *Chahar*, as usual:

> On *Abal* land, rice is usually sown or transplanted, irrigation facilities are always available by means of irrigation channels, and the soil does not contain sand or gravel and is of the best quality and moist, so that two crops can be grown in a year.
> On *Doyam* land, artificial irrigation facilities are not always available,

and crops are sown with the help of rainfall. The soil does not contain sand or gravel, but is of good quality. Two crops can be grown in a year.

On *Sim* land, irrigation facilities are available neither through irrigation channels nor through inundation. Cultivation is dependent solely on rainfall. The soil is slightly sandy, and only one crop can be grown in a year.

On *Chahar* land, the soil is sandy, gravelly, or dry, and crops are sown only with the help of rainfall. Water dries up quickly. The land is situated at a high level, or is terraced. Only one crop can be cultivated in a year. The land is under water for a long time, and rice can be cultivated only in intermittent years.[90]

Bhith or *Pakho* lands were similarly divided into the three grades of *Abal, Doyam,* and *Sim*:

On *Abal* land of *Bhith* or *Pakho* category, the soil is of good quality and fertile, and instead of rice, only dry rice, maize, millet, mustard, rape, and other similar crops can be cultivated.

On *Doyam* land, the soil contains sand or gravel and is of inferior quality. The land has a steep gradient. Crops can be sown only at intervals of one or two years. Only maize, millet, dry rice, mustard, rape, and other similar crops, but not rice, can be grown.

On *Sim* land, the soil is sandy or gravelly. The land has a steep gradient or is situated on a slope, so that plows cannot be used. Crops can be grown only at intervals of one or two years. Instead of rice, only maize, millet, dry rice, mustard, rape, and other similar crops can be sown, or the land is covered with snow for a brief period.[91]

These formulas are essentially the same as those already in use in Kathmandu Valley and elsewhere in the hill region. The only notable difference is that they omit estimates of yields, although taking the multicropping potential of the land into consideration. The grounds on which we regarded the old formulas as unsatisfactory therefore still remain valid. An additional point of criticism stems from the attempt to impose standard grading formulas in regions with such great diversities of terrain, climate, and altitude as Kathmandu Valley, the hill regions, and the Tarai. Moreover, no importance has been accorded such factors as proximity to market areas and availability of

[90] Ministry of Law and Justice, "Jagga Nap Janch Ain" [Land (survey and measurement) act], *Nepal Gazette* (Extraordinary), Chaitra 30, 2019 (April 12, 1963), vol. 12, no. 44a, sec. 10, as amended on Kartik 6, 2024 (October 23, 1967) and Aswin 5, 2029 (September 21, 1972).
[91] Ibid.

transport facilities. It therefore seems justified to conclude that, at least in the Tarai, the new grading formulas have taken away much of the sophistication that the land-tax assessment system had acquired during the early years of the twentieth century.

Reorganization of the Land-Tax Assessment System

Measures to reorganize the land-tax assessment system were started only in 1962.[92] Initially, the purpose was to increase revenue from the land, but soon uniform levels of land taxation on a regional basis also became a goal of official land-taxation policy. In the Tarai and inner Tarai districts, all existing assessments were accordingly increased by 25 percent,[93] leaving the existing inequalities unaffected. The following year, the government decided to standardize land-tax rates in this region at specific levels. The rate was accordingly increased to Rs. 15 per *bigha* on all lands where less than Rs. 10, inclusive of the 25 percent increase made in 1962, was payable per *bigha*, and to Rs. 20 on lands of other categories.[94] Two years later, in 1964, the rate was lowered to Rs. 10 per *bigha* in the hill regions of the inner *Tarai* districts.[95] There were thus only three schedules of rates in the Tarai and inner Tarai districts—Rs. 10, Rs. 15, and Rs. 20 per *bigha*. These rates were further increased to Rs. 18, Rs. 26, and Rs. 34 respectively in 1966[96] and to Rs. 27, Rs. 39, and Rs. 51 in 1968.[97]

In the hill districts and Kathmandu Valley, land-tax assessment rates were increased by 10 percent in 1962,[98] and again by 40 percent over the pre-1962 level in the following year. The conversion rate was standardized at five *pathis* per rupee in all districts where tax assessments were in kind.[99] Between 1963 and 1966, however, all in-kind tax-assessments on *Khet* lands in the hill districts[100] and Kathmandu Valley[101]

[92]Proposals to increase land-tax rates by 10 percent in 1955 and by 100 percent during 1958–59 had to be abandoned in the face of public opposition. *Nepal Gazette*, vol. 4, no. 25, Magh 18, 2011 (January 31, 1955); vol. 4, no. 28, Falgun 10, 2011 (February 21, 1955); vol. 8, no. 7 (Extraordinary), Jestha 2, 2015 (May 15, 1958); and vol. 9, no. 1 (Extraordinary), Baisakh 10, 2016 (April 22, 1959).
[93]Ibid., vol. 11, no. 40B (Extraordinary), Magh 26, 2018 (February 8, 1962).
[94]Ibid., vol. 12, no. 17 (Extraordinary), Aswin 5, 2019 (September 21, 1962).
[95]Ibid., vol. 14, no. 15 (Extraordinary), Aswin 17, 2021 (October 21, 1964).
[96]Ibid., vol. 16, no. 17 (Extraordinary), Shrawan 31, 2023 (August 15, 1966).
[97]Ibid., vol. 17, no. 41A (Extraordinary), Chaitra 26, 2024 (April 8, 1968).
[98]Ibid., vol. 12, no. 17 (Extraordinary), Aswin 5, 2019 (September 21, 1962).
[99]Ibid., vol. 13, no. 10 (Extraordinary), Shrawan 32, 2020 (August 16, 1963).
[100]Ibid., vol. 16, no. 17A (Extraordinary), Shrawan 31, 2023 (August 15, 1966).
[101]Ibid., vol. 14, no. 15 (Extraordinary), Aswin 17, 2021 (October 2, 1964).

were abolished, and the rates were standardized at Rs. 2.60, Rs. 2.20, Rs. 1.80, and Rs. 1.40 per *ropani* of lands of *Abal*, *Doyam*, *Sim*, and *Chahar* grades respectively. The rate on ungraded lands was fixed at Rs. 2.40 per *ropani* in 1964,[102] but reduced to Rs. 1.80 in the hill districts and Rs. 2.12 in Kathmandu Valley in 1968.[103] On *Pakho* lands, after a series of experiments, the rates were fixed at Rs. 4.50, Rs. 2.25, and Rs. 1.13 in Kathmandu Valley and Rs. 3.30, Rs. 1.65, and R. 0.83 in the hill districts for *Hale*, *Pate*, and *Kodale* holdings respectively, and at R. 0.11 per *mana* of seed under the *Bijan* system.[104]

TABLE 4

CURRENT RATES OF LAND TAXATION IN DIFFERENT REGIONS
(PER *ropani*)

Region	Grade of land			
	Abal	Doyam	Sim	Chahar
	Rs.	Rs.	Rs.	Rs.
Tarai and Inner Tarai	3.84	3.31	2.64	2.03
Kathmandu Valley	3.92	3.32	2.72	2.12
Midlands:				
Khet	3.00	2.60	2.20	1.80
Pakho	2.00	1.50	1.00	0.50

Note: The figures are from *Nepal Gazette*, vol. 16, no. 13A (Extraordinary), Ashadh 16, 2023 (July 10, 1966), except for the *Pakho* category, *Chahar* land, which is from *Nepal Rajpatra* [Nepal Gazette], vol. 22, no. 15D (Extraordinary), Ashadh 23, 2029 (July 6, 1972).

In areas where cadastral survey operations have been completed, land-tax assessment rates have been standardized as shown in table 4. This means that land-tax assessment rates have been fixed at a more or less equal level in Kathmandu Valley and the Tarai and a slightly lower level in the hill districts. But although the general level of assessments has been reduced by approximately half in Kathmandu Valley, it has been slightly increased in most of the districts of the hill region. In the Tarai and the inner Tarai districts, the percentage of increase is higher, ranging from about 300 to 1,400 percent. Another significant aspect of the new land-tax assessment system is that the traditional distinction between *Dhanahar* or *Khet* lands and *Bhith* or

---

[102] *Nepal Rajapatra*, vol. 17, no. 41A (Extraordinary), Chaitra 26, 2024 (April 8, 1968).
[103] Ibid.
[104] Ibid.

Pakho lands has been abolished in the Tarai regions and Kathmandu Valley. There are only four schedules in the new system for agricultural lands of *Abal, Doyam, Sim,* and *Chahar* grades (even after the completion of cadastral survey operations). It is therefore incomprehensible why the survey regulations should have made a distinction between *Dhanahar* or *Khet* and *Bhith* or *Pakho* lands and devised formulas for distinguishing between as many as seven grades of land.

The official justification of the new measures stated:

> Current rates of land-tax assessment were not in keeping with the times. They were highest in Kathmandu Valley, followed by the hill region. But the hill region is inaccessible, and agriculture there is an arduous undertaking. Multicropping is not possible because of natural factors, while transport facilities and markets for the sale of agricultural produce are lacking. It would therefore be equitable if land-tax assessment rates were higher in Kathmandu Valley than in the Tarai and the hill region. It is the policy of His Majesty's Government to introduce uniform rates of land-tax assessment all over the kingdom. This measure will reduce land-tax revenue from Kathmandu Valley by approximately 50 percent, but remove the great hardships so far undergone by landowners in this region. It will also put an end to the age-old inequities prevailing in respect to land-tax assessment rates, progressively reduce economic inequalities, and insure social justice.[105]

It is difficult to believe, however, that equity will be assured by introducing uniform land-tax assessment rates on lands of the same quality all over the kingdom without giving due consideration to other economic and geographical factors. Uniformity alone seldom contributes to equity.

PANCHAYAT-DEVELOPMENT TAXATION

Attempts have been made in recent years to mold the land-tax assessment system according to the principle of administrative decentralization by replacing the traditional land tax by the Panchayat-development tax. The objective of this innovation is to "mobilize local resources for local development, accelerate the pace of economic development by vitalizing local Panchayats, and make the land-tax assessment system more equitable." An unusual feature of this tax is that it is collected from landed interests of all categories: owner-

---

[105] *Nepal Gazette*, vol. 16, no. 13A (Extraordinary), Ashadh 16, 2023 (July 10, 1966).

cultivators, nonworking landowners, and tenants. The tax is collected at the rate of 6 percent of the total yield of the main crop from owner-cultivators and at 15 percent of the rent from landowners. Tenants are required to pay this tax at 3 percent or 5 percent of the share accruing to them, depending upon whether rents are above or below 50 percent of the main crop. These in-kind assessments are converted into cash at rates prescribed by the local Panchayat every year. Local Panchayats are responsible also for assessment and collection, but they are allowed to retain only 55 percent of the proceeds. The central government appropriates 35 percent, and the balance of 10 percent goes to the district authorities.[106]

The Panchayat-development tax is thus only a variant of the old in-kind land-tax of the hill region. The in-kind tax-assessment system has been abolished in the hill region, but reintroduced in the form of the Panchayat-development tax. We have seen above what factors led to the gradual conversion of in-kind tax assessments into cash. There is every possibility that the old sequence of events will be repeated. The administrative difficulties involved in the assessment and collection of the tax are formidable. Collection of the tax has been difficult, particularly from tenants, whose tenancy rights are nontransferable and hence cannot be auctioned like landownership rights for the recovery of arrears.[107] Moreover, the experience gained in some areas of Jhapa district during the past few years shows that the objectives of Panchayat-development taxation have not been fully realized. There is evidence that land revenue has even gone down as a result of this measure, at least in a few cases. For instance, at Chandragadhi in Jhapa district, land revenue amounted to Rs. 153,585 before the introduction of the Panchayat-development tax. The tax yielded only Rs. 144,433 in this area during 1971/72, of which no more than Rs. 50,551 (about 35 percent) accrued to the government.[108] As a result, Panchayat-development taxation is still an experiment confined to a few areas of Jhapa and Morang districts in the eastern Tarai region.

Tax on Agricultural Income

Both the old land tax and the Panchayat-development tax are

[106]Ministry of Law and Justice, "Panchayat Vikas ra Jagga Kar Ain, 2022" [Panchayat development and land taxation act, 1965], ibid., vol. 15, no. 14 (Extraordinary), Bhadra 14, 2022 (August 30, 1965).
[107]Ram Bahadur, "Panchayat Development and Land Tax vs. Fixed Rent," *Rising Nepal*, April 16, 1973.
[108]Ibid.

assessed per unit of area, and consequently take no account of the size of the holding or the income of the farmer. A number of efforts have been made in recent years to introduce an element of progression in Nepal's land-tax system, but so far with little success.

In 1959, the government of Nepal imposed a progressive surcharge on holdings that exceeded 25 *bighas* in area or which paid land tax exceeding Rs. 250, whichever the taxpayer preferred.[109] The aim of this measure was to break up large estates rather than to bring in additional revenue. However, it simply led to partition and subdivision, and hence was of little benefit to the peasants.[110] The tax was therefore abolished in 1962.[111] The following year, legislation was enacted prescribing agricultural income as one of the components of general income for the purpose of assessing a progressive income tax.[112] This measure was repealed in 1966 subsequent to a devaluation of the Indian rupee which led to a steep fall in agricultural incomes.[113]

The tax on agricultural incomes was revived in a slightly different form in 1973. Under the new arrangements, income from agriculture will be calculated at rates ranging from Rs. 150 to Rs. 600 per *bigha* according to the grade. Income from holdings in excess of five *bighas* will then be added to income from other sources for the purpose of income-tax assessment.[114] Although the fixed rates of net income from agriculture may be expected to simplify administrative procedure to

---

[109] Ministry of Law, "Arthik Ain, 2016" [Finance act, 1959], *Nepal Gazette*, vol. 9, no. 19 (Extraordinary), Poush 1, 2016 (December 15, 1959), sec. 6, p. 236, and schedule 3, p. 282. According to an official clarification of this measure, "It shall depend on the choice of the taxpayer whether to obtain exemption for 25 *bighas* or for a total land-tax payment of Rs. 250. If the taxpayer prefers exemption for 25 *bighas*, no surcharge shall be collected even if the total tax due on this area exceeds Rs. 250. If he prefers exemption on the basis of a total land-tax payment of Rs. 250, no surcharge shall be collected even if his holding exceeds 25 *bighas*." "Notification of the Department of Land Revenue," *Gorkhapatra*, Bhadra 27, 2017 (September 12, 1960).

[110] Tripurvar Singh Pradhan, "Jagga Karko Natija" [The effect of land taxation], *Nepal Pukar*, Ashadh 15, 2017 (June 29, 1960). A royal proclamation issued on January 5, 1961, stated: "Surcharges on land tax were imposed in order to insure distribution of land among peasants, although these were not expected to yield much revenue. However, the measure produced just the opposite effect." *Nepal Gazette*, vol. 10, no. 20 (Extraordinary), Poush 22, 2017 (January 5, 1961).

[111] Ministry of Law and Justice, "Arthik Ain, 2019" (Finance act, 1962), *Nepal Gazette*, vol. 12, no. 17 (Extraordinary), Aswin 5, 2019 (September 21, 1962), sec. 7.

[112] Ministry of Law and Justice, "Nepal Ayakar Ain, 2019 (Nepal income-tax act, 1963)," ibid., vol. 12 no. 44B (Extraordinary), Chaitra 30, 2019 (April 12, 1963), sec. 2 (b, h).

[113] Ibid., vol. 16, no. 13A (Extraordinary), Ashadh 26, 2023 (July 10, 1966).

[114] *Nepal Rajapatra*, vol. 24, no. 15A (Extraordinary), Ashadh 21, 2031 (July 5, 1974).

a considerable extent, it is still too early to judge the effectiveness of this measure. In any case, the experiment involves no risk to the regular income from land taxation.

Recent land-tax measures have helped the government of Nepal to increase its revenue from the land to a considerable extent. In 1950-51, revenue from *Raikar* land amounted to Rs. 11.3 million.[115] By 1970-71 this figure had reached Rs. 76 million,[116] mainly as a result of the abolition of the *Birta* and *Jagir* systems and higher rates of land taxation. In view of the importance of land revenue in the fiscal system of Nepal, it is scarcely to be wondered at that the government's commitment to uniformity and equity in the field of land taxation should lack conviction, and that it should be proceeding so warily in the implementation of such newfangled experiments as Panchayat-development taxation.

[115] *Nepal Gazette*, vol. 1, no. 26, Magh 21, 2008 (February 3, 1952).
[116] *Nepal Rajapatra*, vol. 22, no. 15D (Extraordinary), Ashadh 23, 2029 (July 6, 1972).

Chapter 9

LABOR SERVICES AND LANDOWNERSHIP

In chapter 8 we dealt with the form and level of the taxes paid by owners of *Raikar* lands in different parts of the country. We saw that payments on such lands were made in kind in most of the hill districts until around the end of the nineteenth century and were gradually commuted into cash. Such in-kind payments were almost in the nature of rents, and were collected by the state in its capacity of landlord. In the same capacity, the state also exacted compulsory and unpaid labor services from cultivators on *Raikar* lands, and on *Raj Guthi* lands and *Kipat* lands owned by communities other than Limbu. These labor services were known as *Rakam*. The majority of cultivators on lands of these categories in the hill districts, including Kathmandu Valley, were required to discharge both fiscal and labor obligations in order to retain their landholding rights.

Origin of the *Rakam* System

The right of the state to exact compulsory, unpaid labor from its subjects for public purposes has traditionally been recognized in Nepal.[1] They were taken into the army, employed in munitions factories, or forced to work as porters for the transportation of military stores. The government also impressed their services to construct and repair forts, bridges, and irrigation channels, reclaim waste lands, capture wild elephants, and supply fuel wood, charcoal, fodder, and other materials required by the royal household. In fact, under this system, which was known as *Jhara*, people could be employed

---

[1]For instance, according to regulations promulgated by King Srinivas Malla (1667-85) of Lalitpur in 1672, compulsory and unpaid labor was utilized to construct bridges and battlements, as well as during war. Dhanabajra Bajracharya, "Malla Kalma Desharakshako Vyavastha ra Tyasprati Prajako Kartavya" [The national-defense system during the Malla period and the obligations of the people], *Purnima*, I, no. 2 (Shrawan 1, 2021 [July 16, 1964]), 31.

without wages in any manner required by the government.[2]

In order to insure that the onerous and gratuitous character of *Jhara* services should not alienate the peasantry, the government of Nepal started providing *Jhara* workers with special facilities of a fiscal and tenurial nature. *Jhara* workers were granted full or partial exemption from the payment of taxes due on homesteads, although their obligation to pay rents or taxes on rice lands remained unaffected. They were also protected from eviction from the lands being cultivated by them so long as they made the prescribed payments and performed the prescribed labor services. Such fiscal and tenurial facilities appear to have long been available to *Jhara* workers. For instance, in 1799, the government of Nepal assigned the services of 88 households at Khokana village in Lalitpur district for the daily supply of fodder and fuel wood to the royal stables. It then directed that these households should not be evicted from the rice lands that they had been cultivating on a taxable basis, and that 50 percent exemption from homestead and other levies should be granted to them.[3]

Obviously, such facilities and benefits could be provided only when the services rendered by *Jhara* workers were regular and specific. The general labor obligations due under the *Jhara* system were therefore commuted whenever possible to specific services to be rendered on a regular basis by the inhabitants of a specified village or area. The system was then known as *Rakam*. Whereas the labor supply required for the construction of roads or the repair of bridges was obtained under the *Jhara* system, *Rakam* services included the supply of fuel wood and charcoal for governmental establishments and the transportation of mail. In other words, *Jhara* labor was impressed for nonrecurring purposes, and *Rakam* supplied regular needs. Under the *Rakam* system, the services of the inhabitants of specified villages or areas were assigned on a regular basis for the performance of labor according to the requirements of the government, and the lands being cultivated by them were converted into *Rakam* tenure.

The imposition of *Rakam* obligations did not of itself create a new form of land tenure. The conversion into *Rakam* tenure of *Raikar* or *Raj Guthi* lands held by *Rakam* workers, and, occasionally, the allotment of additional lands to them, represented essentially administrative measures aimed at insuring the continuity of *Rakam* services

---

[2] Regmi, *A Study in Nepali Economic History*, pp. 103-9.
[3] "Order regarding Supply of Fodder from Khokana," Bhadra Sudi 10, 1856 (September 1799).

and the stability of the *Rakam* population. Records of lands of various categories held by *Rakam* workers were compiled during 1854–56, 1882–83, and finally in 1895–96. The imposition of *Rakam* obligations on a de novo basis appears to have been practically discontinued after the beginning of the twentieth century. It may be presumed that the area under *Rakam* land tenure remained virtually unchanged after 1895–96. Lands acquired subsequently by *Rakam* workers were not registered under *Rakam* tenure, as no arrangements existed to maintain records of *Rakam* lands on a current basis.[4]

Developments During the Rana Period

The traditional pattern of *Rakam* obligations as described above underwent considerable changes under the Rana regime. Technological, administrative, and economic developments led to the obsolescence of several *Rakam* functions and the expansion of several others. The modernization of the Nepali army, which made it almost wholly dependent on extraneous sources for supplies of arms and equipment, dealt a virtual deathblow to the defense industry. Similarly, *Rakam* labor utilized in gunpowder factories was no longer needed after machinery was introduced around 1888.[5] These developments, however, did not necessarily result in the contraction of the *Rakam* system. Inasmuch as *Rakam* obligations were compulsory and gratuitious, the government could hardly be expected to abolish them readily.

Rakam services were gradually diverted to meet the personal needs of members of the Rana family. In 1866, some *Rakam* workers complained: "During the Nepal-Tibet war, we transported arms and military equipment. This year, we have been ordered to transport timber for the construction of a palace."[6] Moreover, supplies of fuel wood and charcoal under the *Rakam* system were diverted to Rana households. To cite another instance, in 1860 mail carriers operating on the Thankot-Kathmandu route became redundant because new forms of mail transport were introduced. They were therefore used as porters for transporting goods during tours and hunting expeditions undertaken by the king or the Rana prime minister.[7] Instead of arms

[4] Regmi, *Land Tenure and Taxation in Nepal*, III, 69.
[5] "Silaute Rakam Land Allotments in Bhaktapur," Jestha Badi 7, 1952 (May 1895).
[6] "Order to Thaple Hulaki Porters in Thankot," Falgun Badi 3, 1922 (February 1866).
[7] "Byang Rakam Regulations for Naikap Village," 1925 (1868).

and ammunition, *Rakam* porters now transported revenues collected from different parts of the country, or timber for the construction of palaces for members of the Rana family and their relatives and favorites.[8] Theoretically, all categories of *Rakam* workers could be employed for military purposes in times of war,[9] but because Kathmandu never fought a war after 1856, this provision became obsolete.

Occasionally, expired *Rakam* obligations were commuted into cash levies,[10] enabling the government to avoid losses resulting from the nonutilization of such obligations and also, sometimes, to finance alternative sources of labor supply. For instance, *Rakam* workers employed in gunpowder factories were obligated to pay a cash levy in lieu of their services when manual labor was replaced by machinery.[11] Similarly, the supply of charcoal was commuted into a cash levy when several magazines in the western hill region were abolished around 1907.[12] In certain cases, the government adopted a more flexible policy and commuted *Rakam* services only at times when these were not required. Some *Rakam* workers thus continued to be employed in gunpowder factories, but each was required to pay a cash levy of R. 0.06 on any day that his services were not required.[13]

On the other hand, administrative and other exigencies occasionally heightened the importance of existing *Rakam* services. With the increasing centralization of the administration, and its gradual extension to the provincial areas, the volume of official correspondence increased considerably and *Rakam* services for the transportation of mail assumed a new importance. The entire internal mail-transportation system was therefore reorganized in 1849-50, and a network of mail outposts was created throughout the kingdom.[14] The trend continued during

---

[8]Law Ministry Records, "Lampahad Kath Katani Bandobast Office Regulations," 1987 (1930).

[9]Ibid., sec. 21 (1).

[10]The trend toward commutation of labor obligations into cash payments had started early in the nineteenth century. Regmi, *A Study in Nepali Economic History*, pp. 115-16, 187.

[11]"Silaute Rakam Land Allotments in Jitpur," 1951 (1894); Law Ministry Records, "Regulations for *Jimmawals* in Kathmandu," Kartik 25, 1995 (November 10, 1938), sec. 37.

[12]"Commutation of Gol Rakam in Pyuthan and Salyan," Shrawan 28, 1972 (August 12, 1915).

[13]"Commutation of Silaute Rakam in Dhankuta," 1951 (1894).

[14]"Order regarding Kagate Hulaki Services in Thankot," Magh Sudi 13, 1906 (February 1850).

subsequent years.[15] In 1913, however, these *Rakam* services were abolished and paid mail-carriers were employed.[16] A cash levy was then imposed on lands held by *Rakam* workers of this category in addition to the land tax so as to compensate the government for the additional expenditure involved.[17]

Rakam AND *Chuni* PEASANTS

Rakam obligations were imposed upon the able-bodied population of the village according to the needs of the government. Minors and old people, lame or crippled persons, and widows were generally exempt.[18] Peasants could therefore be classified into two categories on the basis of whether or not *Rakam* obligations had been imposed on them. Those who were not expected to perform *Rakam* services were known as *Chuni*.

Legislation enacted in 1854 closely tied *Rakam* obligations to landholding. The acceptance of such obligations was left to the choice of the peasant, but nonacceptance led to the forfeiture of his right to cultivate his lands.[19] The voluntary nature of *Rakam* obligations was therefore purely illusory. First, the government imposed such obligations on peasants to fulfill its needs for porterage and other services. It then told them that they were free to reject these obligations, but would have to relinquish their lands if they did so. Occasionally, *Rakam* workers availed themselves of this alternative and relinquished their lands.[20] Most of them, however, obviously found it difficult to take such a step, for means of livelihood outside of the agricultural sector were limited. In subsequent years the Rana government

---

[15] For instance, the establishment of a revenue office in Dolakha in 1879 necessitated the creation of thirteen new mail-transport units between Lyanglyang and Charikot, a distance of approximately thirty-two miles. "Order regarding Creation of Kagate Hulaki Outposts in East No. 2," Kartik Badi 8, 1937 (October 1880).

[16] Law Ministry Records, "Sindhupalchok Revenue Regulations," 1991 (1934), sec. 45.

[17] Hari Lal, *Pahad Mal Bishaya* [On revenue offices in the hill districts] (Kathmandu: Nepali Bhasha Prakashini Samiti, 2008 [1951]), p. 17. Apparently the commutation of the obligation to transport mail into a cash payment was voluntary, for mail-carriers in Jumla were said to have elected to continue under the old system.

[18] Regmi, III, 56-57; Law Ministry Records, "Lampahad Kath Katani Bandobast Office Regulations," 1987 (1930), sec. 18.

[19] Law Ministry Records, "Jagga Pajani Ko" [On land evictions], *Muluki Ain* [legal code], 1870 ed., sec. 95, p. 75.

[20] "Relinquishment of Rakam Lands in Lele, Lalitpur, by Aplu Singh and Others," Chaitra Badi 30, 1910 (March 1854).

revised the policy toward peasants who were unwilling to undertake *Rakam* obligations, and forced them to surrender one-third of their holdings to those who were willing to do so.[21]

Rakam Obligations

Rakam obligations were generally expressed in terms of the number of days to be worked during the year. Most *Rakam* workers were required to serve for six days each month, a total period of 72 days in the year. The six-day period was staggered among a number of work teams in such a way that the government was able to utilize *Rakam* services regularly throughout the year.[22] In the case of mail carriers, each post office was manned by four teams consisting of four *Rakam* workers each, and each team worker remained on duty for approximately eight days in the month.[23] This did not necessarily mean that he actually worked during this period, for his services were utilized only when mail was available for transportation.

Rakam obligations were occasionally expressed in physical terms, such as a stated quantity of fuel wood, charcoal, or the like. If the requirements of the government could not be specified in advance, *Rakam* workers were directed to supply the goods concerned according to need.[24]

For workers employed under the *Rakam* system to process and transport building timber, the government prescribed a continuous period of work during the winter. Work was allotted to *Rakam* workers of different villages according to the total quantity of timber available for transportation. Such work had to be fulfilled on a contractual basis, each *Rakam* worker being liable for porterage services for not more than 75 days during the year. The exact quantity of timber to be transported by each *Rakam* worker through different types of terrain was prescribed, but should any person fulfill the quota allotted to him earlier than scheduled, he was not obliged to work for the full period of 75 days. When *Rakam* workers had to provide porterage or other services during tours and hunting expeditions of members of the Rana

[21]"Order regarding Creation of Kagate Hulaki Outposts in East No. 2," Kartik Badi 8, 1937 (October 1880).
[22]"Bosi Rakam Land Allotment in Panga, Kirtipur," Baisakh Bedi 30, 1912 (April 1855).
[23]"Report on Kagate Hulaki Rakam in Bhaktapur," 1950–51 (1893–94).
[24]"Jangi Megjin and Daura Rakam Land Allotments in Panauti," Shrawan Badi 3, 1912 (July 1855).

family or the royal family, or during military campaigns, this was adjusted against the prescribed 75-day period. The time spent in travelling to the place of work was treated similarly.[25]

A *Rakam* worker was dismissed if he remained absent from duty for more than a year,[26] and he was subjected to a fine of R. 0.25 for each day of absence.[27]

Land Redistribution and Allotment

In an earlier section, it was explained that *Rakam* workers were provided with fiscal and tenurial facilities as a partial quid pro quo for their onerous obligations. It is doubtful to what extent these exemptions provided a satisfactory quid pro quo to *Rakam* workers. In any case, exemptions were meaningful only if *Rakam* workers were actually in possession of lands, or at least possessed a holding large enough to provide them with subsistence. There is evidence that they did not, with the result that the *Rakam* population dwindled in several areas. Faced with this situation, the government initiated measures during 1854–55 to redistribute lands held by *Rakam* workers in Kathmandu Valley. Redistribution was conditional, however, upon the consent of the *Rakam* workers concerned. In several cases, they opposed such redistribution,[28] so that existing inequalities continued.

The actual process of redistribution may be described by reference

---

[25] Law Ministry Records "Lampahad Kath Katani Bandobast Office Regulations," 1987 (1930), secs. 14–21.

[26] Government of Nepal," "Jagga Pajani Ko," *Muluki Ain*, pt. III (Kathmandu: Gorkhapatra Press, 2009 [1952]), sec. 12, pp. 30–31. However, regulations promulgated for *Rakam* workers employed in the transporation of building timber prescribed an equivalent period of compensatory work during the following year, instead of fines. Any *Rakam* worker who remained absent from duty for a period exceeding sixteen days for reasons other than sickness, or who failed to provide compensatory work during the following year, was liable to eviction from his *Rakam* holding. Law Ministry Records, "Lampahad Kath Katani Bandobasta Office Regulations," 1987 (1930), sec. 19(1).

[27] Government of Nepal, "Jagga Pajani Ko," *Muluki Ain*, pt. III (2009 [1952]), sec. 12, pp. 30–31. The figure actually mentioned is four annas, or one-fourth of the 16-anna rupee in circulation before 1903. This is equivalent to R. 0.25 according to the decimal currency introduced in that year. Before this legal provision was enacted, orders and regulations promulgated for different offices often prescribed fines ranging from R. 0.16 to R. 0.32 per working day. "Order to the Lampahad Kath Katani Office regarding Wages and Fines," Jestha 32, 1961 (June 15, 1904).

[28] "Kothabosi Rakam Land Allotments in Kirtipur," Jestha Badi 14, 1911 (May 1854).

to the allotments made to *Rakam* lumber workers at Kirtipur in May 1855. After records of land cultivated by them were compiled, they were asked whether they would agree to have such lands redistributed among themselves so that each family held the same area of land. The *Rakam* workers agreed. A total of 71 families, consisting of 373 members, had been enrolled. Each family then received 20 *muris* of land. In addition, the 373 persons each received four *muris*, irrespective of age, sex, and physical fitness. *Rakam* team leaders received additional allotments totaling 158 *muris*. These allotments required a total of 3,124 *muris*, whereas the total area held by the *Rakam* workers amounted to only 2,378 *muris*. The difference of 746 *muris* was provided by curtailing the surplus lands of other categories of *Rakam* workers in the area.[29]

Redistribution did not always mean, however, that *Rakam* workers were guaranteed a holding large enough to insure subsistence. The size of the new holding depended upon the availability of land, because only such lands were covered by the measure as were actually occupied by the *Rakam* workers at the time of the redistribution. Consequently, although redistribution insured equitable landholdings with reference to any individual *Rakam* in any particular village, there were wide inequalities between different *Rakams* and different villages. For instance, the *Rakam* lumber workers in Kirtipur mentioned above received 24 *muris* of land for each family, but in Panga village, situated a short distance from Kirtipur, another category of *Rakam* workers received 65 *muris* for each family.[30] The government attempted to mitigate such inequalities by curtailing the area being cultivated by *Rakam* workers with unduly large holdings and making the land thus acquired available for redistribution among *Rakam* workers of other categories in the area. In the case cited above, for instance, the *Rakam* workers of Panga collectively lost 164 *muris* of land. Even this did not insure complete equality, however, for some other *Rakam* workers in Panga itself were allotted only 24 *muris*. Apparently, measures aimed at bringing about complete equality were considered impracticable. It is difficult to understand, moreover, why *Rakam* workers whose lands were partly expropriated in this manner consented to redistribution. They seem to have been given a clear option in the matter, and it is inconceivable that they agreed voluntarily to expropriation. Compul-

[29] "Bala Rakam Land Allotments in Kirtipur," Jestha Sudi 8, 1912 (May 1855).
[30] "Byang Rakam Land Allotments in Panga Village," Baisakh Badi 30, 1912 (May 1855).

sion was obviously used to some extent where it appeared that a mild measure of expropriation would not face strong resistance.

Inasmuch as these measures affected only those lands that *Rakam* workers were holding at the time, it is obvious that redistribution alone could not insure a sufficient holding for each *Rakam* household. Subsequently, therefore, the government adopted a different policy ostensibly for the benefit of *Rakam* mail carriers. When it appeared that they possessed no lands at all, or that their existing holdings were inadequate to insure them a subsistence, it asked local landlords either to relinquish a part of their agricultural lands for allotment to the mail carriers, or else undertake the *Rakam* obligations themselves.[31] Apparently this was only a maneuver aimed at imposing *Rakam* obligations on the more substantial landowners of the village in preference to existing *Rakam* workers with meager landholdings, because few landowners would be willing to relinquish their lands through the desire to avoid *Rakam* obligations. It is therefore unlikely that any major accretion in the area of lands held by *Rakam* mail carriers resulted from this policy.

Tenurial Characteristics

Rakam workers cultivated rice lands under *Raikar*, *Kipat*, or *Raj Guthi* tenure. Their obligation to pay rents on such lands remained unaffected. As was noted in chapter 5, most of the *Raikar* area during the nineteenth century had been assigned as *Jagir*, and *Rakam* workers therefore paid rents to *Jagirdars* in the capacity of tenants. *Rakam* tenants were granted a number of tenurial facilities that were not available to cultivators on lands of other categories. To some extent, those facilities were provided in consideration of the dual obligations borne by them—of paying rents on their lands while simultaneously providing labor services to the government. But the foremost objective of the government in providing tenurial facilities to *Rakam* workers appears to have been the desire to check the depopulation of their holdings and the dislocation of *Rakam* services.

The allotment of *Birta* lands to *Rakam* workers was banned in 1853,[32]

---

[31]"Order regarding Creation of Kagati Hulaki Outposts in East No. 2," Kartik Badi 8, 1937 (October 1880).

[32]Government of Nepal, "Jagga Pajani Ko," *Muluki Ain*, pt. III (2009 [1952]), sec. 11, p. 30.

apparently because it impinged upon the *Birta* owners' authority over their tenants. However, *Rakam* workers frequently occupied *Birta* lands when the *Raikar* lands being cultivated by them were granted as such. In order to forestall the dislocation of the services being performed by these *Rakam* workers, *Birta* owners whose lands had been allotted to them were denied the right to resume these for personal residence or cultivation,[33] or to increase rents.[34] *Rakam* workers were thus placed in a more secure position than ordinary cultivators on *Birta* lands.

Rakam workers who cultivated *Raikar* or *Jagir* lands were traditionally exempted from the liability to provide porterage services for transporting rents to *Jagirdars*.[35] Nor were *Jagirdars* permitted to evict defaulting *Rakam* cultivators directly, as this would dislocate *Rakam* services. The local headman of *Rakam* workers was responsible for insuring full collections on behalf of the *Jagirdar*, and also for finding a suitable replacement if eviction was necessary.[36]

Rakam landholding rights were subdivisible and inheritable. Coparceners shared existing *Rakam* obligations in common and were not enrolled on a de novo basis. Children under sixteen years of age who inherited *Rakam* lands were exempt from *Rakam* obligations until they came of age.[37] After records of *Rakam* lands were reorganized during the 1890s, *Rakam* landholders were permitted also to sell them. However, no administrative arrangements were made to insure that *Rakam* obligations devolved on the purchaser. *Rakam* workers were therefore forced to fulfill their obligations even though they were no longer in possession of their *Rakam* lands. Consequently, delinquency in the discharge of *Rakam* services became common,[38] and as a result, transfers of *Rakam* lands were permitted only if the purchaser assumed liability for the appropriate *Rakam* services.[39] Similarly, *Rakam* workers were permitted to appoint tenants to cultivate their lands provided

---

[33] Ibid., sec. 12, pp. 30–31.
[34] "Order regarding Rakam Lands of Ganesh Datta Padhya," Shrawan Sudi 6, 1949 (July 1892).
[35] "Order regarding Transportation of Rents by Rakam Workers," Baisakh 28, 1988 (May 10, 1931).
[36] Government of Nepal, "Jagga Pajani Ko," *Muluki Ain*, pt. III (2009 [1952]), sec. 12, pp. 30–31.
[37] Ibid., secs. 13–14, p. 31.
[38] "Report on Rakam Lands in Thimi," Jestha Badi 9, 1953 (May 1896).
[39] "Order regarding Compilation of Records of Hulaki Rakam Lands," Falgun Sudi 10, 1949 (March 1893).

they continued to discharge the prescribed *Rakam* obligations themselves.[40]

Critique of the *Rakam* System

The basic feature of the *Rakam* system was that peasants were compelled to work without wages to meet the requirements of the government for porterage and other labor services. Their obligations were twofold: payment of revenue on their rice lands and supply of unpaid labor to the government. In consideration of these obligations, they were provided with a number of fiscal and tenurial facilities and concessions, and occasionally, with allotments of agricultural lands. We shall now attempt to analyze to what extent these facilities and concessions provided adequate compensation for the obligations imposed on *Rakam* workers.

It does not require much effort to show that the fiscal concessions provided to *Rakam* workers in the form of full or partial exemption from homestead and other levies were insignificant in terms of the value of the labor services provided by them. Most categories of *Rakam* workers were obliged to work at least 72 days in the year. At the official porterage rate of R. 0.25 per day, this meant that the value of their *Rakam* services was at least Rs. 18.00. However, the total amount paid by a *Rakam* worker in the form of homestead and other levies was hardly R. 1.00 per year.[41] The loss that the *Rakam* system caused to the peasant constituted the profit to the government and was, in fact, the very rationale of the system. If the value of the fiscal concessions did not constitute an adequate return to the *Rakam* worker for his labor, this was so because the government did not intend it to be.

[40] Government of Nepal, "Jagga Pajani Ko," *Muluki Ain*, pt. III (2004 [1952]), sec. 16, pp. 31–32. This law provided: "In case a *Rakam* landholder has given away his *Rakam* land for cultivation to another person on any condition, the provisions of the agreement, if any, shall be followed. Otherwise, the land shall belong to the person who discharges the *Rakam* obligations. In case the *Rakam* worker dies or absconds, and so his position falls vacant, and in case the person who is cultivating the land does not discharge the *Rakam* obligations, he shall not be entitled to get the land on the ground that it was given to him by the *Rakam* landholder. The *Rakam* land shall not be given to another person as long as the cultivator is willing to discharge the *Rakam* obligations. In case he is not so willing, any close relative, or else a creditor, shall get the land if he is willing to discharge the *Rakam* obligations. If neither the cultivator nor any relative or creditor is so willing, the local headman shall allot the land to another person on condition that the *Rakam* services are continued."

[41] Regmi, I, 43–48.

The tenurial facilities provided to *Rakam* workers were largely of a negative character. *Rakam* workers were exempted from the obligation to provide porterage services to transport the rents paid by them to *Jagirdars* because the services exacted by the government from them would otherwise be dislocated. Similarly, security from eviction became a facility of doubtful value after occupancy rights on *Raikar* and *Raj Guthi* lands developed into ownership rights after the beginning of the twentieth century, as will be described in chapter 10. In any case, a *Rakam* peasant paid a high premium for such security in the form of his dual (fiscal and labor) obligations. An ordinary *Raikar* peasant was secure so long as he made the prescribed payments, but his counterpart on *Rakam* land was not secure even if he did so, for he was evicted also if he defaulted in the performance of his *Rakam* obligations. It may thus actually have been easier for *Raikar* peasants than for *Rakam* workers to protect their occupancy rights on the land cultivated by them. Nor was the land-redistribution policy of the government of much help to *Rakam* workers. Redistribution affected only lands actually being held by *Rakam* workers. It may have benefited those with small holdings, but only at the expense of their neighbors. Steps taken to provide *Rakam* workers with adequate holdings at the expense of *Chuni* peasants with large holdings were aimed chiefly at bringing the latter within the ambit of the *Rakam* system.

The *Rakam* system was fundamentally inequitable because it failed to provide an adequate quid pro quo to peasants in consideration of the compulsory and unpaid labor services that they were required to perform for the government in addition to their tax obligations. In fact, it was precisely because of the failure of the system to provide an adequate quid pro quo that the government of Nepal resorted to it to meet its labor requirements during a period when it lacked the resources to pay wages in cash. It is true, of course, that *Rakam* may have seemed to the average peasant to be the lesser of two evils. It usually brought him exemption from *Jhara* obligations, which, in view of their uncertain and arbitrary character, were probably more onerous than *Rakam*. This may explain why, at times, *Rakam* obligations were undertaken on the peasant's own initiative.[42] Nevertheless, the severer inequity of *Jhara* cannot mitigate the essentially inequitable character of the *Rakam* system.

---

[42]"Order regarding Voluntary Registration of Raikar Land under Silaute Rakam," Falgun Sudi 3, 1948 (March 1892).

LABOR SERVICES AND LANDOWNERSHIP
Recent Developments

The *Rakam* system, if carried to its logical conclusion, would have meant the conversion of all *Raikar* and *Raj Guthi* lands into *Rakam* tenure and have provided the state with a vast labor force far in excess of its actual requirements at any time. There is evidence, however, that the government did not favor arbitrary and unrestricted expansion of the *Rakam* system. As early as 1846, it decreed that *Rakam* services should be obtained by persuasion, rather than by force or intimidation.[43] Existing *Rakam* delegations were justified on the ground that they had continued "since former times."[44] The government obviously adopted this policy because various circumstances prevented it from exercising its theoretical right to convert *Raikar* and *Raj Guthi* lands into *Rakam* as it liked. Indeed, seldom during the twentieth century does the government of Nepal appear to have imposed fresh *Rakam* obligations on the peasantry even when faced with a shortage of *Rakam* labor.

The successful functioning of the *Rakam* system depended upon the existence of a system of land tenure in which occupancy rights in the land were based on local residence and personal cultivation. As will be brought out in chapter 10, such a traditional system of land tenure had disintegrated in the hill regions of Nepal by the beginning of the twentieth century. Once private rights in the land became dependent solely on payment of taxes, the correlation between local residence and landownership was broken. The old policy of insuring the continuity of *Rakam* services by tying them up with landholding rights no longer proved feasible, for *Rakam* workers became able to enjoy more or less secure rights in their lands irrespective of the extent to which they fulfilled their *Rakam* obligations. The government was still able to exact compulsory and unpaid services under the *Rakam* system, mainly from the lower-class peasantry who lived in the village and could be rounded up by force, if necessary. But it became more difficult to conscript *Rakam* workers, for it was difficult to locate them outside the village and exact the services due from them.[45] As a result of these developments, the government saw no alternative but to offer

---

[43] "Order regarding Dislocation of Thaple Hulaki Services," Marga Badi 6, 1903 (November (1846).

[44] "Order regarding Supply of Charcoal to British Residency," Chaitra Sudi 7, 1944 (April 1888).

[45] "Order regarding Appointment of Katuwal in Bandipur," Marga 2, 2007 (November 17, 1950).

inducements to *Rakam* workers in the form of wages in cash. There is evidence that by the early 1930s important categories of *Rakam* workers, both in Kathmandu Valley and the hill districts, were being paid cash wages, with the result that the *Rakam* system was fundamentally altered.[46]

ABOLITION OF THE *Rakam* SYSTEM

The practice of compulsory labor tax under the *Rakam* system was inconsistent with the egalitarian ideals of personal liberty and social and economic justice that were ushered in after the end of the Rana regime in 1951. An interim constitution promulgated soon thereafter declared the abolition of compulsory and unpaid labor to be a directive principle of state policy.[47] Although no action was taken immediately to implement this principle, the removal of members of the Rana family, who had been the main beneficiaries of *Rakam* services, from positions of political and administrative authority made important categories of *Rakam* defunct. Several individual *Rakams* were actually abolished during the period from 1957 to 1961,[48] although apparently not effectively, but it was only in 1963 that legislation was enacted to abolish the *Rakam* system in its entirety. By the terms of the new legal code of Nepal, promulgated in that year, "All *Rakams* imposed on the land have been abolished. If taxes have not been imposed on *Rakam* lands, or have been imposed at rates lower than those current in any area, these shall now be imposed and collected at current rates."[49]

The taxation arrangements are apparently being implemented rather slowly, but labor services under the *Rakam* system are no longer a formal obligation of landownership.

[46]Government of Nepal, "Bahi Bujhne Bare Ko" [On audit], *Muluki Ain*, (Kathmandu: Gorkhapatra Press, 2010 [1953], sec. 87, p. 260. Law Ministry Records, "Lampahad Kath Katani Bandobast Office Regulations," 1987 (1930), secs. 16–18, 32.

[47]Government of Nepal, "Nepal Antarim Shasan Vidhan" [Interim constitution of Nepal], *Nepal Gazette*, vol. 4, no. 14, Kartik 30, 2011 (November 15, 1954), art. 20, p. 44.

[48]*Nepal Gazette*, vol. 10, no. 36, Poush 19, 2017 (January 2, 1961); "Rakam Abolition Order," Chaitra 1, 2017 (March 14, 1961).

[49]Ministry of Law and Justice, "Jagga Pajani Ko," *Muluki Ain* (Kathmandu: the Ministry, 2020 [1963]), sec. 6, p. 119. Payments due in consideration of *Rakam* obligations that had been commuted into cash were abolished soon thereafter. Ministry of Law and Justice, "Arthik Ain, 2020" [Finance act, 1963], *Nepal Gazette*, vol. 13, no. 10 (Extraordinary), Shrawan 32, 2020 (August 16, 1963), sec. 6 (5), p. 3.

Chapter 10

PROPERTY RIGHTS IN LAND

The foregoing chapters have dealt with the *Birta* and *Jagir* systems, which conferred ascriptive rights of landownership on individuals. *Birta* owners and *Jagirdars* were accordingly able to appropriate rents on their lands because the state had alienated its sovereign authority of taxation in their favor. Until around the middle of the nineteenth century, a landlord-tenant nexus existed almost exclusively on *Birta* and *Jagir* lands; on *Raikar* lands, a direct relationship between the state and the actual cultivator prevailed in most parts of the country.

The nature of this relationship was subsequently affected by a number of developments, chief among which were the enforcement of legislation protecting the rights of cultivators on *Raikar* lands, and administrative arrangements prescribing the level of rents and permitting their payment in cash rather than in kind. Thanks to these developments, peasants cultivating *Raikar* lands acquired permanent rights in such lands, and the real value of the rents paid by them progressively declined. Peasants were then able to sell their rights to others, as well as to appoint others to cultivate their lands for them on payments of rents. In other words, a *Raikar* cultivator was able to upgrade his status from occupancy to ownership without prejudice to the fiscal authority of the state. This type of landowner was able to achieve his position through the interplay of economic forces within the statutory tenure structure, not through a royal charter or governmental authority bestowing a superior title or ascriptive right.[1]

[1] For an elucidation of this typology see R. P. Dore, "Land Reform and Japan's Economic Development—A Reactionary Thesis," in Teodor Shanin, ed., *Peasants and Peasant Societies* (Penguin Books, 1971), pp. 378–79. In Dore's words, this type of landlord is "characteristically one who achieves his position by *economic* means within the framework of a system of established political order; not by warfare or that milder type of warfare that is politics. Sometimes he is a merchant, sometimes a thrifty farmer who acquires land from the improvidence or misfortunes of others, sometimes a moneylender. He may also exercise some political power, but it is power exercised through the framework of a system of government in which he has no ascriptive right, only the power of manipulation gained by virtue of his superior wealth."

This chapter will be devoted to an analysis of the process of evolution of such private-property rights in *Raikar* land. For the purpose of this analysis, we shall assume that private property in land exists where the opportunities to use and occupy the land are transferable by lease, inheritance, or sale.[2] We shall thus explore mainly three aspects of the agrarian structure: the rights to sell or otherwise transfer *Raikar* lands, accumulate lands in excess of the needs for survival and direct use, and appoint tenants to cultivate such lands.

Traditional Nature of *Raikar* Landholding Rights

An analysis of the traditional nature of *Raikar* landholding rights appears essential in order to help us determine different stages in the evolution of these rights into absolute ownership. The nature of *Raikar* landholding rights traditionally appears to have been different in the central and eastern midlands, the far-western midland and Himalayan regions, and the Tarai.

In the central and eastern midlands, property rights in *Raikar* land were traditionally not recognized by law. Regulations were promulgated during the first decade of the nineteenth century prohibiting the sale and purchase of *Raikar* lands.[3] Individual rights in *Raikar* land were limited to the right to cultivate the land and appropriate a share of the produce. Even this limited right was not permanently available on the same holding, for lands were reallotted periodically under what was known as the *Raibandi* system, under which available rice lands in the village were redistributed among the local inhabitants according to the size of each family. Irrespective of whether it had the opportunity and resources to bring new lands under the plow, a peasant family that had little or no land could thus acquire a subsistence holding through the redistribution of the bigger holdings of its more affluent neighbors. If lands reclaimed by any peasant exceeded the communal share, he was permitted to retain the surplus area. In the event that the area so reclaimed was less than the communal share, the shortfall was met from other cultivated rice lands. If it corresponded to the

---

[2] Kenneth H. Parsons, "The Tenure of Farms, Motivation, and Productivity," in *Science, Technology and Development*, vol. III, *Agriculture* (Washington: U.S. Government Printing press, n.d.), p. 28.

[3] "Judicial Regulations for Areas East of the Dudhkoshi and the Daraundi-Kali and Bheri-Kali Regions," Marga Badi 9, 1866 (December 1809). See also Regmi, *A Study in Nepali Economic History*, pp. 79–80.

communal share, additional rice land was not allotted.[4] The principal feature of this redistribution system was that a family whose rice-land holdings exceeded the per capita share in the village was under obligation to relinquish the excess area without compensation[5] so that "lands were taken away from those who had plenty, and allotted to those who had none." In other words, the state did not recognize the cultivator's property rights in land that was so redistributed.

Irrespective of whether a peasant family obtained land through reclamation or through redistribution in the manner described above, its occupancy rights were recognized by custom so long as it occupied the land and made the customary payments. However, the peasant forfeited all rights to the holding if he vacated it or defaulted in payments.[6] In other words, occupancy rights on *Raikar* lands were based on actual cultivation and payment of the prescribed dues. The emphasis was on continuous occupation, rather than on the retention of occupancy rights merely through the fulfilment of fiscal obligations. This precluded individual control over lands that could not be kept under cultivation. *Raikar* land was therefore used primarily for subsistence, not as a field for monetary investment. Rent-receiving landownership was not permitted under the *Raikar* system.

In the far-western midland and Himalayan regions, on the other

[4] Ministry of Law and Justice, "Jagga Jamin Ko," in *Shri 5 Surendra...Muluki Ain*, sec. 1, p. 19. It appears, nevertheless, that lands were redistributed under the *Raibandi* system much before the promulgation of the legal code in 1854. "Order regarding Raibandi Land Redistribution in Thansing, Nuwakot," Magh Sudi 4, 1902 (January 1846); "Order regarding Appointment of Kaji Jaya Bahadur Kunwar in Dhuwakot, Gorkha," Magh Badi 9, 1903 (January 1847). According to one source, the *Raibandi* system was introduced on *Jagir* lands assigned to the Sabuj and Ser battalions in Palpa, Gulmi, Argha, and Khanchi in 1839. "Order to General Krishna Bahadur Kunwar Rana regarding Raibandi Land Redistribution," Jestha Badi 2, 1905 (May 1848). This cannot be regarded, however, as conclusive evidence that the *Raibandi* system was introduced in that year.

[5] For instance, according to a report submitted by local authorities in Dhor, Tanahu district, in January 1865, "Lands could not be redistributed in this area as in the rest of the country during 1853-54 because of the war with Tibet. When *ryots* who could not get lands as a result complained, both good and inferior lands were joined together and redistributed on *Raibandi* basis according to the size of the family and physical capacity. Narbir Chhetri of Malayagiri village and his mother possessed lands in excess of the average area of 40 *muris*, while Ranjit Bhandari Chhetri of Koldanda village had less than 40 *muris*. Accordingly, 20 *muris* of land was transferred from Narbir Chhetri and his mother to Ranjit Bhandari Chhetri with their consent." "Order regarding Raibandi Land Redistribution in Dhor," Magh Sudi 2, 1921 (January 1865). Also "Order regarding Raibandi Land Redistribution in Ramgha Village, Chundi (Tanahu)," Baisakh Badi 4, 1924 (April 1867).

[6] Regmi, pp. 185-86.

hand, the rights of cultivators on the *Raikar* lands cultivated by them existed in a form that permitted transactions through payment of money. In Dullu and Dailekh, for instance, *Raikar* lands were sold and mortgaged before the Gorkhali conquest of that area around 1789. The Gorkhali rulers do not appear to have interfered with this practice. The ban imposed on *Raikar* land transactions in the central and eastern midlands, therefore, did not apply to the far-western midland and Himalayan regions. Rather, the government promulgated orders from time to time confirming the legality of such transactions in these regions.[7] In the Tarai region as well, private rights in the land appear to have developed in the form of property rights quite early. During the latter part of the eighteenth century, there were large numbers of *Zamindars* in the Tarai region, who paid taxes to the state and had their lands cultivated by sharecroppers.[8] Not all private land rights in the Tarai belonged to *Zamindars*, however, for large numbers of cultivators also obtained allotments of waste lands directly from the local administrators for reclamation. Documentary evidence of their rights to the lands that they had reclaimed was provided in the form of a *Patta*, which specified the area, the duration of the tenure, and the tax payable thereon. These rights appear to have been insecure in actual practice, for local administrators frequently disregarded *Pattas* after lands had been reclaimed and gave these lands to others on higher rents. Legislation was enacted in 1793 granting such *Patta* holders permanent occupancy rights,[9] but available evidence indicates that its implementation was not very satisfactory. Landholders in the far-western midland and Himalayan regions and the Tarai consequently enjoyed rights that were superior to those of cultivators in the central and eastern midlands. Ordinary landholders in the former regions were described as *Chuni*, that is, *ryots* who paid taxes to the government and were listed as taxpayers in the official records.[10] The term used to denote ordinary peasants in the central and eastern

[7]"Order regarding Fiscal and Judicial Matters in Dullu and Dailekh," Aswin Sudi 4, 1879 (September 1822). This refers to regulations promulgated for the Dullu-Dailekh area in 1822, which prescribed: "In case the cultivator listed in the revenue records does not possess the means to pay the revenue due from him, he may sell his lands to his relatives without in any way prejudicing the payment thereof." Presumably, the term "relatives" was interpreted quite broadly in such transactions. See also Naraharinath Yogi, *Itihas Prakash*, II (2), 57-58.

[8]Regmi, pp. 32-33.

[9]"Order regarding Reclamation of Waste Lands in Eastern Tarai Districts," Aswin Badi 8, 1850 (September 1793).

[10]Regmi, p. 31.

midlands was *Mohi*, or tenant farmer. The status distinction is obvious.

The traditional system of *Raikar* landholding in different parts of the Kingdom of Nepal, as described above, was influenced by two important developments during the latter part of the nineteenth century—the compilation of records of private rights in *Raikar* land and the decline in the real value of the land tax.

Records of Rights

Between 1854 and 1868, revenue settlements were revised throughout the kingdom and fresh records of individual rights in land were compiled. Those records listed the cultivator, the area of land held by him, and the total payments due thereon. They were considered to be the ultimate evidence of land-holding rights, superseding all other claims. Cultivators whose names were listed in the revenue records were then placed in a position of comparative advantage, for the registration of their rights made their lands unavailable for others. If the lands were favorably located, or were of high fertility, or if the owner had invested labor and capital in making them productive, a situation emerged in which he could relinquish them to others on payment of rent,[11] or through mortgage or even outright sale.[12] In such circumstances, he was able to retain his rights in the land (subject to the payment of the prescribed taxes, of course) without working on the land personally.[13] In other words, individual rights in land emerged independently of the needs for subsistence and direct use.

As a result of these developments, only unclaimed rice lands or

[11]Law Ministry Records, "Jagga Pajani Ko" [On land evictions], *Muluki Ain* [Legal code], 1870 ed., sec. 38.

[12]Ibid., sec. 51. References to the sale of *Raikar* lands which had been redistributed on *Raibandi* basis in 1854 are contained in "Order regarding Sale of Thaple Hulaki Lands in Syangja," Magh Badi 2, 1921 (January 1865).

[13]"In case *Khet* or *Pakho* land registered as *Raikar* or *Kipat* in course of redistribution under the *Raibandi* system during a revenue settlement is given away by the registered holder to another person for use or cultivation because of lack of means or because of affection, and in case the registered holder has paid taxes due thereon, he shall be permitted to resume the land in the proper season. But in case the cultivator and not the registered holder has paid taxes due thereon to the government or to the *Jagirdar*, the registered holder shall not be permitted to resume the land on the plea that the land has been registered in his name. The land shall remain in the possession of the person who has paid taxes due thereon." Law Ministry Records, "Jagga Pajani Ko," *Muluki Ain*, 1870 ed., secs. 36–37. For an example of such temporary alienation see "Order to Captain Padmadhwaj Khatri Chhetri regarding Land Dispute in Makaikhola, Lamjung," Poush Sudi 9, 1921 (January 1865).

those relinquished by their owners became available for *Raibandi* redistribution.[14] The practice of taking away surplus lands from one family and reallotting them to another family with an inadequate holding consequently became obsolete. The right of the registered landholder to the land that he was cultivating was thus made secure. The trend toward the consolidation of private rights on cultivated lands continued in subsequent years. By 1888, the *Raibandi* system had undergone a basic change. Only waste lands were then allotted to those who possessed insufficient rice lands,[15] with the result that cultivated rice lands remained outside the ambit of the *Raibandi* system. The allotment of waste lands, however, was hardly a special concession to the peasant. Such lands were always available to those who possessed the strength and resources to bring them under the plow.

Legal provisions relating to individual rights in *Raikar* lands, as described above, were applicable uniformly to all parts of the country. Additional provisions were enacted for the Tarai during the early years of the Rana regime in the light of some special problems of that region. As previously explained, the occupancy rights granted to *Patta*-holding peasants were insecure mainly because of administrative highhandedness. The evils of such tenurial insecurity led the government of Nepal in 1857 to allot *Raikar* lands to individual cultivators on five-year leases. Records of individual holdings were compiled and ownership certificates were issued to each allottee. The allotments were nontransferable, but bequests were permitted.[16] The ban on alienation did not last long, however, and in 1870 the unrestricted sale of *Raikar* lands in the Tarai districts was finally permitted.[17]

The possibility of holding land without the obligation of working on it personally appears to have been exploited on a growing scale. The law did not permit the sale of *Raikar* lands, of course, but it provided a loophole by prescribing that the actual cultivator should be regarded as the landholder if he was making payments due on the land. All that

[14]"Appointment of Dalabhanjan Karki Chhetri as *Jimmawal* in Namdu," Shrawan Badi 4, 1924 (July 1867).

[15]Law Ministry Records, "Jagga Pajani Ko," *Muluki Ain*, 1888 ed., pt. III, sec., 2, p. 25.

[16]"Revenue Regulations for Morang District," Marga Badi 6, 1918 (November 1861), sec. 22. The allotments were originally made under *Pota Birta* tenure, obviously with the objective of assuring tenurial security. They were more commonly known as *Nambari*, or bearing serial numbers in the official records.

[17]The 1870 order has been cited in "Order to the Butaul Amini Goshwara Office," Poush Badi 30, 1942 (January 1886).

the registered landholder was required to do to sell his land was to let another person cultivate it and make the prescribed payments.[18] Such extralegal transactions appear to have been quite common.[19] Inasmuch as its revenue was in no way affected by such transactions, the government apparently saw no reason why it should interfere. At the same time, it wanted to insure that the right to sell land did not lead to an exodus of population from any district. In 1868, therefore, legislation was enacted decreeing that the alienation of *Raikar* land through tenancy, mortgage, or otherwise would be permitted only if the registered landholder continued to reside in the same district.[20] It was difficult, however, to define the terms resident and outsider. Obviously, no one could be compelled to live in his village homestead all the year round. In practical terms, therefore, these restrictions applied only to peasants who abandoned their homesteads and shifted permanently to another district. Such a course would be followed only when the lands and homesteads could not attract a buyer. Moreover, the law did not specify how long the erstwhile landholder should continue living in the district for the sale to remain valid.

For all practical purposes, therefore, *Raikar* lands had become salable in Nepal during the early years of Rana rule in Nepal. The 1888 legal code legalized this situation to some extent by providing for the de facto recognition of transfers of *Raikar* holding rights. It did not mention specifically that these rights could be sold, but permitted "relinquishment" with the approval of the local *Talukdar*[21] and thereby sanctioned transactions in *Raikar* lands. The code also recognized transactions in money that resulted in the temporary alienation of *Raikar* lands on the basis of possessory mortgage.[22]

The right to sell and mortgage *Raikar* landholding rights in all parts

---

[18] Law Ministry Records, "Jagga Pajani Ko," *Muluki Ain*, 1870 ed., sec. 37.

[19] Balakrishna Pokhrel, *Panch Saya Varsha* [Five hundred years of Nepali literature] (Lalitpur: Jagadamba Prakashan, 2020 [1963]), pp. 474–476. This refers to a land transfer made in Ramgha village, Chundi (Tanahu district), on an "irrevocable" basis. Significantly, no reference is made to any monetary or other payment.

[20] "In case any landholder vacates his homestead and shifts permanently to another district after 1868, he shall not be permitted to use his *Raikar* lands at his old place in the capacity of a nonresident cultivator. But in case he vacates his old homestead and shifts to another homestead on *Raikar* land in the same district, he shall not be deemed to have settled elsewhere. His *Raikar* lands and homestead shall not be reallotted to his tenants or other persons." Law Ministry Records, "Jagga Pajani Ko," *Muluki Ain*, 1870 ed., secs. 44–45.

[21] Ibid., 1888 ed., pt. III, sec. 7. "Lands shall not be relinquished on payment of the outstanding rents or otherwise without the approval of the *Talukda-* "

[22] Ibid., sec. 2.

of the country was explicitly recognized by law for the first time in 1921,[23] when arrangements were made for the official registration of transactions in *Raikar* lands. Explaining these arrangements, an official notification stated:

> There has been considerable litigation on private land transactions. As such, it has become difficult for simple people to carry on their affairs. It has therefore been decided to have such transactions attested by government offices. This arrangement will check forgery and other illicit practices, including [the sale of the same plot of land] to two or three persons, and thus benefit the people.[24]

Once transactions in *Raikar* land were legally recognized, the restriction that only local residents could hold *Raikar* lands became inoperative. The government could hardly insure that such transactions were conducted only in favor of local residents. The law continued to describe the *Raikar* landholder as a *Mohi*, or tenant farmer, however. A distinction was still drawn between *Birta* ownership rights, which pertained to the land, and *Raikar* rights, which pertained only to the occupancy rights of a tenant farmer.[25] But *Raikar* landholders, though still "holding" land under the state, became de facto owners. Individual rights in *Raikar* land thus acquired exchange value and hence constituted a form of property.

Limitations on Property Rights in Land

By the mid 1930s, *Raikar* landholding rights had evolved to a stage little short of full-fledged property rights. Sale, mortgage, and tenancy were permitted without any restriction, subject only to the condition that payment of taxes due to the state not be disrupted. Lands were foreclosed only in the event of the extinction of the landholder's family, voluntary relinquishment, and tax delinquency. Residential

---

[23]An order for the registration of land transactions was first promulgated in September 1921 (Law Ministry Records, "Order regarding Registration of Land Transactions," Bhadra 24, 1978 [September 8, 1921]), and was later incorporated into the legal code. Government of Nepal, "Registration Ko" [On registration], *Muluki Ain*, pt. III (Kathmandu: Gorkhapatra Press, 2009 [1952]), sec. 7, p. 132. It was initially enforced only in Kathmandu Valley, Palpa, Dhankuta, and all districts in the Tarai.

[24]Law Ministry Records, "Notification regarding Extension of Registration System to Bajhang," 1982 (1926).

[25]Regmi, *Land Tenure and Taxation in Nepal*, I, 20.

qualifications on *Raikar* landholding rights had become practically inexistent.[26]

Nevertheless, the emergence of private-property rights and the contraction of the state's traditional ownership prerogatives in *Raikar* lands were subject to certain qualifications that insured that the concept of state landlordism should not dwindle away to a mere legal fiction. The state's power to acquire *Raikar* lands without compensation was one of these qualifications. Private-property rights on *Raikar* lands were ignored when such lands were taken over by the state.[27] These were essentially rights between individuals, and not between the individual and the state. Moreover, the state's power of taxation implied the power to alienate *Raikar* land as *Birta* or *Guthi*. In the event of such alienation, the individual *Raikar* landholder's right to appropriate the surplus production, after deducting the share due to the actual cultivator, was ipso facto transferred to the beneficiary.

There was another qualification on *Raikar* landholding rights that seems to have been less effective. The law did not permit the *Raikar* landholder to let agricultural lands contained in taxable holdings remain waste on the ground that he was paying taxes, but directed that such lands should be allotted to others.[28] However, unlike the state's authority to acquire *Raikar* lands without compensation or to grant them as *Birta* or *Guthi*, this restriction was difficult to enforce. Because the land remained taxable irrespective of whether it was

---

[26] The latest reference to the obligation of a *Raikar* landholder to reside in the same district where his land is situated is contained in the 1923 edition of the legal code, but not in subsequent editions. Government of Nepal, "Jagga Pajani Ko," *Muluki Ain*, pt. III (Kathmandu: Gorkhapatra Press, 1980 [1923]), sec. 4, p. 21. The following provision remained in the legal code until 1963: "In case anybody makes an offer to construct a homestead on land which is being cultivated by a person who resides in another area, the latter shall be allowed to retain the land if he is willing to construct a homestead there himself. Otherwise, the land shall be allotted to the newcomer." Government of Nepal, "Jagga Pajani Ko," *Muluki Ain*, pt. III (2009 [1952]), sec. 9, p. 30. There is evidence, however, that it was seldom actually enforced.

[27] Compensation was paid for *Raikar* lands acquired by the government only if buildings had been constructed. Government of Nepal, "Jagga Jamin Goshwara Ko" [On miscellaneous land matters], ibid., sec. 5, p. 62.

[28] Government of Nepal, "Jagga Biraune Ko" [On land reclamation], ibid., sec. 8, pp. 24–25. "No person shall, except in the case of land the cultivation of which would affect other holdings adversely, or of land adjoining his homestead and garden, prevent the cultivation of waste land, neither cultivating it himself nor allowing others to do so, on the ground that it forms part of his taxable holding, or that its cultivation will affect his interests adversely. He shall either reclaim such waste land himself or let other persons do so if they are willing. In case he does not comply with the provisions of this law, the land shall be allotted for reclamation to those who are willing."

actually cultivated or occupied, there was presumably little incentive for the government to enforce these provisions strictly.[29]

DEVELOPMENTS AFTER 1951

The political changes of 1950–51 had a far-reaching impact on the nature of *Raikar* landownership rights. The interim constitution promulgated in August 1951 declared the right to "acquire, use, and sell property" to be a fundamental one.[30] In these circumstances, it was perhaps inevitable that the remaining constraints on the evolution of full-fledged property rights in *Raikar* land should have been eliminated one by one.

The 1957 Lands Act was the first important legislative measure aimed at upgrading the status of *Raikar* landholders. It terminated the legal fiction that the *Raikar* landholder was a mere tenant farmer holding lands owned by the state. It defined "registered *Raikar* landholder" as "landowner" and mentioned rent-receiving rights as an essential aspect of landownership rights.[31] The act thus raised the status of the *Mohi* or tenant farmer on *Raikar* land to that of "landowner" and placed him in the same category as a *Birta* owner. Subsequently the government passed two laws that removed the remaining constraints on *Raikar* landownership mentioned above: grants of *Raikar* lands as *Birta*, and nonpayment of compensation in the event of their acquisition for governmental requirements. The system of making *Birta* land grants was abandoned after 1951, with the result that the *Raikar* landowner no longer feared losing his rent-receiving rights through alienation of his land as *Birta* by the state. This security received legislative sanction in 1959, when the Birta Abolition Act decreed: "The *Birta* system existing in the Kingdom of Nepal has been

---

[29]For instance, in Kunchha (Lamjung district), "Practically all over the district, rich and influential people are paying a small sum as land tax and controlling entire hills and extensive highland tracts. They do not reclaim the land themselves, nor allow others to do so. At the same time, a large number of people who have the strength to work are living in wretched conditions because they have no land." Land Reform Commission, "Report on Land-Tenure Conditions in Western Nepal," mimeographed (Kathmandu: the Commission, 2010 [1953]), p. 33.

[30]Government of Nepal, "Nepal Antarim Shasan Vidhan" [Interim constitution of Nepal], *Nepal Gazette*, vol. 4, no. 14, Kartik 30, 2011 (November 15, 1954), art. 17(2) (f), p. 44.

[31]Ministry of Law and Parliamentary Affairs, "Bhumi Sambandhi Ain, 2014" [Lands act, 1957], *Nepal Gazette*, vol. 17, no. 5 (Extraordinary), Shrawan 22, 2014 (August 6, 1957), sec. 2(a).

abolished."[32] The practice of acquiring *Raikar* lands for governmental requirements without compensation had virtually ceased after 1951, but it was not until 1961 that the *Raikar* landowner's right to claim compensation in the event of such acquisition was upheld by law. The Land Acquisition Act, adopted in that year, provided for the payment of compensation to the owners of lands of all tenure categories acquired for governmental requirements and other public purposes.[33] These two measures removed the qualifications on *Raikar* landownership that existed at the end of the Rana regime in 1951. The final stage in the evolution of full-fledged property rights in *Raikar* land in Nepal was thus reached during the period from 1951 to 1961.

Decline in Real Value of the Land Tax

The trend toward the evolution of private-property rights in *Raikar* land, which was the subject of the foregoing section, was accompanied by a progressive decline in the real value of the *Raikar* land tax. In chapter 8, we saw that the tax-assessment system on *Raikar* lands had been fully monetized in all parts of the country by the first decade of the twentieth century. It was also brought out that the Rana government was, as a rule, reluctant to increase land-tax assessment rates. In monetary terms, therefore, those rates remained more or less static for more than a century in all parts of the country. Even after the end of the Rana regime, a decade passed before a meaningful measure to increase land-tax assessment rates was initiated.

Whereas land-tax assessment rates remained more or less static, prices of agricultural produce gradually increased. The result was that the *Raikar* landowner needed a progressively smaller quantity of food grains to meet his fiscal obligations to the state. In 1940, for example, paddy land of the highest grade in Mahottari district paid a tax of Rs. 15 per *bigha*. At the current price of Rs. 4.12 of paddy per maund, the total payment, in terms of grain, amounted to 3.6 maunds.[34] In 1961 the tax-assessment rate was the same, but the price

[32]Ministry of Law, "Birta Unmulan Ain, 2016" [Birta abolition act, 1959], ibid., vol. 9, no. 19 (Extraordinary), Poush 1, 2016 (December 15, 1959), sec. 3.

[33]Ministry of Law, Justice, and Parliamentary Affairs, "Jagga Prapti Ain, 2018" [Land acquisition act, 1961], ibid., vol. II, no. 48 (Extraordinary), Bhadra 9, 2018 (August 25, 1961), sec. 3.

[34]Department of Industrial and Commercial Intelligence, "Audyogik Survey Report" (Industrial survey report for Mahottari, Sarlahi, and other districts), mimeographed (Kathmandu: the Department, 2005-6 [1948-49]), p. 14.

of paddy had increased about ninefold, to Rs. 37.50 per maund. The *Raikar* landowner therefore was able to meet his tax obligation by selling only about half a maund of paddy. A similar decline in the real value of the land tax occurred in the hill districts. In most of the districts of that region, revenue settlements were last conducted during the period from 1854 to 1868. Where these settlements were revised, tax-assessment rates were fixed at a level sufficient to fetch the existing amount of revenue. The real value of tax-assessment rates naturally declined when prices of agricultural commodities rose.

In those districts of the hill region where the land tax had been assessed in kind, collections were made in cash and the conversion rates fixed for that purpose were not tied to the prices of agricultural commodities. When the conversion system was first introduced, during the early 1840s, the rates of conversion evidently were higher than the current level of prices of agricultural produce, at least in a few cases.[35] In 1910, the rates were fixed on a long-term basis according to prices that prevailed during the harvesting season of 1907 and 1908. They were meant to apply solely to land-tax payment, and not to payment of rents on *Jagir* lands and public transactions,[36] which suggests the existence of a discrepancy between conversion rates and the market prices of agricultural produce. This discrepancy gradually widened as prices soared and the conversion rates remained more or less static. The result was that the real value of the land tax progressively declined. An example will help to make the point clear. An official survey made in Kathmandu district in 1950 disclosed that the average assessment amounted to 19.25 *pathis* of paddy and 2.50 *pathis* of wheat in addition to a cash tax at R. 0.12 per *ropani* of rice lands of the highest grade. At the official conversion rates, this meant a total payment of Rs. 4.77 per *ropani*.[37] In 1910, when the conversion rates were fixed, the cultivator might have found it necessary to sell the full quantity of the in-kind assessment to meet his fiscal obligations. But in 1961, when paddy sold in Kathmandu at approximately Rs. 40 per *muri*, he had to sell no more than about 3 *pathis* for this purpose. The real value of the assessment thus fell from about 22 *pathis* of food grains to 3 *pathis* during this fifty-year period.

In all parts of the country, therefore, the income of the *Raikar* land-

[35] Regmi, *A Study in Nepali Economic History*, p. 181.
[36] Law Ministry Records, "Order regarding Schedule of Rates for Commutation of In-Kind Land-tax Assessments," Ashadh 2, 1967 (June 16, 1910).
[37] Law Ministry Records, "Kathmandu Tax Assessment Order," 2007 (1950).

holder increased considerably as a result of static tax assessments and the rising prices of agricultural produce. If he was able to make a subsistence living before, it was now possible for him to make an actual profit on his holding. The government's loss was the landowner's gain. He was now able to meet his fiscal obligation by selling a very small portion of the produce. This increased income could, of course, have been utilized for increased consumption. But two other alternatives proved to be equally attractive. Landowners found that the increased income could be used to yield a nonrecurring gain in the form of its capital value. In other words, the right to appropriate this additional income could be sold to bring in a capital gain. Alternatively, the increased income could be employed to provide increased leisure. The landowner then sublet the land on a rent of half of the produce and appropriated the increased income without actually working on the land himself. His total earnings decreased, no doubt, but he was free to take up other occupations. The actual form taken by this choice depended upon a number of subjective factors that are not pertinent to the present discussion. The end result was the same, however—the emergence of an intermediary class of interests on the land between the actual cultivator and the state. This development was due primarily to the discrepancy between a rigid level of taxation and the rising market prices of agricultural commodities. It resulted in a clear distinction between the taxing powers of the state and the right of the landowner to appoint a tenant to cultivate his land and receive rents. Rent, as the value of this newly acquired property right, was paid to the owner,[38] and the sovereign rights of the state were limited to taxation, police power, and eminent domain.

Property Rights in *Birta* Land

The gradual emergence of the right to sell or mortgage occupancy rights and the progressive decline in the real value of payments due on

---

[38] Parsons writes: "The rent of land is derived from the use and enjoyment of land, made secure by property relations which give security of expectations regarding the indefinite residuum of opportunity to use the land. Property, and consequently rent, are deductions from sovereignty when viewed from the public perspective of history. The distinction between rent and taxes disappears when private property in land is wiped out along with the indefinite residuum of opportunity for the independent exercise of the will." Kenneth H. Parsons, "Agrarian Reform Policy as a Field of Research," in *Agrarian Reform and Economic Growth in Developing Countries* (Washington: U.S. Department of Agriculture, 1962), pp. 19–20.

the land, which were described in the previous sections, were trends that were by no means confined to *Raikar* land. Available evidence shows that these trends affected *Birta* lands in more or less the same manner.

As explained in chapter 3, *Birta* land grants traditionally meant a virtual abdication by the state of its internal sovereign authority. *Birta* grants thus placed the recipient in a position of overlordship vis-à-vis the cultivator. In other words, such grants created a new layer of land interests above the cultivator, depressed his status, and exposed him to demands for higher rent payments.[39] The government generally remained unconcerned over this situation, as its fiscal interests were not directly affected. It promulgated orders from time to time prohibiting the eviction of cultivators by *Birta* owners only when it felt that such practices were likely to result in depopulation.[40] Comprehensive legislation defining the nature of the relationship between *Birta* owners and their tenants was enacted for the first time in 1854. It granted absolute rights to *Birta* owners to evict their tenants, resume the lands for personal cultivation or residence, or increase rents. The only consideration shown to the tenant was that rents should not be increased if he had reclaimed the *Birta* land through his own efforts. If he had not done so himself, he was allowed to continue tilling the land only so long as the *Birta* owner did not receive a higher offer from another prospective tenant. In the event such an offer was received, the tenant could protect himself from eviction only by matching it.[41] The tenure of a *Birta* tenant consequently was extremely insecure.

The unlimited authority exercised by *Birta* owners over their tenants under the 1854 legal code no doubt enhanced their status and helped them to maximize their income. However, such insecurity also discouraged prospective tenants and so hampered efforts to open up new *Birta* lands. The government therefore enacted legislation in 1906 defining the nature of the relationship between a *Birta* owner and his tenant in more specific terms.[42] In regard to the level of rents and tenurial security, the 1906 law placed *Birta* lands in more or less the same category as *Raikar* lands. It reconfirmed the existing general

---

[39] Regmi, *Land Tenure and Taxation in Nepal*, III, 69.
[40] "Order regarding Taxes and Tenancy Rights in Parbat," Marga Sudi 5, 1860 (December 1803); "Order regarding Tenancy Rights in Dolakha," Chaitra Sudi 15, 1873 (April 1817).
[41] Law Ministry Records, "Jagga Pajani Ko," *Muluki Ain*, 1870 ed., secs. 10, 12-24.
[42] Government of Nepal, "Jagga Pajani Ko," *Muluki Ain*, pt. III (2029 [1952]), sec. 20, pp. 33-38.

provision that tenants should not be evicted so long as they paid the stipulated rents. *Birta* owners in the hill regions were now permitted to increase rents only to the level prevailing on *Raikar* lands in the area, so that competitive bidding was prohibited. In the Tarai, on the other hand, rents could be fixed at any level by mutual consent, or, in the absence of such consent, increased to a maximum of 10 percent above the level of payments due on *Raikar* lands. The *Birta* owner's right to resume lands for personal cultivation or for residential purposes was limited to 5 *ropanis* in each village in the hill regions and 1.5 *bighas* in the Tarai; provisions made at the same time insured that the tenant from whom lands were acquired in this manner was left with a subsistance holding.

However, the level of taxation prevailing on adjoining holdings of *Raikar* land was ambiguous. Where assessments were in kind, and collection was made in cash at conversion rates that were low in comparison with current prices of agricultural produce, the term could be used to mean either the level of assessments or that of actual collection. Naturally, therefore, *Birta* owners in several hill districts, including Kathmandu Valley, took advantage of this ambiguity to determine their rents on the level of in-kind assessments prevailing on adjoining *Raikar* holdings, instead of on the level of actual collection. In the Tarai, however, the application of such rent-control measures appears to have been easier because both assessments and collections on *Raikar* land in this area were in cash. Moreover, in many cases a new class of tenants had emerged on *Birta* lands who subsisted on the difference between what they paid to the *Birta* owners and what they received from the actual cultivators as rent. This law therefore did not directly safeguard the interests of the actual cultivator in the Tarai. Where an intermediary class of tenants existed between the *Birta* owner and the actual cultivator, the law regulated only the relationship between the *Birta* owner and his tenant, and set no limit to the rents that the actual cultivator might be required to pay the intermediary tenant. Rising prices tended to reduce the real value of the *Birta* owner's monetary income, whereas the intermediary tenants appropriated rents in kind from the actual cultivator. The difference between their payments to *Birta* owners and their actual receipts thus progressively widened. Certain categories of *Birta* owners were required to pay taxes to the state, but the intermediary tenants had no obligation of this nature.

In this situation, the intermediary class became rich at the expense of both the cultivators and the *Birta* owners, so that tenancy rights on *Birta* lands became more tangible and profitable than *Birta* ownership rights themselves. To the extent that it was applicable and effective, therefore, the 1906 law encouraged subinfeudation and defeated its own stated purpose by exposing cultivators to the extortions of an intermediary class. Even in the absence of subinfeudation, where the *Birta* owner had direct relationship with the cultivator, the 1906 law set a limit to the latter's rent liability and created conditions favorable to the emergence of an intermediary class.

The position of intermediary tenants on *Birta* lands was buttressed also by the provisions of the 1906 law that permitted them to sell or otherwise alienate their rights without prejudice to the rights of the *Birta* owner. Tenancy rights on *Birta* lands thus became salable like any other form of property. The trend toward the development of intermediary property rights in *Birta* lands culminated with the legal recognition of the *Birta* tenant as "landowner" by the 1957 Lands Act.[43] The abolition of the *Birta* system in 1959 finally converted this type of rights in land into *Raikar* landownership rights.

Economic Differentiation

The emergence of property rights in land, and the opportunity to acquire such rights through money, created a number of problems that are familiar to the current agrarian scene: economic differentiation in the agrarian community; cleavage between ownership of land and its actual use, which gave rise to tenancy; and landlord-tenant disputes. In a situation where landholding rights were circumscribed by the need for subsistence and direct use, the size of holdings was perforce limited by these factors. But when landholding became a field for monetary investment and a source of income without the obligation to cultivate it personally, the size was limited only by the amount of resources available to acquire *Raikar* lands. Land thus became a commodity, available for purchase by any prosperous farmer who could procure sufficient funds.

Economic differentiation in the agrarian community was not, of course, the product solely of the emergence of property rights in land. We have already seen that in both the far-western hill region and the Tarai, *Raikar* land could be held without reference to the needs of subsistence. In Doti district, for example, influential persons

[43] Sec. 2.

controlled large areas of waste lands, whereas others complained that they did not have adequate lands for subsistence.[44] Similarly, in Morang, where large areas of cultivable waste lands were available, several families were actually landless.[45] Even in the central and eastern hill regions, where the *Raibandi* system might have been expected to check concentration of landholding to some extent, at least two circumstances prevented the equitable distribution of the available lands. One was that only *Raikar*, *Raj Guthi*, and *Kipat* lands were covered by the system, leaving *Birta* lands unaffected. As a result, *Birta* ownership may, at least in some areas, have provided the steppingstone to the emergence of a rich agricultural class and progressive economic differentiation among the peasantry. The other circumstance was that only rice lands were redistributed. Inequalities in the ownership of dry lands therefore persisted. Moreover, the actual process of redistribution cannot but have been affected by the social and political power wielded by village headmen, local landowners who were in the service of the government, or people enjoying top positions in the caste hierarchy. Even assuming that the allotments were more or less equal, it would be reasonable to suppose that they appropriated the best lands in the village, thereby laying the foundation for growing economic differentiation in the future. There is evidence that often influential persons were able to appropriate land allotments in excess of the actual needs of their families.[46]

The emergence of private-property rights in *Raikar* land intensified this trend toward inequality of landholding all over the country. An example from Tanahu district in the central hill region will make this point clear. In that area, cultivated *Raikar* rice lands were redistributed "in proportion to physical capacity and size of the family" during the period from 1854 to 1860. Information about the size of allotments in different parts of the district is not available, but in one area, Dhor, it appears to have amounted to 40 *muris* per family in 1865.[47] A family could then possess a larger area only if it had reclaimed lands through its own efforts. After about a century, in 1961, the situation had

[44] "Order regarding Cultivation of Agricultural Lands in Doti," Ashadh Badi 4, 1872 (June 1815).

[45] "Revenue Regulations for Morang District," Shrawan Sudi 2, 1855 (July 1798).

[46] In one case in Kaski district, for instance, a village headman was alleged in 1862 to have appropriated allotments for twenty-four persons, even though there were only nine members in his family. "Complaint regarding Raibandi Land Redistribution in Musadi Village, Kaski District," Ashadh Sudi 2, 1919 (June 1862).

[47] "Order regarding Raibandi Land Redistribution in Dhor," 1921 (1865).

changed drastically: 28.0 percent of the agricultural households had been able to control as much as 77.8 percent of the rice lands in Tanahu district, whereas the remaining 22.2 percent was in the hands of 71.9 percent of the agricultural households. There were 366 households, or 1.5 percent, who had holdings of more than 160 *muris* each.[48] This trend was by no means confined to Tanahu. According to a recent study of Thak village, in Mustang district, "in 1883 most households had a plot of rice land, and few had a large number of plots. There was more inequality by 1933, with a larger group of middling and wealthy households. By 1968 there was again more equality amongst those who held some rice land; the largest landholdings of 1933 had been split up. But there were also signs of a fast-growing section of the population who had no rice land at all."[49] The following 1961 agricultural-census statistics[50] illustrate this process of economic differentiation in the agrarian community on a nationwide basis:

Size of holdings	Percentage of agricultural households	Percentage of total cultivated area
Below 10 *ropanis*	46	10
10–20 *ropanis*	29	15
20–60 *ropanis*	17	36
Above 60 *ropanis*	8	39

These statistics show that 46 percent of agricultural households cultivated farms of less than 10 *ropanis* each, covering only 10 percent of the total cultivated area. These are the small peasants, who cultivate little land and therefore cannot meet their needs with income from farming alone. The middle peasants, those who cultivate between 10 and 20 *ropanis* of land, constituted 29 percent of agricultural households, but controlled only 15 percent of the total cultivated area. Their holdings, however, are large enough to cover their average household

[48]Statistics compiled from Central Bureau of Statistics, *Rashtriya Krishi Gananako Parinam, Tanahu* [Results of the National Agricultural Census for Tanahu district] (Kathmandu: the Bureau, 2023 [1966]), table 6, p. 6. The 1865 statistics related to *Raikar* and *Raj Guthi* lands, while those for 1961 covered lands of all tenure categories, including *Birta*.

[49]A. D. J. Macfarlane, "Population and Economy in Central Nepal: A Study of the Gurungs," (Ph.D. thesis, London University, 1972).

[50]Ministry of Food and Agriculture, *Farm Management Study in the Selected Regions of Nepal, 1968–69* (Kathmandu: the Ministry, 1971), p. 14. These statistics are based on the findings of the 1961 national agricultural census.

needs. Lastly, there are the big farmers, with farms of over 20 *ropanis*. They accounted for only 25 percent of agricultural households but controlled as much as 75 percent of the total cultivated area.

Such concentration meant that units of ownership were large, whereas units of actual cultivation were not always of the optimum size. As one study notes:

> The existence of large-scale property ownership does not secure any of the advantages of large-scale operation or investment. The tenants secure no benefit of working with better equipment, or with better seed: their methods of work are the same as those of the small owner. Landowners are less interested in maintaining the fertility of the soil, or in increasing agricultural production, than in holding wealth in a secure form.[51]

Inequality in landownership may, in part, be explained by factors that have no connection with trends in relations among different classes of the agrarian population. These include the reclamation of waste lands by families who possess the capacity and the resources to do so and who consequently increase the size of their holdings. Additional factors are subdivision and fragmentation, which explain why holdings decline in size. In Nepal, however, the emergence of property rights in land, which made it a field for monetary investment and acquirable through purchase, mortgage, and renting, appears to have played a more prominent role in accentuating agrarian inequality.

Acquisition of agricultural lands by the more prosperous sections of the agrarian community means, of course, that the poorer elements lose ownership rights in the lands they till. Such loss of landownership rights in Nepal was due primarily to indebtedness. The growing scarcity of cultivable lands and increasing fragmentation and subdivision of holdings progressively undermined the economic condition of the peasants in all parts of the country. Because the majority of peasants occupied small subsistence holdings, any adverse trend in production made it difficult for them to meet their fiscal and domestic obligations, thereby driving them toward indebtedness.

The problem of agrarian indebtedness had become both chronic and ubiquitous even during the early years of the nineteenth century, and it worsened when the *Adhiya* system was discarded in favor of the *Kut* system. Rents then soared to unprecedented heights in most parts

[51]United Nations, *Land Reform* (New York: U.N. Department of Economic Affairs, 1951), p. 18.

PROPERTY RIGHTS IN LAND 189

of the country, and the share of the surplus agricultural production left in the hands of the peasants progressively dwindled.[52] Yet another factor that encouraged agrarian indebtedness was the monetization of the land tax. Monetization meant that the peasant had to sell a portion of his crop to raise the money he needed to pay taxes. Such payment no longer meant a division of the crop between the landlord and the peasant at the threshing ground itself. There was an interval between the time when the crop was harvested and the time when payments fell due. Inasmuch as most peasants lived on the margin of subsistence, this interval intensified the propensity to consume. Official regulations therefore admitted that if peasants did not pay land tax immediately after crops were harvested, they would have nothing left at the end of the year.[53] But a time lag between harvesting of crops and payment of land taxes in cash, however short, was inevitable, and it encouraged delinquency in payment and eventual recourse to a moneylender.[54]

Even at present, there is evidence that the net annual income of a farmer in the hill region is not sufficient to repay his outstanding debts. An agricultural-credit survey conducted by the Nepal Rashtra Bank during 1969–70[55] yielded the following statistics regarding the average income, indebtedness, and repayment of an agricultural household in the hill region:

Size of farm	Net income	Indebtedness	Repayment
Large (above 20 *ropanis*) ...	Rs. 1,020	Rs. 1,314	Rs. 14
Medium (10 to 20 *ropanis*) ...	Rs. 489	Rs. 777	Rs. 2
Small (below 10 *ropanis*) ...	Rs. 347	Rs. 509	Rs. 6

The economic pressure on the peasantry was further aggravated by high rates of interest and other extortionate payments. The survey found, for example, that private moneylenders, who supplied more than 90 percent of the total agricultural credit during 1969–70, often charged interest of as much as 50 percent yearly, in addition to an initial discount on their loans at rates ranging from 5 to 25 percent.[56]

[52] Regmi, *A Study in Nepali Economic History*, p. 98.
[53] Regmi, *Land Tenure and Taxation in Nepal*, I, 144.
[54] Balakrishna Pokhrel, op. cit. (in n. 19 above), p. 570. This gives the text of a bond concerning a loan of Rs. 12 obtained by one Kalu Jaisi from the poet Bhanubhakta Acharya in 1860 for payment of land taxes in Tanahu district.
[55] Compiled from Nepal Rashtra Bank, *Agricultural Credit Survey, Nepal* (Kathmandu: the Bank, 1972), II, 95, 120, 266.
[56] Ibid., IV, 151–58.

Such practices insure that indebtedness is both chronic and accumulative.

The alienable character of *Raikar* land gave a new dimension to the problem of agrarian indebtedness. Previously, a peasant was able to obtain a loan from the village moneylender only on personal security by bonding himself, or by offering crops as security, for property rights in *Raikar* land had not evolved and therefore it could not be offered as collateral. But when transactions in *Raikar* land rights were permitted by law and such land consequently assumed the nature of a commodity, few peasants were able to withstand the pressure to offer it as collateral for a loan. Most often, land was so offered under the system of possessory mortgage, which meant that the creditor took possession of the land in lieu of interest until the loan was repaid. Possessory mortgage freed the debtor from the obligation to pay interest regularly or to repay the principal loan within a definite time limit, but imposed the burden of indebtedness on him without providing the means to redeem it. The situation became more difficult for small peasants when they were compelled to mortgage their holdings for sums far below their productive capacity and to assume the burden of a very high rate of interest. This excerpt from a law enacted during the 1880s testifies to the nature of the problem:

> In case a peasant cultivating *Raikar* lands in Kathmandu Valley, the hill regions, or the Tarai obtains a loan [from a creditor], and the latter then takes up his land for cultivation, the peasant may complain: "My holding, which can produce much [grain], is being cultivated [by the creditor] on payment of a small sum of money. I do not have the capacity to pay back the loan."[57]

The law prescribed that in such circumstances the holding should be sold by auction to the highest bidder. At the same time, it insisted that this course be followed only if the original transaction was not legally valid. The measure was ineffectual in actual practice, and it did not remain long in the statute book.

Even when mortgages were simple and not possessory, so that the moneylender did not take the land into his actual possession, prosperous farmers were able by this means to grab lands belonging to weaker peasants. By taking recourse to exorbitant and compound rates of interest, and, not infrequently, various other devious means, they ultimately enlarged the original loan to a figure that was quite beyond

[57] Law Ministry Records, "Jagga Pajani Ko," *Muluki Ain*, 1888 ed., sec. 38.

the debtor's capacity to repay, and then attached his holding. Holdings thus became larger by absorbing smaller holdings.[58]

Finally, a prosperous farmer was able to increase his holdings by renting lands belonging to others. Because of the low credit-worthiness of the small peasant and the landless agricultural laborer, cultivated land available for renting tended to pass into the hands of middle and big farmers. In Tanahu district, for instance, 7,360 agricultural families of a total of 23,844 were cultivating land in the capacity of tenants in 1961. On the other hand, 3,238 families, or about 44 percent of the total, who had holdings of forty *muris* or more of both owned and rented land, had acquired as much as 89,032 *muris*, or 71.1 percent of the total rented area. In other words, a little less than three-fourths of the total rented area had passed into the hands of middle and big farmers. In contrast, more than half of the 256 families of "pure" tenants, that is to say, "landless" peasants whose farms consisted solely of rented land, had holdings of only one to eight *muris* each.[59] Available evidence indicates that this trend was by no means confined to Tanahu.

The evolution of the agrarian structure in Nepal during the latter part of the nineteenth century consequently followed a pattern familiar to students of agrarian conditions in most countries of South Asia: a rising population and growing demand for land, increased security of tenure, subletting, and the emergence from the peasantry of a class of petty landlord-rentiers.[60]

Incidence of Tenancy

The emergence of landownership rights independent of the needs

---

[58] In one village in the far-western hill region, "Change was also the result of a chronic shortage of cash, needed for paying taxes and purchasing certain essential commodities which had to be imported. Those in a position to obtain cash—particularly the Brahmins, who received it from their clients—were able to become extremely wealthy and powerful. They lent money to members of other castes and took land on mortgage in return; they also bought land in the village. Much of the land which was sold and mortgaged belonged to untouchables, who had only limited access to cash. The latter became progressively poorer and more dependent upon the Brahmins for the wherewithal to make ends met. The only way out of the vicious circle of indebtedness and landlessness was for untouchables to migrate to India for varying periods in search of unskilled work," A. Patricia Caplan, *Priests and Cobblers* (San Francisco: Chandler Publishing Co., 1972), p. 1; see also p. 22.

[59] Central Bureau of Statistics, op. cit. (in n. 48 above), table 6, p. 6.

[60] Barrington Moore, Jr., *Social Origins of Dictatorship and Democracy* (Penguin Books, 1967), pp. 362-63.

for subsistence had a profound effect on the nature of *Raikar* tenure. *Raikar* landownership rights were now prized not because they yielded an opportunity for personal labor and subsistence, but because they created a new avenue for profitable investment and were therefore a source of unearned income. This, in turn, led to a cleavage between ownership of land and its actual use. The size of holdings was now determined by what a farmer could reclaim, or acquire through mortgage, outright purchase, or otherwise, not by the needs of his family or by its working capacity. But, given the average size of the family and the level of agricultural technology, it was obviously impossible for an agricultural family to cultivate personally the entire area it could accumulate. Frequently, a farmer could give up agriculture altogether as an occupation, and concentrate on moneylending and other enterprises. In this manner emerged the landlord-tenant hierarchy in Nepal.

It is important to assess the true importance of the problem, however, because not all lands were affected by the trend toward the emergence of tenancy. Table 5, which gives the total area of cultivated land and that under tenancy in 1961 in the different regions, shows that during that year only 27.64 percent of the total was under tenancy.[61] The data in the table indicate that the overall incidence of tenancy was higher in Kathmandu Valley and the Tarai region than in the hill regions. In the western midland and Himalayan regions, in particular, only 19.14 percent of rice land and 6.55 percent of unirrigated land were under tenancy in 1961.

The incidence of tenancy is obviously governed by one or more of several factors, chief among which are agricultural productivity and size of holdings. It can hardly be a coincidence that agricultural productivity is higher in Kathmandu Valley and the Tarai regions than in other parts of the country. The conclusion that the incidence of tenancy varies in proportion to productivity is proved also by the fact that only 16.50 percent of the total unirrigated agricultural area in the kingdom is cultivated by tenants, whereas the percentage is 35.65 in respect to rice lands. The reasons for the correlation between tenancy and productivity are not difficult to understand. The sharing of the produce of the land between landowners and tenants obviously depends on the quantity available; where the output of land is too low to

[61]Central Bureau of Statistics, "Sample Census of Agriculture," mimeographed (Kathmandu: the Bureau, 1962), table 2. Only 98 percent of rice lands and 86.55 of unirrigated lands contained in agricultural holdings were actually cultivable.

TABLE 5

TOTAL AREA OF AGRICULTURAL HOLDINGS IN NEPAL AND SHARE THEREOF CULTIVATED BY TENANTS, 1961

Region	Total area in agricultural holdings (in thousand muris)		Area cultivated by tenants (in thousand muris)		Percentage of total area	
	Irrigated (rice) land	Unirrigated land	Irrigated (rice) land	Unirrigated land	Irrigated (rice) land	Unirrigated land
Eastern midlands and Himalayan regions	3,836	11,292	1,627	1,967	42.41	17.41
Eastern inner Tarai	1,843	2,094	615	223	33.36	10.64
Eastern Tarai	46,509	15,105	16,186	3,040	34.81	20.12
Kathmandu Valley	1,417	865	591	201	41.70	23.23
Central inner Tarai	1,788	2,602	413	269	23.09	10.33
Western midlands and Himalayan regions	3,500	12,374	675	815	19.28	6.58
Western inner Tarai	3,006	1,765	1,340	672	44.57	38.01
Western Tarai	9,981	4,077	4,590	1,267	45.98	31.07
Western Tarai far-western midlands and Himalayan regions	1,847	6,688	431	691	23.33	10.33
Far-western Tarai	10,447	3,718	3,554	1,064	33.82	28.61
Total	84,174	60,580	30,022	10,209	35.01	16.85
Grand total—144,754			40.231		27.79	

provide subsistence to the tenant and an income to the landowner that he considers sufficient, the land will not be given to a tenant for cultivation.[62] The importance of the size of holdings in determining

[62] Donald. S. Zagoria, "The Ecology of Peasant Communism in India," *American Political Science Review*, LXV, no. 1 (March 1971), 144: "In India, and in other parts of monsoon Asia, there is a link between the cultivation of irrigated food crops, particularly wet-rice, on the one hand, and heavy rural population concentrations, tenancy and uneconomic dwarf-holdings on the other."

the incidence of tenancy is demonstrated by the fact that in the western Tarai region, where the size of individual holdings is larger than in any other part of the kingdom, as much as 45.98 percent of the total area of cultivated land is under tenancy. It is clear that a landowner who has been able to accumulate an area larger than he can cultivate personally has the option either to appoint tenants for this purpose or employ hired labor. The use of hired labor, however, presupposes a situation in which labor is cheap and easily available or its net product is high. Otherwise, tenancy is the sole alternative.

Landlord-Tenant Relations

Under conditions of subinfeudation, landownership assumed the form of a rent-collection function, devoid of any positive contributions to farm management or real investment. Having no direct function in the processes of agricultural production, the landowner was able to concentrate on moneylending or pursue nonagricultural occupations such as trade and service. The evils of absentee landlordism thus emerged "through the neglect or atrophy of the management function among the owners of land."[63] There was, moreover, little control of the landowner's power over his tenants. The government considered that tenants as a class were hardly important, because it was the landowner who paid taxes on land. A legal and administrative framework that visualized a direct relationship between the state and the actual cultivator virtually ignored this class. The tax-assessment records maintained by the government contained only the names of taxpaying landowners and not those of tenants who actually cultivated the land. According to the law existing at the end of the Rana regime in 1951, restrictions on the eviction of *Raikar* landholders were generally applicable also in the case of tenant cultivators. Eviction was permitted in the event of noncultivation or nonpayment of rents, but only during prescribed seasons.[64] These restrictions were generally ineffective, because of the lack of enforcement machinery at the local level. In any case, the law permitted tenant cultivators to relinquish their lands voluntarily.[65] Usually, it was difficult to ascertain whether such voluntary relinquishment did not actually involve a measure of

---

[63] Parsons, (op. cit. (in n. 2 above), p. 28.
[64] Government of Nepal, "Jagga Pajani Ko," *Muluki Ain*, pt. III (2009 [1952]), sec. 5, p. 29.
[65] Ibid., sec. 7, p. 29.

compulsion. Rana legislation also gave to a tenant cultivator the preemptive right in prescribed circumstances to purchase the lands being cultivated by him and to redeem alienations made in favor of others.[66] This was a meaningless provision, however, for the actual value of land transactions was usually overstated in official documents.

No arrangement existed in any part of the country to control rents, and their level was determined by such factors as productivity, local custom, and population pressure.[67] The proportion of the rent to the total yield varied from two-thirds in the eastern Tarai to one-third in the sparsely populated areas of the far-western Tarai.[68] Sometimes in the hill districts, including Kathmandu Valley, the best land in the village fetched a rent amounting to two-thirds of the crop.[69] Elsewhere, an equal division of the gross produce between the landowner and the tenant was the custom generally followed.[70]

To sum up, the agrarian system that existed in Nepal at the end of the Rana regime encouraged social and economic differentiation in the agrarian community and a trend toward the concentration of landownership and toward absentee landownership. It thus failed to protect the rights and interests of those who worked on the land. There was no adequate protection against arbitrary evictions, and no practical limits to the rents that tenants might be compelled to pay the landowner. As one study notes while describing the evils of the traditional form of tenancy in Asian countries:

> In the first place, the tenant has little incentive to increase his output, since a large share in any such increase will accrue to the landowner, who has incurred no part of its cost. In the second place, the high share of the produce taken by the landowner may leave the peasant with a bare

[66]Government of Nepal, "Sahu Asami Ko" [On creditors and debtors], ibid., sec. 10, p. 113.

[67]In Dang-Deukhuri, for instance, "With an increasing number of persons dependent on income from virtually the same amount of land under cultivation as formerly, over most of the districts, and without there having been much intensification of methods of production, rents have risen. The actual tiller receives less income from the land than before. Less of the surplus crop can be sold by the tiller, because more is paid in rent. Especially in Dang, rents had been rising steadily when Land Reform was implemented in 1965." Charles Mcdougal, *Village and Household Economy in Far-Western Nepal* (Kirtipur: Tribhuwan University, n.d., [1968]), p. 113.

[68]Tek Bahadur Panthi, *Hamro Arthik Samasya* [Our economic problems], (Kapilavastu: Bishnumaya Devi Panthi, 2019 [1962]), pp. 40-41, 48-49.

[69]John T. Hitchcock, *The Magars of Banyan Hill* (New York: Holt, Rinehart and Winston, 1966), p. 19.

[70]Regmi, I, 14-15.

subsistence minimum, with no margin for investment; in a bad year, he gets more heavily in debt; in a good year, he can reduce his indebtedness. Thirdly, it means that wealth is held in the form of land, and that the accumulation of capital does not lead to productive investment. In Asia, the landowner is also a moneylender, and in this capacity depends more on interest on loans to small cultivators than on increased income from the improvement of land.[71]

It is against this background that we shall attempt, in the following chapter, to analyze recent land-reform programs and their impact on the structure of agrarian society in Nepal.

[71] United Nations, *Land Reform*, p. 18.

Chapter 11

THE IMPACT OF LAND REFORM

Social and economic justice, together with a higher standard of living for the people, were adopted as directive principles of state policy in Nepal for the first time in 1951, after the downfall of the Rana regime. Because of the importance of agriculture in the social and economic life of Nepal, efforts to apply these principles were naturally concentrated in the agrarian field. The government of Nepal realized that the existing agrarian system had failed in important respects to protect the rights and interests of those who work on the land, and that a higher standard of living for the people was not possible without the development of agriculture. We shall now consider the extent to which recent land-reform programs have changed or modified the agrarian structure described in chapter 10.

OBJECTIVES OF LAND-REFORM POLICY

In the initial stage of post-1951 land reform, the government of Nepal envisaged it primarily as an instrument of social justice. Land-reform policy therefore aimed at ameliorating the condition of the peasantry and stemming the tide of social unrest. An official statement issued in 1952 declared:

> Unless the land-tenure system is improved, the economic condition of the peasantry and agricultural production will not improve. Land-ownership is passing from the hands of peasants to those of money-lenders and other rich people. But the actual cultivators do not have security of tenure. This has reduced agricultural production and increased the number of landless peasants.[1]

Steps to ameliorate the condition of the peasantry were considered urgent because, in several districts, particularly in the western Tarai, "these developments [were] leading to an agrarian revolution."[2]

[1] *Nepal Gazette*, vol. 1, no. 22, Poush 23, 2008 (January 6, 1952).
[2] Ibid.

Nevertheless, it did not prove overly difficult for the government to forestall the anticipated "revolution." Official commissions were sent to several districts in the Tarai to recommend measures for resolving landlord-tenant disputes,[3] particularly those concerning unauthorized appropriation of ownership rights by *Jimidars* and the sharing of crops. The major recommendations of these commissions were that a ban should be imposed on the eviction of cultivators, that conditions of tenancy should be stipulated clearly in writing, and that landowners should issue receipts for the rents paid to them by their tenants.[4] These were clearly ad hoc arrangements aimed at defusing the situation and they had no significant impact on the systems of landownership and tenancy. Moreover, no action was taken to ameliorate the condition of the peasantry in the hill regions, possibly because no "agrarian revolution" was apprehended there at the time.

The 1957 Lands Act,[5] the first major land-reform measure undertaken in Nepal during the post-1951 period, fully reflected the imprint of this hesitant approach. Its main objective was to define the nature of the relationship between landlord and tenant without introducing any structural changes in the agrarian system. It sought to grant security of tenure to tenants, regulate the rents paid by them to landlords, and prohibit extra impositions in money or labor. The measure was largely ineffective because of the lack of implementation machinery at the local level, as well as of records of tenants.

After 1961, there was a marked change in official thinking regarding the scope of land-reform policy. Land reform was considered to be of crucial importance in the successful implementation of the economic and political goals of the Panchayat system that was introduced in that year. Simultaneously, the government of Nepal realized that such steps as protection of tenancy rights, control of rents and interest rates, and imposition of ceilings on landholdings should be supple-

---

[3] These commissions were sent to the western and far-western Tarai districts of Palhi, Majhkhand, Sheoraj, Taulihawa, Banke, Bardiya, Kailali, and Kanchanpur. "Notifications of the Ministry of Food and Land Administration," ibid., no. 23, Poush 30, 2008 (January 13, 1952), and no. 41, Jestha 6, 2008 (May 19, 1952). Reports of the commissions have been summarized in Nepali Congress, *Kisanharuko Nimti Nepali Congressle Ke Garyo?* [What has the Nepali Congress done for the peasants?] (Kathmandu: Nepali Congress, n.d.), pp. 10-26.

[4] Ibid., p. 11.

[5] Ministry of Law and Justice, "Bhumi Sambandhi Ain, 2014" [Lands act, 1957], *Nepal Gazette*, vol. 7, no. 5 (Extraordinary), Shrawan 22, 2014 (August 18, 1957). Amended on Poush 1, 2016 (December 15, 1959), Marga 21, 2018 (December 6, 1961), and Magh 24, 2018 (February 6, 1962).

mented by arrangements for the supply of credit, fertilizers, and irrigation facilities and for the development of cooperatives.[6] It also realized that the vast sums of money invested in land purchases should be diverted toward development in other spheres of the economy.[7] This line of thinking laid greater stress on the need to accelerate growth in nonagricultural spheres than on the egalitarian ideal of social justice. It aimed at "diverting inactive capital and manpower from the land to other sectors of the economy in order to accelerate the pace of national development."[8] Only secondary importance was given to the need to improve the standard of living of the peasantry through equitable land distribution and the provision of agricultural know-how and resources. The government recognized that land reform is only one of the several components of economic development. Tenurial reforms, therefore, constituted only a secondary aspect of the land-reform program introduced during 1963–64, the final goal being nothing else than to give impetus to industrial development.[9]

[6] National Planning Council, *Tesro Yojana, 2022–27* [Third plan, 1965–70] (Kathmandu: the Council, 2022 [1965], p. 73.
[7] Ministry of Economic Planning, *Economic Affairs Report*, I, no. 2 (May 1963), p. 9.
[8] Ministry of Law, "Bhumi Sambandhi Ain, 2021" [Lands act, 1964], *Nepal Gazette*, vol. 14, no. 18 (Extraordinary), Marga 1, 2021 (November 16, 1964), preamble. This law replaced the 1957 Lands Act and the 1963 Agricultural (New Arrangements) Act.
[9] The program may therefore be called agrarian reform rather than land reform. "Although land reform and agrarian reform may be considered as the same phenomenon, it seems useful to distinguish between the two terms, the latter being considered the more comprehensive. A land-reform program is directed toward the redistribution of wealth opportunity and private power as manifest in the ownership and control of land. Agrarian reform has come to have the broader meaning, at least in the discussions of policy in the United Nations and the U.S.A., of the reconstruction or reformation of the whole structure of the agricultural economy by the creation of appropriate institutions and public services designed to strengthen the economic position of the independent farmer." Kenneth H. Parsons, "Agrarian Reform Policy as a Field of Research," in *Agrarian Reform and Economic Growth in Developing Countries* (Washington: U.S. Department of Agriculture, 1962), p. 17. For a summary of different interpretations of the concept of land reform see United Nations, *Progress in Land Reform* (New York: U.N. Department of Economic Affairs, 1954), p. 49. An incisive comment on this confusion is made by Doreen Warriner, who has rightly stressed that "it is important not to blunt the edge of the policy by widening it too much." She adds: "Because the conception of land reform has broadened to include a variety of measures to improve land tenure and agricultural organization, the emphasis shifts from the foundation to the accessories, and the original—and still essential—aim of greater social and economic equality tends to be obscured. The integrated approach sometimes seems to offer everything except the land." *Land Reform and Development in the Middle East* (2d. ed.; London: Oxford University Press, 1962), pp. 3–6.

The 1964 Land-Reform Program

A comprehensive land-reform program was accordingly introduced throughout the country in three stages during the period from 1964 to 1966. The program aimed both at remolding agrarian relations and mobilizing capital from agriculture. With the objective of insuring "the equitable distribution of cultivated land," ceilings were imposed on both landownership and tenancy holdings. Tenancy rights were provided to all peasants cultivating agricultural lands belonging to others at the time of the enforcement of the program, and to all those who subsequently cultivated the main crop at least once. Agricultural rents were generally fixed at a maximum of 50 percent of the main crop. These provisions were first applied to *Raikar* lands alone, and were extended to *Raj Guthi* lands with in-kind revenue assessments in September 1972.[10] In addition, efforts were made to mobilize capital by introducing a compulsory-savings scheme and a taxation system covering both landowners and tenants, and by intercepting the repayment of moneylenders' capital.

The land-reform program has thus had a twofold objective. On the one hand, it aims at establishing cultivators on the land "as freemen and citizens, operating land which they own or hold securely, and owning at least an equitable share of the product of the land."[11] On the other, it seeks to divert both investment capital and surplus manpower from agriculture for the development of the nonagricultural sector.[12] We shall now examine the main components of the program: ceilings on landholding, security of tenancy rights, rent control, and compulsory savings and credit provisions.

Ceilings on Landholding

One of the factors that hastened the pace of land-reform activity

---

[10] Ministry of Law and Justice, "Guthi Samsthan Ain, 2029" [Guthi Corporation act, 1972], *Nepal Rajapatra*, vol. 22, no. 30A (Extraordinary), Aswin 5, 2029 (September 21, 1972), secs. 26–30.

[11] Kenneth H. Parsons, "The Tenure of Farms, Motivation, and Productivity," in *Science, Technology and Development*, vol. III, *Agriculture* (Washington: U.S. Government Printing Office, n.d.), p. 31.

[12] An official report states: "From agriculture must come Nepal's nonfarm labor force and most of the investment capital which she herself provides for development. Unless processes are set in motion which will draw labor and investment capital from agriculture and set them to work in nonagricultural sectors, economic growth will not take place." Ministry of Economic Planning, *Economic Affairs Report*, I, no. 2 (May 1963), p. 9.

during the post-1961 period was the realization that a situation in which "the ownership of land is concentrated in a very small number of people, while the majority of cultivators are exploited," was inimical to both economic development and democracy.[13] An attempt was therefore made to diffuse rights to use the land by imposing ceilings on the holdings of both landowners and tenants.

The 1964 Lands Act prescribed that a family (the term being defined to include parents, minor children, and unmarried daughters below thirty-five years of age) would be permitted to own not more than 25 *bighas* of land in any part of the country, in addition to prescribed areas for residential purposes. Ceilings prescribed for both agricultural and residential purposes in different parts of the country[14] are given in table 6. The Lands Act also imposed ceilings on tenancy holdings in various regions. These ceilings amount to 4 *bighas* in the Tarai and the inner Tarai, 10 *ropanis* in Kathmandu Valley, and 20 *ropanis* in the hill regions. Tenants are not entitled to additional areas for residential purposes. These arrangements are applicable also to "mixed" farmers, that is, those who cultivate their own lands as well as lands rented from others.[15]

TABLE 6

CEILINGS ON LANDHOLDING IN DIFFERENT REGIONS

Region	Agricultural lands	Residential lands	
		Urban areas	Rural areas
Tarai and inner Tarai regions (in *bighas*)	25	1	3
Kathmandu Valley (in *ropanis*)	50	5	8
Hill regions (in *ropanis*)	80	10	16

Source: See chap. 11, n. 14.

Land in excess of the prescribed ceilings is acquired by the government on payment of compensation at prescribed rates. The rates have been fixed at ten times the land tax for agricultural lands, and

---

[13] *Nepal Gazette*, vol. 10, no. 20, Poush 22, 2017 (January 5, 1961).
[14] Lands Act, 1964, sec. 7.
[15] Ibid., sec. 8.

five times the tax for nonagricultural lands.[16] Ten percent of the amount of the compensation is payable in cash within one year of acquisition and reallotment, and the balance in the form of bonds bearing interest at 3 to 5 percent, which may be utilized after ten years to purchase shares in development programs undertaken by the government. These bonds are accepted in payment of deposits or as security to His Majesty's Government, and as collateral to any autonomous corporate body for the purpose of obtaining industrial loans; they may also be sold or transferred. Surplus lands acquired under the program are redistributed, subject to the prescribed ceilings, to tenants currently cultivating them or members of their family, owners of adjoining holdings, and other tenants, in that order of preference. Landless persons come at the bottom of the list, because the main purpose of this measure is to consolidate existing holdings into economic units, rather than to create a multitude of uneconomic holdings.

By July 1972, the government of Nepal had acquired a total area of approximately 50,000 hectares of surplus lands under this program. This amounts to approximately 3 percent of the cultivated area. Only 22,000 hectares, however, have actually been redistributed, to about 10,000 peasant families.[17] The slow progress in reallotment has been attributed to the fact that revenue surveys have not been completed and therefore accurate boundaries of the surplus lands have not been ascertained.[18] It is also possible that the entire area declared as surplus is not cultivable. Complaints of irregularities in the land-redistribution program have been made and they seem to be substantiated by the fact that high-powered official commissions were deputed to probe into such irregularities in late 1971.[19]

[16] *Nepal Rajapatra*, vol. 21, no. 30, Marga 6, 2028 (November 23, 1971).

[17] Ram Bahadur, *A General Study on Land Reform, Land Administration and Socio-Economic Activities* (Kathmandu: Lands Department, Ministry of Land Reform, 1972), pp. 9, 19, 34. In November 1973, the order of priority for land redistribution under the 1964 Lands Act was changed to provide that "His Majesty's Government may assign third priority to prescribed public institutions after tenants and owners of adjoining holdings in the allotments of lands in excess of the prescribed ceilings." Ministry of Land Reform, "Bhumi Sambandhi (Athaun Samshodhan) Niyam Haru, 2030" [Lands (eighth amendment) rules, 1973], *Nepal Gazette*, vol. 23, no. 30, Kartik 27, 2030 (November 12, 1973).

[18] National Planning Commission, *Fourth Plan (1970–75)* (Kathmandu: the Commission, 1972), p. 106.

[19] *Gorkhapatra*, Aswin 21, 2028 (October 7, 1971). A similar commission was deputed to Bardiya district in April 1973. *Nepal Gazette*, vol. 23, no. 3, Baisakh 18, 2030 (April 3, 1973). The extent of such irregularities necessitated the addition of the following provision to the 1964 Lands Act in October 1968: "His Majesty's Government may

Security of Tenancy Rights

As defined in the 1964 Lands Act, a tenant is "a peasant who obtains land from a landowner on any condition and cultivates it through his personal labor, or the labor of his family." In other words, only actual cultivators were recognized as tenants. The rights of intermediaries, that is, those persons who obtained land from a landowner and sublet it to actual cultivators, were abolished without compensation. Existing tenants, or those who raised the main crop at least once, were entitled to permanent tenancy rights on the agricultural lands tilled by them. Their eviction was permitted only if they did anything to reduce the value or productivity of the land, defaulted in the payment of rents, or discontinued cultivation for one year. In any case, landowners were permitted to evict tenants for these offenses only through legal action.[20]

Landowners were allowed to resume their lands for residential purposes within specified limits, but were required to pay compensation to the tenant at 25 percent of the value of the land so resumed. Resumption of land for agricultural purposes was permitted without payment of compensation only if the landowner had given his land for cultivation to a tenant because he was serving in the army, or was a minor, a chronic invalid, or insane, and subsequently became able to cultivate the land personally. However, individual action to resume lands cultivated by tenants was ruled out in all cases.[21] Even relinquishment of tenancy rights was not permitted without official sanction.[22]

The law thus sought to make the tenant secure on his holding so long as he paid the prescribed rents and cultivated the land regularly and properly. Nevertheless, it took care to insure that tenancy rights did not develop into salable property rights. A tenant was not permitted to sell his holding, or alienate it through gift, donation, or other means. Nor could tenancy rights be auctioned in settlement of

---

institute investigations in case it is satisfied that any person has appropriated, on the basis of false particulars or in contravention of the rules framed under this law, lands which have been acquired or confiscated by His Majesty's Government under this law. Lands which have been [wrongfully] appropriated by any person in this manner may be confiscated and then reallotted in the prescribed manner." Ministry of Law and Justice, "Bhumi Sambandhi (Dosro Samshodhan) Ain, 2025" [Lands (second amendment) act, 1968], *Nepal Rajapatra*, vol. 18, no. 21 (Extraordinary), Kartik 9, 2025 (October 25, 1968), sec. 10, pp. 108-9.

[20] Lands Act, 1964, secs. 25, 29.
[21] Ibid., secs. 27, 28.
[22] Ibid., sec. 26 (1) (a).

any governmental or private claim or penalty.[23] With the aim of checking fragmentation, the law also prescribed that after the death of a tenant, tenancy rights on the lands tilled by him should accrue to the surviving husband or wife or son, "whosoever is trusted by the landowner."[24] Tenancy rights were hence not subdivisible.

Rent Control

Legal provisions for the protection of tenancy rights are not enough, however. Unless rents are controlled, such provisions become ineffective, for landowners can simply increase rents to a level beyond the capacity of the tenant to pay and then evict him on the ground of delinquency in payment. Since 1957, therefore, the government of Nepal has prescribed ceilings on rents that tenants are required to pay to their landowners, so as to provide a just share of output to the tenant and thereby increase total production. The government believed that in the absence of rent-control measures the tenant would have no incentive to increase production. Accordingly, the trend of official policy has been not only to impose ceilings on agricultural rents, but also to reduce such ceilings progressively. The 1957 Lands Act prohibited landowners from charging rents in excess of 50 percent of the total produce in cash or in kind. At the same time, it prescribed that collection should be made at a lower rate, if any, prevalent according to custom, law, or mutual agreement between the landowner and the tenant.[25] The 1964 Lands Act retained this provision for all parts of the country except Kathmandu Valley, where it fixed rents at speci-

TABLE 7

AGRICULTURAL RENTS IN KATHMANDU VALLEY (IN *pathis* PER *ropani*)

Grade of land	Rice lands (*Khet*)	Unirrigated lands (*Pakho*)
Abal	23	10.12
Doyam	18.75	7.25
Sim	13	4.37
Chahar	8.62	2.87

Source: See chap. 11, n. 26.

[23] Ibid., sec. 26A.
[24] Ibid., sec. 26 (1).
[25] Ibid., sec. 3.

fic rates, shown in table 7, according to the grade of the land.[26] Official estimates indicate that these figures amounted to roughly one-third of the total produce.[27]

Until October 1968, half of the total annual produce from all crops grown on the land was the maximum amount that a landowner could collect as rent from his tenant in areas other than Kathmandu Valley. At that time, the ceiling was reduced to half of the main crop.[28] The government also assumed the power to determine the average output of the main crop and then fix the rent at a specific rate on the basis of half of that quantity. So far, rents have been fixed under this provision at the rates shown in table 8 in the districts of the eastern Tarai and in Chitaun in the inner Tarai.[29] Rents at these rates are payable in paddy on rice lands and maize on dry lands, irrespective of the actual crop grown. There is evidence that these rates amount to less than 50 percent of the main crop,[30] but they were deliberately kept low because

TABLE 8

AGRICULTURAL RENTS IN SOME TARAI AND INNER TARAI DISTRICTS (IN MAUNDS PER *bigha*)

Grade of land	Category of land	
	Khet	Pakho
Abal	15	8.5
Doyam	11.5	6.5
Sim	8.5	4.5
Chahar	5.5	—

[26] Ibid., sec. 33.

[27] His Majesty's Government, *The Budget Speech, 1961* (Kathmandu: Department of Publicity and Broadcasting, 1961, p. 8. These rates had initially been applied to *Birta* lands in Kathmandu Valley which had been converted into *Raikar* under the 1959 Birta Abolition Act. Ministry of Law and Justice, "Birta Unmulan (Samshodhan) Ain, 2018" [Birta abolition (amendment) act, 1962], *Nepal Gazette*, vol. 11, no. 40 (Extraordinary), Magh 24, 2018 (February 8, 1962), sec. 2.

[28] Ministry of Law and Justice, "Bhumi Sambandhi (Dosro Samshodhan) Ain, 2025" [Lands (second amendment) act, 1968], *Nepal Rajapatra*, vol. 18, no. 21 (Extraordinary), Kartik 9, 2025 (October 25, 1968).

[29] *Nepal Rajapatra*, vol. 21, no. 20, Bhadra 14, 2028 (August 30, 1971), and vol. 23, no. 26, Aswin 29, 2030 (October 15, 1973).

[30] In the eastern Tarai region, the average yield of paddy is 33 maunds per *bigha*. Central Bureau of Statistics, *Pramukh Bali Ko Utpadan Dar* [Average yields of main crops], (Kathmandu: the Bureau, 2022 [1965]), p. 27. The yield on lands of *Abal* grade is therefore much higher.

"the cultivator will have to bear all costs of cultivation himself."[31] Moreover, landowners are under obligation to grant remissions if the tenant is unable to cultivate the land, or if crops are not good in any year because of adverse circumstances or natural calamities.[32]

Compulsory Savings and Credit Provisions

The main aim of the land-reform program is to divert inactive capital and manpower from the land to other sectors of the economy in order to accelerate the pace of national development. Attempts were made to attain that goal through the introduction of a compulsory-savings scheme and interception of the repayment of moneylenders' capital. The 1964 Lands Act prescribed that every landowner and tenant should make in-kind savings on a compulsory basis from the main crop grown on the land owned or cultivated by him. These savings are deposited with local committees formed for the implementation of the land-reform program, and interest is paid on them at 5 percent. Refundment is made after five years wholly or partly in cash, or in government-loan bonds, or in shares, stock, or debentures of agricultural-credit agencies.[33] Table 9 gives the rates of these compulsory savings.[34]

TABLE 9
RATES OF COMPULSORY SAVINGS IN DIFFERENT REGIONS

Category	*Tarai region* (*per* bigha)	*Hill region* (*per* ropani)
Landowners and tenants paying less than 50 percent of the annual produce as rent	14 *seers*	2 *manas*
Landowners and tenants getting less than 50 percent of the annual produce as rent	6 *seers*	1 *mana*
Owner-cultivators	20 *seers*	3 *manas*

Source: See chap. 11, n. 34.

[31]Ram Bahadur, "Kut Nirdharan" [Assessment of agricultural rents], *Gorkhapatra*, Kartik 10, 2028 (October 27, 1971).
[32]Lands Act, 1964, sec. 35.
[33]Ibid., secs. 40–43.
[34]Ministry of Land Reform, "Bhumi Sambhandhi Niyam Haru, 2021" [Lands rules, 1964], *Nepal Gazette*, vol. 14, no. 21 (Extraordinary), Marga 8, 2021 (November 22, 1964). Rule 26, as amended on Baisakh 13, 2028 (April 26, 1971).

During a period of approximately five years, from November 1964 to April 1969, a total amount of Rs. 120 million was collected throughout the kingdom under the compulsory-savings scheme. Rs. 80 million are being used for the supply of agricultural credit through village-level committees.[35] The balance of Rs. 40 million has been deposited with a central agency formed by the government to administer the compulsory-savings scheme and finance industrial and other enterprises "from which the agricultural and rural sector can derive direct and immediate benefit."[36] Collection of compulsory savings was suspended, however, in early 1969 because of allegations of large-scale defalcations.[37]

In addition, arrangements were made to intercept the repayment of loans previously advanced by moneylenders to peasants for agricultural purposes; the proceeds were to be eventually refunded to the moneylenders concerned. Similarly, landowners were not permitted to take back from tenants oxen and other agricultural resources given to the latter for purposes of cultivation.[38] The objective was to mobilize the agricultural resources previously involved in private moneylending operations and institutionalize the agricultural-credit system. Of perhaps greater importance were provisions aimed at scaling down the volume of agricultural indebtedness by controlling rates of interest. If the creditor had already realized interest double the amount of the principal, the loan was canceled. If he had collected interest at a rate exceeding 10 percent on both ordinary loans and possessory mortgages, the excess was deducted from the principal amount. In the event that lands had been utilized on possessory mortgages and income appropriated in excess of 10 percent of the amount of the loan, the excess amount so appropriated was deducted from the principal. These provisions have resulted in the redemption of agricultural loans amounting to approximately Rs. 40 million and the restoration of mortgaged lands totaling about 12,000 *bighas*.[39]

IMPACT OF THE LAND-REFORM PROGRAM

The 1964 land-reform program has made the most incisive intervention in systems of landownership and tenancy in the history of

[35] Figures obtained from the Department of Land Reform.
[36] *Nepal Rajapatra*, Magh 8, 2024 (January 22, 1968).
[37] *Gorkhapatra*, Chaitra 29, 2025 (April 11, 1969).
[38] Lands Act, 1964, secs. 45–46.
[39] Figures obtained from the Department of Land Reform.

Nepal and has had profound social and psychological consequences. We are here concerned, however, only with the impact of the program on the agrarian structure.

With the imposition of ceilings on landholding, the existing concentration of landownership has been broken, both through the redistribution of lands in excess of the ceilings and through voluntary transfers in anticipation of land reform. Big landowners no longer constitute a dominant economic class in the agricultural community.[40] Of perhaps greater importance is the fact that land is no longer available for unlimited acquisition through monetary investment.

The land-reform program has also conferred greater security of tenure on tenants and made it possible for them to appropriate the major portion of the produce. Intermediary tenants have been eliminated, and the right of landowners to evict their tenants or to increase rents at their discretion has been taken away. Land reform has thus made tenants "free men, no longer trepidly dependent on their landlords for land and the means to till it."[41] Their rights are clearly defined by law and are actually being enforced by courts in their favour.

Nevertheless, the land-reform program has had little impact on the agrarian structure that has been described in the foregoing chapters. The program has made tenants more secure on their holdings and also has reduced the rents payable by them to their landowners, but it has strengthened the position of landowners as rent receivers without imposing any obligation on them beyond collecting rents after crops are harvested. Nor has the acquisition of lands in excess of the prescribed ceilings affected the nature of the landholding system per se. Land still remains a profitable field for investment, and the demand of the upper classes of the rural community for land remains undiminished. Along with the tendency to resume lands for personal cultivation, the progressive displacement of the small peasant, and the growing pressure of the population, this is likely to result in the progressive proletarization of the peasantry. The problem could be solved, in part, by "diverting manpower and other resources"[42] from land to other sectors of the economy, but the land-reform program has not had much success in bringing this about.

[40] Zaman, *Evaluation of Land Reform in Nepal*, p. 31.

[41] James B. Hunt, "The Political Repercussions of Land Reform on the Economic Development of Nepal," in Department of Land Reform, *Bhumi Sudhar* [Land reform], Jestha 2023 (June 1966), p. 23.

[42] Lands Act, 1964, preamble.

One defect of the 1964 land-reform program is that it fails to take into account the different categories of property relationships in land. Large areas of agricultural lands are cultivated personally by the owner. No restriction exists on the emergence of tenancy on such lands. Certainly it would be a more realistic policy to forestall such a development than subsequently to seek to protect tenants by reducing rents and making tenancy rights secure. Yet restrictions on the emergence of tenancy on owner-cultivated lands can scarcely be imposed unless these categories of tenure relationships are defined by law. Owner cultivation and tenancy are land-tenure forms so different in their impact on land use and rural life that it appears incongruous to lump them together under the same reform policy.

The purpose of rent control was, together with increased land taxation, to "squeeze the income from the land available to the non-tiller owner to the point where other investments in the nonagricultural sector look more favorable."[43] A new role was envisaged for the landowning class in the development of the nonagricultural sectors of the economy.[44] Realities belie this enthusiasm, however. Despite the land-reform program, agricultural land is still not only a profitable avenue of investment but is deliberately being made so from the viewpoints of both current returns and capital gains. One observer of the land-reform program points out that the new rates of agricultural rents in the eastern Tarai have been fixed at a level that insures an income to the landowner not less than he would have obtained by investing his capital in other fields.[45] He adds:

> A rent of 15 maunds of paddy, commuted into cash at Rs. 40 per maund, will yield Rs. 600 to the landowner. After deducting Rs. 51 as land tax, his net income will amount to Rs. 549. Assuming that the average price of rice land of *Abal* grade is Rs. 5,000 per *bigha*, the return

[43] Quentin W. Lindsey, "Budabari Panchayat: The Second Year after Reform," in Department of Land Reform, *Bhumi Sudhar*, p. 32.

[44] "The landlord class should be utilized in the future course of development, but through clear and rigorously enforced land-reform policies its retarding influence upon tiller decisions should be eliminated.... Land-reform policies will push the managerial talents and capital of the landlord class away from land; positive measures to utilize their resources in construction of transport and hydroelectric power systems, in manufacturing and trade, and in public service, must be deliberately framed." Quentin W. Lindsey, "Agricultural Planning in Nepal," *Economic Affairs Report*, V, no. 1 (February 1967), pp. 44–45.

[45] Bahadur, op. cit. (in n. 31 above). A recent evaluation of the land-reform program, undertaken under the auspices of the FAO, arrived at the same conclusion. Zaman, *Evaluation of Land Reform in Nepal*, pp. 70–71.

on the landowner's investment will amount to approximately 10 percent, that is, not less than he would have obtained from other sources.

A landowner therefore has little reason to divert his capital from land to the nonagricultural sector.

The 1964 Lands Act provides a number of benefits to the tenant that are certainly illusory. The tenant is permitted to construct buildings and other fixtures on the land for purposes of cultivation even without the landowner's consent. He may remove such assets in the event of the termination of his tenancy rights, if the landowner does not offer him compensation. On the other hand, it is most unlikely that the landowner should make such an offer, inasmuch as it is physically impossible for the tenant to remove "walls, enclosures, drains, bridges, irrigation channels, wells, huts, etc." from the land.[46] Moreover, the landowner has been given the right to resume specified areas of land for residential purposes, on payment of compensation to the tenant amounting to 25 percent of the value of the land,[47] but no provision has been made to insure that under such circumstances the tenant is not displaced. The landowner is even entitled to resume land from a tenant who is in possession of an area equal to or less than the area permitted to be resumed, so that the latter may be rendered landless. Legislation enacted for *Birta* lands in 1906 during the Rana regime had permitted *Birta* owners to resume lands for personal residence or cultivation on condition that the tenant be fully compensated for it and not be deprived of his entire holding. Restoration of this enactment to cover all categories of landowners would have been of greater advantage to tenants.

Available evidence suggests, in fact, that legal provisions aimed at protecting tenancy rights have actually had the effect of increasing the area under informal tenancy. In other words, actual cultivators continue to be tenants, but without any right to be enrolled as such in the records of rights compiled under the land-reform program. A recent survey found that 66.17 percent of landlord holdings was personally cultivated by the landlords.[48] This percentage appears unduly high, but it is not difficult to understand the reasons for such distortion. As early as 1961, the government of Nepal had found it difficult to compile accurate statistics on landholding and agriculture because

[46]Lands Act, 1964, sec. 26.
[47]Ibid., sec. 27.
[48]Zaman, p. 36.

the "rumour of land reform was in the air."⁴⁹ Inasmuch as the 1964 Lands Act was enforced throughout the country in stages, landowners had ample opportunity to evict their tenants where possible. In many cases, they were also able apparently to suppress the claims of their tenants and register themselves as cultivators so as to evade the rent-control provisions of the new law.⁵⁰

Nor is this all. It is axiomatic that if it is not profitable to let agricultural land, land will eventually cease to be let. The landowner may easily find a way to evict his tenant, or simply buy him off by taking advantage of the provision for voluntary relinquishment of tenancy rights, and then resume the land for personal cultivation. The introduction of improved agricultural methods and mechanized techniques appears to make this choice feasible and profitable. The tenant would thus be degraded to the status of a landless laborer, whereas the landowner would reap all the benefits of capitalist farming.

The experience of countries such as India shows that the introduction of modern agricultural techniques without any changes in the agrarian structure has an adverse effect on the mass of the peasantry, who lack necessary resources to adopt such techniques or are institutionally precluded from taking advantage of the new agricultural trends.⁵¹ Moreover, any employment opportunities created as spread effects of the green revolution "may have become more precarious, with less permanent employment (but increased seasonal work) and fewer opportunities for renting land."⁵² Increased productivity alone, therefore, when achieved within a tenure structure of great inequalities, does not improve the lives of the great mass of peasants. Frequently, a one-sided emphasis on production linked with a neglect of institutional issues exacerbates existing inequalities.⁵³ The green revolution, therefore, is no substitute for land reform, and reform becomes increasingly imperative as the rate of adoption of new technologies accelerates. This conclusion is largely substantiated by a recent study of Thak village in Mustang district:

---

⁴⁹Central Bureau of Statistics, "Sample Census of Agriculture," mimeographed (Kathmandu: the Bureau, 1962), p. 111.

⁵⁰Zaman, p. 36.

⁵¹Wolf Ladejinsky, "Ironies of India's Green Revolution," *Foreign Affairs*, 48 (1970), 758-68, cited in Peter Dorner, *Land Reform and Economic Development* (Penguin Books, 1972), p. 26.

⁵²Dorner, p. 26.

⁵³Ibid., p. 27.

Even at present there is barely ample work to keep the resident population busy, despite huge labor migration of adult males. At the most optimistic of estimates, the introduction of new agricultural methods, especially artificial fertilizers and high-yield grains, could increase the labor demand by some 50 percent. At present rates of population growth this would put off the problem of wide-scale unemployment by about ten to fifteen years. In fact, it is likely that there will be increasing under/unemployment within a few years. The first to suffer will be the lower castes.[54]

It is true, of course, that the imposition of ceilings has checked the tendency to accumulate lands and so has prevented the undue concentration of landownership in a few hands. This measure has already led to the redistribution of some cultivated lands, as we have noted. It may also be possible to reduce the ceilings in the future, thereby making an additional area available for redistribution, but this process cannot continue indefinitely. Moreover, holdings will be subdivided in the course of time, and the owner of the subdivided holding may decide to invest in additional lands up to the ceiling. Naturally, no single landowner will own lands in excess of the prescribed ceilings, but the landowning class as a whole is likely to grow, and this growth will inevitably be detrimental to the small peasant. Particularly in the hill region, where the majority of Nepal's peasant families live, the small peasant has a very precarious hold on his land, for he may have to sell it at any moment to settle his debts. As one study notes,[55] in Asian systems of land tenure it is very difficult to make ownership stick. Because farms are very small, and because consumption perpetually tends to outrun production, the cultivator is always under pressure to resell his holding. The result is that so long as the pressure on the land increases, it is difficult to make ownership secure and permanent. This necessitates the expansion of other occupations.

What the land-reform program has sought to achieve is not a revolutionary change in property relations among the different classes that compose the agrarian community through the abolition of nonworking landownership rights. Its aim has been limited to the mitigation of a few of the undesirable features of the traditional

---

[54]A. D. J. Macfarlane, "Population and Economy in Central Nepal: A Study of the Gurungs" (Ph.D. thesis, London University, 1972).

[55]Doreen Warriner, "Land Reform and Economic Development," in Carl K. Eicher and Lawrence W. Witt, eds., *Agriculture in Economic Development* (reprint; Bombay: Vora and Co., 1970), p. 298.

pattern of landownership rights, such as unlimited concentration of landed property and the landowners' virtually unrestricted power over the occupancy rights and earnings of their tenants. The landowners' rights in the land have been left basically intact, but adequate concession has been made to the peasants' expectation of tenurial security and an increased share in the produce.[56]

Land Reform and Class Coordination

Authoritative statements have in fact been made from time to time since 1961 in Nepal that land reform is not meant to cause hardships to the landowning class. A royal proclamation states:

> The land-reform program is not meant to benefit one class at the expense of the other. It is based on the principle of class coordination, not class conflict. A situation in which the majority of the people are poor, hungry, and naked is dangerous not only for national security and independence but even for the rich and landed classes themselves.[57]

In other words, the purpose of land reform is simply to inhibit concentration of landownership, bring about a redistribution of agricultural incomes, and provide some measure of tenurial security to the cultivator, leaving the traditional agrarian structure unaffected. This is in line with the basic objective of the existing political system to promote the welfare of the people by creating a social order that is just, democratic, dynamic, and free from exploitation "by integrating and consolidating the interests of different classes and professions."[58]

The existing economic differentiation in the agrarian community

---

[56] In the words of a Marxist economist, "Such agrarian reforms as that undertaken by Stolypin in Tsarist Russia, those carried out before the Second World War in Eastern and South-eastern Europe, or those currently enacted (or talked about) in some countries of Latin America, Southeast Asia, and the Near East, proceeding in an 'orderly manner,' represent handouts on the part of the governments largely controlled by landowning interests, are calculated to appease a restive peasantry, and are usually combined with lavish compensations of the feudal landlords. They frequently serve not to break the feudal grip on the state but rather to strengthen it. They tend therefore to accentuate all the negative repercussions of agrarian reforms without leading the way to industrial development and to the reorganization and rationalization of the agricultural economy resulting therefrom." Paul A. Baran, *The Political Economy of Growth* Penguin Books, 1973), p. 307.

[57] *Gorkhapatra*, Poush 2, 2021 (December 16, 1964).

[58] "First Amendment to the Constitution of Nepal," *Nepal Gazette*, vol. 16, no. 45 (Extraordinary), Magh 14, 2023 January 27, 1967), art. 4.

214   THE IMPACT OF LAND REFORM

has been petrified in the process of such integration and coordination. This conclusion is substantiated by an analysis of the process and impact of the imposition of ceilings on both ownership and tenancy holdings. The government's aim in imposing such ceilings was to limit the concentration of landownership and tenancy rights and divert capital from land to other fields of investment. However, landowners and tenants have not been placed on an equal footing. Landowners have been allowed to own residential areas in addition to agricultural lands within the prescribed ceilings, but tenants have been denied this facility. Moreover, a tenant will be able to cultivate a maximum of four *bighas*, that is, a farm a little smaller than has been considered to be an economic holding in the Tarai.[59] An owner-cultivator, on the other hand, may cultivate a farm 625 percent larger, amounting to 25 *bighas*. A landowner whose surplus lands are acquired is entitled to compensation, but a tenant who loses his surplus land does not have a similar right. Compensation will be paid to him at one-fourth of the value of the land only if the government considers this necessary.[60] The economic gulf between landowners and tenants is therefore too wide to be bridged easily.[61] Class coordination has been interpreted in a manner that makes it synonymous with preservation of the status quo. The principle of coordination in the interests of landowners and

---

[59]"After careful calculations based on available data on farming in Nepal and Northern India, 4.2 *bighas* of land was found to be a reasonable economic holding for an average farmer-family consisting of three adults and two children." Department of Agriculture, "Resettlement Project: Nawalpur," mimeographed (Kathmandu: the Department, 1963), p. 13. The reference is to an owner-cultivated holding. For tenant-cultivated holdings, the area will have to be twice as large to be economic, if half of the produce is paid as rent.

[60]Lands rules, 1964, rule 15.

[61]An official report on the first year of land reform in the Budhabare Village Panchayat area of Jhapa district largely substantiates this conclusion. The net after-tax income from a typical four-*bigha* tenant-cultivated farm in this area was estimated at Rs. 688 for the tenant and Rs. 1,304 for the landlord, a difference of approximately 200 percent. The net after-tax income of a landlord owning 25 *bighas* of land was estimated at Rs 8,150, i.e., slightly less than twelve times the maximum earnings of a tenant from his four-*bigha* farm. This disparity has been aggravated because the tenant is not allowed to increase his income, for he is not allowed to cultivate more than four *bighas* of land, whereas the landlord is free to engage himself in other occupations. Significantly, the report notes that "the landlords seem to have little room to complain." Ministries of Land Reform, Panchayat, and Economic Planning, "Report on the Successful First Year of Land Reform in Budabari, Jhapa," mimeographed (Kathmandu: 1961), p. 1. According to an FAO survey conducted in 1972, the average size of the sample landlord household was 18.33 hectares, whereas that of the holdings of owner-cum-tenant and tenant cultivator was 1.64 and 1.74 hectares respectively. Zaman, *Evaluation of Land Reform in Nepal*, p. 33.

peasants, so that the interests of neither class are basically affected, is at best an elusive and unrealistic one.

Forest-Land Policy

The anomalous situation created by the government's unwillingness to reject the principle of nonworking landownership is highlighted by a number of recent developments. Several inaccessible areas in the Tarai regions have been opened up by the construction of roads and highways and, thanks to the eradication of malaria, are no longer as forbidding to prospective settlers from the hill regions as they were previously. To these "pull" factors has been added the "push" factor of growing population pressure in the hill regions.[62] As a result, there has been a steady migration of the agricultural population from these regions to waste and forest areas in the Tarai. In many cases, however, influential people had managed to obtain grants of such lands in their names.[63] The "landowners" thus had their lands reclaimed without any effort or expense on their part, and the pioneering peasants became nothing more than tenants. Agrarian conflict was the inevitable result.

The government's reaction to this problem has been more drastic than the general spirit of the 1964 Lands Act would warrant. The Forest Areas Lands Act, which has been enforced in the eastern Tarai districts of Morang, Sunsari, and Jhapa, has terminated the rights of a landowner on lands in forest areas that have been cultivated not personally by him but by a tenant, on payment of compensation at a rate not exceeding five times the amount of the land tax. Lands acquired in this manner are allotted to the actual cultivators at the rate of not more than four *bighas* for each family on payment of the stipulated price.[64] Nonworking landownership has thus been abolished in this case. Nevertheless, the allottee is permitted to alienate the land after he has paid the price, and he may even appoint a tenant to cultivate the land. There can hardly be better proof to substantiate the view that such superficial reforms can bring about no basic changes in the agrarian structure of Nepal.

---

[62]Charles Mcdougal, *Village and Household Economy in Far-Western Nepal* (Kirtipur: Tribhuwan University, n.d. [1968]), pp. 5-6, 118-19.

[63]*Gorkhapatra*, Kartik 7, 2028 (October 29, 1971).

[64]Ministry of Law and Justice, "Jhora Kshetrako Jagga Sambandhi Ain, 2028" [Forest areas lands act, 1971], *Nepal Rajapatra*, vol. 21, no. 33A (Extraordinary), Aswin 6, 2028 (September 22, 1971).

216   THE IMPACT OF LAND REFORM

PURCHASE OF LANDOWNERSHIP RIGHTS

Authoritative statements have been made from time to time that peasant proprietorship is the ultimate goal of land reform in Nepal.[65] Notwithstanding a decade of land reform, however, owner-cultivated lands are gradually lapsing into tenancy. The number of tenants has increased, and new tenancy farms have emerged at many places.[66] The failure of the land-reform program to bring about any major land redistribution, the preponderance of subeconomic farms, and the growing pressure on the land appear to make such a trend inevitable.

In an attempt to counteract this trend, the government of Nepal has initiated a scheme under which loans are supplied to tenants desirous of buying the lands tilled by them. The scheme has been started on an experimental basis for the benefit of tenants cultivating an area of less than 15 *ropanis* in Kathmandu Valley and five *bighas* in the Tarai.[67] The apparent purpose of this measure is to improve the status of the peasant without remolding the existing agrarian structure and without using coercive methods against the landlord class. It is evident, however, that it will not have a significant impact on the land-holding system, even though it may help a few peasants to upgrade their status. Its success depends on the landlord's willingness to accept a price that the tenant can afford to pay. Even if he is ready to sell his lands, he may do so to another nonworking landlord who can afford to pay a higher price. If the measure is to result in a large-scale transfer of ownership rights, the price of land must be fixed at a level that the tenant can pay. Such a price must inevitably be lower than the market value of the land. In any case, the measure is intended to benefit only the upper-middle-class peasantry who have the ability and creditworthiness to obtain loans.[68]

---

[65] "Since Nepal's economy is predominantly agricultural, it is necessary to create a land system which will enable the actual cultivator to get a fair return for the labor, and thereby maximize agricultural production, make such production useful for the people, and mobilize resources from agriculture for development. Otherwise, an atmosphere in which the intermediary class can exploit [the actual cultivator] will continue. Fresh consideration will therefore be given to the present land-reform program and efforts will be made to gradually make the cultivator owner of the land he tills." National Planning Commission, "Panchaun Yojanaka Adharbhut Siddhanta Haru" [Basic principles of the fifth plan], *Gorkhapatra*, Falgun 22, 2029 (March 5, 1973).

[66] Ram Bahadur, "Bhumi Sudhar: Samasya ra Nirakaranka Upayaharu" [Land reform: problems and solutions], *Gorkhapatra*, Jestha 23, 2029 (June 5, 1972).

[67] *Gorkhapatra*, Falgun 13, 2028 (February 25, 1972).

[68] "In Asian countries, the market price of land is too high in terms of what it pro-

THE IMPACT OF LAND REFORM
A Compromise Formula

The land reform that has been introduced in Nepal may be regarded as a compromise formula whose rationale has been succinctly described by Gunnar Myrdal:

> Legislation [which] leaves the landlord in possession of his land while attempting to ameliorate the tenants' plight, is a compromise solution, both politically and economically. The hope is that these changes will afford tenants both greater means and stronger inducements to improve cultivation, while leaving a surplus at the disposal of landowners. Protective tenancy legislation can also be viewed as a device to reconcile the modern concept of the landlord as an absolute owner and cultivator of the land with the traditional concept of the landlord as a tribute-receiver debarred from interfering with the peasants' right to occupancy and cultivation.[69]

Demographic realities make such compromise formulas ineffective. Most of Nepal's rapidly growing population depends on agriculture for its livelihood and this situation is likely to persist indefinitely.[70] The demand for land as a means of subsistence will therefore increase progressively. Progressive fragmentation and subdivision of agricultural holdings may be expected to lead to the emergence of a growing number of suboptimum farms and the use of labor in agriculture to the point where its marginal productivity becomes zero.[71] Such a stage

---

duces to allow the tenant to purchase his land. If agriculture becomes more prosperous, either as a result of higher prices or better harvests, the sharecropping tenant will not be able to buy his holding, because the landlord benefits equally from the increased income, and the tenant's position in relation to the landlord has not improved. There is no price which the tenant can afford to pay which the landlord will be willing to accept. If the tenant is to acquire ownership, the price of land must be fixed at a level which he can pay, and this will inevitably be much lower than the market value of the land. All land reforms involve expropriation to some extent for this reason." Warriner, "Land Reform and Economic Development" in Eicher and Witt, op. cit. (in n. 55 above), p. 286.

[69] *Asian Drama: An Inquiry into the Poverty Nations* Penguin Books, 1968), II, 1323.

[70] Folke Dovring, "The Share of Agriculture in a Growing Population," in Eicher and Witt, p. 97. According to Dovring, "in most of the less developed countries today, there is no reason to expect reduction of absolute numbers in the agricultural population within the near future." In 1970, a national seminar on land reform in Nepal arrived at a similar conclusion. *Report of National Seminar on Land Reform* (Kathmandu, 1971), p. 159.

[71] N. Georgescu-Roegen, "Economic Theory and Agrarian Economics," in Eicher and Witt, p. 166.

may, in fact, already have been reached in some areas of Nepal. Control of rents and protection of rents, in these circumstances, will be elusive goals. A reform program that seeks to improve the status and earnings of the cultivator within the framework of the existing agrarian system is naturally restricted in its scope. High rents and insecure tenancy rights are but symptoms of the pressure of population on the land. Rent, as the price for the use of land, is high because the demand for land as a means of subsistence is high. Tenancy rights are insecure for the same reason. In the words of an Indian economist:

> The tendency for tenancy to persist and for rents to remain high cannot simply be outlawed so long as the pressure of population on land, and hence the demand for a patch of land to eke out a living, remains as intense as it is. In economic terms, so long as the growing demand for land presses against an inelastic supply, rent, as the price for the use of land, is bound to remain high. An agrarian revolution cannot simply be legislated into being.[72]

This economist then stresses the futility of a land-reform program restricted to rent control and security of tenancy rights:

> While some land reforms are essential for economic development, economic development is essential for the success of many land reforms. Until economic development gathers a certain momentum some of these reforms cannot be made effective; and when it does gather momentum their aims would be realized without legislation. As the man-land ratio in agriculture improves, tenancy would diminish and rents would fall even without any law.[73]

Nepal's experience in the sphere of land reform fully demonstrates the truth of these statements. Almost a decade has passed since land reform

---

[72] Raj Krishna, "Land Reform and Development in South Asia," in Walter Froehlich, ed., *Land Tenure, Industrialization and Social Stability: Experience and Prospects in Asia* (Milwaukee: Marquette University Press, 1961), pp. 222-23. A U.N. Study on land reform contains a similar conclusion: "In the conditions which prevail in these countries [Asia, the Middle East and Latin America], control of rents by legal restrictions to enforce maximum rates of payment has proved extremely difficult to enforce. Owing to the pressure of population on the land, the landlord is in a strong bargaining position in relation to the cultivators and can exact his own terms. For the same reason, legislation to provide conditions of secure tenure has also proved extremely difficult of enforcement." United Nations, *Land Reform* (New York: U.N. Department of Economic Affairs, 1951), p. 68.

[73] Op. cit., p. 223.

THE IMPACT OF LAND REFORM 219

was initiated, but "unregulated tenancy" persists, and the new rates of rents are sufficiently below the traditional level of half of the produce to enable tenants to sublet their lands and appropriate the difference without working on the land themselves.[74] Moreover, evictions of tenants have not been effectively checked even in Kathmandu and the adjoining districts.[75]

Criticism of the land-reform program for its failure to make any real dent in the existing pattern of agrarian relations might have been offset to some extent had it succeeded in "diverting inactive capital and manpower from land to other sectors of the economy in order to accelerate the pace of national development."[76] Available evidence shows that it has not. Its performance has been all the more disappointing because it has not been able to generate adequate resources for self-sustained growth in the agricultural sector. A recent agricultural-credit survey, conducted by the Nepal Rashtra Bank in 32 districts covering 78.44 percent of the total cultivated area in the kingdom, proves the truth of these statements. The survey found that during 1971–72, when the area covered by improved methods of farming amounted to approximately 5 percent of the total cultivated area, medium- and long-term agricultural credit supplied by agricultural financing institutions amounted to Rs. 50 million. On the assumption that the area covered by improved farming methods would increase by about 3 percent every year, agricultural-credit needs were estimated at Rs. 80 million in 1972–73 and Rs. 350 million in 1981–82. Taking the carry-over of unrepaid loans into consideration, total long- and medium-term credit requirements in 1981–82 were estimated at Rs. 577 million. However, total collection of compulsory savings during the period from 1972–73 to 1981–82 was estimated at only Rs. 150 million, or 25.9 percent of the total requirements. Assuming that Rs. 100 million would be obtained from the Agricultural Development Bank and Rs. 25 million through the mobilization of rural savings, the shortfall was estimated at Rs. 202 million. The report adds, significantly, that this shortfall "will have to be met mostly by

---

[74] Bahadur, op. cit. (in n. 17 above), p. 28.

[75] *Gorkhapatra*, Bhadra 16, 2028 (September 1, 1971), Kartik 21, 2028 (October 7, 1971) and Kartik 24, 2028 (October 10, 1971). In November 1973, the chairman of the official Nepal Peasants' Organization told a press conference in Kathmandu: "There is no evidence that any major change is occurring in the fields of agriculture. Eviction of tenants has become a serious problem." *Gorkhapatra*, Marga 3, 2030 (November 18, 1973).

[76] Lands Act, 1964, preamble.

external borrowings."[77]

Reforms in the tenancy system alone can hardly insure that the productive resources of the land are utilized to the maximum possible extent, or that sufficient capital is generated to insure self-sustained growth in agriculture. By the very nature of his status, a tenant would need a higher cost-benefit ratio to induce him to invest adequate labor and capital in the land than would an owner-cultivator. As studies in countries adjoining Nepal have shown, the cost-benefit ratio for the use of fertilizers at the initial stage may be as high as 1:4. Such an apparently attractive ratio becomes badly diluted, however, because the tenant alone bears the entire additional investment in fertilizers. The ratio, in effect, drops to 1:2 if 50 percent of the increased production is paid as rent. Consequently, whereas a cost-benefit ratio of 1:2 may be profitable enough for an owner-cultivator, it has to be 1:4 for a tenant to yield the same net gain from a given capital outlay.[78] It has been calculated that if a tenant cultivator tilling a four-*bigha* farm in the Tarai, who bears all costs of production himself and pays half of the crop as rent, invests Rs. 530 in fertilizers, the net increase in his income (after paying 50 percent of the additional production also as rent) will be only Rs. 480. In other words, the tenant will lose Rs. 50 by using fertilizers.[79]

Nor can the disadvantages of tenant farming from the viewpoint of increasing agricultural productivity be offset solely through such palliative measures as rent control. Rent control does not automatically lead to increased production if the increased income of the tenant is not available for investment in the land. Claims have been made that agricultural production has increased in Kathmandu Valley because rent has been fixed in terms of an absolute amount of the main crop and limited to that crop only, so that tenants need not share the benefits of increased production with the landowner.[80] Notwithstanding this reform in the system of rent payment, productivity is higher on owner-cultivated farms than on those cultivated by tenants,

---

[77] Nepal Rashtra Bank, *Agricultural Credit Survey (Summary and Recommendations)* (Kathmandu: the Bank, 1972), pp. 216–18.

[78] M. A. Zaman, "A Socio-Economic Case for Peasant Ownership in Nepal" (mimeographed; Kathmandu: Ministry of Agriculture, 1972), pp. 13–14.

[79] James B. Hunt, "The Effects of Land Reform on Achieving the Agricultural Production Targets of the Third Plan," *Economic Affairs Report*, vol. 3, no. 3 (August 1965), p. 5.

[80] Quentin W. Lindsey, "Land Reform and the Food Problem," in Department of Land Reform, *Bhumi Sudhar*, pp. 14–15.

as shown in table 10, which gives statistics of average yields in selected areas of Kathmandu Valley after the introduction of the 1964 land-reform program.[81]

TABLE 10

AVERAGE YIELDS OF PRINCIPAL CROPS IN KATHMANDU VALLEY, BY TENURE STATUS (IN KG. PER HECTARE)

Crop	Owner-cultivated farms	Tenant-cultivated farms	Percentage of higher production on owner-cultivated farms
Paddy	3259.84	2703.52	120.57
Wheat	2640.34	1687.64	156.45
Maize	2218.44	1306.56	169.79
Millet	1118.26	749.90	149.12

Source: See chap. 11, n. 81.

If it is argued that the reduction of rents to approximately one-third of the total yield in Kathmandu Valley has led to increased production, one may also point out that in large areas of the far-western Tarai, rents customarily amount to approximately the same percentage without any apparent positive effect on productivity.

The Objective of Land Reform

We may conclude that in the situation existing in Nepal at present any program of land reform can be meaningful only if it fulfills two objectives: elimination of nonworking landownership, and mobilization of capital. In other words, land reform must insure that land belongs to those who actually cultivate it, and that surplus agricultural production becomes available for use as productive capital. According to an observer of the Indian scene:

> If you do not totally reject the principle of nonworking cultivators you cannot prevent the village oligarchs from acting as landlords. As soon as you leave the door barely open for property income to nonworking proprietors—which you do when you permit landownership to

[81] Zaman, "A Socio-Economic Case for Peasant Ownership in Nepal," p. 32, table 6.

exist unassociated with labor in the fields—you allow all the evils of concentration of power at the village level to come trotting back in. As long as some peasants are without land or very short of land, they will be at the mercy of those who are allowed to have land without working it.[82]

He therefore suggests:

> Lands and the fruits thereof are to belong to those who do the tilling, the tillers being defined as those who plough, harrow, sow, weed, and harvest. In consequence, the income from land is to be brought to an end (not necessarily overnight, but within a stipulated period of time). This will result in a major redistribution of rural income, to the advantage of those who work in the fields, and to the disadvantage of those who do not. In the process, income arising from property rights in land will dwindle, and, in the course of time, fade away and disappear.[83]

Gunnar Myrdal advocates an essentially similar approach to the problem of land reform by recommending the elimination of "sharecropping as a system of tenancy, absentee landownership, and the prevalence of cultivators who in fact are not doing any cultivation." He also advocates "a deliberate policy choice in favor of capitalist farming by allowing and encouraging the progressive entrepreneurs among the group of peasant landlords and privileged tenants to reap the full rewards of their strivings." He points out that "this might encourage more such farmers to act in the same way and, in particular, to give up relying on sharecropping." Simultaneously, Myrdal lays emphasis on the need for "additional measures to protect agricultural workers" by giving them " a small plot of land and with it dignity and a fresh outlook on life, as well as a minor independent source of income." Finally, Myrdal suggests a higher tax on nonresident landowners and legislation to ban land transfers to noncultivators and nonresident persons.[84]

These recommendations would mean putting land into the hands of those who actually cultivate it. This would be quite appropriate, for, in essence, the land problem facing Nepal at present is the product of an aristocratic and bureaucratic tradition that has viewed land as a

---

[82]Daniel Thorner, *The Agrarian Prospect in India* (Delhi: University Press, 1956), p. 82.
[83]Ibid., p. 79.
[84]*The Challenge of World Poverty* (Penguin Books, 1971), pp. 119–21.

source of unearned income rather than as a means of production. The challenge of economic development puts us under the obligation of inverting this outlook. The ownership and control of land must be reorganized for maximizing collective interests, rather than those of an individual or a select class of the society.

Chapter 12

THE FUTURE PATTERN OF LANDOWNERSHIP

Our study of landownership in Nepal has concerned mainly three categories: ascriptive and communal ownership (*Birta, Guthi, Jagir,* and *Kipat*), *Jimidari* landownership, and *Raikar* landownership. In view of the importance of *Raikar* landownership in Nepal's current land system, we have also outlined the fiscal and labor obligations attached to such ownership.

The central theme in this historical account of Nepal's land system is the position of the peasant at the lowest rung of the community of agrarian interests. It was the quantum of agricultural production in excess of the barest subsistence needs, extracted from the peasant through the authority of the state, that financed military campaigns in the process of political unification, sustained the Rana body politic, and enriched the aristocracy and the bureaucracy, with enough pickings left for the village overlords. The peasant therefore carried "the greatest burdens of taxation and of military mobilization."[1] He was unable to change his lot, because he constituted "politically the most passive and inarticulate, and the least organized, stratum," whose internal political activities were "largely isolated and insulated from the central political processes of the society."[2] In this concluding chapter, we shall try to assess the measure of success attained by recent land-reform measures in upgrading the position of the peasant in the agrarian community and examine in outline prospects for the future.

THE TRADITIONAL LANDED ELITE

This analysis properly begins with a brief description of the nature and composition of Nepal's traditional landed elite. Nepal's landed

---

[1] S. N. Eisenstadt, *The Political System of Empires* (New York: Free Press, 1963), p. 207.
[2] Ibid.

elite traditionally comprised *Birta* owners and *Jagirdars*, in whose roles the aristocracy and bureaucracy served their economic interests. This combination of political and economic power was not due to the fact that a landowning class had been able to capture political power. Rather, it was a system under which the political elite was able to utilize its political power to acquire an economic base in landownership. Probably as a consequence of this use of political power for economic enrichment, the Rana rulers were able to establish a polity that may appropriately be described as a centralized agrarian bureaucracy, or a society that depends upon a central authority for extracting the economic surplus from the peasantry.[3]

The Rana aristocracy and the bureaucracy exploited this economic base through the cooperation of village overlords (*Jimidars* and *Talukdars*) instituted for the purpose. These village overlords functioned as intermediaries between the aristocracy and bureaucracy in Kathmandu and the peasant society at the local level, thereby strengthening the "institutional links binding peasant society to the upper classes."[4] It was perhaps natural that this institutional link was forged quite early during the Rana period, during the early 1860s, as we saw in chapter 7. The village overlords, especially the *Jimidars* of the Tarai, long remained one of the main bastions of Rana rule in Nepal.

In essence, therefore, Nepal's traditional land system represented a coalition between the aristocracy and the bureaucracy on the one hand and local overlords on the other to wring agricultural surpluses from the peasantry and share the proceeds. The system worked fairly well in its basic objective of channeling agricultural surpluses from the peasantry to the aristocracy and the bureaucracy. Each side needed the other. The landowning class needed village overlords to collect rents and control the peasantry, and the village overlords needed the political backing provided by the landowning aristocracy and bureaucracy.

The Role of Nonascriptive Landownership

Cracks appeared in this system, probably around the beginning of the twentieth century, when feudalistic relationships between village

---

[3] Barrington Morre, Jr., *Social Origins of Dictatorship and Democracy* (Penguin Books, 1967), p. 459.

[4] Ibid., p. 478.

overlords and the land magnates of the aristocracy and the bureaucracy on the one hand, and between peasants and village overlords on the other, were replaced by capitalistic relationships in which the central political authority had, at best, a secondary role. *Jimidari* rights, as explained in chapter 7, soon developed into property rights. Village overlords realized that they no longer needed the political backing of the central authority to control and exploit the peasantry. The emergence of de facto ownership of land, which was described in chapter 10, reduced the importance of ascriptive rights. The right granted to village overlords to use forced and unpaid labor from the peasantry could now be achieved through nonascriptive landownership and moneylending. The growth of the nonascriptive landowning class was thus a factor that countervailed the traditional authority of the village overlords. That class, moreover, owed little to the central political authority for its growth and sustenance. The Rana regime consequently had to face "loss of the support of an upper class of wealthy peasants because these [had] begun to go over to more capitalist modes of cultivation and to establish their independence against an aristocracy seeking to maintain its position through the intensification of traditional obligations."[5]

The loss of the support of an important segment of the agrarian society was possibly one of the main causes of the downfall of the Rana regime in early 1951. Because ascriptive rights in land were acquired through political power and privilege, the collapse of the political system was inevitably followed by changes in the land system. The abolition of ascriptive forms of landownership such as *Birta* and *Jagir* was therefore inevitable. These reforms led to a divorce between political power and landownership and so had a deep impact on Nepal's social structure. Land policies were no longer attuned to the class interests of the political elite. For the first time, it became possible to view land and agriculture from the larger perspective of the nation's

---

[5]Ibid. According to Eisenstadt (op. cit., p. 34), "In most of these [historical bureaucratic] societies several tendencies developed which undermined or limited these traditional-ascriptive economic frameworks. The most important of these tendencies to differentiation in agriculture was manifested by the development of independent private peasant property, and then of some measure of mobility of manpower and labor. In most cases, there were a relatively widespread weakening of ascriptive community rights in land and a growing of some measure of individual (or small family) property rights—although these rights were often still severely limited either by the traditional fetters of various kinship and community rights or by obligations to agricultural overlords or to the state."

social and economic development rather than as a means to increase the earnings of privileged classes in the society.

Land Reforms under the Panchayat System

From one point of view, the history of Nepal's landownership system may be said to be an account of how successive regimes have tried to establish a political base among different classes in the society. Trends in land policy after the introduction of the Panchayat system in 1961 substantiate this conclusion. The land-reform program constitutes an effort to widen the political base of the Panchayat regime. The village assembly, the lowest unit of Panchayat polity, has as its members all local residents who have attained the age of twenty-one years. Moreover, peasants have been recognized as a class with a constitutional status, whereas landowners have been denied this status. Panchayat polity, in fact, seeks to maintain a political base directly among such primary segments of the population as the peasantry. To this end, land reform has aimed basically at uplifting the status and earnings of the peasant at the cost of the landlord. The introduction of the land-reform program has shown that the government can take the risk of alienating the landowning class for the benefit of the peasantry and agricultural development as a whole. The principle of coordination between the interests of landlord and peasant may therefore prove to be only a tactic aimed at stifling potential opposition from the landowning class. This is what the progressive reduction in the level of agricultural rents may indicate, together with increased land taxation and the graduated taxation of agricultural incomes. As these measures gain momentum, ceilings may be further lowered.

Available evidence indicates nevertheless that the upper rural classes have been the main beneficiaries of land reform and the new technology that has been introduced in its wake. On the other hand, the lower strata of the peasantry have been almost left out of the new order, although their expectations have been aroused to a considerable extent. This has engendered the possibility of a conflict of interests between these two segments of the agrarian society. As one study puts it:

> Where the upper class assumes the initiative in exploiting the gains inherent in the new technology, it develops an interest in freeing itself

of obligations to the peasants and in gaining full control over land. Whenever the upper rural classes become actively engaged in management they will seek to shed social obligations, gain a free hand in controlling land use, and obtain the services of a "law-and-order" state in protecting their property.[6]

But a free hand in controlling land use can be gained only at the expense of the lower strata of the peasantry. Possibly for this reason, "in most underdeveloped countries land and tenancy reforms have been a sham, except when carried out in a revolutionary situation of some sort."[7]

A basic contradiction exists, in fact, between the social and economic goals of land reform. The adoption of the new technology and of intensive methods of agricultural production requires capital investment on a scale that the lower strata of the peasantry may not afford. In chapter 11, we saw that the introduction of modern agricultural techniques usually has an adverse effect on the mass of the peasantry. Rising productivity in one sector of the agricultural economy may therefore coexist with stagnation and even decline in the other. It appears doubtful, in these circumstances, that traditional systems of landholding will insure the realization of the social and economic goals of land reform. At the same time, it should be stressed that "unless those who work the land own it, or at least are secure on the land as tenants, all the rest is likely to be writ in water."[8] It may, therefore, be worth while to suggest a remodeling of the landholding system in the light of the kingdom's new social and political philosophy.

The deficiencies of the post-1961 land-reform program in upgrading the status of the peasantry have led several observers of the current agrarian scene to suggest that Nepal's landholding system needs such remodeling despite the changes brought about by land reforms during the post-1961 period. Opinion among these observers has

---

[6]Peter Dorner, *Land Reform and Economic Development* (Penguin Books, 1972), p. 74. Dorner quotes (pp. 26-27) the following passage from Ladejinsky: "There are too many tenants or share-croppers to deal with them summarily without courting a good deal of trouble, but the old squeeze whereby tenants are reduced to sharecroppers and eventually to landless workers is being accelerated as more of the bigger owners become involved with the new technology. The basic provisions of tenancy reform are less attainable than before the advent of the green revolution." Wolf Ladejinsky, "Ironies of India's Green Revolution," *Foreign Affairs*, 48 (1970), 764.

[7]Gunnar Myrdal, *The Challenge of World Poverty* (Penguin Books, 1971), p. 221.

[8]Ibid., p. 128, quoting Ladejinsky, "Agrarian Reform in Asia," *Foreign Affairs*, 42 (1964), 446.

largely been in favor of abolishing tenancy and instituting a system of peasant proprietorship.[9] Nevertheless, experience has shown that peasant proprietorship can easily degenerate into landlordism under favorable economic, fiscal, and demographic conditions. No student of Nepal's land system during the past two centuries can possibly avoid this conclusion. As was brought out in chapter 10, *Raikar* tenure was essentially a system of peasant proprietorship at the middle of the nineteenth century. Certainly, the system of landlordism to which it has partially evolved since then is not the consequence of any deliberate administrative effort. One can therefore hardly advocate a repetition of the old sequence of developments in the name of agrarian reform.

A Scheme for Panchayat Landownership

We began our study with the truism that in any society, systems of land tenure develop within the framework of its political philosophy and its general policies toward property in land. Nepal has adopted the Panchayat system as its political philosophy. This system stresses class coordination and guarantees the freedom to acquire, use, and alienate property. It also aims at protecting every class or individual from unjust economic pressure and enabling the common people to participate in the economic growth of the nation. These objectives of the Panchayat system may best be fulfilled through a synthesis between individual landownership and the collective authority of local Panchayats. Such a synthesis may be brought about through the institution of a new form of landownership, under which every local Panchayat is owner of lands used for agricultural and other productive purposes in the area under its jurisdiction. These lands will be used by individuals on payment of rent to the Panchayat at about 25 percent of the main crop. The Panchayat will then bear the burden of the land tax payable to the government in the capacity of landowner. Individual landholders will be free to sell their holdings, but only to resident cultivators. It would be out of place, however, to discuss the administrative and other ramifications of the Panchayat land-tenure system at this stage.

[9]For a strong advocacy of the system of peasant proprietorship in Nepal see Ram Bahadur, *A General Study on Land Reform, Land Administration and Socio-Economic Activities* (Kathmandu: Lands Department, Ministry of Land Reform, 1972), pp. 29–30, and M. A. Zaman, "A Socio-Economic Case for Peasant Ownership in Nepal" (mimeographed; Kathmandu: Ministry of Agriculture, 1972).

The categories of lands that may be acquired in this manner depend upon how rapidly the government is determined to change the nation's agrarian structure. If it is necessary to proceed cautiously, Panchayats need not immediately take over all lands situated in their areas. A beginning may be made with surplus lands acquired by the government under the ceiling provisions of the 1964 Lands Act. These lands should now be taken under Panchayat ownership, instead of being allotted to individuals. Panchayats may also acquire the rights of absentee landowners with the compulsory savings collected by them under the land-reform program. This will be a good investment, for lands thus acquired will yield rents. It is also possible that some landowners may wish to sell their lands to Panchayats. In any case, they should not be permitted to transfer their lands to others.

Panchayat ownership, once established on any plot of land, cannot revert to the old system. A progressively larger area will therefore accrue to Panchayats in the course of time. Considerable resources will be available for agricultural and other development from the rents accruing to Panchayats. Surplus agricultural production will be available for investment, instead of being consumed by parasitic landlords. Moreover, the disappearance of village land magnates will have a beneficial effect on the structure and working of the political system itself. The peasant will become proprietor of the land in the real sense of the term.

The justification of a system of Panchayat landownership is not confined to egalitarian considerations. For countries such as Nepal, the manner in which surplus agricultural production is used constitutes a crucial factor determining the pace of economic progress. During the eighteenth and nineteenth centuries, this surplus was largely channeled toward the maintenance of a military establishment with the objective of territorial expansion. During the Rana regime, it was used for the maintenance of a parasitic aristocracy and a bureaucracy in whose decision-making process the welfare of the masses was not a relevant factor. At present, economic progress has replaced territorial expansion or the sustenance of oligarchic interests as the national goal. Such progress is impossible unless surplus agricultural production is used for productive purposes. The present pattern of landownership does not insure its use for such purposes. Nor has land reform made any significant contribution to the realization of this objective. Panchayat landownership, in these circumstances, may prove to be an effective means for converting surplus agricultural production into productive capital.

FUTURE PATTERN OF LANDOWNERSHIP

The transformation of the existing pattern of landownership on Panchayat lines is, of course, not an easy task. It is a drastic solution to the problem of using surplus agricultural production for economic progress. However, the economic condition of the country is critical enough to justify such decisive steps, and, "as long as powerful vested interests oppose changes that lead toward a less oppressive world, no commitment to a free society can dispense with some conception of revolutionary coercion."[10]

[10] Moore, p. 508. Gunnar Myrdal (op. cit., p. 218) expresses a similar view: "There is little hope in South Asia for rapid development without greater social discipline, which will not appear without legislation and regulations enforced by compulsion."

GLOSSARY

Abal: First grade of land for purposes of tax assessment. On rice lands of *Abal* grade, rice is usually sown or transplanted, artificial irrigation facilities are always available, and the soil is moist and of the best quality, so that two crops can be grown in a year. On unirrigated lands of *Abal* grade, the soil is of good quality and fertile, and, instead of rice, only dry rice, maize, millet, mustard, rape, and similar other crops can be cultivated.

Adhiya: A system of sharecropping in which the landowner (or the state) appropriated half of the produce as rent (or tax).

Amanat-Guthi: *Raj Guthi* endowments that are administered by an official agency, now the Guthi Corporation.

Bhatha: An east-west zone in the eastern Tarai region, situated on the Nepal-India border.

Bhith: Unirrigated agricultural lands and homesites in the Tarai region.

Bigha: A unit of land measurement used in the Tarai, comprising 8,100 square yards, or 1.6 acres or 0.67 hectare. A *bigha* is divided into 20 *katthas*.

Bijan: A system under which land taxes on unirriagated lands in the hill regions are assessed on the basis of the estimated quantity of seed maize needed for sowing.

Birta: Land grants made by the state to individuals, usually on an inheritable and tax-exempt basis; abolished in 1959.

Chahar: Fourth grade of land for purposes of tax assessment. Rice lands of *Chahar* grade are dry, sandy or gravelly, and crops can be sown only if there is rainfall. They are situated at a high level, or are terraced, or remain submerged under water for a long time, and rice can be grown only in intermittent years. Only one crop can be grown in a year.

Chardam-Theki: A cash levy payable on rice lands in the hill regions, including Kathmandu Valley; it has been abolished.

Chaudhari: A functionary responsible for revenue collection at the *Parganna* level in the Tarai region before the emergence of the *Jimidari* system.

Chuni: (1) Peasants who were not under obligation to provide unpaid labor (*Rakam*) services for governmental purposes. (2) Landholders in the far-western hill districts and the Tarai who were listed as taxpayers in the official records.

Chhap-Birta: A category of *Birta* grants that were usually made on a lifetime and taxable basis.

233

GLOSSARY

Chhut-Guthi: *Raj Guthi* endowments administered by individuals; abolished in 1972.

Dhanahar: Irrigated lands in the Tarai regions where rice can be grown.

Dhokre: Agents who purchased *Tirjas* from *Jagirdars* and collected rents on *Jagir* lands.

Doyam: Second grade of land for purposes of tax assessment. On rice lands of *Doyam* grade, artificial irrigation facilities are not always available. The soil is of good quality and two crops can be grown in a year. Unirrigated lands of *Doyam* grade contain sand or gravel and are steeply inclined. Crops can be sown only at intervals of one or two years.

Duniya-Guthi: *Guthi* endowments founded and administered by individuals.

Ghiukhane: A cash levy payable on rice lands in the hill regions, including Kathmandu Valley; it has been abolished.

Guthi: An endowment of land made for any religious or philanthropic purpose.

Guthi-Birta: Lands granted as *Birta* for use as *Guthi*.

Guthiyar: A functionary responsible for the management of *Guthi* endowments.

Hale: An unirrigated holding in the hill regions which can be plowed by one ox team in one day.

Jagera: *Raikar* lands not assigned as *Jagir*.

Jagir: *Raikar* lands assigned to government employees and functionaries in lieu of their emoluments; abolished in 1952.

Jagirdar: The beneficiary of a *Jagir* land assignment.

Jhara: Forced and unpaid labor obligations due to the government.

Jimidar: An individual responsible for land-tax collection at the village level in the Tarai region.

Jimidari: A *Jimidari*'s holding.

Jirayat: A plot of taxable land attached to a *Jimidari* holding as part of the *Jimidar*'s emoluments.

Khet: Irrigated lands in the hill regions, including Kathmandu Valley, on which rice can be grown.

Kipat: A system of communal landownership prevalent among the Limbus and other Mongoloid communities in the hill regions.

Kodale: An unirrigated holding in the hill regions that was too small to be plowed by oxen and hence had to be dug with a spade.

Kut: A system of sharecropping under which the landowner (or the state) appropriated a specific quantity of the produce or a stated sum in cash as rent (or tax).

Mahant: The head of a Hindu monastery.

Majh: An east-west zone in the eastern Tarai region situated between the *Sir* (northernmost) and *Bhatha* (southernmost) zones.

Mana: A volumetric unit equivalent to 0.3 kg. of paddy, 0.42 kg. of wheat or maize, or 0.41 kg. of millet; 8 *manas* make one *pathi*.

Muri: (1) A unit of land measurement equal to 1,369 square feet; 4 *muris* of land make 1 *ropani*. (2) A volumetric unit equivalent to 48.77 kg. of paddy, 68.05 kg. of wheat or maize, or 65.78 kg. of millet; one *muri* consists of 20 *pathis*.

Pakho: Unirrigated high land or hillside land in the hill regions, including Kathmandu Valley, on which only dry crops such as dry rice, maize, and millet can be grown.

Parganna: A revenue subdivision in the eastern Tarai region, comprising a number of villages.

Pate: An unirrigated holding in the hill region, including Kathmandu Valley, which is roughly half of a *Hale* holding in size.

Pathi: A volumetric unit equivalent to 2.43 kg. of paddy, 3.4 kg. of wheat or maize, or 3.28 kg. of millet; one *pathi* consists of 8 *manas*.

Patta: A land-allotment certificate in the Tarai region.

Pota: A tax imposed on certain categories of *Birta* lands in Kathmandu Valley.

Prajajat: A generic term used before 1951 to denote certain communities of Mongoloid origin, such as Bhote, Chepang, Darai, Majhi, Haya, Danuwar, Kumhal, and Pahari, who were not eligible for recruitment in the army.

Raikar: Lands on which taxes are collected from individual landowners, traditionally regarded as state-owned.

Raj Guthi: *Guthi* endowments under the control or management of the Guthi Corporation.

Rakam: Unpaid and compulsory labor services due to the government from peasants cultivating *Raikar* (including *Jagir*), *Kipat*, and *Raj Guthi* lands; abolished in 1963.

Ropani: A unit of land measurement in the hill districts, including Kathmandu Valley, comprising an area of 5,476 square feet or 0.05 hectare; one *ropani* is equal to 4 *muris* of land.

Seba Birta: A category of *Birta* grants, mostly in Kathmandu Valley, made to individuals for the performance of specified services.

Seer: A unit of weight equivalent to 1 kg. or 2.2 lbs.

Sim: Third grade of land for purposes of tax assessment. On rice lands of *Sim* grade no irrigation facilities are available, but rice can be cultivated if there is rainfall. The soil is slightly sandy and only one crop can be grown in a year. On unirrigated lands of *Sim* grade, the soil contains sand or gravel, and the gradient is steep, so that plows cannot be used. Crops can be grown only in intermittent years. Often the land is covered by snow for brief periods.

Sir: An east-west zone in the eastern Tarai region adjoining the Churia hills, north of the *Majh* zone.

Talukdar: A village-level revenue-collection functionary in the hill region.

Tirja: A letter of authority issued to a *Jagirdar* entitling him to collect rents on his *Jagir* lands.

Tiruwa: A category of taxable *Birta* grants, mostly in the Tarai region.
Ukhada: A form of *Jimidari* landownership in the western Tarai districts of Rupandehi, Kapilavastu, and Nawal-Parasi; abolished in 1964.
Zamindar: An intermediary class of landowners in some parts of northern India who were responsible for the collection of revenue from peasants living in the villages under their jurisdiction.

BIBLIOGRAPHY AND SOURCE MATERIALS

Archival Materials

The records of the Lagat Phant (Records Office) of the Department of Land Revenue in the Finance Ministry of His Majesty's Government provided the basic source materials for this study. These records consist of official copies of regulations, orders, notifications, and the like promulgated by the government of Nepal since the last quarter of the eighteenth century. All unpublished documents cited here have been obtained from that source, unless otherwise stated.

Archival materials have been obtained also from the following sources:
(1) Library, Ministry of Law and Justice of His Majesty's Government.
(2) Ministry of Foreign Affairs (Jaisi Kotha) of His Majesty's Government.
(3) Amalkot Kachahari (Pashupatinath Temple) Office.
(4) Bhandar Tahabil (Pashupatinath Temple) Office.
(5) Pashupati Goshwara (Pashupatinath Temple) Office.
(6) Guthi Lagat Janch Office.
(7) Kathmandu Guthi Tahasil Office.

Materials obtained from these sources have not been individually listed in the bibliography. Full references to all documents actually used have been given at the appropriate places in the footnotes.

Books and Articles

Nepali

Acharya, Baburam. *Nepalko Samkshipta Vrittanta* [A concise account of Nepal]. Kathmandu: Pramod Shamsher and Nir Bikram "Pyasi," 2022 (1966).

Bahadur, Ram, K.C. "Bhumi Sudhar: Samasya ra Nivaranka Upayaharu"

[Land reform: problems and solutions]. *Gorkhapatra*, Jestha 23, 2029 (June 5, 1972).

———. "Kut Nirdharan" [Assessment of agricultural rents]. *Gorkhapatra*, Kartik 10, 2028 (October 27, 1971).

Bajracharya, Dhanabajra. *Licchavi Kalka Abhilekh* [Inscriptions of the Licchavi period]. Kathmandu: Institute of Nepal and Asian Studies, Tribhuwan University, Ashadh 2030 (June 1973).

———. "Malla Kalma Desharakshako Vyavastha ra Tyasprati Prajako Kartavya" [The national-defense system during the Malla period and the obligations of the people]. *Purnima*, vol. 1, no. 2, Shrawan 1, 2021 (July 16, 1964).

Bhandari, Krishna Prasad. "Pallokirat Ko Jagga" [Land in Pallokirat]. *Samyukta Prayas*, Bhadra 15, 2016 (August 30, 1959).

Central Bureau of Statistics. *Pramukh Baliko Utpadan Dar* [Average yields of main crops]. Kathmandu: the Bureau, 2023 (1966).

———. *Rashtriya Janaganana 2018 Ko Parinam* [Results of the 1961 national population census]. 4 vols. Kathmandu: the Bureau, 2026 (1969).

———. *Rashtriya Krishi Gananako Parinam, 2018* [Results of the 1961 national agricultural census]. Separate volumes for different districts. Kathmandu: the Bureau, 2023 (1966).

Devkota, Grishma Bahadur. *Nepalko Rajnaitik Darpan* [Political mirror of Nepal]. Kathmandu: Keshav Chandra Gautam, 1960.

Government of Nepal. *Madhesh Jilla Jillako Jimidar Patuwarika Naunka Sawal* [Regulations for *Jimidars* and *Patuwaris* in the Tarai districts]. Kathmandu: Gorkhapatra Press, 2012 (1955).

———. *Madhesh Malko Sawal* [Revenue regulations for the Tarai districts]. Kathmandu: Gorkhapatra Press, n.d.

———. *Muluki Ain* [Legal code]. Various editions published during the period from 1853 to 1963, including: Ministry of Law and Justice, *Shri 5 Surendra Bikram Shah Devaka Shasan Kalma Baneko Muluki Ain* [Legal code enacted during the reign of King Surendra Bikram Shah Dev], Kathmandu: the Ministry, 2022 (1965).

———. *Muluki Sawal* [Administrative regulations]. 3d ed. Kathmandu: Gorkhapatra Press, 2010 (1953).

Harilal. *Pahad Mal Bishaya* [On revenue offices in the hill districts]. Kathmandu: Nepali Bhasha Prakashini Samiti, 2008 (1951).

His Majesty's Government of Nepal. *Bhumi Sudhar Ke Ho?* [What is land reform?]. Kathmandu: Department of Publicity and Broadcasting, 2017 (1960).

———. *Shahi Kar Ayog Ko Report* [Report of the Royal Taxation Commission]. Kathmandu: Department of Publicity and Broadcasting, 2018 (1961).

———. *Shri 5 Maharajadhiraj Bata Bakseka Ghoshana, Bhashan ra Sandesh Haru* [Proclamations, speeches, and messages of His Majesty]. Kathmandu:

Department of Publicity and Broadcasting, 2019 (1962).

Lamsal, Devi Prasad, ed. *Bhasha Vamshavali* [Genealogy in the vernacular language]. Kathmandu: Nepal Rashtriya Pustakalaya, Department of Archeology, 2023 (1966).

Lohani, Gobind Prasad. *Nepalma Bhumi-Sambandhama Sudhar Tarf Bhayeko Gatividhi ra Ajasammako Upalabdhi* [Developments in the field of land reform in Nepal and the achievements made so far]. Kathmandu: Department of Publicity, Ministry of Publicity and Broadcasting, 2023 (1966).

Naraharinath Yogi. *Itihas Prakash* [Light on history]. 4 vols. Kathmandu: Itihas Prakash Mandal, 2012-13 (1955-56).

———. and Acharya, Baburam, eds. *Rashtrapita Shri 5 Bada Maharaja Prithvi Narayan Shah Devako Dibya Upadesh* [Divine counsel of the Great King Prithvi Narayan Shah Dev, father of the nation]. 2d. rev. ed. Kathmandu: Prithvi Jayanti Samaroha Samiti, 2010 (1953).

National Planning Council. *Trivarshiya Yojana, 2019-22* [Three-year plan, 1962-65]. Kathmandu: the Council, 2019 (1962).

———. *Tesro Yojana, 2022-27* [Third plan, 1965-70]. Kathmandu: the Council, 2022 (1965).

Nepali, Chittaranjan. *Janaral Bhimsen Thapa ra Tatkalin Nepal* [General Bhimsen Thapa and contemporary Nepal]. Kathmandu: Nepal Samskritik Sangh, 2013 (1956).

———. *Shri 5 Rana Bahadur Shah* [King Rana Bahadur Shah]. Kathmandu: Mrs. Mary Rajbhandari, 2020 (1963).

Nepali Congress. *Kisanharuko Nimti Nepali Congressle Ke Garyo?* [What has the Nepali Congress done for the peasants?]. Kathmandu: Nepali Congress, n.d.

Panthi, Tek Bahadur. *Hamro Arthik Samasya* [Our economic problems]. Kapilavastu: Bishnumaya Devi Panthi, 2019 (1962).

———. "Ukhada Byabastha Bare Ek Adhyayan" [A study of the *Ukhada* system]. *Naya Samaj*, Shrawan 17, 2020 (August 1, 1963).

Pokhrel, Balakrishna. *Panch Saya Varsha* [Five centuries of Nepali literature]. Lalitpur: Jagadamba Prakashan, 2020 (1963).

Poudyal, Bhola Nath. "Yaksheshwara Mandira" [The temple of Yaksheshwara]. *Purnima*, 5, Baisakh 2022 (April 1965), pp. 16-21.

Pradhan, Madan Bahadur. "Butaul Jillako Bhumi Samasya" [Land problems of Butaul district]. *Kisan*, vol. 1, nos. 2-3, n.d.

Pradhan, Tripurvar Singh. "Jagga Karko Natija" [The effect of land taxation]. *Nepal Pukar*, Ashadh 15, 2017 (June 29, 1960).

Rajvamshi, Shankar Man. "Lalitpurka Mallarajaka Tadapatra Tamasukharu" [Palm-leaf bonds of the Malla kings of Lalitpur]. *Ancient Nepal*, July 1969, pp. 29-33.

———. "Siddhinarasimha Mallaka Tadapatra Tamasukharu" [Palm-leaf bonds of Siddhinarasimha Malla]. *Ancient Nepal,* July 1968, pp. 23-26.

———. "Srinivasa Malla ra Yoganarendra Mallaka Tadapatra Tamasukharu" [Palm-leaf bonds of Srinivasa Malla and Yoganarendra Malla]. *Ancient Nepal,* October 1968, pp. 29-33.

———. "Yogaprakasha Mallaka Tamapatra, Tadapatra ra Tamasukharu" [Copper and palm-leaf inscriptions and bonds of Yogaprakasha Malla]. *Ancient Nepal,* October 1969, pp. 25-32.

———. ed. *Puratattwa-Patrasangraha* [A collection of ancient documents]. 2 pts. Kathmandu: Department of Archeology and Culture, His Majesty's Government, 2018-19 (1961-62).

Sharma, Bal Chandra. *Nepal Ko Aitihasik Ruprekha* [An outline of the history of Nepal]. Varanasi: Krishnakumari, 2008 (1951).

Sharma, Janak Lal. "Chitwandekhi Janakpursammaka Kehi Puratattwik Sthal" [Some archeological sites from Chitaun to Janakpur]. *Ancient Nepal,* January 1968, pp. 1-10.

———. "Varahakshetra Ra Anya Kehi Sthal" [Barahakshetra and some other sites]. *Ancient Nepal,* July 1968, pp. 27-35.

Shrestha, Pushpa Lal. "Birta Unmulan" [*Birta* abolition]. *Navayug,* Bhadra 31, 2017 (September 15, 1960).

English

Baden-Powell, B. H. *Land Revenue and Tenure in British India.* Oxford: Clarendon Press, 1913.

Baer, Gabriel. *A History of Landownership in Modern Egypt, 1800-1950.* London: Oxford University Press, 1962.

Bahadur, Ram K. C. *A General Study on Land Reform, Land Administration and Socio-Economic Activities.* Kathmandu: Lands Department, Ministry of Land Reform, 1972.

———. "Panchayat Development and Land Tax vs. Fixed Rent." *Rising Nepal,* April 16, 1973.

Baran, Paul A. *The Political Economy of Growth.* Harmondsworth, Middlesex: Penguin Books, 1973.

Bista, Dor Bahadur. "The People." In Pashupati Shumshere J. B. Rana and Kamal P. Malla, *Nepal in Perspective.* Kathmandu: Center for Economic Development and Administration, 1973.

Bose, Atindra Nath. *Social and Rural Economy of Northern India.* 2 vols. Calcutta: Firma K.L. Mukhopadhyay, 1961.

Bottomore, T. B. *Elites and Society.* Reprint. Harmondsworth, Middlesex: Penguin Books, 1971.

Buchanan (Hamilton), Francis. *An Account of the District of Purnea in 1809-10.* Patna: Bihar and Orissa Research Society, 1928.

———. *An Account of the Kingdom of Nepal, and of the Territories Annexed to This Dominion by House of Gorkha.* Reprint. New Delhi: Manjusri Publish-

ing House, 1972.
Burn, Sir Richard, ed. *Cambridge History of India*. Vol. III. Delhi: S. Chand and Co., 1957.
Caplan, A. Patricia. *Priests and Cobblers: A Study of Social Change in a Hindu Village in Western Nepal*. San Francisco: Chandler Publishing Co., 1972.
Caplan, Lionel. *Land and Social Change in East Nepal: A Study of Hindu-Tribal Relations*. Berkeley and Los Angeles; University of California Press, 1970.
———. "Some Political Consequences of State Land Policy in East Nepal." *Man*, vol. 2, no. 1, March 1967.
Central Bureau of Statistics. "Sample Census of Agriculture." Mimeographed. Kathmandu: the Bureau, 1962.
Chaudhari, Dipak. "German Research on Sherpas." *Rising Nepal*, March 23, 1973.
Clauson, Gerard. *Communal Land Tenure*. F A O Agricultural Studies, no. 17. Rome: Food and Agriculture Organization, 1953.
Chemjong, Iman Singh. *History and Cultures of the Kirat People*. 3d. ed., Panchthar: Tumeng Hang and Chandraw Hang Zobegu, 1966.
Dore, R. P. "Land Reform and Japan's Economic Development—A Reactionary Thesis." In Teodor Shanin, ed., *Peasants and Peasant Societies*. Harmondsworth, Middlesex: Penguin Books, 1971.
Dorner, Peter. *Land Reform and Economic Development*. Harmondsworth, Middlesex: Penguin Books, 1972.
Dovering, Folke. "The Share of Agriculture in a Growing Population." In Carl K. Eicher and Lawrence W. Witt, eds., *Agriculture in Economic Development*. Reprint. Bombay: Vora & Co., 1970.
Dutt, Romesh. *The Economic History of India*. 2 vols. Delhi: Publications Division, Ministry of Information and Broadcasting, Government of India, 1963.
Eicher, Carl K., and Witt, Lawrence W., eds. *Agriculture in Economic Development*. Reprint. Bombay: Vora & Co., 1970.
Eisenstadt, S. N. *The Political System of Empires*. New York: Free Press, 1963.
Froehlich, Walter, ed. *Land Tenure, Industrialization and Social Stability: Experience and Prospects in Asia*. Milwaukee: Marquette University Press, 1961.
Fürer-Haimendorf, Christoph von. *The Sherpas of Nepal*. Calcutta: Oxford Book Co., 1966.
———, ed. *Caste and Kin in Nepal, India and Ceylon*. Bombay: Asia Publishing House, 1966.
Gaige, Frederick H. "The Role of the Tarai in Nepal's Economic Development." *Vasudha*, vol. XI, no. 7, Ashadh 2025 (June 1968).
Georgescu-Roegen, N. "Economic Theory and Agrarian Economics." In Carl K. Eicher and Lawrence W. Witt, eds., *Agriculture in Economic Development*. Reprint. Bombay: Vora & Co., 1970.

Government of Nepal, *Draft Five-year Plan: A Synopsis.* Kathmandu: the Government, 1956.

Gupta, Sulekh Chandra. *Agrarian Relations and Early British Rule in India.* Bombay: Asia Publishing House, 1963.

Gurung, Harka. "Geographic Foundations of Nepal." *Himalayan Review,* special issue, 1968.

———. "Geographic Setting." In Nepal Council of Applied Economic Research, *Nepal: A Profile.* Kathmandu: the Council, 1970.

———. "The Land." In Pashupati Shumsher J. B. Rana and Kamal P. Malla, eds., *Nepal in Perspective.* Kathmandu: Center for Economic Development and Administration, 1973.

Habib, Irfan. *The Agrarian System of Mughal India.* Bombay: Asia Publishing House, 1963.

Hagen, Toni. *Nepal: The Kingdom in the Himalayas.* Berne: Kimmerley and Frey, 1961.

Hamilton, Francis. See Buchanan.

Hazeltine, H.D., "Mortmain." *Encyclopaedia of the Social Sciences.* XI, 40–49.

Hicks, John. *A Theory of Economic History.* London: Oxford University Press, 1969.

His Majesty's Government of Nepal. *The Budget Speech, 1961.* Kathmandu: Department of Publicity and Broadcasting, 1961.

Hitchcock, John T. *The Magars of Banyan Hill.* New York: Holt, Rinehart and Winston, 1966.

Hodgson, Brian H. "Some Account of the System of Law and Police as Recognized in the State of Nepal." *Journal of the Royal Asiatic Society of Great Britain and Ireland,* vol. I, 1834.

———. "On the Law and Legal Practice of Nepal, as regards Familiar Intercourse between a Hindu and an Outcast." *Journal of the Royal Asiatic Society of Great Britain and Ireland,* vol. I, 1834.

Hunt, James B. "The Effects of Land Reform on Achieving the Agricultural Production Targets of the Third Plan." *Economic Affairs Report.* Vol. 3, no. 3, August 1965.

———. "The Political Repercussions of Land Reform on the Economic Development of Nepal." In Department of Land Reform, Ministry of Land Reform, Agriculture, and Food, *Bhumi Sudhar* [Land Reform]. Kathmandu: the Department, Jestha 2023 (June 1966).

Jha, Hit Narayan. *The Licchavis.* Varanasi: Chowkhamba Sanskrit Series Office, 1970.

Jha, J. C. "History of Land Revenue in Chhotanagpur." In Ram Sharan Sharma, *Land Revenue in India.* Delhi: Motilal Banarsidass, 1971.

Jhabvala, Noshirvan H. *Principles of Hindu Law.* 7th ed. Reprint. Bombay: C. Jamnadas and Co., 1964.

―――. *Principles of Mahomedan Law.* 8th ed. Reprint. Bombay: C. Jamnadas and Co., 1964.
Joshi, Bhuwan Lal, and Rose, Leo E. *Democratic Innovations in Nepal: A Case Study of Political Acculturation.* Berkeley and Los Angeles: University of California Press, 1966.
Karan, Pradyumna P., et. al. *Nepal: A Physical and Cultural Geography.* Lexington: University of Kentucky Press, 1960.
Kirkpatrick, Colonel, *An Account of the Kingdom of Nepaul.* Reprint. New Delhi: Manjusri Publishing House, 1969.
Kumar, Satish. *Rana Polity in Nepal.* Bombay: Asia Publishing House, 1967.
Lambton, Ann K. S. *Landlord and Peasant in Persia.* London: Oxford University Press, 1953.
Landon, Perceval. *Nepal.* 2 vols. London: Constable and Co., 1928.
Lévi, Sylvain. *Le Népal.* 3 vols. Paris: Ernest Leroux, 1905-8.
Lewis, Arthur W. *The Theory of Economic Growth.* London: George Allen and Unwin, 1963.
Lindsey, Quentin W. "Agricultural Planning in Nepal." *Economic Affairs Report,* vol. V, no. 1, February 1967.
―――. "Budabari Panchayat: The Second Year after Reform." In Department of Land Reform, Ministry of Land Reform, Agriculture, and Food, *Bhumi Sudhar* [Land reform]. Kathmandu: the Department, Jestha 2023 (June 1966).
―――. "Land Reform and the Food Problem." In Department of Land Reform, Ministry of Land Reform, Agriculture, and Food, *Bhumi Sudhar* [Land reform]. Kathmandu: the Department, Jestha 2023 (June 1966).
Lohani, Prakash C. "Industrial Policy: The Problem Child of History and Planning." In Pashupati Shumshere J. B. Rana and Kamal P. Malla, eds., *Nepal in Perspective.* Kathmandu: Center for Economic Development and Administration, 1973.
Mcdougal, Charles, *Village and Household Economy in Far-Western Nepal.* Kirtipur: Tribhuwan University, n.d. [1968].
Ministry of Food and Agriculture (Economic Analysis and Planning Division). *Agricultural Statistics of Nepal.* Kathmandu: the Ministry, 1972.
―――. "Farm Management Study in the Selected Regions of Nepal, 1968-69." Mimeographed. Kathmandu: the Ministry, 1971.
Ministries of Land Reform, Panchayat and Economic Planning. *Report on the Successful First Year of Land Reform in Budabari, Jhapa.* Mimeographed. Kathmandu, 1961.
Misra, B. R. *Land Revenue Policy in the United Provinces.* Banaras: Nand Kishore and Bros. 1942.
Mookerji, Radha Kumud. "Indian Land-System." In Government of Bengal, *Report of the Land Revenue Commission, Bengal.* Vol. II. Alipore:

Bengal Government Press, 1940.
Moore, Barrington, Jr. *Social Origins of Dictatorship and Democracy: Lord and Peasant in the Making of the Modern World.* Harmondsworth, Middlesex: Penguin Books, 1967.
Moreland, W. H. *India at the Death of Akbar.* Reprint. Delhi: Atma Ram and Sons, 1962.
Mukerji, Karuna. *Land Reforms.* Calcutta: H. Chatterjee and Co., 1952.
Myrdal, Gunnar. *Asian Drama: An Inquiry into the Poverty of Nations.* 3 vols. Harmondsworth, Middlesex: Penguin Books, 1968.
———. *The Challenge of World Poverty: a World Anti-Poverty Programme.* Harmondsworth, Middlesex: Penguin Books, 1971.
National Planning Commission. *Fourth Plan (1970–75).* Kathmandu: the Commission, 1972.
Nepal Council of Applied Economic Research. *Nepal: A Profile.* Kathmandu: the Council, 1970.
Nepal Rashtra Bank. *Agricultural Credit Survey, Nepal.* 4 vols. Kathmandu: the Bank, 1972.
Nepali, Gopal Singh. *The Newars.* Bombay: United Asia Publications, 1965.
Nicholls, William H. "The Place of Agriculture in Economic Development." In Carl Eicher and Lawrence Witt, *Agriculture in Economic Development.* Reprint. Bombay: Vora & Co., 1970.
Panday, R. S. "Nepalese Society during the Malla and Early Shah Period." In R. S. Varma, ed., *Cultural Heritage of Nepal.* Allahabad: Kitab Mahal, 1972.
Parsons, Kenneth H. "Agrarian Reform Policy as a Field of Research." In *Agrarian Reform and Economic Growth in Developing Countries.* Washington: U.S. Department of Agriculture, 1962.
———. "The Tenure of Farms, Motivation, and Productivity." In *Science, Technology and Development*, vol. III, *Agriculture*, Washington: U.S. Government Printing Office, n.d.
Patel, G. D. *The Land Problems of the Reorganized Bombay State.* Bombay: N. M. Tripathi (Private) Ltd., 1957.
Pauw, E. K. *Report on the Tenth Settlement of the Garhwal District.* Allahabad: North Western Provinces and Oudh Government Press, 1896.
Raj, Jagadish. *The Mutiny and British Land Policy in North India, 1856–68.* Bombay: Asia Publishing House, 1965.
Raj, Krishna. "Land Reform and Development in South Asia." In Walter Froehlich, ed., *Land Tenure, Industrialization and Social Stability Experience and Prospects in Asia.* Milwaukee: Marquette University Press, 1961.
Rana, Padma Jung. *Life of Maharaja Sir Jang Bahadur of Nepal.* Allahabad: the author, 1909.
Rana, Pashupati Shumshere J. B., and Malla, Kamal P., eds. *Nepal in Perspective.* Kathmandu: Center for Economic Development and Administration, 1973.

Report of National Seminar on Land Reform. Kathmandu, 1971.
Regmi, Mahesh C. *A Study in Nepali Economic History, 1768–1846.* New Delhi: Manjusri Publishing House, 1971.
———. *Some Aspects of Land Reform in Nepal.* Kathmandu: the author, 1960.
———. *Land Tenure and Taxation in Nepal.* 4 vols. Berkeley and Los Angeles: University of California Press, 1963–68.
Rose, Leo E. *Nepal: Strategy for Survival.* Bombay: Oxford University Press, 1971.
Rosser, Colin. "The Newar Caste System." In Christoph von Fürer-Haimendorf, ed., *Caste and Kin in Nepal, India and Ceylon.* Bombay: Asia Publishing House, 1966.
Sastry, R. Shama. *Kautilya's Arthasastra,* 8th ed. Mysore: Mysore Printing and Publishing House, 1967.
Shanin, Teodor. ed. *Peasants and Peasant Societies.* Harmondsworth, Middlesex: Penguin Books, 1971.
Sharma, Ram Sharan, ed. *Land Revenue in India.* Delhi: Motilal Banarsidass, 1971.
Singh, Suresh. "The Munda Land System and Revenue Reforms in Chhotanagpur during 1869–1908." In Ram Sharan Sharma, ed., *Land Revenue in India.* Delhi: Motilal Banarsidass, 1971.
Sinha, Narendra Krishna. *The Economic History of Bengal.* 2 vols. Calcutta: Firma K. L. Mukhopadhyay, 1962.
Sinha, Ram Narayan. *Bihar Tenantry (1783–1833).* Bombay: People's Publishing House, 1968.
Sinha, U. N. "The Genesis of Political Institutions in Nepal." In R. S. Varma, ed., *Cultural Heritage of Nepal.* Allahabad: Kitab Mahal, 1972.
Snellgrove, David. *Buddhist Himalaya.* Oxford: Bruno Cassirer, 1957.
Stiller, Ludwig F. *The Rise of the House of Gorkha.* New Delhi: Manjusri Publishing House, 1973.
Thorner, Daniel. *The Agrarian Prospect in India.* Delhi: University Press, 1956.
United Nations. *Land Reform: Defects in Agrarian Structure as Obstacles to Economic Development.* New York: U.N. Department of Economic Affairs, 1951.
———. *Progress in Land Reform.* 2 vols. New York: U.N. Department of Economic Affairs, 1954.
Varma, R. S., ed. *Cultural Heritage of Nepal.* Allahabad: Kitab Mahal, 1972.
Warriner, Doreen. *Land Reform and Development in the Middle East.* 2d ed. London: Oxford University Press, 1962.
———. "Land Reform and Economic Development." In Carl K. Eicher and Lawrence W. Witt, eds., *Agriculture in Economic Development.* Reprint. Bombay: Vora & Co., 1970.
Weiner, Myron. "The Political Demography of Nepal." *Asian Survey,* vol. XII, no. 7, July 1973.

Wilson, H. H. *Glossary of Judicial and Revenue Terms*. 2d. ed. Delhi: Munshiram Manoharlal, 1968.
Workman, H. B. "Monasticism." *Encyclopaedia of the Social Sciences*. X, 584–90.
Wright, Daniel. *History of Nepal*. Reprint of 1877 ed. Kathmandu: Antiquated Book Publishers, 1972.
Zagoria, Donald S. "The Ecology of Peasant Communism in India." *American Political Science Review*, vol. LXV, no. 1, March 1971.
Zaman, M. A. "A Socio-Economic Case for Peasant Ownership in Nepal." Mimeographed. Kathmandu: Ministry of Agriculture, 1972.
———. *Evaluation of Land Reform in Nepal*. Kathmandu: Ministry of Land Reforms, 1973.

Unpublished Materials

Nepali

Acharya, Baburam. "Nepalko Bhumi Byabastha" [Nepal's land system].

English

Department of Agriculture. "Resettlement Project, Nawalpur." Mimeographed. Kathmandu: the Department, 1963.
Department of Industrial and Commercial Intelligence. "Audyogik Survey Report (Industrial survey report for Mahottari, Sarlahi, and other districts)." Mimeographed. Kathmandu: the Department, 2005–6 (1948–49).
Land Reform Commission. "Report on Land Tenure Conditions in Saptari, Mahottari, and Sarlahi." Typescript. Kathmandu: the Commission 2010 (1953).
———. "Report on Land Tenure Conditions in the Western Tarai." Mimeographed. Kathmandu: the Commission, 2010 (1953).
———. "Report on Land Tenure Conditions in Western Nepal." Mimeographed. Kathmandu: the Commission, 2010 (1953).
———. "Reports of the Land Reform Commission." Mimeographed. Kathmandu: the Commission, 2010 (1953).
Macfarlane, A. D. J. "Population and Economy in Central Nepal: A Study of the Gurungs." Ph.D. thesis, London University, 1972.
Raimajhi, Thir Bahadur. "Industrial survey report of Saptari and Biratnagar" (English trans. of "Saptari ra Biratnagar Ko Audyogik Survey Report"). Kathmandu: Department of Industrial and Commercial Intelligence, 2006 (1949).
Sharma, Hridaya Nath. "Industrial survey of Butaul district." (English trans. of "Butaul Jillako Audyogik Sarvekshan"). Mimeographed. Kathmandu: Department of Industrial and Commercial Intelligence, n.d. [1949].

BIBLIOGRAPHY AND SOURCE MATERIALS

NEWSPAPERS AND PERIODICALS

Nepali

Gorkhapatra (daily). Published by the government-owned Gorkhapatra Corporation.
Kisan (monthly). Published by the former Nepal Peasants Association.
Naya Samaj (daily).
Navayug (weekly). Organ of the former Nepal Communist Party.
Nepal Kanun Patrika (monthly). Journal of the Supreme Court of Nepal.
Nepal Gazette. Official Gazette of His Majesty's Government. Renamed *Nepal Rajapatra* after January 27, 1967. The miscellaneous laws, regulations, orders, and notifications published from time to time by His Majesty's Government in the *Nepal Gazette* and actually used for the purposes of this study have been cited in full at appropriate places in the footnotes.
Nepal Pukar (weekly). Organ of the former Nepali Congress Party.
Nepal Rajapatra. See *Nepal Gazette*.
Prachin Nepal (English title, *Ancient Nepal*). Journal of the Department of Archaeology, with Nepali and English sections.
Purnima (quarterly).
Rashtravani (weekly). Organ of the former Gorkha Parished Party.
Samyukta Prayas (weekly). Organ of the former United Democratic Party.

English

Ancient Nepal. See *Prachin Nepal*.
Asian Survey (monthly).
Contributions to Nepalese Studies (semiannual). Journal of the Institute of Nepal and Asian Studies, Tribhuwan University.
Economic Affairs Report. Published irregularly by the Ministry of Economic Planning.
Himalayan Review. Published by the Nepal Geographical Society.
Journal of the Royal Asiatic Society of Great Britain and Ireland.
Nepal Statistical Bulletin. Published irregularly by the Central Bureau of Statistics, National Planning Commission Secretariat, His Majesty's Government.
Regmi Research Series (monthly). Mimeographed. Privately published by Regmi Research.
Rising Nepal (daily). Published by the Gorkhapatra Corporation.
Vasudha (monthly).

INDEX

Abal. See Grading systems
Achham, 3, 26n, 99n, 134, 139
Adhiya. See Land-tax-assessment systems
Agrahara, 22n
Agricultural income-tax, 153–154
Agricultural land:
  categories of: *Khet*, 126–128, 131–137, 139, 141, 143, 148, 150–152, 174n, 204–205; *Pakho*, 99, 126–127, 132–133, 139–141, 143, 146, 148–149, 151–152, 174n, 204–205; *Dhanahar*, 143–144, 147–148, 151–152; *Bhith*, 143–144, 148–149, 151–152
  taxes on: *Ghiukhane*, 135–136; *Chardam-Theki*, 135
  zoning system in the Tarai, 145
Argha-Khanchi, 3, 172n
Arun River, 89, 100

Baglung, 3, 25, 134, 140
Baitadi, 3, 133, 134, 140
Bajhang, 3, 128, 133, 134, 147
Bajura, 3, 26n, 128, 134, 140
Bandipur, 84, 134.
Bangladesh, 2
Banke, 2, 8, 31, 124n, 198n
Bara, 2, 27, 124n, 143
Baramu, 88, 98n, 99n
Bardiya, 2, 8, 31, 117, 124n, 146, 198
Bengal, 29n, 110n
Bhadgaun. *See* Bhaktapur
Bhairahawa, 5
Bhaktapur, 3, 5, 8, 52n, 84, 133, 134, 147
Bhatha. See Agricultural land, zoning system in the Tarai
Bhith. See Agricultural land categories
Bhojpur, 3
Bhote, 7, 88, 98n, 99n
Bihar, 8, 29n, 30n, 110n
Bijan system. *See* Land-tax-assessment systems
Biratnagar, 5
Birganj, 5
Birt, 22n
Birta, categories of: *Chhap*, 35; *Tiruwa*, 35; *Pota*, 34–35, 175n; *Seba*, 99. *See also* Landownership forms
Birta-Abolition Act, 42–43

Birta Taxation, 34–35, 40–44
Brahmans, 6, 8, 22n, 23, 27, 30, 31n, 50n, 51, 52, 191n

Calcutta, 2
Chahar. See Grading systems
Chardam-Theki. See Agricultural land taxes
Chaudhari, 105, 108
Chepang, 7, 88, 98n, 99n
Chhap Birta. See *Birta* categories
Chhathum, 133, 134, 139
Chhetri, 6, 8, 27
Chhut Guthi. See *Guthi* categories
China, 1, 2
Chitaun, 3, 205
Chuni. See Tenant categories
Compulsory Savings, 200, 206ff
Conversion rates, 138–139, 181

Dailekh, 3, 25, 124n, 128, 132n, 134, 173
Dandeldhura, 3, 134, 140, 141
Dang, 3, 145, 195n
Danuwar, 8, 20, 88, 99n
Darai, 98n
Darchula, 3
Debutter, 46
Dhading, 3, 84, 134
Dhanahar. See Agricultural land categories
Dhankuta, 3, 88, 139, 177n
Dhanusha, 2, 57
Dharan, 5
Dhokre, 80, 81
Dolakha, 3, 134, 139, 140, 160n
Dolpa, 4, 76n
Doti, 3, 13n, 25, 26n, 99n, 128n, 134, 185
Doyam. See Grading systems
Dudhkosi River, 100
Dullu, 22, 23, 50n, 124n, 128n, 132n, 173
Duniya Guthi. See *Guthi* categories

East India Company, 29n
Egypt, 54n
England, 33

Forced-labor system, 7, 18, 41, 156, 157, 167, 214n
Forest Areas Lands Act, 215

INDEX

Gandaki River, 4
Ganges plain, 2
Garhwal, 47n
Ghiukhane. *See* Agriculture land taxes
Gorkha, 3, 4n, 7, 8, 9, 26, 36, 58n, 66n, 74, 123, 133, 134, 138, 139, 147, 148
Gosthi, 47
Grading systems, 132-136, 143, 147-149, 151-152, 204-205
Gulmi, 3, 134, 172n
Gurung, 7, 8, 27
Guthi, categories of: *Duniya*, 58-59, 63, 65; *Raj*, 58-63, 69-70, 121n, 156-157, 164, 167-168, 186, 187n, 202; *Chhut*, 60-61, 70; *Amanat*, 60-61; *Sanam*, 48n. *See also* Landownership forms
Guthi Corporation, 59-62, 69-70
Guthi Corporation Act, 61, 62, 121n

Hale. *See* Homestead categories
Hale-Pakho. *See* Homestead categories
Hanumannagar, 143
Hayu, 88, 99n
Himachal Pradesh, 8, 73
Himalayan region, 6, 171-173, 192-193
Himalaya, 1-4
Homesteads, categories of: *Hale*, 127, 139-142, 151; *Pate*, 127, 139n, 141-142, 151; *Kodale*, 127, 139-142, 151; *Hale-Pakho*, 133; *Kodale-Pakho*, 133
Humla, 4, 128

Ilam, 3, 88, 95, 97, 133, 134
India, 1-2, 4-6, 9, 13, 17, 29n, 46-47, 54n, 71, 73, 94, 106, 107, 124, 127n, 145, 147, 211

Jagera. *See* Landownership forms
Jagir. *See* Landownership forms
Jajarkot, 3, 51, 134, 138
Jamuna-Sutlej region, 73
Janakpur, 57
Jhapa, 2, 143, 148, 153, 214n, 215
Jhara. *See* Forced-labor system
Jimidars, 104, 106-123, 145-146, 198, 224-226
Jirayat, 107, 108, 110, 115, 118, 120-122
Jumla, 3, 25, 26n, 49n, 66n, 128, 132n, 134

Kabhrepalanchok, 3, 84, 134, 140
Kailali, 2, 8, 31, 109, 124n, 144, 148, 198n
Kami, 7
Kanchanpur, 2, 8, 31, 109, 124n, 144, 148, 198n
Kapilavastu, 2, 112, 122
Karnali region, 128, 134
Karnali River, 4
Kaski, 3, 186n

Kathmandu, 3, 5, 8-10, 19, 22, 24, 29, 34, 44, 47n, 48, 49n, 52, 57, 61, 66, 67, 72, 74, 83-85, 92, 100, 101, 104-106, 116, 121, 123, 126-127, 132, 133-139, 141-142, 147, 149-152, 156, 158, 169, 177, 181, 184, 190, 192-193, 195, 201, 204-205, 216, 219-221, 225
Khajahani, 119, 144, 148
Khas, 7
Khet. *See* Agricultural land categories
Khotang, 3
Kipat. *See* Landownership forms
Kirtipur, 134, 141, 163
Kodale. *See* Homestead categories
Kodale-Pakho. *See* Homestead categories
Koshi River 4
Kumhal, 7, 88, 98, 99n
Kunchha, 133, 134, 138
Kut. *See* Land-tax-assessment systems

Lalitpur, 3, 5, 8, 24n, 47n, 50n, 53n, 84, 85, 134, 141, 156n, 157
Lamjung, 3, 58n, 130, 179n
Lands Act, 198, 201, 206, 210, 211, 215, 230
Land Acquisition Act, 180
Land ceilings, 200-202
Landownership, forms of: *Raikar*, 16-21, 24, 25n, 32, 35, 37-44, 57-58, 61-62, 64-65, 68, 71, 76, 79-80, 84-86, 91-103, 121n, 122, 137-139, 156-157, 164-194, 202, 205n, 229; *Birta*, 16-21, 22-46, 50n, 53-56, 58-59, 64-76, 86-88, 91-92, 94, 99, 104, 108, 112, 115, 123, 127, 155, 164-165, 170, 177-179, 182-187, 205, 210, 224-226; *Guthi*, 16-21, 23n, 24, 27, 29-30, 36, 46-59, 63-70, 73, 87, 122, 127, 178, 224; *Jagir*, 16-21, 22n, 38, 58, 69, 71, 88, 92, 104, 123, 127, 129-131, 137, 141, 155, 164-165, 170, 174n, 181, 224, 225-226; *Jagera*, 17, 20, 58, 71, 79-80, 82, 131; *Kipat*, 19-21, 36, 73, 87-103, 123, 156, 164, 174n, 186, 224; *Rakam*, 18-21, 38, 156-169
Land redistribution, 171-172, 200-202
Land reform, 200ff, 227-228
Land-tax-assessment systems: *Adhiya*, 127-131, 188; *Kut*, 129-131, 134, 188; *Bijan*, 139-141, 151; crop-asssment system in the Tarai, 124-125; ox-team units, 125
Land-tax rates: on newly-reclaimed *Khet* lands, 136; on *Pakho* holdings, 141-142; at the end of the Rana period, 147-148; current rates in different regions, 150-151; rates of Panchayat development tax, 152-153
Lepcha, 88
Licchavi, 22n, 47
Limbu, 7n, 20, 27, 88-89, 93-97, 99, 101-103, 156

INDEX

Magar, 7, 8, 27
Mahabharat Mountains, 3, 4
Mahottari, 2, 51, 57, 128, 144, 147, 148
Majh. See Agricultural land, zoning system in the Tarai
Majhi, 7, 88, 98n
Majhiya, 88
Majhkirat, 100, 101, 134.
Makwanpur, 3, 74n, 126n, 144, 146n
Malla, Jaya Prakash, 22n, 24n
Malla, Jayasthiti, 23n, 132n
Malla, Prithvi, 22n, 50n
Malla, Siddhinarsimha, 50n
Malla, Srinivas, 156n
Mallas, 28, 47n, 57, 66, 67
Manang, 4
Mechi River, 89
Midlands, 3-4, 6-7, 125, 134, 141, 147, 151, 171-174, 192-193
Mohi. See Tenant categories.
Morang, 2, 22, 57, 118, 124n, 128, 141, 143, 145, 148, 153, 186, 215
Mughal revenue system, 124, 125
Mugu, 4
Murmi, 99n
Mustang, 4, 187, 211
Myagdi, 3
Myrdal, Gunnar, 14, 217, 222

National Planning Commission, 11
Nawal-Parasi, 2, 118, 122
Nepal-British War, 8
Nepal-China War, 52
Nepalganj, 5
Nepali Congress, 9
Nepal Rastra Bank, 189, 219
Nepal-Tibet-Sikkim trijunction, 93
Nepal-Tibet War, 36, 52, 158
Newar, 48
Nuwakot, 3, 84, 134

Okhaldhunga, 3, 134
Orissa, 29n

Pahari, 88, 98n
Pajani, 73n
Pakho. See Agricultural land categories
Palhi-Majhkhand, 118, 144, 198n
Pallokirat, 88-89, 92-103
Palpa, 3, 84, 134, 172n, 177n
Panchayat development taxation, 152-153, 155
Panchayat landownership, 229ff
Panchayats. *See* Panchayat system
Panchayat system, 9, 10, 103, 122, 152-153, 198, 227, 229-231
Panchthar, 3, 88
Panga, 163

Parbat, 3
Parsa, 2, 57, 143, 148
Pashupatinath Temple, 52
Patan. *See* Lalitpur
Pate. See Homestead categories
Patta, 173, 175
Pokhara, 5, 133, 134, 138
Pota Birta. See Birta categories
Prajajat, 7
Punjab, 73
Pyuthan, 3, 134

Rai, 20, 88, 100, 101
Raibandi, 171, 172n, 174n, 175, 186
Raikar. See Landownership forms
Rajasthan, 7
Raj Guthi. See Guthi categories
Rajput, 7
Rakam. See Landownership forms
Ramechhap, 3, 134, 140
Rana, Bir Shamsher, 31, 32
Rana, Chandra Shamsher, 49n, 83
Rana, Dhir Shamsher, 52
Rana, Jang Bahadur, 9, 30, 31, 32n, 67, 108
Rana, Ranoddip Singh, 30, 31
Ranas, 9, 11, 25-28, 30-34, 36-37, 39, 42-45, 53, 55-57, 60, 75, 77, 82-83, 85-86, 94-102, 108-109, 116, 118, 120, 121, 123, 130, 131, 133-135, 138, 141, 146-147, 158-161, 169, 175, 180, 194-195, 197, 210, 225-226, 230
Rasuwa, 4
Rautahat, 2, 32n, 57, 143, 148
Record of rights, 174-175
Rohani, 98n
Rolpa, 3
Rukum, 3
Rupandehi, 2, 118, 122
Ryotwari system, 107n

Sagarmatha, 4.
Salyan, 3, 13n, 84, 134
Sankhu, 132, 133, 141
Sankhuwa-Sabha, 3, 88
Saptari, 2, 32n, 57, 119, 128, 146
Sarki, 7
Sarlahi, 2, 31n, 57, 143
Sen, Bisantar, 71n
Sen, Kamadatta, 22n
Sen rulers, 57
Shah, Drabya, 58n
Shah, Pratap Simha, 25n
Shah, Prithvi Bir Bikram, 31n, 52
Shah, Prithvi Narayan, 8, 25n, 34, 37, 47n, 53n, 56, 73-74, 85, 90n
Shah, Rajendra Bikram, 49n
Shah, Ram, 123
Shah, Rana Bahadur, 52n

252 INDEX

Shah, Surendra Bir Bikram, 9n, 31n, 51
Shah rulers, 9, 25, 28, 56, 57, 66, 105, 128, 134, 173
Shakya, 47
Sheoraj, 119, 144, 147, 148, 198n
Sherpa, 46n, 88, 100n
Sikkim, 1
Sim. See Grading systems
Sindhuli, 3
Sindhupalchok, 3, 84, 134, 140
Sir. See Agricultural land, zoning system in the Tarai
Siraha, 2, 57, 143, 148
Siwalik Hills, 3, 145
Solukhumbu, 3, 46n, 55n, 100n
Sri Lanka, 2
Sunsari, 2, 57, 215
Sunuwar, 20
Surcharge on land tax, 154
Surkhet, 3, 147
Switzerland, 2
Syangja, 3, 134

Talukdar, 106, 107, 108, 110n, 176, 225
Tamang, 20, 27, 88, 89
Tanahu, 3, 172n, 176n, 186, 187, 189n, 191
Taplejung, 3, 88
Tarai region, 2-6, 12-13, 24, 40, 57, 97, 105-114, 118-119, 121, 123-125, 128, 141, 143, 171, 173, 177n, 184-185, 192-195, 197-198, 201, 205-206, 209, 214-215, 220, 225

Taulihawa, 198
Tenancy, 92-93, 203 ff
Tenants, categories of: *Mohi*, 174, 177, 179; *Chuni*, 160, 167, 173
Terhathum, 3, 88, 134
Thakuri, 7n
Thami, 88
Thapa, Bhimsen, 28n, 53n
Thapa, Mathbar Singh, 28n
Tibetan Autonomous Region, 1, 4, 6
Tibrikot, 3, 49n, 51n
Tirja, 76, 77, 78, 80, 81
Tiruwa Birta. See *Birta* categories

Udaipur (India), 7
Udayapur (Nepal), 3
Ukhada, 112, 113, 122
United Provinces. See Uttar Pradesh
Uttar Pradesh, 8, 145

Vijayapur, 22n, 71n
Vritti, 22n

Waqf, 46, 54n

Yakha, 88

Zabti system, 125n
Zamindar, 106, 107, 145n, 173

www.ingramcontent.com/pod-product-compliance
Lightning Source LLC
Chambersburg PA
CBHW021659230426
43668CB00008B/674